REKINDLE THE FIRES OF WONDER TOWARD THE ANIMAL WORLD AND ALL OF NATURE

Many ancient myths and stories speak of a magical time and place in which there were no boundaries between humans and animals. Animals and humans spoke. Wild and tame had no meaning. And always the divine revealed itself in Nature.

The natural world and the animals within it speak to us everyday: by their appearances, behaviors, movements, and characteristic patterns. When we know what to look for, we can use them as omens—not in a superstitious sense, but in the development of true prophecy and higher perception.

Through this book you will realize how intricately every aspect of nature is woven into your life. You will awaken to the ancient knowledge of spirit animals and how to determine their roles within your life. They will touch a primal part of your heart and soul—and stir long dormant embers. They will become your friends, your teachers and your companions.

"Animal Speak teaches that our relationship with the animals on this earth is not merely a physical one, it involved our mystical side as well. The lessons learned will benefit the animals in your life by increasing your communication with them and therefore your respect for them. But even more so, the lessons teach how, through animals, one can learn to communicate with and respect oneself better. The author teaches that the animals that enter and exit our lives everyday offer us guidance and support if we will be open to it. Having spent years studying the biology and natural history of animals, with Animal Speak I begin my study of the whole animal."

—**Mark Mazzei**
Animal Rehabilitation Supervisor
Brukner Nature Center
Troy, Ohio

About the Author

Ted Andrews is a full-time author, student, and teacher in the metaphysical and spiritual fields. He conducts seminars, symposiums, workshops, and lectures on ancient mysticism, focusing on translating esoteric material to make it comprehensible and practical for everyone.

Ted is certified in basic hypnosis and acupressure, and is involved in the study and use of herbs as an alternative path in health care. He is active in the holistic healing field. Trained in piano, Ted also employs the Celtic harp, bamboo flute, shaman rattles, Tibetan bells, the Tibetan Singing Bowl, and quartz crystal bowls to create individual healing therapies and induce higher states of consciousness.

Ted is a clairvoyant and works with past-life analysis and synthesis, aura interpretation, dreams, numerology, and the tarot. He is a contributing author to various metaphysical magazines, with published articles on various topics including Occult Christianity, Working with Our Angelic Brethren, and the Metaphysical Mirrors within Our Lives.

To Write to the Author

If you wish to contact the author or would like more information about this book, please write to the author in care of Llewellyn Worldwide and we will forward your request. Both the author and publisher appreciate hearing from you and learning of your enjoyment of this book and how it has helped you. Llewellyn Worldwide cannot guarantee that every letter written to the author can be answered, but all will be forwarded. Please write to:

Ted Andrews
c/o Llewellyn Worldwide
P.O. Box 64383, Dept. L028-1,
St. Paul, MN 55164-0383, U.S.A.

Please enclose a self-addressed, stamped envelope for reply, or $1.00 to cover costs.
If outside U.S.A., enclose international postal reply coupon.

ANIMAL-SPEAK

The Spiritual & Magical Powers
of Creatures Great & Small

TED ANDREWS

1999
Llewellyn Publications
St. Paul, Minnesota, 55164-0383, U.S.A.

FIRST EDITION
Sixteenth printing, 1999

Cover art by Victoria Lisi
Photography by Margaret K. Andrews
Book design by Constance Hill
Interior illustrations by Winston Allen, on pp. 5, 6, 14, 16, 42, 51, 70, 84, 90, 92, 98, 103, 105, 107, 109, 215, 369

Library of Congress Cataloging-in-publication Data
Andrews, Ted. 1952–
    Animal-speak : the spiritual & magical powers of creatures great & small /
Ted Andrews.
        p.   cm.
    Includes bibliographical references and index.
    ISBN 0-87542-028-1
    1. Shamanism—Miscellanea. 2. Animals—Miscellanea. 3. Human-animal communi-
cation—Miscellanea. 4. Totems—Miscellanea. I. Title.
  Miscellanea. I. Title.
BF1623.A55A53 1993   93-28673
133.9'3—dc20   CIP

Llewellyn Publications
A Division of Llewellyn Worldwide, Ltd.
P.O. Box 64383, St. Paul, MN 55164-0383

Printed in the United States of America

DEDICATION

So often we are touched in ways that seem small and insignificant at the time, but which prove to be wonderful catalysts and blessings later. It is with great joy, love, and gratitude that I dedicate this book to the following:

To Quenda Healing Woman for her love, her very dear and treasured friendship, and her sharing of Owl Medicine,

To Ann Konik who with contagious enthusiasm opened the splendor and joy of hawking to me,

To Kin Quitugua who shared with me the power of HAWKQUEST and the magic of birds of prey in educating the public,

To Brukner's Nature Center and all who work there for the opportunity of more intimate contact and educational experiences with animals and nature. To them also goes a special thanks for permission to photograph the animal residents and use the photographs in this book.

A special thanks goes to Mark Mazzei, Debbie Brill, and Terri Menoche of Brukner Nature Center for their help and guidance.

To my sister Theresa for her love for and work with animals.

To Pagan Alexander for her indexing assistance and input on such short notice.

To Constance Hill for her creative designs and editorial work.

Especially to the one who knew that the white bear would take you "East of the Sun and West of the Moon."

Other Books by Ted Andrews

Crystal Balls & Crystal Bowls
Dream Alchemy: Shaping Our Dream to Transform Our Lives
Enchantment of the Faerie Realm
The Healer's Manual
How to Develop and Use Psychic Touch
How to Heal with Color
How to Meet and Work with Spirit Guides
How to See and Read the Aura
How to Uncover Your Past Lives
Imagick
Magical Dance
The Magical Name
The Occult Christ
The Sacred Power in Your Name
Sacred Sounds: Transformation Through Music and Word
Simplified Magick

TABLE OF CONTENTS

PART THREE — UNDERSTANDING ANIMAL MEDICINE

PART FOUR — THE EXOTIC LANGUAGE OF INSECTS AND REPTILES

INTRODUCTION

ON LEARNING ANIMAL-SPEAK

Nature has filled my life. I was fortunate in spending most of my childhood among woods, ponds, creeks and fields. Animals have always come to me in dreams and in waking. They have guided me in life decisions and they even spoke to me of my father's death.

I have seen the wolf in the wild, eye-to-eye, and I have encountered moose, bear, porcupines, and otters. I have held hawks, owls, and even a golden eagle upon my arm, and I have been nipped by a fox. I have fed vultures and marveled at the bellowing of elk on a distant hill.

Crows call to me every morning, and ravens guided me once when lost. I have held a fragile seahorse in my hand, and followed a great green moray eel to a depth of 150 feet, and hawks always watch over me when I travel.

And with it all, I am always amazed at the wonder of nature, its multiplicity, and especially at what it is saying to me about my own life at the time of such encounters. I look for what it is trying to teach me. I know nature speaks to us if we listen. Every animal has a story to tell. Every flower blossoms with reminders to be creative, and every tree whispers with its rustling leaves the secrets of life.

As a life-long student of mysticism, with a formal background in literature and linguistics, I have found within most scriptures and mythologies of the world a vein of lore surrounding the spirit of animals and the belief that the divine forces speak to humans through the natural world. Humans were as much a part of the natural world as the natural world was part of them. Animals and Nature are not the domain of any one society or segment of society. All peoples are touched by them.

Today it is not uncommon to hear people speak of trying "to get back to nature," to get "in touch with the Earth once more." The truth is, we have never been out of touch. We are always connected to the Earth and it to us. Everything we do repercusses upon it, and everything within it repercusses on us. Unfortunately, most choose to ignore it or are unable to recognize it. The saddest part is that when we fail to reverence any aspect of nature and our intimate connection to it, we are failing to reverence intimate aspects of our own self.

I am part of the natural world. As part of it, I have a responsibility to know as much about the environment in which I am living. The more I understand it, the more I understand myself. I have made a point of trying to understand my environment and all life—human and animal—within it. To some, this may make me an amateur naturalist, but I am simply trying to speak the language of life.

If you were to move to a foreign country, you would have to learn the language of that country to survive and be productive. The more you understood the intricacies of that language, its dialects and uses, the more effective you would become within your life. The easier it becomes for you to survive and grow.

The natural world is part of your environment and your life, and if you truly wish to become productive and creative within your world, you will need to learn some of its languages. And the easiest and most enjoyable to learn is Animal-Speak.

There are many myths of a magical time and place in which there were no boundaries between humans and animals. Humans were at peace with the animals and spoke their language. It reflected a time of mingling between divine and human. Wild and tame had no meaning. Animals and humans could speak together, sometimes humans learning the animal tongue and sometimes animals learning the human tongue.

In our quest for the scientific and rational, we have come to look at nature and its elements as objects separate from us and simply to be studied. For many, this scientific approach to nature has destroyed the mysticism and spirituality surrounding it. It has burst its bubble of mystery. Nothing could be further from the truth. What science uncovers about nature should amaze us and fill us with even greater wonder at the magnificent expression of life in all its varied forms. It should teach us how intricately every aspect of nature is woven into our own existences.

The animal world has much to teach us. Some animals are experts at survival and adaptation. There are times when we can use those same skills. Some animals never get cancerous conditions. Wouldn't it be wonderful to learn their secrets? Some are great nurturers and protectors. Some have great fertility and others have great gentleness. Some embody strength and courage, while others can teach playfulness. The animal world shows us the potentials we can unfold. But to learn from them, we must first learn to speak with them.

Animals have often been attributed with fantastic qualities, and if nothing else, this attribution helps us to appreciate the natural world more fully. Every animal is a gateway to the phenomenal world of the human spirit. What most fail to realize though is that what they think of animals reflects the way they think of themselves.

When we learn to speak with the animals, to listen with animal ears and to see through animal eyes, we experience the phenomena, the power, and the potential of the human essence, and it is then that the animals are no longer our subordinates. They become our teachers, our friends, and our companions. They show us the true majesty of life itself. They restore our forgotten childlike wonder at the world, and they reawaken our lost belief in magic, dreams and possibilities.

If you talk to the animals
they will talk with you
and you will know each other.
If you do not talk to them,
you will not know them,
And what you do not know
you will fear.
What one fears one destroys.
— Chief Dan George

PART ONE

SYMBOLS IN THE NATURAL WORLD

Realizing that visible bodies are only symbols of invisible forces, the ancients worshipped the Divine Power through the lower kingdoms of Nature . . . The sages of old studied living things to a point of realization that God is most perfectly understood through a knowledge of His supreme handiwork—animate and inanimate Nature. Every existing creature manifests some aspect of the intelligence or power of the Eternal One . . .[1]

1 From *The Secret Teachings of All Ages* by Manly P. Hall (Los Angeles: Philosophical Research Society, 1977), p. LXXXV.

CHAPTER ONE

THE SPIRITUAL AND MAGICAL ROLES OF NATURE

There was a time when humanity recognized itself as part of nature, and nature as part of itself. Dreaming and waking were inseparable realities; the natural and the supernatural merged and blended. People used images of nature to express this unity and to instill a transpersonal kind of experience.

In the past shamans, priests, and priestesses were the keepers of the sacred knowledge of life. These individuals were tied to the rhythms and forces of nature. They were capable of walking the threads that link the invisible and visible worlds. They helped people remember that all trees are divine and that all animals speak to those who listen.

The early priest/ess-magicians would adopt the guise of animals—wearing skins and masks—to symbolize a reawakening and endowing of oneself with specific energies. They performed rituals in accordance with the natural rhythms of the seasons to awaken greater fertility and life. To them, every species and every aspect of its environment had the power to remind them of what they could manifest within their own life. It was an aid to bridge the natural world to the supernatural, awakening the realities of both within the environs of their own lives.

Though these rituals and behaviors may seem primitive and even silly to the rational minds of modern society, they are no less powerful today. And the laws which govern them—physical and spiritual—are no less viable. Different societies expressed these laws in their own unique ways, but probably the most distinctly expressed is the ancient Hermetic Law of Correspondence: "As above, so below; as below, so above."[2]

This principle teaches that all things are connected and have significance. We cannot separate the physical from the spiritual, the visible from the invisible. "This Principle gives one the means of solving many a dark paradox and the hidden secret of Nature. . . . The ancient Hermeticists considered this principle as one of the most important mental instruments by which man was able to pry aside the obstacles which hid from view the Unknown . . . (it) enables man to reason intelligently from the Known to the Unknown."[3]

It is for this reason that a study of Nature Totems is essential for understanding how the spiritual is manifesting within our natural life. A totem is any natural object, being, or animal to whose phenomena and energy we feel closely associated with during our life.

We can use animal imagery and other nature totem images as a way to learn about ourselves and the invisible world. We do not have to believe that these images and totems are beings of great intelligence, but there are archetypal powers that reside behind and oversee all manifestations in Nature. These archetypes have their own qualities and characteristics which are reflected through the behaviors and activities of animals and other expressions of Nature.

When we pay attention to and acknowledge a nature totem, we are honoring the essence that lies behind it. We are opening up and attuning to that essence. We can then use it to understand our own life circumstances more clearly. We can share in its power or "medicine." Nature totems—especially animals—are symbols of specific kinds of energy we are manifesting and aligning with in our life. The animal becomes a symbol of a specific force of the invisible, spiritual realm manifesting within our own life. The characteristics and activities of these totems will reveal much about our own innate powers and abilities. By studying the totem and then learning to merge with it, we are able to call upon its archetypal energy whenever needed.

Terrestrial animals have always had a strong symbology associated with them. They have represented the emotional side of life, often reflecting qualities that must be overcome, controlled, and/or re-expressed. They are also symbols of power—powers associated with the invisible realm that we can learn to manifest within the visible.

Birds have often been considered the symbols of the soul. Their ability to fly reflects the ability within us to rise to new awareness, bridging the earth and the heavens. As totems, birds each have their own peculiar characteristics, but they can all be used to stimulate greater flights of hope, inspiration and ideas.

Aquatic life can also be a totem. Water is an ancient symbol of the astral plane and the creative element of life. Various fish and other forms of aquatic life symbolize guidance to specific expressions of intuition and creative imagination. They can reflect the feminine side of our essence.

---

2   Three Initiates, *The Kybalion* (Chicago: The Yogi Publication Society, 1940), p. 28.
3   *The Kybalion*, Ibid., pp. 29-30.

The Masked Sorceror

A prevalent symbol associated with Shamanism, its image is taken from a prehistoric cave painting. Early man, surrounded by mysterious forces, responded to them through imitation. Man attempted to bring the divine in accord with humanity. Priests used totems and images to assist in coming face to face with the mystery. Through dance, costume, and so forth, the priest or priestess would take complete identity with the deity and its powers. This is the symbol of the prophet, medicine person, and the manifestation of the powers of nature. Images such as this invoke a presence which helps one to transcend the physical. Wearing the skins of the animals was a means of appeasing its spirit and honoring its power.

Insects are also a part of Nature, and they can be totems for us as well. From the bee of fertility in Egyptian myths, to the Mantis of the African Bushmen, to the many tales of the Spider Woman who created the universe, they hold a dynamic place within the spiritual scheme of Nature.

By studying and reading about the animals, birds, fish, insects, reptiles, etc., you encounter in your life, you can understand more about the circumstances you also encounter. You can learn much about the kind of energies you are most likely to confront and those you are most able to manifest within your own day-to-day life circumstances. You will learn how to draw upon those energies most effectively in dealing with life situations.

Nature has bestowed upon its inhabitants a natural ability for adaptation. This enables the animal to live in a particular place in a particular way. There are both physical and behavioral adaptations. A common example is the manner in which some animals may adapt to the cold, either through growing thicker fur or even migrating.

An animal such as a mountain goat has a dynamic adaptive ability for surviving in its mountain environment. Its feet are developed in such a manner that they can grip more strongly and securely. It also has more red blood cells, which assists it in surviving the colder temperatures in the mountains. By learning how our totems adapt to survive can assist us with our own lives by applying those same principles to our life circumstances.

This book's purpose is five-fold:

1. It will help you to determine your Nature totems.

2. It will help you in learning how to honor, attune, and invoke their energies more effectively into your life.

3. It will assist you in discovering the hidden powers and significance of yourself, as is reflected by your totem.

4. It will help you in applying the skills and adaptive powers of your totem to your own life environment.

5. It will help you to learn the language of Nature (physical, spiritual, and magical) as it speaks to you every day, to read and apply what it says (through signs and omens), and in doing so help you to develop a greater reverence and respect for all life, and greater power and control in your own.

The true shaman, the true naturalist, works to reconnect conscious human life with Nature and Spirit through totems and ritual. The images of the animals and the expressions of Nature help us to transcend our normal, waking consciousness so that we can more easily attune to ethereal realms and beings. The first step begins with realizing that all vision and imagery, originating in Nature or the inner mind, has validity on some level.

The Symbolism of Animal Totems

Characteristics and activities of these specific animal forms and images will reveal much about our own innate powers and abilities.

What gets most of us into trouble is interpreting what is seen in the mind or in Nature itself. Reading, studying, and learning about what you see and experience is what will facilitate relating them to yourselves. Don't accept Nature totems without question. Put them through the verification process that you will learn later in this book.

Don't discard a totem simply because it may not seem glamorous or as powerful as your ego wanted. The totem may be quite appropriate for empowering your life. Sometimes it is only through study and exploration of the specific totem that its significance will become clear. Remember that searching out the significance of Nature's expression to you is a way of honoring it.

Humanity has lost that instinctive tie to the rhythms and patterns of Nature, and with that loss has come a loss of the reality of magic. Nature tries to show us everyday that *all* forms of life can teach us. As we learn to listen to Nature, we break down our outworn perceptions. We find that magical creation is the force of life inherent in all things. And it is this, above all else, that Nature teaches to those who will learn from Her.

CHAPTER TWO

AWAKENING TO YOUR SPIRIT TOTEMS

The reality of spirit beings and their assistance to those in the physical has been a part of every major religion. The Greeks spoke to spirits and gods through oracles. The Bushmen of Africa developed ritual and myth from the movements and activities of animals such as the eland and mantis. The Native Americans imitated animals in dance and ritual to establish links with the spirit realm. Belief in the spiritual realms of life and all of its varied manifestations is universal. The most common belief in many societies is that spiritual guides often use animals or animal imagery to communicate their purpose and roles to humans.

In our modern, rational society there is a tendency to scoff at such possibilities. Spirit beings—whether in the form of saints, angels, ancestral contact, fairies and elves, demons, and even animal totems—fill our ancient myths and scriptures. When beliefs are as universal as these, some credence should be given them.

Their descriptions show them to be as diverse as the humans we meet on a daily basis. They serve many functions upon the planet. They help us to recognize our own innate abilities. They help empower us and protect us. Their energies can be used to help heal, inspire, and grow.

One of the most common forms spirit guides take are in the form of animals. Most ancient societies studied the natural world in order to understand the supernatural. Gods and goddesses were often depicted as animals. Throughout this book we will examine how nature—in the guise of animals—is a means by which the spiritual links with the physical. We will examine the symbolic and mythical aspects attributed to animals and how that should speak to us personally.

A totem is any natural object, animal, or being to whose phenomena and energy you feel closely associated with during your life. In this book we will be focusing predominantly upon spirit totems in the guise of animals. The study of animal totems is essential for understanding how the spiritual realm is manifesting within your natural life.

We can use animal totems and their images to learn about ourselves and the invisible world. We do not have to believe that these images and totems are beings of great intelligence, but there is an archetypal power that resides behind, oversees, and manifests through these creatures. These archetypes have their own qualities and characteristics which are reflected in the behaviors and activities of the animals.

A shaman works to reconnect conscious human life with nature and spirit through animal totems. The image of the animal helps the shaman to transcend the normal, waking consciousness so that he or she can more easily attune to the more ethereal realms and beings. By discovering your animal totem, studying it and then learning to merge with it, you will be able to call its energy forth whenever needed. You will be able to connect with specific archetypal forces and patterns through the animal and understand the patterns of your own life more effectively. When you honor the totem, you honor the essence that lies behind it—be it an actual force or a specific spirit being who uses the image and form of the animal to communicate with you.

Ancient priests and priestesses used animals totems to assist them in coming face to face with the spirit world. They would imitate the animals in posture, dress, and dance, creating rituals around it so as to invoke and share in the energy manifesting in the world through that animal. The animal became a totem—a power or medicine. It became a symbol of a specific kind of energy. When they awakened to that totem and honored it, they released the archetypal energies behind it into their lives.

You can learn to access that same energy. By doing so, you begin to learn the language of nature and open yourself to her secrets. The first step, though, is to determine what your animal totem(s) might be. There are techniques to help you identify your personal animal totems. Most are simple and require little more than increased observation and the application of your own creative imagination. That is what this book will help teach you.

Most people equate the imagination with unreality. Nothing could be further from the truth. The imagination is a power of the mind to create and work with images. It is this ability which can open us to other realms, assist us in healing, help us to discover lost knowledge and to open to higher vision and even prophecy.

Through creative imagination we begin to see the spiritual energies surrounding and interplaying with the physical world. What we consider imagination is a reality in some form on levels beyond the normal sensory world. With creative imagination, we create a new kind of awareness, a new kind of experience in color and form. This triggers higher forms of inspiration and intuition, giving us a higher understanding of the conditions of our lives and the spiritual energies affecting it. Images are the tools to link with the spiritually creative world. It is what helps you to identify your spirit totems and awaken their energies in your life.

As you begin to identify and recognize your animal totems, you will begin to understand your life more effectively. You will be able to develop a more unique view of yourself, along with a new look at reality. You will find yourself filled with new inspiration, and you will find yourself more creative within your life. The more you understand your totem, the more you will understand yourself.

DO YOU KNOW YOUR ANIMAL TOTEMS?

(Begin the process of discovering your animal totems by examining the animals you have been most interested in and the times of your life that interest was piqued. Use the following questionnaire to help you determine which animals are probably totems to you in your life.)

1. Which animal or bird has always fascinated you? (We are drawn to that which most resonates with us. Those animals which fascinate us have something to teach us.)

2. When you visit the zoo, which animal do you wish to visit the most or first? (As a child, this is especially important. Children are more naturally open and thus are able to more easily recognize the animal that will be important to them.)

3. What animal(s) do you see most frequently when you are out in nature? Have you had encounters with animals in the wild? (The animals we encounter, in the city environment or in the wild, have significance for us. We can learn from them, even if only about survival within that environment.)

4. Of all the animals in the world, which are you most interested in now? (Our interests in animals change. Yes, we usually have one or two that are lifetime, power animals, but others become prominent when there is something important or specific to teach us.)

5. What animal most frightens you? (That which we fear the most is often something we must learn to come to terms with. When we do that, it then becomes a power. Some shamans believe that fears will take the shape of animals, and only when we confront them without fear do their powers/medicine work for us instead of against us. Such an animal becomes a shadow totem.)

6. Have you ever been bitten or attacked by an animal? (Historically, if a shaman survived an attack, it was believed that the animal was the shaman's spirit totem and the attack was the totem's way of testing the shaman's ability to handle the power.)

7. Do you have dreams with animals in them or are there animal dreams you have never forgotten? (This is especially important if the dreams are

recurring or if at least the animal image in the dream is a recurring one. Children often dream of animals, and attention should be given to these animals. They will often reflect specific spirit totems of the child.)

THE BASICS OF ANIMAL TOTEMS

Animal totems go by a variety of names. They are called spirit animals, power animals, totem helpers and others. Regardless of how people refer to them, certain beliefs are common:

1. Every animal has a powerful spirit.

2. This spirit may be its own, or that of a being who uses the animal image to communicate messages of the world to humans.

3. Every animal has its own talents. A study of its talents will reveal the kind of medicine, magic, and power it can help you to develop within your own life. Remember, every animal has a specialty.

4. Lifelong power animals are usually wild, not domesticated, animals. There are a few exceptions, but even these exceptions are often just links to the true power animal. For example, people may have dogs or cats as totems. These have their own medicine and power, but the domesticated animal may only be a softened form of its wild counterpart. A dog may be a link to the wolf, coyote, or any of the wild canine family. A cat may be a link to a member of the wild feline family, such as panthers, lions, tigers, and such. For many, beginning with the domesticated form of the totem is a way of laying a foundation so that some day they will be able to handle and work more effectively with its true power form.

5. The animal chooses the person, not the other way around. Many believe that they can just choose an animal and start communicating with it. Usually ego gets in the way at these times. The individual chooses the animal he or she believes to be most glamorous and powerful, rather than what is harmonious to the individual. The results are ineffectual and often frustrating. No animal is better or worse than any other. Every animal's medicine is unique. It is always much better to be powerful in mouse medicine than to be clumsy and ineffectual in eagle medicine. You will find your greatest success in the animal that comes to *you*.

     When I was about four years old, a spirit wolf came to me. At the time I shared a bedroom with two older brothers and one who was two years younger. On this particular night, my father had taken my two older brothers to a ball game, and I was to sleep in the room alone with my younger brother.

I was in bed when I saw lights against the wall. There was a soft film and then an older woman and a wolf stepped into the room. I started screaming and calling to my mother who came running down the hall and into the room. As I blurted out about the wolf and the lady, she kind of smiled and tucked the blankets in around me, all the while telling me that I was just having a bad dream.

I knew it wasn't a dream though, as the woman and the wolf were standing about three feet behind my mother. She just shushed me, saying to go back to sleep because she didn't want to wake up my brother Tom. She then left.

She no sooner left and the woman and the wolf drew closer. Both seemed to be smiling gently, but that didn't matter to me at the time. I started calling out to Mom again. She opened the door and again tried to tell me there was no one there that it was all a dream. This time she told me to come sleep in her bed, telling me, "They can't get you in here."

Her words had no effect, for the woman and the wolf followed us into her room. I just pulled the covers over my head and tried to pretend they weren't there.

I would see the wolf often from that time on, and occasionally the woman, who called herself Grandmother. I eventually became more and more comfortable with them, but I never told anyone again about them because I knew they would not believe me. It would be years later before I was able to put it all together and realize who and what they were.

Wolf encounters still continue to this day—not only in my dreams, but as spirit beings around me. I have also been privileged to meet the wolf in the wild.

6. You must develop a relationship with your totem. To communicate with them demands respect. You must learn their point of view. Animals won't just warm up to you immediately. They must learn to trust you and your limitations, and you must learn to trust them and their limitations. This takes time, patience and practice.

7. You must honor your totem for its medicine to be effective in your life. The more you honor them—the more significance you give them within your life—the more powerful and effective they become. Some of the ways you can honor them and draw them closer into your life is by:

Hanging pictures of them,

Drawing pictures of them,

Reading and learning as much about them as possible,

Buying figurines of your totem for yourself or purchasing small tokens and images of your totem and giving them to friends as gifts. These fetishes are a reminder of the power and spirit of your animal totem.

Donating to wildlife organizations with time and/or money.

Dancing to honor your totem is a powerful link. Learn to mimic its behaviors. If it's a turtle, learn to creep like a turtle. If it's a lion, learn to crouch like a lion. If it's a bird, imitate its hopping or flying. And most importantly, keeping the animal alive within your imagination. See yourself as the animal totem using its qualities in appropriate places within your life. *Remember that the imagination is a real link to your totem.*

8. Once you learn to work with the medicine of your power animal, it then becomes a doorway to connecting with others of the animal realm. You are not limited to just one totem. Each can teach or add something to your life that the others can't. Working with your power animal will help teach you how to align with others. This way if you need greater strength, you can call up the image and draw upon the energy of a bear. If you need speed, you can connect with the energy of cheetah. Through your power animal, you learn to align with and shapeshift to the energies of other animals and beings.

9. Although there are one or even several totems that are strongest in your life and remain with you through most of it, others do play a role. You may have a totem for a day. You may have a totem that assists you through a particularly rough period in your life.

One may come to you and stay with you through a cycle of several years. Another may be present when you do creative work. You are likely to have different totems for different areas of your life. There's no limit to the totems you can work with. The key though is to connect strongly and fully with at least one. This expands the consciousness and opens the bridge to others more easily.

Owls came to me often in my dreams during childhood. Then at about the age of 12, the visits became less frequent. Before I was out of high school they had stopped. Years later, the owl came once more into my dreams. I asked it where it had been.

"I can not stay while the heart is closed."

I remember looking at it, puzzled, and I am sure the owl smiled at my response. "I am silent when around you, but I will return when the heart is open and that which you allowed to help close your heart is gone. You have needed others more than me through these years."

I then saw movement behind the owl, and I saw all of the great cats that had visited me so often in my dreams since my teenage years—the panthers, the cougars, and the tigers. I then was shown an image of my father and the way he often treated my brothers and I, and I awoke. Years later, the owl began to show up in my dreams again—always at a distance and always silent—usually in dreams replaying childhood gatherings.

In 1989 my good friend Quenda Healing Woman gifted me with some owl teachings. My eyes filled with tears and my throat became tight.

Images of death and funerals filled my mind. I knew then my father would soon pass away.

Two months later my father died of cancer. And the owl visits me regularly once more in my dreams.

10. More than one person can have the same totem. I know a number of individuals who work with wolf medicine. There are common factors in the way each works, but there are also differences. The archetypal energies and spirit reflected in the wolf will manifest for each uniquely, because each person is unique. The role the totem plays will be specific in many ways to the individual.

Individuals who are in close relationships may share a totem. That totem becomes a guide to making the relationship stronger and more productive. The totem may watch over the couple. Totem sharing is not limited to couples. Healing and meditation groups often share a totem animal, to oversee the activities.

A wolf is a totem that my wife and I both share. It works with each of us individually in separate ways, but also as a couple. A number of years back, my wife and I took a canoe trip at the time of my birthday into northern Ontario. On midnight of my birthday, we were awakened by distant wolf howls.

This was unique for they were rarely heard at this time of year. The howling continued off and on all night. Each time it picked up, it would come from a different direction. It was one of the best birthday presents I had ever received.

On another occasion we also made a trip to Superior National Forest, hoping to physically connect with the wolf totem. People visit Superior year after year with no wolf contact, but we felt if the wolf were truly our totem we should have faith and try. As we prepared to leave the area, disappointed, a beautiful wolf stepped out from the trees and stood about 30 feet in front of us. It turned and stared, its eyes locked on ours for what seemed an eternity. Then it crossed and followed us in the shadows of the trees before disappearing once more into the woods, leaving us thrilled and blessed.

MEETING YOUR ANIMAL TOTEM

The exercise that follows is one that will assist you in meeting your animal totem. We will be using the creative imagination to help open the animal realm to you more effectively. Don't worry that you might be making it up. You would not be imagining it if it did not have some significance to you.

It is important to be relaxed and to not perform the exercise with any preconceived notions. Let the animal totem present itself to you. Let it choose you,

Awakening to Your Animal Totem
Learning to draw upon the energies of your animal totem through the use of creative imagination is essential to awakening the magic and power of its medicine.

rather than you choose it. Keep in mind that the totem will have symbolic significance to you. The more you learn about it and meditate on how it might reflect your own life, the easier it will become to access its energies.

In exercises such as these, most people get into trouble with the interpretation of the images encountered. Your nature totem may be a bird, a mammal, or even an insect or reptile. Read, study, and learn about your nature totem to facilitate your being able to relate it to yourself. Don't just accept the totem without question. The imagination is a wonderful tool, but if not used properly, it can mislead. Put your totem through a simple verification process:

- How does it feel?
- What emotions/sensations does it arouse in you?
- Is it an animal you that interested you in the past?
- What does it make you think of?
- What is your heartfelt response?

Do not haphazardly discard it, simply because it is not as glamorous as what your ego may have wanted. The totem may be quite appropriate to you, but you will not know until you study and explore more closely the qualities and characteristics of it. Use the dictionaries in this book to assist you, but do not limit yourself to them. Do your own exploration. Searching out the significance of the totem and its application to you and your life circumstances is a way of honoring it. It is the first step in opening a communication that can lead to true animal-speak.

If after your studying and exploration you cannot find its application to you, perform the exercise again. If you have a totem appear with fangs showing or it is in any way frightening, simply come out of the exercise. There will be no harm. You can end wherever you wish. You can experience as much as you wish. Totems teach that there is but one moment and you are in charge of that moment.

Keep in mind too that frightening images are more often than not projections of your own fears. They may also be expressions of resistance. It is amazing sometimes how programmed we are not to accept anything that can't be rationally explained in the moment. Most people have some degree of programming of the idea—"Better the devil you know than the one you don't."

When you start exploring the inner realms and their play upon the outer world through nature, it can be a little disturbing. There is often a sense of being vulnerable and unprotected, of having no control. If you find yourself encountering fear and resistance, think about your favorite pet, and imagine taking it along with you in the exercise. This will calm you, and its energy is always loving and protective to you on the inner realms.

With exercises such as those that follow, individuals often wonder if they are experiencing a true shamanic journey. The difference is simply in the depth of experience. In a true shamanic journey, you are actually in it, feeling it and experiencing it first hand. It will not always follow a prescribed pattern. In meditational exercises, such as the following, you often observe yourself experiencing the situation or imagining how it would be experienced. With time and practice the meditation can become a doorway to a true journey.

Most exercises to discover one's totem can follow a basic pattern:

1. Relaxation.

2. Entering a cave or tree.

3. Leaving the cave or tree to enter a meadow or natural area.

4. Experiencing peacefulness of nature.

5. Allowing the totem to enter the scene.

6. Allowing the animal to speak to you—its movement, sounds, form, color, etc, will give you a message about its power. You may even hear its thoughts in your own. Allow it to tell you or show you how it has helped you in the past and how it will do so in the future.

16

7. Give thanks to it for making itself known, and ask it for some tangible confirmation in the next week or so that it is truly your animal totem. Such confirmations can come in many ways. You may see its face in the markings of a stone. It may come to you in a dream. You may encounter figurines, pictures or television. programs on it, but if it is truly your totem, there will come some confirmation of its presence in tangible form, in a quantity that is more than coincidence.

8. Move back to the cave or tree and step back through it to its other entrance point. Then step out from it.

9. Take four or five slow, deep breaths and allow yourself to feel grounded and connected.

10. Begin your verification process. Research and study the totem and its qualities. Meditate and contemplate on its qualities as they apply to you and your life circumstances.

Preparation

Drums and rattles are effective instruments to use, although they are not crucial. If drums and rattles are used, the rhythm should be slow and steady. You should allow the drum beat to lead you. I recommend you not do any imaging, but simply sit and feel the drumbeat for at least five minutes. This relaxes you and brings your body rhythms into synchronization with the drum. If you do not have drums or a rattle, you may use some soft music that is repetitive and nonintrusive.

Make sure you will not be disturbed. Take the phone off the hook, lock the door, and/or do whatever is necessary so that you will not be interrupted. Make yourself comfortable. Sit or lie down, whichever is easiest for you, but make sure your back is straight so that the blood can flow freely up the spine. Close your eyes and breathe deeply. Then begin to perform a progressive relaxation. Focus on each part of your body, sending warm, soothing sensations through it. Begin at the feet and work your way to the top of your head. Take your time with this. The more relaxed you are, the more effective the exercise will be. Don't worry if your mind wanders. Just bring it back to where you left off and continue. Then simply imagine the scenes that follow.

Exercise

As you relax, you find yourself growing lighter and lighter. The surroundings seem to fade, and you are wrapped in the warm dark cloak of your own energy and mind. It is safe, warm and comfortable.

In your mind's eye you begin to see soft light, and slowly the view opens. You find yourself at the edge of a crystalline pool of water. The sky above is blue, and there is a soft haze on the distant horizon. Above you, the sun and the moon can be seen together in the sky. You are not sure if it is dusk or dawn, but you know it is one of those powerful "Between Times," a time in which there is a thinning of the veils between the physical and the spiritual.

To your right, at the end of the pool, is a waterfall. The spray from it is cool and misty, and where it touches the pool, water ripples outward, distorting all reflections. It gives the area a surreal appearance.

You look about you at the green grasses and the distant trees, and all is silent. It is as if nature is in a state of quiet anticipation. You look back to the waterfall and you notice a dark area behind it. You move toward it, and as you stand close to the waterfall, you see a cave half-concealed behind it. You step carefully behind the waters and into the muted darkness of the inner cave.

You are surprised, for it is illuminated with soft torches. The light given off from them give the open chamber a warmth. Somehow it looks familiar, and it makes you feel as if you were expected.

To the back of that chamber is a tunnel that is also lit with torches. You glance over your shoulder to the area beyond the waterfall, and then walk further into the cave. It is as warm and comfortable as it first appeared, and as you step further in toward that back tunnel, you feel a slight giddiness, and a soft childlike laugh slips out. For the first time in a long time, you feel like a child, about to open and explore wondrous treasures of the world.

You step from the chamber onto the path of the tunnel and begin to follow it slowly. It is well lit, and you are not at all uncomfortable. You reach out and touch the walls with your hands, and you are surprised at their warmth. It is as if you could feel the life blood of the earth itself flowing through its walls.

As you move further along, the tunnel widens and grows taller. The torches are fewer and more distant, but you notice that it seems to be getting lighter still. Then you pass a couple of torches that are not even lit. You stop and touch them, just to confirm they have not recently gone out, and then as you look ahead, you see the reason. The tunnel has widened so greatly that the sun is able to penetrate almost fifty yards back.

You can see beyond the end of the tunnel. There is a distant river and lush green grass. The sunlight sparkles off of it as it would the morning dew on a summer's day. Across the field is the edge of a rich, deep-green forest. You pause only a moment, and then you run the last fifty yards and burst from the tunnel into the warm sunlight of this beautiful meadow.

The sun is warm upon your face, and the grass soft beneath your feet. Your nose is teased with the fragrance of honey and spring wildflowers. The air is sweet, and you tilt your head back and stretch your arms wide. You spin and swirl and laugh at the beauty and lightness of this meadow.

Next to the river is a large, ancient oak tree. Surrounding it is the greenest and most lush grass you have ever seen. You run to it and sit down beneath it. You stretch out, and roll in its softness, and you inhale its sweetness. Then you sit up. Next to the tree is a stone, shaped as if carved into a chair.

You sit down upon it, and as you do, you find that it fits your form perfectly. It makes you giggle with wonder. You breathe deeply, and from this chair you look about you. It is quiet and peaceful, and you know that this meadow is a place where wildlife must surely come, and for a moment you envy the animals and the birds for having such a place of beauty.

You sit upon that stone chair and you enjoy the beauty of nature. It is as if with each breath you become more and more a part of it, and it becomes more and more a part of you.

Then suddenly your breath catches. You see a movement out of the corner of your eye at the edge of the forest. You hold your breath. Maybe you will get to see some wildlife. Then from among the trees comes movement.

It may soar above you or it may step out into the meadow. You sit still. watching, as an animal appears in your vision. Don't force it. Allow it to show itself to you. And as it does, its eyes seek you out and hold your gaze.

Never have you seen anything so wonderful, so unique. Such animals have always seemed so wild and out of touch. There is no fear as it moves closer, only recognition and wonder. Surely this must be a dream! Then, as if in response to your thoughts, it makes a sound, a movement, a gesture and you fix your eyes upon it. In that moment you begin to understand. You catch glimpses of memories of how it may have helped you in the past. You now know why you have always been fascinated with it. And then it begins to move toward that tunnel. It pauses and turns to look back at you, as if telling you it is time to go on. You stand and begin to follow it. As you approach the mouth of the tunnel, it waits. It is so close; with a few steps you could touch it.

Carefully, gently you extend your hand out to it, but before your hand gets close enough to actually touch it, it jumps and is heading back to the edge of the forest. It pauses, looking back at you once more and then disappears into the green.

You understand. It will take time to develop a relationship. There is much you have to learn from each other. Until then you must be patient. You smile a sweet sadness, and then move back into the tunnel following it back to the waterfall.

As you step from the cave and behind the waterfall, you look into the crystal pool. You see your reflection rippling, and then behind your reflection you see the form of your animal totem. You catch your breath and you laugh, thanking it for opening to you. As you do, its image disappears, and the scene around you begins to fade. You are again in the warm darkness of your own mind. The image of your totem is strong within you, as you breathe deeply and allow yourself to come back to your surroundings.

CHAPTER THREE

THE MYSTERY AND MAGIC OF PREDATOR AND PREY

The average person rarely understands his/her connection to and impact upon the environment. Most people live in the cloistered environments of the city, away from the wild or the truly natural world. Our trees and lawns are manicured. Our food is bought already prepared and packaged. Many see animal life as being either cute little Teddy Bear figures, or as "wascally wabbit" types as found on television and in cartoons. The only contact many have with truly wild animals are those which have adapted to living within city environments—the squirrels, raccoons, robins, and such.

Because of this, it is not surprising that most people do not feel a part of the natural world. There is little connection to it, and thus even less concern for it. For some it may hold a small fascination, but for many more there is a lack of reverence, respect, and understanding for it. The world is merely a distant, abstract object full of different creatures and plants, with no life or purpose of its own other than to take care of us.

Seven of my years of teaching were spent in a special, alternative education program in the inner city. Our goal was to take students who had behavioral, social, financial, and academic problems and train them for entry-level positions in the work field. Most of the students were unable to function within the regular high schools and probably would never finish their formal education. Illiteracy was widespread, and criminal records were not uncommon. And most had traveled no further than to where the city buses could carry them.

During my last year with this program, I arranged a number of field trips. One of these trips was to the Cincinnati Zoo, about fifty miles away. Only a handful had ever been to a zoo, and they had not been there since they were very little children. The response was amazing.

I have never seen such pure wonder, awe, and excitement. Every time I turned around, students were running up to me, breathlessly describing some "weird" animal they had seen. I was being tugged in every direction to "Come see this!" Eyes that often seemed cold and vacant became wide and alive. Students who rarely smiled bubbled over. Those who were usually fighting were open and friendly. And all of them, who were so used to proving they were tough and adult, got to experience part of the wonder of childhood discovery that they had lost or never had.

It spoke to each of them intimately. On the bus back conversations were fresh and lively, even when some lighthearted arguing ensued over each of their favorite animals. Soon the conversations diminished and the students settled into a quiet contemplation. As we got closer to the school, postures changed.

Some of the changes were subtle. Quiet contemplation shifted to masks of stoicism, and eyes became vacant and unreadable once more. Other changes were not so subtle. Some students began to fidget. Conversations began once more, but no longer were they lighthearted and focused on the fun of the zoo. Some suddenly seemed to be embarrassed by their own behavior at the zoo and their childlike excitement over the animals. They began to posture to the others on the bus and play it off. Some were quietly nervous with eyes darting, searching the faces of others to discover if the day's childlike release would come back to haunt them. Smiles disappeared, and there were even a few eyes that were moist. It was a moment of sweet sadness.

The trip had created a memory that they would be able to draw upon the rest of their lives, but it also reminded them of how different the world was than they had ever perceived it. It reminded them that there was so much to be discovered outside of the neighborhood. It was then that I realized they had truly experienced a kind of culture shock.

They were not prepared for the immersion into the strange animal world. Yes, they knew what zoos were, and they had seen animal and zoo depictions on television, but it was not the same. Their experience stirred wonder, bewilderment, and even disorientation, but it also triggered a new reading of their present reality. The world was no longer the same. It no longer was confined to the concrete and sidewalks of the city's neighborhoods. It was much greater and more complex than they had ever imagined, and this scared them.

Although this is a somewhat extreme situation—albeit not uncommon—it did reveal that most people have distorted perceptions of the natural world. Animals are alien life forms to most people. Their behaviors and activities appear strange, mysterious, and entirely disconnected to human life. The wrong assumptions about animals and the natural world abound in today's society.

Probably the most mysterious, and thus the most misunderstood, aspect of the natural world is the mystery of predator and prey. Most assume when you mention predator and prey that the reference is to those who kill and those who are killed. The truth is that, in the animal world, most fall in between these two extremes. Sometimes the predator is also the prey. A snake will swallow a frog, but then it is plucked up and eaten by a red-tailed hawk.

When we study the process of predator and prey and learn of its natural and spiritual significance, our misconceptions begin to crumble. We begin to understand that there is a power and magic in the animal world, especially in its relationship to us. We begin to realize that every species is linked to every other—animal and human—in the ecosystem in staggering ways.

Predators and prey are found everywhere. A predator can be defined as one who has the ability to take live prey. Humans have often exalted in the beauty, power, and majesty of predator animals. We have exalted in their wild freedom. Birds of prey have been commanding symbols of authority and awesome omens of battle.

There has always been a contest between predator and prey in the natural world, and life is always the prize. Owls search for mice. Warblers search for insects, and hawks search for warblers. The predation process takes time, patience and skill. It sharpens the senses. The strongest, most alert and knowledgeable will survive. Animals grow stronger and wiser trying to avoid being caught.

When you work with spirit totems from the natural world, the mystery and power of predation will be awakened within your own life. Understanding it to its fullest extent will be necessary to work its magic within your own life circumstances and environment. Predation in the natural world holds four primary lessons for humans. Each of these lessons has its own corresponding form of magic.

On a mystical level, each can also be related to one of the four directions and to one of the four elements. These correspondences are, of course, general. They are not locked in stone. They simply provide a jumping-off point for understanding and working with predation from a practical, magical perspective. It also reflects the universality and balance found within the mysteries of predation in the natural world that can be yours if you learn to work them. Understanding these lessons, their correspondences, and their magic is the key to making your life more creative, healing, and spiritual through the use of spirit totems.

THE LESSON OF LIFE, DEATH, AND REBIRTH

MAGIC	:	CREATION
ELEMENT	:	FIRE
DIRECTION	:	SOUTH

Life and death are the two most creative processes we experience. And yet both are filled with mystery and superstition. Life is difficult for most to understand and death is difficult for most humans to accept. We have built a tremendous fear around it. The processes involved in both life and death are complex. Birth and death are the greatest changes we can encounter, but they are not the only ones.

When we examine birth and death, we want to view them as changes or transitions, not as final states. Change occurs on many levels and at many different times within our lives. Changes are blessings. They are signal flares of new growth. Loss and gain are relative terms, but it is always our fear of death or change that prevents us from exploring new ways. The changes we go through on a daily basis are miniature mirrors of the entire life, death and rebirth process.

Many ancient traditions involved rites of passage, symbolic rituals of birth, death, and rebirth. A person would die to one stage of life to be reborn to a new. Every day we are challenged in some way to let go of the old and create the new. Each of us is challenged by our life circumstances.

When you work with spirit animals and totems, this mystery will become more defined. You will begin to see the little deaths and rebirths in your life on a daily basis. You will begin to see them in the same rhythms and patterns of your totem. You will begin to see how you can use the life and death process to end aspects of your life and to create new ones.

Predation in the natural world can teach us how to develop no fear of death while maintaining a high regard for life. Those in the natural world do not worry about death. Their focus is on living. If death approaches, they fight fervently, not giving in and living to the fullest. Each day and moment is taken for what it is. Every day's activities is lived with the same fervor and intensity as the next. There is a sense of living in a perpetual present. There is no past, and the future takes care of itself. Every day is a new creation in which the natural energies of the animal are applied with fresh vigor.

Many have difficulty reconciling predation with anything other than cruelty. We must remember, though, that predation links predator and prey, killer and victim, together. In the ancient Qabalistic tradition there is a term that can be loosely applied to this. It is "tsimtsum" which refers to God's self-limitation. Judgment is separated from mercy, and creation necessitates judgment, untouched by any softening influence.

"As a free act of love in which God gives of his essence for the purpose of creation . . . untouched by the softening influence of the power of mercy. If God had created the world through the combined powers of judgment and mercy, it would not have been the world as we know it. The lion would not hunt the deer out of compassion, and in so doing would die of starvation and condemn to extinction all of the predators who depend on his hunting skills for survival. We would not eat other forms of life and would probably deny ourselves the eating of an apple out of compassion for the tree. As it is, the interaction of life forms upon the planet creates a perfect balance in nature. The lion only kills when he's hungry. Only man kills for pleasure. The lion, in accordance with the immutable cosmic laws, is exercising perfect judgment. Man is not." [1]

Predation teaches us that there is no life without death, and there is no death without rebirth. Death always has a loss and a gain balance. It is the working with the old and the new, the process of giving and taking. Predation teaches us that all life is sacred and essential to all other life.

As we work with our individual totems, we will begin to see how the predation process in its life within the wild reflects our own life within our environment. There will be parallels. There will be times best to feed and times best to rest. Times best to play and times best to hunt. These parallels will help you to take advantage of changes and opportunities that present themselves. Examining the prey of your individual totem, be it another animal or something of the plant kingdom, will help you in seeing how to create rebirth in your life.

Shamans often work with balanced medicines. For example, one who works with owl medicine would do well to study skunk medicine as well. Skunk is the favorite food of the great horned owl. A peregrine will capture a duck. A robin yanks a worm. A wolf pack brings down a moose. Predation links predator and prey, knitting them together in a complex intimacy.

By examining the combined qualities (the medicine) of both predator and prey, the powers of death and rebirth become more accessible. The balance of totems (predator and prey) enables you to recognize the natural rhythms of the death and rebirth process and use it more effectively. By working with the energies of both the predator totem and its prey as a totem will make life transitions less chaotic and disruptive. As a result your life becomes more creative and productive.

The magic of creation involves learning to use the deaths within your life as opportunities for rebirth. It involves learning to use the cycles of life—the ups and downs, the highs and lows to your advantage. As you will see, every animal has a natural cycle. Some are more definable, but there are times in which the animal is more or less active. If the animal is your totem, applying its rhythms and natural cycles to your own life will make you more productive.

This is the primary reason that fire, and its direction of South, is associated with this lesson. Fire is destructive as well as creative. It purifies, and it burns away the dross so that the gold can shine forth. It is the mystery of the phoenix who rises from the ashes. Fire is the element of the heart, the center of passions and love that can help us to recreate our lives. It is the element of regeneration and

---

1   Gonzalez-Wippler. *A Kabbalah for the Modern World* (St. Paul: Llewellyn Publications, 1987), p. 134–135.

resurrection, and it is this lesson which enables us to use the fires of our experience to create positive changes in our life.

Creation is a process, not a final goal. Change within your life reflects that the creative process is active. Most people ask for changes in their life, but fail to recognize them for what they are. They find them difficult and oftentimes chaotic. Transitional periods involve movement. This movement, and any of its ensuing difficulties and chaos, forces us to be our most creative, while reminding us that life is always in a perpetual process of creation. We can either choose to participate in it or ignore it. If we participate, especially through work with spirit totems, the lessons of death and rebirth are learned and our lives are filled with the magic of creation.

Magical Exercises

1. This simple meditation/visualization is powerfully effective. For it, you must have knowledge of some predator and its most common prey. If you already have a totem that is a predator use it, otherwise choose a predator from the world of animals that has always fascinated you.

   Visualize a bad habit, an uncomfortable situation, or something negative in your life as the prey animal. Then visualize yourself as the predator. See yourself swallowing the habit, eliminating it, and becoming stronger as a result.

   Use the predator's natural hunt cycle in this visualization. If it hunts primarily at night, perform the exercise at night. If it hunts during the day, perform it then.

   Only spend about 5–10 minutes a day on this exercise, but put a lot of feeling and passion into it. Within a week, you will begin to notice a difference. Make sure you see yourself, stronger, healthier and more empowered as a result.

2. A variation of this exercise can be used to effect changes in your life as well. Again use the predator and prey images. In this case though, the prey will represent a change you wish to make in your life or the things you wish to acquire but which have eluded you to this point. The change should be visualized in the form of a prey animal which is smart and has eluded you up til the present.

   Visualize—imagine—yourself hunting, stalking, and giving chase to the prey. Visualize the feel of the chase and the capturing of the prize. VIsualize and imagine yourself stronger, happier and more fulfilled as a result.

   Sometimes the changes we wish to make are intricate and have several steps. Each step can be seen as a prey animal, with the following step a larger prize. For example, if your predator is a red-tailed hawk, you might visualize the first step as a mouse, the second as a snake, and the third as a jack rabbit.

Decide on a realistic time frame when you would like to see the complete change accomplished, along with the time frame for each step of the change. Visualize this predator and prey activity for about five minutes each day until each step is accomplished, and then move on to the next. You will be surprised at how much more quickly and easily your goals are accomplished.

Lesson of Life, Death, and Rebirth

The turkey vulture epitomizes this lesson. It may be a scavenger, but by cleaning up after death, it prevents disease from infecting other animals and the environment. It thus sustains life and enables rebirth.

(Photo courtesy of Brukner Nature Center, Troy, Ohio.)

THE LESSON OF ADAPTATION

MAGIC	:	SHAPESHIFTING
ELEMENT	:	WATER
DIRECTION	:	WEST

Adaptation is the natural ability of an animal to live in a particular place in a particular manner. There are physical adaptations and behavioral ones as well. A fox will use its long ears to dissipate heat in the summer and its bushy tail to cloak its face and nose from the cold in the winter. This is a physical adaptation. A mule deer will always vary the path and the trails it follows to a food source, rarely using the same one twice. This helps keep it safe from predators by making its movements less predictable. This is a behavioral adaptation.

The result of both forms of adaptation is life. If a predator becomes too specialized, it can become endangered. The snail kite of southern Florida is a good example. It feeds only on large marsh snails. With the loss of good marshlands, the kite's primary food supply has dwindled, and it is now an endangered species.

On the other extreme is the coyote which will eat just about anything. The coyote is found throughout the country. It can be found in cities, plains, mountains, and deserts. It will kill its own prey or scavenge off the kills of others. It is also known to root through garbage cans to find food. Its ability to adapt to the environment and find food and shelter wherever it can has enabled it to survive and thrive.

Most predators fall between these two extremes. Most rely on a few species. Most are able to adapt and change their appetites if conditions demand it. The manner in which your totem adapts and survives within its environment provides clues as to how best you can adapt and survive within your own environment.

Different animals adapt in different ways—even those of the same environment. For example, in hotter climates, the totems may become more nocturnal. If you have one of these animal totems, it may tell you that you would work more effectively at night.

Some animals in hotter climates have large ears to help dissipate excess body heat, such as in the case of a desert fox or hare. Individuals who have fox totems and who are having difficulty with the heat during the summer would do well to wear their hair behind their ears. Since a fox dissipates heat through its ears, those who are connected to fox medicine will find that this also works for them.

Other animals in hotter climates may use panting to dissipate heat. Those with such a totem should learn new breathing methods and rhythms to assist them in their own hot environments. Those breathing methods and patterns will help them dissipate heat not only from the climate, but also from any particular heated situation that may arise, helping them to keep cool.

A study of the survival technique of your totems will provide clues to activities (behaviors) or physical attributes you could focus upon to survive more effectively in your own life. If a kestrel is your totem, for example, you may need to pay more attention to the subtle movements around you. Most birds of prey respond strongly to movement. A kestrel can spot a beetle move from 100 feet up in the sky. Paying close attention to subtle movements will enable you to recognize and take advantage of opportunities when they present themselves.

Once you have discovered your totem, learn how it adapts to its environment. Then practice applying that same kind of adaptation to your environment. That totem provides clues as to the best way for you to successfully adapt and be productive in your life environment.

Water, and its direction of West, is most appropriate to this particular lesson. Water will take the form of its container, and it will follow the path of least resistance. It is the element that reflects the shifting of emotions through the use of imagination. Water can absorb and concentrate life in varying degrees.

Adaptation is the ability to shift to meet the needs of the waters within our life. We must be able to shift like the waters around us. We must be able to ride them and flow with them, without becoming engulfed by them.

Water is often associated with intuition, dreams and inner vision, and journeys. It is one of the most ancient forms of transportation. Water that does not flow becomes stagnant. This is a reminder to always use our natural abilities to flow and change according to need. Water will adapt itself to its environment.

Imitation of your totem's adaptation abilities is a step leading to the magic of shapeshifting. Shapeshifting is natural, instinctual to all humans. In the story I related of the students on the field trip, the behavior change on the bus trip back was a natural example of adaptation. They began to shift out of the fun and safety of the trip to postures and attitudes that they would need to survive once back within their own life environment.

Every day, you shift your energies to meet daily trials, responsibilities, and obligations. You learn early in life when and how to smile. You know when to be serious or when to be studious. You have learned what activities and postures make you more or less vulnerable. Shapeshifting is not just transforming yourself into some beast as is often related in ancient myths and tales. It is a matter of controlling and utilizing your energy to the fullest to meet whatever the life situation requires. Learning to assume the posture and attitude of your totem will facilitate this, and that is part of what this book will teach you.

A shapeshifter is one who can relate to and adjust behaviors to work and live as conditions warrant. The shapeshifter is one who manipulates his/her aura and energies for growth. The shapeshifter is gentle according to need, and still capable of great strength. The shapeshifter can adapt to change—pleasant or otherwise. The shapeshifter can find the creative possibilities within limitation, and by the shapeshifting overcome the limitation.

Learning to shift your consciousness, to align with and adapt your energies to that of your totem—imitating its manner and behaviors—will help you to survive. Remember that your totem would not come to you if there were not something it could teach you. Imitating the adaptive behaviors of your animal totems and applying them to your own life circumstances is the first step to being able to shapeshift your life.

Magical Exercises

For this exercise, you will not need to know your individual totem. It is primarily an exercise in proving to you that you can adjust your energy field—your aura—for particular effects.

An old axiom teaches that all energy follows thought. Where you put your thoughts—that is where energy goes. We can change the shape, colors, and intensity of our auric field by our thought patterns. The following exercises can assist you in developing this ability. This is a preliminary work for the ultimate ability of shapeshifting.

- Stand against a wall and see yourself as becoming its color. Imagine yourself blending into it and becoming a part of it. Try this with a couch and against backgrounds of different patterns and colors.

- Practice seeing yourself as invisible. One way to assist this process is by seeing your aura as a haze or fog around you, hiding you.

- When you are comfortable with the above, use them in a group situation (meeting, party, etc.). Before you arrive, make yourself invisible, or take a seat somewhere and imagine yourself as part of the furniture.

The results of the above are always interesting. You will be surprised at the comments you receive. Such things as, "Oh, I didn't know you were here," or "When did you arrive? I didn't see you come in" are not uncommon. You will also be surprised at how many people bump into you, apologizing for not seeing you, as you imagine yourself as part of the furniture or walls. With practice you can learn to be as noticed or unnoticed as you desire.

THE LESSON OF USING YOUR POTENTIAL

MAGIC	:	MANIFESTATION
ELEMENT	:	EARTH
DIRECTION	:	NORTH

Every animal is unique unto itself. Each species has its own characteristics, its own strengths and its own weaknesses. These natural abilities are often reflective of your own innate abilities. The totems that come to you are often symbolic of potentials within you that can be developed and used to your benefit. Keep in mind the principle of correspondence discussed earlier.

The animals which are our totems are mirrors to us. They reflect lessons we need to learn and abilities we can most easily develop. We can use them to

The Lesson of Adaptation

The red fox is a wonderful example of this lesson and its corresponding magic. The fox's ability for camouflage and focused attention has enabled it to survive, in spite of extensive hunting and human encroachment upon its territory throughout its history.

(Photo courtesy of Brukner Nature Center, Troy, Ohio.)

understand ourselves and our life circumstances. The animal becomes a symbol of a specific force that is able to be manifested by you. It is a medicine for healing your self and your life, and it is a power that can be accessed to help manifest your dreams.

Once you discover your totem, which this book will help you to do, study it. Learn its individual characteristics and behaviors. These same characteristics and behaviors can be developed by you to make your life more productive. In this way the animal becomes your teacher. Just as predator and prey become stronger and wiser in developing their skills, you will do likewise.

For those of you who learn to work with animals and the spiritual and archetypal energies symbolized by them, members of the predator and prey community will come into your life at some point as an individual totem. When this occurs, give it the significance it truly deserves. A study of your totem's individual predation process will provide insight into your own ability to learn, to survive, and to develop to your fullest potential. It will provide the clues to the most effective ways for you to work the magic of manifestation within your life.

Predators waste little. A mountain lion or bear will eat its fill and then bury the hide and remains for later. Another, such as the wolf, will gorge itself, knowing that food is not always readily available. All of us can learn from the predator's penchant for little or no waste. It reminds us to use our abilities to the fullest and not to waste what we do have.

Most predators hunt alone. If your animal totem is one of these, it may reflect that you too will best develop or utilize your abilities alone. Others develop cooperative hunting techniques. Wolves will hunt in packs, and even Harris hawks hunt in groups.

A friend in Colorado, Kin Quitigua, runs an educational program called Hawkquest. He uses his Harris hawks to teach the predator and prey lessons, and he is often asked by the U.S. Wildlife Department to rehabilitate other birds of prey.

The first time I met Kin he was working with a golden eagle whose parents had been killed and so it had never learned to hunt. He was using his Harris hawks to imprint it with hunting techniques so that it could eventually be released into the wild. I was astounded at the cooperative hunting technique employed by his two hawks the first time I saw one of his demonstrations. One would fly low, flushing the jackrabbits into the open, and the other would come from on high to add power to the kill. It was a remarkable demonstration of their cooperative abilities.

Individuals with totems that develop cooperative behaviors should learn to utilize the same behaviors within their own life. Prairie dogs live in a community and are master architects, each adding to their rooms and each watching and sounding alarms for others within their community. A prairie dog may not seem like a glamorous totem, but it has abilities that are unique.

Those who find the prairie dog as their totem will have the ability to develop and manifest those same kind of abilities within their own life circumstances. This will be most easily accomplished within a community setting of some sort, rather than as a loner. (Refer to chapter eleven for more specific information on the individual abilities of the prairie dog and other animals.)

The life skills of your totem will help you in more skillfully handling your own life. In the predation process, successful attack is accomplished with specific skills such as speed, ambush, or teamwork. The technique your totem uses is a technique you can learn to apply more successfully within your own life. Those animals preyed upon also have a number of defenses. Some use safety in numbers, such as prairie dogs and musk ox. Some develop an armor, as in the case of an armadillo or porcupine. Some use camouflage and invisibility. Some use just a vicious attack or great vigilance. Remember that you must look at the predator and its most common prey. Both have qualities that will be beneficial for you to develop. Both can teach you things that you can apply to your life circumstances.

The more you understand about your totem's individual characteristics and behaviors, the more you will understand about your own natural and often hidden abilities. When you begin to recognize these abilities and then use them in your everyday life, you honor yourself and the spirit of your totem animal. It is at this point that you begin to realize that manifesting what you need is not as difficult as you once believed.

Once you "be" who you are (reflected in part by your totem), then you must do what is necessary to be you. As long as you persist, you will succeed in manifesting what you need or desire. A hawk is a hawk. It behaves like a hawk and not like a duck. Because of what it is, it is able to recognize opportunities essential for, and unique to, its life. If it fails to catch its prey, it does not worry about being unable to eat. It persists. It does not change. It works to become a more effective predator, for that is where its success lies.

What blocks most people from manifesting their dreams in life is their fear of being who they are. Sometimes this is a fear of non-acceptance from others. Sometimes it is a fear of failing. Sometimes it is simply because their whole life has conditioned them to live in a manner entirely alien to who they really are. When we are afraid, we are more likely to miss or neglect opportunities when they appear. When you are true to yourself and your instincts and your potentials, there will be no fear.

Recently, at Brukner Nature Center in Troy, Ohio, where I do volunteer work, an immature red-tailed hawk was brought in for rehabilitation. It had a broken wing. Part of my job is to clean the cages and feed the animals. In order to clean the cages, many of the animals have to be removed, especially if they are in rehabilitation.

This young hawk never shows fear. Upon moving it to a clean cage, it ruffles its feathers impressively and it stares intensely as if to show you that even when caged and hurt it is no less magnificent and powerful than before. It strikes fast and strong with its talons when you reach for it. Even with the heavy gloves on, its talons will occasionally penetrate and cling. This hawk is always true to itself.

In spite of a broken wing, in spite of being confined indoors in an alien environment, it is true to its natural behavior and instincts. It doesn't put on airs; it doesn't try to pass itself off as something it is not. These qualities are what will enable it to survive in the wild. And that is what makes it a magnificent creature!

When you begin to behave in the manner most natural to you and use—if only in simple ways—your innate abilities, your life begins to work. Animals never get hung up on fruitless repetition of behaviors and patterns that are doomed to fail. They don't put on airs. When you begin to be true to your higher self, your own magnificence begins to manifest, and people begin to notice a "newness" about you. They may not be able to define it, but it is a nobility manifesting from the true essence within you.

Earth is the element, with its direction of North, associated with this lesson. This element is symbolic of wisdom, patience, and prosperity. Part of the lesson is that we can receive from Mother earth all that we need. By being true to yourselves, we will have what we need. Mother Earth is where we have come to learn and to grow. It is where we learn to free ourself from our limitations. It is here that we begin our quest for the Grail of Life, which is the quest for our true essence and how best to manifest that essence within our life.

The ancient mystery schools taught the axiom "Know thyself and thou shalt know the world!" It is this precept that is inherent within the third lesson of predation. That which we know, we share in. When we know ourselves and the treasures within us, we become open to the treasures of the Earth.

Every animals' abilities are unique. Every human's potential is unique as well. There are many philosophies, systems, and teachers to help us come to greater awareness of our innate abilities. We do not have to limit ourselves to just one. We can gain something from them all.

This lesson and its magic involves learning from whatever source you can find. It involves extracting it, reshaping it and synthesizing it into what works for you as an individual. It involves using what you learn in the manner that is best for you. It is then that your ability to manifest becomes truly empowered.

Most people fail at magical practices because they try and manipulate people and situations around them. Magic works best when applied upon oneself. Instead of working from the outside in, work from the inside out. Be and do what is most natural for you, and then the world does not need to be manipulated. You find more joy, satisfaction, and fulfillment in yourself, and thus the world reinforces it.

A hawk who misses catching a rabbit does not try to become a weasel or raccoon. It learns to use its natural abilities—its eyes, its speed, its strong talons—more effectively. Each time it hunts, it grows stronger and wiser. Even if it does not succeed, it still has no fear. It just hunts more intensely at the next opportunity. It knows instinctively that there are always other opportunities. When we come to understand and learn to use our own talents, we instinctively know there will be opportunities to apply them—even to adapt them. If the hawk doesn't catch the rabbit, it may catch the snake or the mouse. It takes advantage of its opportunities.

Our totems help us to recognize our opportunities in life. They help define who we are and how to succeed. Their individual abilities reflect our own innate ones. When we learn to live to the highest of our innate abilities, we realize that the world has within it everything we need for fulfillment. Wondrous opportunities begin to manifest so frequently that we can not ascribe them to mere coincidence. You will find you will be able to manifest more than what you need to live a joyful existence.

The Lesson of Using Your Potential

A groundhog has the unique ability to form elaborate dens with many exits and entrances. It can also slow its entire metabolism in response to seasonal changes (hibernation). This "death without dying" can be learned and used by those with this totem.

(Photo courtesy of Brukner Nature Center, Troy, Ohio.)

The same skills your totems use to survive and to capture prey can help you to become more aware and sensitive in your relationship to the earth. By letting your totems teach you and help awaken that which is within you, you will be more attuned to the world and more able to partake of the blessings within it.

Magical Exercises

1. This first exercise is more of a self-awareness and self-examination exercise than anything else. Familiarize yourself with your totem's unique abilities. The dictionaries in this book and your own research should help you to pinpoint two or three specific qualities.

   Take a few moments to relax and think back over your life, starting from now, in five-year increments. Try and determine times in your life when you exhibited those same qualities successfully. Also try to see those times in your life in which you could have, or should have, demonstrated those same characteristics beneficially. This will help develop rapport with your totem, and it will help you to be more aware the next time such an opportunity presents itself.

2. Part of learning to work with this lesson and its magic of manifestation, requires that you learn to receive from the Earth. Everything we have is available to us, and it is often offered. Everyday gifts and opportunities are offered to us, but we either refuse them or do not recognize them. We have forgotten to receive from the Earth, and that is what predation can teach us.

   Unfortunately, in our present society, we hold strong to an unbalanced view of martyrdom. We are taught that if we do not suffer we cannot grow. We are programmed not to be selfish. We are drilled in our religions and our society to give and give. We are never taught that there are times to receive as well as times to give.

   Because of this most people have forgotten to receive. We refuse to receive both big and small. We don't realize that for manifestation of our dreams to occur, we must be able to receive. People are paid a compliment, and they say such things as, "What, this old thing?" or "Oh, no, I am really such a mess today." People offer to help and we say, "No, thank you, I can handle it myself."

   If we don't receive the little things—the compliments, the assistance, etc.—the universe does not send us the big things. It is the receiving of the little things that starts the magnetic pull which brings the bigger things into your life. Take time over the next few weeks to receive what is offered to you. Observe how often it occurs, and how often you would have turned it down. Try not to feel guilty, and don't try and figure out how you can pay it back. Just receive the gifts, joyfully and freely. You will have more than enough times to give back in more appropriate and opportune ways later.

   A predator knows how to receive. When the Earth presents a prey opportunity, it goes after it. If it doesn't, it will not eat. As you learn to recognize and acknowledge your potential, even greater opportunities to manifest it will present themselves to you.

THE LESSON OF RESPONSIBLE RELATIONSHIPS

MAGIC	:	HIGHER VISION & PROPHECY
ELEMENT	:	AIR
DIRECTION	:	EAST

The intricate web of connections of all life—whether predator or prey—is reflected most strongly through trophism or the feeding process. Solar energy is transformed by plants into food which then goes through the food chain. Plants manufacture food from the soil and the sun. Grasshoppers eat the plants. Frogs eat the grasshoppers, and so on.

This is a predatory transaction, the energy being passed from the eaten to the eater. This is why many societies believed that when you ate what you killed, its energy and essence became part of your own. Everything feeds upon and is fed upon by other life forms. The connections are real and significant.

"At each step along the way, energy is lost, through respiration, body heat, and other natural functions of living creatures. Thus as the food chain advances through ever higher trophic levels, the number of individuals at each level decreases, like the diminishing point of a pyramid. There can never be as many wolves as there are caribou, or as many swallows as insects. The predators are forever outnumbered."[2]

Humans are at the top of the food chain, and this should give us pause for thought. With the destruction of land and the killing of many species of animals, through pollution of the land and the air, by the time the energy of the food reaches us, what condition is it in? Over hunting, destruction of habitat, pollution, pesticides, etc. all interfere with the natural predation balance. Interference with the balance of natural predation tends to weaken the species through overpopulation and undernourishment.

This is reflected in the human world, just as it is in the natural. Just as in predators and prey within the natural world, every human action is followed by a reaction from all other worlds—whether positive or negative. The predator and prey process should teach humans that all action entails responsibility. There are relationships beyond what we may initially perceive.

Most ancient societies recognized this interaction. All life was honored, and human life was no more sacred than any other life. Rituals and ceremonies were performed before, during and after hunting. These rituals grew out of a recognition of the intimate relationship between an individual and the spirit of the animal.

---

2   Weidensaul, Scott. *American Wildlife* (New York: Gallery Books, 1988), p. 163.

In some rituals, participants would ask permission to hunt. Others were designed to reverence and show appreciation for the lives of the animals and to express thanksgiving for the food. Bones were often placed in trees or on the earth, near where the animal was killed, in thanksgiving and to ask pardon for taking its life. If an animal spirit assisted them, it was honored.

"'Little Sister,' he cried out. 'Thank you for guiding us here. Thank you for taking care of us all this way. Wherever we go we will remember your kindness. We shall wear your feathers when you give them to us. We will hold your people in regard and tell our people always to treat you well. I hope you have many children. Wah-hey!'

"The Flicker flew up in the air, flashing the gold beneath her wings one last time, and then flew back into the forest."[3]

People are beginning to recognize the interconnectedness of all life. There are many ways that other life forms—animal, plant, and mineral—enrich our own. They reflect the environmental health of the planet. There is the utilitarian value— i.e. food, clothing, and such. There is an educational value and aesthetic and spiritual value. Contact with a diversity of life expands our vision of life.

As we begin to see the expansiveness of life, a greater, more spiritual vision opens up. This vision can even become prophetic. At some point in our growth we must come to see beyond the immediate circumstances of our life. We must see the larger repercussions of our life upon all other lives. We are not separate. We are related to all things.

This higher vision is the magic of this lesson of predation. It is also why the element of air and its direction of East is associated with it. Air and the East are associated with creativity, inspiration, and higher awareness. The element of air is often representative of the powers of the mind, of new wisdom and higher intuition. It is the power of self-mastery through appropriate use of strength of will.

Air links the Earth and the heavens. It is a symbol of the unity of all things. It is what ties all life on this planet together. Nothing can live without air. It is the subtle influence of relationships. The links are not always visible, but they are always present.

The element of air is the expansion of the mind. It is learning to control the workings of the mind and to see the links between the Earth and the heavens, the animals and humans and all life. As we will see in part two, all birds are associated with the element of air to some degree. Birds of prey, especially, teach the lesson of relationships. They help us to understand that there is more than just an earthy aspect to predation. They teach the intricacies of all life, and how to fly to those heights that bring new perspectives on our life and our relationships.

Before a major decision were made in many Native American societies, the long range relationships and effects had to be considered. The repercussions upon all life for as distant as seven generations were often considered. This kind of

---

3 Excerpts from *Crow and Weasel* by Barry Lopez. Text copyright 1990 by Barry Holstun Lopez. Reprinted by permission of North Point Press, a division of Farrar, Straus & Giroux, Inc.

The Lesson of Responsible Relationships

The eagle is a powerful example of this lesson. Long a symbol of higher spiritual vision, it is at the top of its food chain. It is dependent upon the balance of prey animals beneath it. The prey that eagles eat are often poisoned with pesticides that do not always kill eagles, but often result in their laying eggs too fragile to survive. Humans are at the top of the food chain as well, and we need to look more closely at this relationship.

(Photo courtesy of Brukner Nature Center, Troy, Ohio.)

vision goes beyond mere foresight. As you learn to recognize connections and repercussions in your own life, you can learn to follow the ripples of actions and events to the past or future. This awakens prophecy.

Most psychic activity can be tied to this lesson of predation. Divination is the ability to gain knowledge of future or otherwise unknown events. Most psychics who make accurate predictions are able to do so because of their ability to see relationships. They are able—through whatever means they use—to see the pattern that has brought an individual to the point he or she is currently at. If the person continues that same pattern of action, there are likely to be specific, discernible repercussions. Since few people change their patterns, the percentage of correct forecasts can be high for someone capable of divining the patterns. Determining that line of relationships is part of higher divination.

Among the Lakota Sioux of the Great Plains, reverence is given to an ancient holy woman by the name of White Buffalo Calf Woman. Legend tells how she appeared at a time when the Indians did not truly know how to live. When she appeared, she spoke to the people in a special medicine lodge built specifically for her.

She presented the people with the sacred pipe and taught them how it would lead them always in the right direction. The bowl represented the buffalo and all humans, and its stem represented all things that grow upon the Earth. She taught them how to use the pipe and of the sacred mysteries of relationships it symbolized. She taught them how the pipe would help them to walk like a living prayer, and with it all could become one—the earth, the sky, the two-legged, the four-legged, the winged ones, the trees, the grasses, and all living things.

This lesson of predation teaches us—like White Buffalo Calf Woman—that all things, all people, all events, and all times are connected. When we can see those relationships, and follow them to the past and to the future, we are manifesting the magic of higher vision and prophecy.

Magical Exercises

1. For any relationship to work there must be three elements: silence, respect, and sharing. Relationships teach us silence. Silence enables us to listen and to experience the relationship as it truly is. It enables us to know when to speak and act for the greatest benefit. Relationships also teach us respect for other lives, and to only take that which is truly needed. Relationships also teach us sharing. They teach us how we can best live in the world with one another.

   This exercise will give you an opportunity to examine your predatory role in relationships. Allow your totem to lead you along a road to your past. You will stop at each of your most important relationships. Observe yourself in these relationships objectively, and allow your totem to show you whether you were in the role of predator or prey or if there was a sharing of the roles.

   After examining several of these, you should begin to see a pattern that you usually fall into. When you can see that pattern, allow your totem to lead you back to the present. Then allow your totem to show you the one quality above all else that it can teach you in order to have balance in relationships. Allow your totem to melt into you, to heal and balance, and open your eyes to a new awareness.

2. Choose an incident from your present, positive or negative. This can be an event, an outburst, anything that seems to stand out for you in the past three months. As you focus upon it, close your eyes, and envision your totem approaching you.

Allow your totem to lead you back to the day of that event. Observe it, replay it in your mind. Then allow your totem to lead you further back, to show you something that helped lead to that event. Do this at least four times.

Some people find that there are large jumps in time in this exercise. They go back five, sometimes even ten years, and find themselves replaying a situation from the past that does not seem connected at all. There is almost always a connection though. The emotion or behavior in the past event may be part of a pattern that led to what you experienced recently.

Simply observe. When you return you will have time to contemplate and make the connections. Again allow your totem to lead you back to the present, past those events. You may wish to have it speak to you, but do have it melt into you to heal and strengthen, to bring clarification, in the days that follow, on the relationships of events.

It is a good idea to write down the events you encounter in this visualization. Writing them down will help to draw their essence out of that ethereal mental realm and help you to clarify them in your own mind.

Do not be discouraged if you do not achieve results at first. Persist. As you develop your relationship with your totem through such exercises as these, the ability to use them for both past and future exploration will develop.

Eventually, you can use this same process to explore the impact present events will have upon the future. This is a little more difficult, because it is sometimes difficult to be objective. There can be a tendency to project what we want to have occur upon the mind, rather than see the effects that are actually being set in motion.

Work with the past first. When you begin to have more and more success with it, you can begin to use the process to follow the ripple effects to the future. You will learn to do this for yourself and also for others. This can be used to trace past-life connections to the present, and present-life connections to future lives.

Persist and practice. Remember that relationships demand patience and time to develop. Each time you practice, it will become easier. The more you honor and work with your totem, the more you will find opening to you.

CHAPTER FOUR

READING SIGNS AND OMENS
IN NATURE

Ecology is the study of the interaction between living things and their environments. We can never truly separate ourselves from the environment, but we can learn to read it so that we can use the knowledge of it to our benefit. The ability to read nature is what enables us to recognize true omens within our life.

An omen is an event which may indicate a particular destiny. People from around the world have believed in omens at some point. They have held strong the idea that the changing aspects of Nature reflect changes that are likely to occur within their own life. This is connected to that ancient Law of Correspondence we discussed earlier. What affects us on one level, affects us on another. The divine forces speak to humanity through Nature and its varied expressions.

Omens border upon an instinctual perception, an innate resonance with natural elements that we do not consciously recognize or acknowledge any more. As you develop animal-speak, you will begin to see relationships and patterns in Nature and animal behaviors, along with their correspondences to your life. You will know automatically that certain birds or animals are likely to be seen daily. You will come to expect certain kinds of behavior from them because of what you have come to learn of them—including their natural behaviors, sounds, rhythms, and activities.

The difficulty, though, is being able to define, explain, and apply the omen of Nature to your individual life. For this to be effective, you must be knowledgeable about your environment and the animals within it. You must develop practice in seeing relationships, without forcing the correspondences. You must begin to recognize that nothing is by accident or coincidence—that all things, all people, all animals have significance to us. You must be able to recognize that the supernatural world often reflects itself within the natural world.

It is easy to become superstitious in reading the signs of nature within your life. Most people see omens and superstitions as the same thing. The reading of omens is founded upon a knowledge base of the environment and the animals and other natural elements within it. The changing aspects of the normal, natural elements in your environment can then reflect changes in other areas of your life. The changes are interpreted from a strong knowledge base and with reason. Remember that correspondences in reading the signs of nature do not need to be forced when there is a solid base of knowledge. They reveal themselves naturally.

Superstitions, on the other hand, are beliefs or notions in the significance of an event or thing that is not based upon knowledge or reason. Superstitions often involve irrational fears and behaviors. Superstitions often involve actions that are taken to avoid bad luck. Relationships and correspondences between natural elements and one's own life are not formed from a base of knowledge.

VALENTINE'S DAY SUPERSTITION

It was often believed that a woman could determine the kind of man she would marry by the first bird she saw on Valentine's Day.

Blackbird = priest, a clergyman or a religious figure.
Dove = a good-hearted man.
Goldfinch = a rich man (especially if it was a yellow goldfinch).
Sparrow = a happy man.
Hawk = a soldier, a warrior or brave man.
Crossbill = an argumentative or bad-tempered man.
Robin = a sailor.
Bluebird = a happy man.
Owl = a man who would not live long.
Woodpecker = the woman will never marry.

These are superstitions and not true omens. A thorough knowledge of the birds in the individual's environment may prove that there is a greater likelihood to encounter certain birds every day, while never encountering others. An unusual or untoward behavior of a bird may provide indication of something unusual in the offing, but would not indicate one's future mate. Such beliefs, though, can be amusing entertainment and add fanciful fun to days like Valentine's Day.

The best example to define the difference between omens and superstitions can be found in the behavior of the short-eared owl. Communities and societies often experience times in which rodent and other prey populations erupt. In some localities, voles (meadow mice) suddenly erupt and seem to overrun the place. Such times were often depicted as unfortunate, evil, and even outright plagues. This perception of evil manifesting through an overpopulation of rodents was further augmented in places where overnight a horde of short-eared owls would also seem to materialize out of nowhere.

For the superstitious person, one with no knowledge base, this may appear to be an extraordinary revelation of evil from Nature; especially so since both rodents and owls have a long history of being perceived negatively. For those who have a good knowledge base of both of these animals, the interpretation would be entirely different.

Many predator and prey species have years in which populations plummet and years in which populations erupt. Many rodents are subject to boom-bust cycles. For their natural predators, this cycle is often matched. Short-eared owls have an instinctual knack for appearing overnight in a horde, to descend upon abundant food sources. Such appearances are not reflections of evil manifesting. Rather their appearance serves as a boon to help restore the balance of nature.

"This ability is shared by other birds. The California gull—the species the Mormons of Salt Lake City memorialized in marble for saving their crops from a cricket plague—has it. . . . A few years ago voles swarmed over Amherst Island on Lake Ontario. Short-eareds by the dozen poured in out of the void; more amazingly, they brought along a retinue: great gray owls, snowy owls, hawk owls, boreal owls and saw-whet owls in unprecedented numbers . . ."[1]

Correspondences will naturally deepen as your own knowledge base grows. The relationships between what you are experiencing in Nature and what you are experiencing in your own life do not need to be forced. You must be careful of not allowing your desire to divine the future to override common sense. Although it is usually safe to assume that the events within Nature can and do reflect something about the events within your own life, only a true knowledge base will allow those mirrors to be clear.

The most common misinterpretations occur because of your own fears. In the case of the boom in the vole population and the appearances overnight of short-eared owls, some may begin to believe that their life is about to be overrun with pests. Since even today many harbor the ancient superstition of the owl as an evil agent of the devil, the perception that their life is about to be plagued is what will be assumed.

In truth, the exact opposite would be a more correct interpretation. The abundance of both voles and owls reflects a cycle of boom beginning to manifest, a boom that has balance to it. But this kind of interpretive ability only comes with knowl-

---

1   Wolfe, Art. *Owls — Their Life and Behavior* (New York, Crown Publishers, Inc., 1990), p. 117.

edge. To one who is knowledgeable or takes time to learn about what is being observed, the natural world can shed light on most life circumstances.

It is also easy to read into Nature what you want to read and not what truly is. Many want to see every expression of Nature as a supernatural sign. The events and observations that are unusual, out of the context of normal patterns, or not part of your daily contact will often have the most significance for you. These kinds of circumstances will speak most strongly.

As you begin to study and observe Nature within your life, you must learn of its usual manifestations and patterns. Note the kinds of animals you encounter and their usual behaviors. The more you learn of the usual, the easier it will be for you to recognize the unusual, no matter how subtle. When something is different, then Nature is calling to you to pay attention.

Animal-speak requires that you realize Nature most often speaks to you in a natural manner. A person who wishes to get a message across uses a variety of techniques—language, vocal and facial expressions, tonality, volume, etc. If the message is an important one, the voice takes on a different tone—one of urgency or tension. You know the message is important because the tone of voice is not the usual. Nature and animals in Nature speak to us in the same manner. If the message is important, the expression of Nature will take on noticeable, although often subtle, expressions.

READING ANIMAL SIGNS

Nature speaks to us constantly. Through its shapes, colors, textures, smells, and varied expressions of animal life, it communicates to us about the world and our life. The symbolism of Nature will vary according to its context, so you must come to know its natural context.

Every animal has distinguishing features, movements, shapes, and colors. Each has its own unique relationship with humans. A good number of these are outlined for you in the dictionaries found within this book, but they are guidelines only. You must develop your own dictionary. Just as different groups of people who speak the same language may have different dialects and accents, it is the same with animal-speak. You must learn the dialect that is best for you.

In ancient Rome certain officials were charged with observing and interpreting natural omens for guidance in public affairs. These individuals were known as augurs. "Julius Caesar was a respected augur." Although originally augurs were bird talk experts who listened to what birds said, the term eventually came to be applied to anyone who used animals and their language for divination purposes. A particular branch of this came to be known as auspices in ancient Rome. Auspices was a method of reading the future in the activities of birds and animals.

The ancient augurs studied Nature. They learned to read her signs and to understand her language. Every augur had his or her own specialty, some working with birds and some with other animals and expressions of Nature. Regardless of the area of expertise, each augur had to come to terms and develop a new understanding of Nature.

If you are to learn animal-speak and develop your own ability for augury, you must lay a new foundation for relating to Nature. Nature speaks everyday, but few ever truly listen. If you were speaking to someone, and they never acknowledged it, soon you would quit speaking to them entirely. If you truly wish to learn animal-speak, you must re-establish the lines of communication with Nature. You must let it know you are ready to listen once more.

There are ten related steps to facilitate your ability to reopen communication and to develop augury. They are simple and can be applied within any living environment—swamp, city, forest, mountain, river, farm fields, grasslands, etc. By consciously working with them, you will send a message to the universe, and especially to all of Nature, that you are now open to receive communication. And all it takes to hear what Nature has to say is to be open to listening. These ten steps are:

1. Experience Nature first hand. Take walks in the woods or parks. Take binoculars to the beach. Seek out marsh lands. Don't assume that your environment is without Nature's elements. Try to identify birds by their calls. Try to identify different trees by their leaves.

2. Begin with an examination of the wildlife endemic to your environment. The plants, trees, and animals of your environment have much to teach you about survival. Although some may feel that the expressions of Nature within the city are nothing to shout about, a chipmunk can be quite as remarkable as a grizzly. Trees and flowers have long been symbols of mysticism and magic— each with its own qualities and characteristics. On the following two pages are lists of trees and flowers with the basic characteristics associated with them. For further information, you may wish to consult an earlier work of mine, *The Magical Name*.

3. Orient yourself to your landscape. As you will see in chapter five, the landscape can reveal much. It can be as symbolic as the animal life within it. Look at the spatial symbolism of your yard or home. What does its shape say about you? What is the form or pattern of the terrain? Does it appear soft to the eye? Hard? Broken? Sloped? Ask yourself what kind of qualities are necessary to live in such a terrain?

4. Pay closer attention to physical signs of Nature. These were often considered the most important elements of augury, and they can be powerful fetishes. The three most common signs read by ancient augurs were: (a) appearances of birds and animals, (b) feathers, fur, stones, or any physical fetish; and (c) the calls, chatter, and other sounds of animals. Pay attention to when they are most noticeable and where.

5. When you are out in Nature, pay attention to what seems to stand out most strongly. Some days a particular flowery fragrance may stand out. On other

days, it may be the continual cawing of crows. On another, you may notice a particular tree. That which you most notice when out in nature has spoken to you. Take note of it, greet it—acknowledge it. Then research it. What are the qualities and characteristics associated with it? These qualities will either reflect those awakening within you, or those you may need to awaken. Ask yourself, "Where can I apply these qualities? What are they saying about me and my life?"

THE SYMBOLIC QUALITIES OF TREES

Apple = magic, youth, beauty, and happiness
Ash = sacrifice, sensitivity, and higher wisdom
Aspen = determination, overcoming fears and doubts
Beech = tolerance, past knowledge, softens over-criticism
BIrch = new beginnings, cleansing of past, vision quests
Cedar = healing, cleansing, protection
Cherry = death and rebirth, new awakenings
Cypress = understanding of role of sacrifice
Elder = birth and death, renaissance of Faerie Realm
Elm = strength of will, intuition
Hawthorne = fertility and creativity, magic
Hazel = hidden wisdom, dowsing and divination
Heather = healing from within, immortality, and initiation
Holly = protection, overcoming of anger, spiritual warrior
Honeysuckle = learning from the past, discrimination, change
Lilac = spiritualization, realization of true beauty
Maple = balance, practical expression of psychic, promise
Oak = strength and endurance, helpfulness, continuity
Orange = clarity to emotions, release of trauma
Palm = protection, peace, opportunity
Pine = balance of pain and emotions, creativity
Spruce = new realizations, healing, intuition
Sycamore = communication, love, learning to receive
Walnut = eases transitions, following a unique path
Willow = magic, healing, inner vision and dreams

6. When you begin to take greater notice of Nature and apply what you experience, it is beneficial to pay special attention to colors. Are there specific colored flowers or plants that stand out, or which are continually encountered? What are the colors of the bird(s) you notice? Is there a significant color to any animal you come across? Keep in mind that color can be a most significant clue to the kind of energies you are likely to experience.

    As you will see, the colors of animals can provide dynamic insight into the qualities and energies manifesting within your life. The color reflects much about that totem's energies and its applications for you. The black of the crow

---

SYMBOLIC QUALITIES OF FLOWERS

Baby's Breath = modesty, sweet beauty

Basil = integration, discipline and dragon force

Begonia = balance, psychism

Buttercup = self-worth, the power of words

Cactus = manifestation of riches and beauty

Carnation = deep love, healing, love of self

Clover = luck, love and fidelity, kindness

Daffodil = power of inner beauty, clarity of thought

Dahlia = higher development, self-worth, and dignity

Daisy = increasing awareness, creativity, inner strength

Gardenia = purity of action and purpose, emotional help

Geranium = happiness, healing, and renewed joy

Gladiola = receptivity to divine will

Hibiscus = femininity, sexuality and warmth, new creation

Hyacinth = overcoming of grief, gentleness, inner beauty

Iris = higher inspiration, psychic purity

Lavender = magic, love, protection, healing, and vision

Lily = birth, godly mind, and humility

Marigold = fidelity, longevity, loving sacrifice

Morning Glory = Breaking down of the old, spontaneity

Rose = love, strength through silence, passion

Rosemary = power, clarity of thought, sensitivity

Snapdragon = will force, creative expression, clairaudience

Sunflower = opportunities, self-actualization, happiness

Violet = modesty, fulfillment, psychic sensitivity

may reflect mystery or the ability to bring light out of the dark. The red fox that comes into your life may reflect an awakening of the kundalini.

A study of the meaning of colors will help you in determining the significance of what you experience in Nature—whether it is the color of your animal spirit or some other aspect of Nature. Color is an expression of energy, and it can be symbolic of something positive or negative.

Do not be concerned if you only experience animals of muted and earthy colors. Keep in mind that most animals have colors that assist them in survival. The more muted colors may reflect a form of camouflage that serves to protect the animal. Be sure to ask yourself, "What purpose does this color serve for this animal?" Ask yourself whether you need to develop the positive aspect of the color or whether the color is a reminder to do something about its negative expression.

The following list will provide some insight into colors and their significance. In the bibliography are several books which also will help in defining the meaning of colors. Remember that in Nature there will often be subtle nuances to color tones, so be flexible in your interpretations.

COLORS	POSITIVE QUALITIES	NEGATIVE QUALITIES
Black	protection, birth, magic	secretiveness, sacrifice
Blue	happiness, calm, truth	depression, loneliness
Brown	grounded, new growth	lack of discrimination
Green	growth, healing, abundance	uncertain, miserly, greed
Grey	initiation, imagination	imbalance, secretiveness
Orange	warmth, joy, creativity	pride, agitation, worry
Red	sex, passion, strength	anger, aggression, impulse
Violet	alchemy, humility, spirit	obsession, misunderstood
White	purity, sharing, truth	scattered, overextended
Yellow/ Gold	communication, optimism, inspiration	needing clarification, overcriticalness

7. Yet another means by which you can begin to develop your ability to augur is by paying attention to the numbers associated with the animals you encounter. Numbers, like colors, have a deep and ancient symbolism associated with them. The numbers can help you to pinpoint the best area(s) to apply the energies of your totem. It can also help you to understand more clearly what Nature is trying to communicate to you.

For example, you may, upon walking in Nature, have three crows fly overhead. Later you may see even more crows, again in groups of three. To some the crow may be a symbol of the great void, the dark, but the numbers in which they appear will alter that interpretation. Three is the number of creativity and new birth, so seeing three crows may reflect that there is going to be a new birth, a new coming out of the void, a bringing of light out of the darkness.

The mysticism of numbers can help you in understanding animal-speak. The more you open yourself to developing a wider vocabulary of Nature— colors, numbers, plants, animals, etc.—the more it will speak to you and the more you will understand. How many of a particular bird or animal do you regularly see? Does a bird or animal, such as a crow, call out to you? If so, how many times? Is there a pattern to the sounds it makes—a natural numerical rhythm?

Pay particularly close attention to appearances of animals not often seen. This is especially significant if they appear more than once, and in a small time-frame. I have had days where a red fox would run across my path—on foot and while in my car—several times. Since a fox is gifted at camouflage and is hard to see, its appearance—especially more than once—had significance. On such occasions, I examined the qualities of the fox, the number of times it appeared and its direction of movement; all of which I was able to apply to what was unfolding within my life at that time.

A study of the significance of numbers, particularly the science of numerology, will help you to develop an expanded vocabulary for communicating with Nature. In the study of numerology, the greatest emphasis is upon the single digits of one through nine. The list in the following chart will provide some insight into the meaning of numbers:

NOS.	POSITIVE ASPECTS	NEGATIVE ASPECTS
1	beginnings, originality, leader	arrogance, dominance
2	feminine, dreams, cooperation	sensitivity, meddling
3	creativity, birth, mystical	gossipy, moody
4	foundations, patience, builder	stubborn, rigid
5	versatile, change, activity	scattered, overindulgent
6	home, service, family	jealous, worrisome
7	wisdom, seeker, truth	faithless, critical
8	power, money, infinity	careless, greedy, authoritarian
9	healing, understanding	gullible, hypersensitive

(All double digit numbers can be reduced to one of these nine by adding the two digits together. For example, 23 = 2+3 = 5.)

8. Yet another way of laying a foundation by which you can begin to develop animal-speak and the gift of augury is by paying attention to the directions in which animals appear. As we discussed in the previous chapter on predators and prey, each direction or quarter of the world has its own significance and meaning.

Different societies associated certain qualities with each of these directions. Some of these associations developed into superstitions. For example, a bird call heard first thing in the morning from the North was believed to reflect tragedy. From the South, it reflected a good harvest. From the East, it reflected good loving, and from the West, good luck.

As you develop your personal relationship with Nature and animals, you can ask your totems to appear in the direction that is most significant of their purpose. For this to work most effectively, you must have a strong idea as to what each direction symbolizes and represents for you. Then the animal that appears to you in that quarter of the world or from that direction will be a totem that will help you develop the qualities associated specifically with that direction.

For example, if you associate the West with healing and a red fox appears to you from that direction, it can be safely assumed it will help you with healing. To understand specifics, you must look at the individual qualities of the animal. Since a fox is associated with camouflage and invisibility, it may reflect that you are coming into a time to heal that which has been camouflaged or invisible to you.

In the following chart are some of the more common associations with each direction. You do not have to agree with them. Develop your own correspondences. Then when an animal appears to you from that direction, you will know its role within your life.

DIRECTION	CHARACTERISTICS AND ENERGIES OF THE DIRECTIONS
East	Healing, creativity, illumination, divination and intition, new birth and sunshine, new learnings, strength of will, communication, expression of new.
West	Vision, dreams, quests and journeys, emotions, imagination, creative arts, the feminine, higher compassion, inner spiritual renewal, goals.
South	Purification, faith, strength, awakening inner child, overcoming obstacles, playfulness, change, protection, self-sufficiency, trust, resurrection.
North	Teaching, abundance, balance, sacred wisdom and knowledge, gentleness, thankfulness, drawing forth inner treasures, empathic intuition, trust, alchemy.

Aside from the four directions of the world, attention should also be given to the position of the animals to yourself, along with any movement in relation to yourself. Does the animal appear on your left or your right? Does it move from left to right? Right to left? Toward you? Away from you? All of these have significance.

The right side is generally considered more masculine and assertive, while the left side is considered more feminine and receptive. If the animal appears on your left, it may reflect that its energies are still within and are not yet expressed. On the right, it may indicate that they are being expressed or need to be. If it moves from right to left, crossing your path, it can indicate its energies coming into your life; maybe even being born within you.

Decide for yourself what each direction means, and which movements will indicate what. Take five minutes a day for a week and meditate on these associations. By doing so, you are programming your mind to understand the movements. You are also sending out to Nature the guidelines for communication with you. (Refer to #10 for further information on this process.)

9. Another means by which Nature will speak to you is through the kind of activity the animals may be involved in when encountered. We have spoken of the importance of their directional movement, but their activities or lack of activity can also speak to us strongly. To understand this fully, you must understand the pattern of activity the animal is usually involved in.

A lack of movement or activity may be a reminder for you to take a break or rest from your own activities. If you encounter squirrels that seem to be playing and chasing, rather than gathering and storing, it may tell you to take some play time for yourself. On the other hand, if you encounter two animals squabbling, it may reflect conflicts that are present or soon to arise within your own life. The animals and the kind of squabbling will help you define and pinpoint where in your life this is likely to occur.

I have four large canines in my home—two golden retrievers, a German shepherd, and a mixed breed who thinks she's a golden retriever. Each has a unique personality, and each I often use for clues to what I should watch for in my own life. Each has periods when their own presence and behavior stands out from the others.

The oldest is a golden retriever who is the alpha dog. She knows it and doesn't have to force her dominant role. The other dogs sometimes try to cut her off when coming into the house or when getting water. She always remains calm. She is always the lady. She simply knows and trusts in her position in the household. At those times where this behavior stands out, it causes me to sit back and regroup myself. It is often a message to just be patient and wait. It reminds me that my position is not threatened.

The other golden retriever, Cheyenne, loves the outdoors and playing. She has always been a bit of a loner. At those times when she desires to be more sociable and playful, she will sit in front of me and begin swatting me with her paw. No matter what I may be doing, she will persist. If the pawing doesn't work, she will begin to gently bite my feet, or go up into the bedroom and grab one of my socks and toss it around in front of me. If that doesn't work, she begins romping with the other dogs between my legs. This is usually a clue for me to take a break from work. It reminds me that I need some play time and some socializing. It often reflects that I am too busy working or dealing with other people only on a work level and not for the simple enjoyment of socialization. My German shepherd, Akasha, likes to think she is the queen. She hates feeling left out or having the other dogs go first in anything. When we first got our hybrid, Avalon, she took over the mothering. At times she becomes very aggressive and dominant toward Avalon—sometimes too aggressive. When these occasions occur, I sit back and look at where I might be becoming too aggressive or pushy in my own life. More often than not, I can easily pinpoint the area.

Avalon, the mixed breed, has been a wonderful addition to the house. She keeps all of the other dogs active and playful. She likes to show the other dogs that she can get away with things they can't. She teases and aggravates. She steals and hides things. And she is always playful. At times when she is overly so, it reminds me to keep the kid in me alive and find some time for play. With practice you can learn to see the relationships between animal activities and your own life. The more you understand the behavior patterns of the animals you encounter the easier it will be for you. This is effective with both animals in the wild and those you may have as pets.

10. The last technique for developing the ability of animal-speak and augury is probably the most important. If you want Nature to speak to you and give you signs, you must ask it to. You must make a conscious effort to align yourself with Nature.

Meditate outdoors. Send thoughts and prayers to Mother Nature, asking for signs and communications. Pay attention to what you see, hear, feel, and smell each time you step outdoors. Try to find connections between what you experience and your life circumstances. I heard once that the best way to make a friend is to ask a favor. By asking a favor you are honoring that person and giving respect for what he or she can do. You acknowledge that person's unique ability. Ask Nature to teach you how to speak its language. It is the best favor you can do for the Earth and for yourself.

As you develop your ability to understand what Nature says to you, you can begin to ask for specific kinds of communications. One way in which this works is through your animal totems. Once you have developed attunement with them, you can ask them to communicate to you in special ways—ways that you will always know as messages.

The hawk is one of my totems. Over the years I have developed the ability to see and hear hawks everywhere I go. Whenever I travel, I always ask for hawk's protection and vision to assist me and guide me on my trip. I also ask that hawk show that it has heard my prayers by showing itself to me in the first hour of my trip. Hawk has never failed me. I always have several hawks that will appear alongside of the road in that first hour. They will be sitting on sign posts, on branches of trees overhanging the road or may just fly across my path. Each time I see hawk, I greet it and honor it.

If I travel at night, I ask hawk to send me some other totem to show that the journey is protected and blessed—since hawks do not fly at night. I may spot deer, owl, or some other night animal in numbers that tell me hawk is watching out for me.

As you develop your relationship with your totem, you can ask that it appear to you in specific ways for specific messages. For example, with my hawks, I ask that they let me know where police are on the highway, or if the road is clear. When I notice a hawk while driving, I pay attention as to whether it is looking at me, behind me, in front of me, soaring over head, on the right side of the road, the left side, etc. Over the years this has developed into a wonderful and effective vocabulary with hawks that enables me to know road conditions and the presence of police radar. It has never failed me, and it is very accurate. For this to work, you must develop the relationship and ask for the signs.

CHAPTER FIVE

AUGURY AND THE MEANING OF LANDSCAPES

As mentioned in the previous chapter, one of the ways in which you can come to understand Nature and what she says to you through animals is by examining the symbolism of the habitats. The landscape, the habitats, the countryside in which animals are observed and experienced can add much to your understanding of the role they will play in your life as totems. Keep in mind that the inner, spiritual forces often unfold as forms within Nature. This means then that a mountain crest has much greater significance than just being the top of a big hill.

Different worlds—different landscapes—reflect different states of beings. We can discover much about our own state of being by orienting ourselves to the landscapes within our life. Many societies recognized the importance of landscape and spatial shapes and forms. They saw them as dynamic symbols. We can discover much about our own life situation by orienting ourself to our landscape and the life within it. To do this appropriately, we must consider:

- The predominant elements and character of the whole, natural and artificial, i.e. the trees, flowers, ground, etc.,
- The spatial symbolism,
- The form or pattern of the terrain (soft, hard, broken, sloped, etc.),
- The relationship of a specific area to the whole region,
- The general cyclic pattern (seasonal, yearly, etc.),
- The predominant colors,
- The predominant wild life.

These are just some of the basic characteristics to consider. In the context of this book, we do not have the means to explore all of these aspects intricately with all their symbolic implications. We will try to give you an overview that you can begin to build upon for yourself.

In the East (India and Tibet particularly), the use of geometric shapes is called yantra and geomancy. A study of the symbolism of geometric shapes will yield much fruit in regard to the shapes within your own environment—be it the shape of a room, a yard, or a park. Although geomancy is often considered divination in Western Traditions, it has a much wider history and application to environments.

In China, feng shui is art that uses ancient wisdom to assist in arranging furniture and buildings to achieve the greatest harmony with Nature. This Chinese practice is based on principles of design, ecology, mysticism and architecture. "For all the mystery that surrounds it, feng shui evolved from the simple observations that people are affected, for good or ill, by surroundings."[1]

The Chinese, as with many societies, saw a dynamic link between landscapes and humans. They believed that Nature reacts to every change and that reaction resounds within the life of the human. Feng shui is a language of symbols associated with landscapes—rural, city, towns, and even in the rooms of a home. To the feng shui person, the shape of the landscape could leave an imprint upon an individual's life, affecting the character or the prosperity. It can be read and interpreted in very significant ways that need to be considered if we are to become fluent in speaking and understanding the language of Nature.

In feng shui, the environment takes on a symbolic quality. Mountains could be watchdogs or dragons, rivers could be serpents, and hills could be barriers. Trees could reflect longevity and protection, and flat, riverless plains are often considered devoid of energy. Looking at the symbolic qualities of the landscape, in conjunction to the animal totems, can reveal much more information.

This process can be applied in both rural and city environments. In the city, high buildings replace mountains, and roads replace rivers. The size, the shape, and the colors of buildings and skyscrapers affect the natural flow of energy and reflect much about what kind of energy will manifest in your life. The directions of roads and the angles can help define this as well.

Behind my home is a slight hill, and at the top of the hill is a line of apartment buildings that are like the vertebrae of the dragon. Separating the apartments from my home on this hill was thick foliage and trees of rich green which would indicate to a traditional feng shui person that this is a spot of high energy. It is a spot where a variety of animals gathered—raccoons, opossum, crows, woodpeckers, owls and a variety of other birds and small mammals.

Unfortunately, this past year, the city demanded that the apartment owners clear out the trees and foliage. Though they gutted the area, it took little more than a month before it was green and growing wild again, in spite of their efforts to seed it with plant life that could be more easily controlled. Even new trees were

---

1 Rossbach, Sarah. *Feng Shui—The Chinese Art of Placement* (New York, E. P. Dutton, 1983), p. 2.

stretching upward, all attesting to the positive flow of power in this area. It simply reinforced the impression that the dragon my home is nestled against is both very powerful and very beneficent.

SYMBOLOGY OF THE LANDSCAPE

By examining the shapes and contours of your environment and the environment of your totems, you will uncover so much more about yourself and the role your totem has within your life. Examine the landscape in which you encounter and observe animals in the wild. Try to determine some of its symbolic qualities as well. This will help you to understand the significance of the wildlife you encounter that is endemic to that area. To do this effectively, you must learn to use strong imagination, common sense, along with both psychic and practical knowledge. The following list will help you in this process:

The City Environment

In modern society, most people find themselves living within the city environment. This will not prevent you from learning to read Nature and to develop animal-speak. Cities do, of course, have their own unique lessons.

Cities often contain many lessons associated with community and learning to live with variety, flexibility, and adaptability. Examine the variety of people, conditions and such within your environment. Examine the shape of your city. What does its shape reflect? Does the main city building (government offices) face East, West, North, or South? (Remember that directions are symbolic of qualities.) Does your home in the city face the East, West, North, or South? What is the symbolic shape of your house or yard?

To the feng shui person or one skilled at reading landscapes, rectangular or square shapes are often considered best. They reflect balance. What do the street patterns closest to you seem to reflect? A backyard higher than the front is often considered more auspicious. Are there plant life or trees flourishing near your home? This reflects healthy energy.

Remember that cities and homes have their own metabolism. Those living within them will take on many of the same characteristics of their home, their yard, their neighborhood and their city. They will embody and reflect the qualities of these landscapes.

Cities also have their own indigenous wildlife. Those animals that survive and live in the city are very adaptable. Be careful about making biased judgments about city animals. Even the rat can have wonderful, symbolic characteristics. In Chinese astrology, the rat possesses characteristics that range from humorous to meticulous and often change directions. As with any animals, city animals should be examined for all their characteristics.

Forest Trees and Plants

Forests have a very ancient symbolism about them. This symbolism is often complex but always connected to the feminine forces within the universe—creation and birth. The kind of forest, its thickness and predominant tree and plant growth will provide insight.

Forests are places where vegetation and animals thrive—free of the controls of society and culture. It is hard to find forests that are not touched by human culture in some way, but it is always a good point to make occasional trips to forested lands. It is freeing to our own consciousness.

Forests are symbols of the unconscious. They reflect the untapped primal forces to which we do have access. Individuals who have a terror of forests may find that they are really afraid of freedom, their own creative forces, or the perils of loosening the unconscious.

The rules of life in the forest are very different and alien especially to a city dweller. The lessons of predator and prey are magnified to a greater and purer degree. The forest, though, is a place where our own creative forests can come alive and thrive without the limitations or restrictions of society and other people in our life.

Gardens and Plants

For the city dweller, gardens and plants are essential to maintaining contact with Nature in some degree. They are a symbolic reminder of growth—a reflection of Nature in miniature.

A garden is a point where Nature is controlled and subdued. It is Nature, enclosed. It is also a symbol of the feminine energies, the ability to create and nurture life. The kind of garden you maintain (vegetable, herbal, etc.) and the kind of animal life that visits it can be very insightful. It can often reflect how well you are consciously using your innate creative energies and abilities.

As your garden grows and produces, you will see movement and growth in corresponding areas of your life. If you house an indoor garden, at some point you may wish to transplant it outdoors so it can grow free and uninhibited. It can also be a means of inviting animals contact. This will strengthen your connection with Nature and animals.

Caring for your garden is a means of symbolically saying you are open to Nature and what it has to offer. It is an outer reflection of your willingness to commune with Nature. Inevitably, someone will say, "I can't make anything grow. Every time I plant something, it dies." Death is a part of Nature and should not discourage you. It may also reflect that you are trying too hard or attempting to grow something of which you are not yet capable.

Just like the development of anything beneficial, it requires time. Trying to develop immediate communion with Nature or assuming you will pick up augury or animal-speak quickly and easily is what creates superstition and disappointment. Remember that seeds need time to germinate and take root. But also remember that as you work to align with any aspect of Nature, you open the doors to align with all.

House and Home

Your house, and the animals found within and around it, can tell you much about your life. Do you have pets? What are their basic qualities and characteristics? What kind of relationship do you have with them? It is amazing how many irresponsible pet owners exist in the world. If you can't work responsibly with a domesticated animal, you will have even less success with the wild. What kinds of birds and animals do you most often see around your house?

Your home reflects and affects you as well. Traditionally, it is the place of wisdom, and it often reflects the human body and thought process. What rooms do you spend the most time in? What are the shapes of those rooms? What are the conditions of those rooms? Neat? Messy? Dirty? Clean? Warm? Comfortable?

Apartments and homes have some of the greatest impacts upon city dwellers. It should be a place in which you are comfortable and safe. The more at ease and safe you feel, the more animal life will feel safe and comfortable coming around. What feeling do you get when you step through your front door? When you step out into your yard, what do you primarily feel?

Your home or house and the animals around it will tell you much. If you are looking to move, it is a good idea to look at the birds and animals that seem to gather in that environment. Where the animals appear can also reflect much. If they are most abundant and frequent in the front yard, this may reflect the "front" you present or that part of you which is open to the public or predominant in the front of your mind. If the animals gather most in the back, they may reflect your private aspects—that which you have kept hidden—the inner consciousness. Every aspect of the home, interior and exterior, can provide clues to understanding what Nature is saying to you.

For example, if squirrels seem to gather or be seen most often in the front of your home, it may reflect that you appear to everyone to be a very busy person—working, gathering, and staying active. If they are seen most often in the back, it may reflect that you are privately gathering a working on many busy things that most people do not see. Remember that we are always looking for relationships.

Marshland

Marshland has a wide variety of animal and plant life. It is an environment in which many water fowl will gather. As we will see in part two, water fowl reflect the ability to move beyond the emotional or passionate stages of life. They can be symbols of bringing fresh air into our emotional life.

Marshes are also areas of decomposition. They are combinations of water and earth in a passive form. Decomposition is part of the transitional process—the tearing or breaking down of the old is necessary before the new can be built. It can reflect the alchemical process active within your life, especially if your totem is one which resides or is discovered in marshland.

In the tales of King Arthur and the Knights of the Round Table, Sir Gawain is one who would finally achieve his quest for the Holy Grail. Part of his journey and testing occurred in marsh landscapes. Those who have a totem from marshlands would do well to read the story of Gawain.

Meadows and Valleys

Meadows are areas of abundant animal life and vegetation. They are usually near a stream or river, so it is good to examine the symbolism of rivers as well as meadows. The water source usually nourishes the meadow. A traditional meadow has some trees, but most importantly it has waves of grass and wildflowers, lending the meadow a soft appearance.

The soil is usually very fertile and well nourished, and the totems of this landscape can help show you how to add fertility and nourishment to your own life. They may also reveal places where it is lacking. Be sure to examine the predominant colors, flowers, and the overall shape of the meadow. Remember that meadows are places of silent and soft growth.

Valleys are often equated with meadows, but there is a difference. A valley is more of a low-lying area. It is one of great fertility, and it is often contrasted with deserts, the place of purification. Valleys are long symbols of new life, new fertility, and a neutral zone beneficial for developing creativity. The totems associated with this environment will help you in that development. In legend and lore, valleys were often the home of priest and priestesses of the community.

Mountains

Mountains often reflect power and a loftiness of spirit. Those animals found around or indigenous to them will reveal ways to discover your own spiritual power. Mountains have height and a verticality which is traditionally masculine in its symbolism. This mass and shape reflects the sexual aspects of masculinity, along with outward expressions or assertiveness. To the Chinese, mountains were symbolic of greatness and generosity. Mountain ranges often took the symbolism of dragons.

Mountains can reflect the alchemical process active within your live. The animal totems that you encounter in such environments will reveal the means by which you can best work with the process in your own personal circumstances. Many myths speak of mountains which are hollow inside, serving much the same function as an oven—baking and tempering the spirit of those who enter. The hollowness and the interior have been described as the land of the dead and the home of the fairies. Again, it reflects that the totems associated with it are those which will open new dimensions to us.

The mountain reminds us of the spiritual attainment that is ours as we overcome our obstacles. The height of many mountains gives rise to thoughts of them being a world axis, linking heaven and Earth. Castles were often built upon mountains, providing a point where humans could commune with the divine or could draw the heavenly powers out of the sky and into manifestation on the Earth. Mountains are symbols for higher meditation, spiritual elevation, and communion with the blessed spirits.

Muddy Terrain

Terrain predominantly comprised of mud or animals encountered at times when mud is prevalent (after rains, etc.) are very significant. Mud is the union of earth and water. This combination reflects transition and transformation.

Mud is the substance of birth. It is the medium for the emergence of matter. This landscape reflects that there is a new stimulation occurring in some area of your life. The animal totem will help you to define that area.

Mud can also be a reminder to recharge and strengthen our connection to primal earth. The totem that appears may provide the clues to how best to accomplish this. Mud usually reflects the opportunity for new germination within your life.

On the other hand, excessive amounts of mud, or animals stuck in mud can warn of the same thing. Are you bogged down in a particular area of your life? Are your emotions bogging you down? Are you stuck in old emotions and unwilling to grow and move on?

Ocean, Seas and Rivers

Water is always significant. It is the primal life source. Many myths and scriptures speak of how all life sprang from the seas. The ocean is a symbol of womb, mother, and woman. The totems associated with it are tied to those same symbolic qualities.

Ocean, and water in general, is a dynamic force. It is constantly in transition, and it can reflect the same within your life. The totems of it can reveal how best to work with those transitions. The ocean is also the sum total of possibilities.

The ocean and great seas are symbols of the subconscious mind and even the unconscious mind. Totems tied to them can help us to awaken the deeper levels of the mind. Water reflects our spiritual life and our emotions. The quality and activity of the water in seas, oceans and rivers will reveal much. about these aspects of ourselves.

Rivers have an ancient symbolic connection to animal life, creation and the flow of time. Rivers are places where animals will gather to drink. The movement of the river is often used as a metaphor for the passing of time. Totems linked to or encountered by rivers may often help you in working with your past and/or your future.

Because rivers flow, they reflect a continual evolution. The quality of the river water, the speed of its movement, and the animal totem associated with it will help you to define the areas of your life undergoing evolution and how to work with that process most effectively.

Rocky Terrain

Rocky terrain can reflect many possibilities, all colored by the totem and its activity within that area. Rocks have been depicted in story and myth as obstacles that need to be climbed over. They are often symbols for the true self. Of course, different rocks and stones have different meanings—each with its own unique qualities. Rocky terrains, especially high upon mountains, were often considered the dwelling place of gods and goddesses because they were so inaccessible.

On the other hand though, they also can reflect solidness, stability, and sturdiness. They can be a point from which we can gain a new perspective. Many people can't resist standing or climbing rocks to gain a view of the surrounding terrain.

In learning animal-speak, we begin by looking at the animals. But we do not stop there. If we truly want to understand how the divine is expressing itself to us through Nature, we should also examine the environment in which the totem is discovered, along with its natural habitat if it is different from where it was encountered.

In the course of your life, you will encounter a range of habitats, climates, and animals. All of these will be saying something to you. Asking yourself the following questions will help you in developing your ability to understand what Nature is telling you through the animal world. It will help you to develop animal-speak into a true gift of augury:

- What are the characteristics and qualities of the animal totem?
  Is it migratory or endemic to the area?
- What is its natural habitat and what does that indicate?
- What is the symbolic nature of the habitat in which you encounter your totem?
- What is the climatic condition in which it appeared? Where does it usually season?
- What is this environment and animal saying to you about you and your life?

PART TWO

WINGED ENCHANTMENT

If men had wings and bore black feathers, few of them would be clever enough to be crows.

—Henry Ward Beecher

CHAPTER SIX

BIRD TOTEMS AND THE
INITIATION OF AIR

Birds have an ancient mythology and mysticism. In most societies, animals were visible signs of invisible forces, and people realized that you could only understand the Divine through its creations. This was especially true of birds. The behaviors, the characteristics, and the other qualities of the birds took on both natural and supernatural significance.

Birds were often thought of as deities or the thoughts of deities. In Norse mythology, the god Odin had two ravens as messengers, Hugin (Thought) and Munin (Memory). In Central American mythology, the god of the air, Quetzlcoatl, is most often depicted as a feathered serpent. In Native American tradition, the Thunder Bird is a spirit creature of great creative power and might. The Egyptian god Horus is usually depicted with a hawk's head, while Maat, the Egyptian goddess of truth, is often shown with a vulture feather. To the Hindus, birds represented a higher state of being.

Legends, folklore, and mythology are filled with winged creatures that touched humanity in many ways. Pegasus is the Greek winged horse. Harpies were birdlike women, and the ancient griffin is a combination of animals with great wings and a bird's head. The phoenix is a mythical bird that is burnt in the fires of sacrifice and then rises from its own ashes. Most tales of angelic contact depict these beings with wings, reflecting birdlike characteristics.

To primitive humans, birds were gods. Birds could make the thunder and bring the rain. Their feathered wings and their flight stirred the imagination of humans. Because of this unique ability to fly, much mystical and symbolic significance came to be applied to birds. Birds foretold of death and they could bring either good or ill luck. Birds were often seen as angels and teachers, or devils and destroyers. Many believed they were the souls of the dead. In a catechism class I attended when I was very young, a nun told a story of how a child would become a bird if it died before it was baptized.

Birds are one of the most ancient forms of life upon the planet. Many scientists believe that birds evolved from reptiles over 140,000,000 years ago. The oldest bird known to humanity is the archaeopteryx, Greek for "ancient wing."[1] The fossil of this bird, dated from the late Jurassic period, shows that it had a lizard-like tail, jaws with sharp teeth, and claws on the outer joint of its wings.

Flight is a means of leaving the earth and rising to the heavens. It is a means of descending out of the sky to land upon the Earth. Birds are the bridge between humans and the divine, the Earth and Heaven. They are the symbols of transcendence, the rising above lower natures. They reflect a taming or rising above a juvenile nature. Often times liberation from any state of being that is too fixed, final or immature is reflected through bird symbology and appearances. They are the ultimate symbols of transcendence and release from any pattern of existence to a more superior one.

Birds reflect a union of the conscious mind with the unconscious. They reflect the achievement of full realization. Because of their ability to fly, they are associated with aspiration, flights of intuition, beauty, and levitation. Birds are a source of creative imagination, and they have the ability to awaken within us our own flights of magic.

Each bird has its own unique qualities and characteristics. Examining those you encounter will do much in helping you recognize and use your own creative faculties. Each has the ability to help you in your life, to realize that everyday of your life presents opportunities to soar to new heights.

I believe there is a very good reason that crows are found everywhere. Traditionally, they were symbolic of magic. They squawk and call out to everyone. This should remind you constantly that magic is around you at all times, just calling out for you to use it within your own life. The behaviors, movements, and activities of the crows you specifically encounter will help you to understand how to apply magic in your life.

Learning to attune and recognize the spiritual significance of birds will help you open new faculties of perception—past, present, and future. Birds hold the knowledge of speaking with all animals. They hold the knowledge of how to make our ideas concrete and effective. As you approach periods in your life where you will be able to make new leaps in higher consciousness and new expressions of your true essence, birds will become more prominent. They will become signs, guideposts, protectors, and teachers.

As you begin to study and honor the birds you encounter at such times, you will find yourself being gifted with feathers. You will find them everywhere you

---

1   Bantock, Nick. *Wings* (New York, Random House, 1991), p. 5.

go. You will also be presented them by others in your life who may not know why they are giving you such a present but only that it *feels* right for you. These gifts should be honored.

Feathers have long been associated with the wind, the mind, new flights, and all creator gods/goddesses. They are a form of supplementary language, and, as signs and gifts, they serve specific functions, the most common of which are:

- A direct connection to gods, goddesses, and specific divine forces,

- A form the god/goddess (divine force) takes when traveling,

- A signal between human and human,

- Qualities and characteristics within or around you which you must deal with,

- A medicine or quality you can develop,

- A link to teachers of specific aspects of Nature including animal, angelic, and/or Faerie Kingdom beings.

- Omens and signs,

- Tools for prayers, petitions, and alignment with specific natural forces,

- A reflection of new changes and new leaps of consciousness about to unfold for you,

- A call to unfold the wings of enchantment within your life.

Most of these will be explored in detail in the next several chapters. Always keep in mind that a bird's wings and its feathers make it a part of heaven. Every feather is a special gift and a promise. Every feather can connect you with the specific archetypal energies of *any* bird. You don't have to have a hawk feather to link with hawks. Honoring and using any feather available will help you in your alignment.

This is because all feathers relate to the human spirit and its innate connection to the Divine. Even though there are general applications for any feather, each individual bird and its feathers must be examined for its own unique qualities, if you are to understand its function within your own life circumstances. You must examine its characteristics and behaviors and draw the connections to your own life. As you do this, the forces that manifest through that bird and its feathers, will begin to manifest more dynamically to you.

This is when you begin to understand the process of alchemy that is beginning to unfold within your life. Alchemy is the process of burning away the dross to reveal the gold beneath. You will begin to see the leaps into higher consciousness that are about to unfold. Birds and feathers have often been used as traditional symbols for the alchemical process—especially through the force of activation. The location and the action of the bird(s) will help you to determine how the alchemical process will manifest in your life.

In alchemy there is a two-step process to create distillation, the purifying and condensing of a substance so as to extract its truest essence. One step is usually through volatilization, a heating up to dissipate and evaporate what is non-essential. The second step is through precipitation and condensation, the extracting of the essence after the non-essential aspects have evaporated.

Winged Enchantment

Whether a hawk, an eagle or a tiny hummingbird, all birds awaken a sense of wonder and enchantment by their ability to fly. They remind us that we all can rise above our circumstances. They are the ultimate symbols of transcendence.

The volatilization is symbolized by a bird flying skyward, and the condensation through the bird swooping earthward. The colors, the behaviors, and all aspects of the bird must be examined, though, to determine its true power and how it reflects the alchemical process in your life. What aspects of your life does this bird totem show as non-essential and needing to be evaporated? What aspects of your life need to be condensed and extracted for greater power and magic?

Birds are the primary symbols for the Initiation of Air. This initiation reflects a period in which you begin to open to higher knowledge and wisdom, with an increased ability and opportunity to use it to raise yourself up. The Initiation of Air is the learning to open more fully to Divine ideas, ideas that link normal consciousness to the universal. It speaks of opportunity to develop and manifest the highest forms of intuition. If left undeveloped, it will manifest in lower forms of psychism. The Initiation of Air is the opening to realms beyond physical time and space.

Through this initiation you learn to understand and control the workings of the mind. This understanding does not come through a mere collection of knowledge. It is understanding based on higher wisdom and sensitivity, founded in transmuting psychic perceptions into spiritual intuition.

Air is what separates Heaven and Earth. It is the realm of birds, who move easily between both. Air and birds are thus a link between your own spirituality and your physical consciousness.

Air in motion is a force. It is the wind. This wind and the ability to fly and soar upon it resides within the mind. Birds reflect the archetypal energies most actively playing upon the mind, while also reminding you to learn to ride those winds. They remind you that you can fly if you learn to use your own wings your inspiration, creativity and your intuition.

Air is also essential to life. You live through breathing and you breathe in air. Whatever air is blowing around you is what you will take into yourself. This initiation reflects new learning in control of your surroundings and your life. Learning to control what you allow in your life is what your bird totems can teach you most effectively.

Strength and self-mastery—with a new sense of responsibility is part of this initiation. Learning to bridge and open to new energies and dimensions is what birds often reflect. Birds are calls to creative expression that will enable you to rise over certain elements of your life.

Birds are the extended kin of human. They are unique among most animal life. Like humans, they stand upon two feet. (The bear, because of its ability to walk on two legs, is also considered extended kin to humans.) They are more than just part of Nature and part of the Divine. They are the agents of both. When you begin to work with birds and receive from them, the mysteries of both the Earth and the Heavens open to you. Birds invite us to new flights of spiritual awareness and creativity. The following chapters will show you how to accept that invitation.

The Eagle Dancer

Costumes and movements are employed to awaken the archetypal force behind various animals. Eagle dances were employed by many groups of people. The eagle is a powerful totem because it soars out of sight. It is believed to have a close relationship with the sun. Its power is often sought in healing. The feathers in the costume, along with the movements mimicking flight, help manifest its energy. The different feathers are symbols of different qualities of energies of the eagle. Flight feathers are for strength, and fluff feathers symbolize the breath of life.

CHAPTER SEVEN

WORKING WITH BIRD MEDICINE

Birds are a part of our everyday life. Most people pay little if no attention to their presence. And when they do, most attention from a spiritual perspective is focused upon the birds of prey, of which there are about 420 different kinds.[1] Birds of prey are often considered the aristocrats of the bird world. They have long been commanding symbols of authority, evoking feelings of beauty, power and majesty. Their piercing eyes, sharp beaks and strong talons reflect a noble power, so most people find it easy to exalt in them.

An examination of the medicine and power of birds though should not be limited to birds of prey alone. Almost every bird has had some ancient and symbolic association with it. Woodpeckers were symbols of magic and rhythm, and the raven was the bringer of light to the Athapaskan Indians of Alaska. To the ancient Hermeticists the pelican was a bird of self-sacrifice, because of a folk tale of how it fed its young from the blood of its own breast.[2] Birds have been symbols and signs for pagans, Christians, seers, prophets, and native people all over the world.

All birds are governed by instinct and reflex. They have an ability to react automatically to whatever data presents itself to them. It is part of their survival instinct. This same ability to respond automatically from an instinctual and/or intuitive level is what any bird totem can teach us to do. In this way we can learn to use our innate intuition to ride the currents of our life more effectively, instead of being bounced around by them.

---

1   Wexo, John. *Zoo Books — Birds of Prey* (San Diego, Wildlife Education, Ltd., 1980), p. 2.
2   Cirlot, J. E. *A Dictionary of Symbols* (New York, Philosophical Library, 1971), p. 252.

You must be careful about misconceptions of the majesty and power of birds. If you truly intend to work with the medicine and energies associated with this expression of Nature, you must come to a greater understanding of birds in general. This is the first step in developing animal-speak with birds.

Birds have a make-up that is unique among animal life. Although the idea of being "birdbrained" is considered synonymous with stupidity, this is a misconception. Birds are wonderful teachers. Their brains are simply adapted to the life they live. Their consciousness is in their own life process, from moment to moment. How many humans can say the same thing? If humans had the ability for singularity of focus that birds do, so much more could be accomplished.

The bird's body is, of course, designed for lightness. This is essential to flight. There are only a few birds that cannot fly—the ostrich and the penguin being the prime examples. Even the bones of birds are hollow and filled with air to promote lightness and flight.

Their entire metabolism is accelerated, to accommodate the lightness necessary for flight. Those who align with bird totems can use the bird to help adjust their own metabolism. Working with bird medicine will result in a tremendous lightness of spirit, if not in body. This lightness is a freeing of the consciousness, and can be used to develop the ability to leave the body (astral projection).

The digestive system of birds is very rapid, and it is often more complete than in other animals. Those working with bird totems can take clues from the specific eating habits of their bird(s) to effect changes in their own digestive system. Elimination—regular and complete—will be essential to develop that same lightness for flight within your life. Most birds have no structure for storage of wastes, reinforcing the need for complete elimination in those working with bird totems—especially to instill new flights.

Their accelerated metabolism causes many birds to burn food much more quickly. Thus they often eat more often, but in smaller amounts. Nutritionists today recommend frequent meals of lesser amounts throughout the day as much healthier for the human body than the traditional three full meals per day. Many birds focus on high-octane foods for the greatest amount of releasable energy. A hummingbird burns its food at a rate in relation to its weight that is 50 times that of the human; because of that it is constantly searching out sugars and nectars from flowers and plants.

Many birds also have the ability to develop a torpid state where the body requires less food. They slow down the speed at which they live. The heartbeat slows, breathing is reduced and their temperature drops. In many ways this is similar to a hibernation state found among mammals. For the birds, though, it enables them to go further on less. They are able to utilize all the energy of the food they do take in.

These same abilities can be developed by those who align with their bird totems. Examine the eating and digestive habits of your birds. You will find as you work with it, that your metabolism and your digestive system will begin to reflect those same rhythms and patterns. If a bird comes into your life as a totem, it will reflect a corresponding change in diet, metabolic rate, and digestion that may be necessary for your overall health and growth. It may even reflect its necessity for your next step in your spiritual development. Remember to always ask yourself, "What is this bird trying to teach me?"

Working with bird totems can teach you new methods of breathing that can speed up or slow down your metabolism as is needed. Birds use air and oxygen to force combustion of food. Learning new techniques of breathing to extract greater energy from your own food and body is part of what birds can teach. Experiment with new breathing patterns. Study the breathing rhythms of your totems, and try to duplicate or imitate them. You will find it beneficial for those times you need to draw upon that bird's energy.

Birds do not run out of breath. They literally fly into it. To make our lungs expand, we contract our diaphragm. When we relax, the rib cage moves to its regular size and we exhale. Most birds breathe in the opposite way. Their muscular effort expels air, rather than drawing it in. When they relax fresh air is automatically drawn in.

This is a technique that we can develop to some degree. We cannot duplicate the process, as we have a very different muscularity. A bird's pectoral muscles also operate their lungs. Ours do not. Birds also have what we could call a one-way air system. They breathe in and through the body, thus there is always fresh air in the lungs. For those with bird totems this is very important. You must—for your own physical and spiritual health—have fresh air in the lungs regularly. Being outside and performing deep breathing exercises on a regular basis will be very empowering to you. It will be necessary to your overall health.

This fresh air contact is most effective for those with bird totems if it involves activity. Taking a walk outdoors, rather than just sitting and breathing, is more effective. A bird's most powerful breathing activity occurs in flight, for as it moves its pectoral muscles (the muscles that control the wings) the lungs allow air to enter. Practice trying to increase and slow your breathing rate. Keep in mind, though, that humans will not be able to duplicate the breathing rate of birds. The average human breathes about 16 times per minute, and during exercise that will increase by five or six times. A pigeon at rest breathes 29 times a minute and in flight about 450 times.

By working with breathing and relaxation, we eliminate stress. We also find that it takes less effort to accomplish the things we work on in our life. There is a very ancient and powerful mysticism associated with breath. Yoga is one discipline that has taught the value of varied breathing techniques to fill the body with prana or energy. The Chinese discipline of chi kung involves learning to channel inner energy into greater outer expression through proper breathing. Taoism has its specific teaching regarding breath and the health of the body. There are many techniques that can be used to relax the body, increase its energy, to stimulate brain function, and to correct many health problems.

Breath and air are life, and birds hold the secrets to both, for it is their natural realm. We cannot explore all of their breath techniques in this volume, but in the bibliography are some sources that can help you get started. Remember that birds hold the secrets to the power of breath. The more you learn about birds and your specific bird totem, the more you will be able to align with and access the archetypal forces that manifest through it.

All birds, in general, have excellent vision. Their vision is much improved over humans, giving them a tremendous ability to judge distances. This visual perspective is part of what our bird totems can teach us. They can help us to see more clearly that which is at a distance; thus they are wonderful tools for developing higher forms of intuitive discrimination.

Many birds have eyes on both sides of the head. This enables them to see things approaching from more directions at the same time. Does your totem? If so, then it can help teach you to see in various directions at the same time (including the directions of time—past, present, and future). Other birds have eyes paired in front and they see the world as we do. The most common example of this is the owl.

The bird's neck has much flexibility, enabling it to extend its vision to a wider area. Keeping the neck lose and flexible will be essential for anyone with a bird totem. Regular massages and stretches will not only find your physical vision improving, but also your intuitive vision as well.

The neck area has great symbolic significance. It is the point of connection between the head and the trunk of the body—the upper and the lower. It is a bridge between the two. The bridge is an ancient symbol associated with the joining or opening to new realms. The neck can reflect flexibility in thoughts and perceptions.

If you have a bird come into your life as a totem, maybe it is because you have been too inflexible. Are you being too rigid? Are you afraid to see what's ahead or behind you? Are you refusing to see others' points of view? Are you ready to open to new vision? To new realms?

Usually bird totems also indicate a more creative outlook on the world and your life. Many birds, especially birds of prey, have three eyelids. They have an upper eyelid, like ours. The owl especially moves the upper eyelid much in the same manner as humans, giving it a human appearance. Birds can also have a lower eyelid. This one is usually closed while sleeping. Hawks close their eyes by moving the lower eyelid up. There is a third eyelid, called the nictitating eyelid. It moves side to side to moisten and clean the surface of the eye, and to protect it against the wind when flying.

Three is a traditional number for creativity and new birth. Since it is associated in this case with the eyes, it would reflect new vision. A little meditation on the eyelids will elicit some dynamic insight into the way vision is going to shift in your own life.

It is always a good idea to study the flight patterns and behaviors of your bird totems. This will elicit much information. Aspects of this will be covered in the next chapter on "Feather Magic." All birds fly in two basic ways: (1) by flapping the wings and (2) by gliding and soaring. Most utilize a combination of the two. They also will use the natural currents to gain altitude. Anyone with a bird totem should learn to recognize and utilize the natural currents in their own life. This, more than anything, will bring you the greatest success. There are times to flap and times to glide. As you learn your bird's natural rhythms, you will find your life taking that rhythm upon itself. When that occurs, you will find you expend less energy and accomplish more.

Migration is common to many birds. Migration is simply the movement from one climate zone to the next for food. Birds know when to start, what route to take, where they're going, when to start the return journey, etc. They don't have to follow older birds who have made the trip before. They are born with the route somehow imbedded in them. Many scientists feel it is a kind of cellular knowledge that gives them an inborn directional and timing device.

If you have a totem which is migratory, study its patterns. This totem will help you in developing your own innate directional and timing device to accomplish and fulfill yourself most completely. It will help you in your own migration to those "food" sources most beneficial to you—be they actual food, jobs, other people, or even lovers.

Some birds do not have to migrate. They have developed an adaptive ability that affects survival in their own climate zone. Other birds which are not thought of as migratory may do so on occasion, reminding us not to get too locked in at any time. Remember that flexibility is part of what birds can teach us. Birds of prey are often not thought of as migratory, but even they do migrate when necessary. Usually, though, it is only as far as is necessary.

All birds are weather sensitive. With time and practice you too will develop an awareness of how your bird responds to changes in weather before the condition occurs. All birds can teach you how to recognize weather changes, and even how to create your own changes. Of course, this entails great responsibility.

When my father passed away several years ago, my brothers and I traveled to South Carolina for a special funeral service before bringing the body back to Dayton, Ohio, for burial. On the night of the service, the weather turned very nasty, with sleet and ice. Everyone was worried about roads freezing, planes being missed, and other hazardous problems by the time we left for Dayton the next morning. I tried to tell everyone not to worry about it—that it would be all right, but nobody, of course, listened.

That night, I did a particular meditation that I have used in the past to move the line of problem weather out of the travel road. Although I don't use this exercise often, it is very effective. It is an exercise that involves my bird totems and other aspects. I had not used it in a while because I have found over the years that if I shift weather away from one area, it has to go somewhere else, so there is some very grave responsibility involved in using the exercise. On this night, I was coming down with a cold, I was tired and a little drained, so I was not being as careful as I should. Rather than dissipate the weather conditions, which requires more effort, I just shifted them out of the path I felt everyone would be taking back to Dayton.

The next morning the roads were clear, only one semi-slick spot was found, and it was melting by the time we hit it. Though overcast, there was no snow or rain, and by noon the clouds were breaking up and the sun was beginning to shine.

When my brothers and I reached Dayton, we were informed that my mother's plane flight had been snowed in. She and my sister were flying back with my father's body for the funeral service and burial in Dayton. I came to realize that she had not intended to fly out of the airport that I assumed she would. Rather, her flight was scheduled from an airport directly in line with where I had pushed the negative weather conditions. It was believed at that time that the flight would not be able to get out until the next day, which would throw all of the funeral arrangements into chaos.

I obviously had to do some corrective work. It was accomplished, and the flights were restored later that day. It did reinforce in me the need to be extra cautious in using these natural forces. Their energies are powerful and much can be accomplished by them, but there is a grave responsibility. It can be too easy to create problems. If I had not worked with my totems for a long time and known how to access their own unique energies none of this could have been accomplished. With practice and persistence, birds can teach great wonders.

The more you begin to look at both the general and specific characteristics of your totem, the more you will understand some of its language. You will come to know what it is saying to you about your life. Once you start seeing the obvious correspondences, then the subtle make themselves known more easily. The rest of this chapter will help you in beginning to truly understand what the birds are saying to you—about you and your life.

EXERCISES FOR UNDERSTANDING
THE LANGUAGE OF BIRDS

Birds are often seen as omens, objects of worship, and even forecasters of weather. They communicate to anyone who will learn to listen appropriately. Each person though, based upon a solid knowledge, must learn to sense how the truth of the bird's communication translates into his or her life. Information comes to us through Nature and all of its creatures. The body and mind knows and senses that what we see is significant. The flight of the bird and its direction is not accidental or without meaning. The time of flight, the place the bird appeared, and how other birds and animals responded are messages rich in meaning for us. Nature reflects the Divine within the physical world. The animals in Nature are the shadows of those mirrored reflections.

Exercise 1: Beginning the Day

Walt Whitman once wrote:

> There was a child went forth every day,
> And the first object he look'd upon, that object he became.
> And that object became part of him for the day or a
>   certain part of the day,
> Or for many years or stretching cycle of years. [3]

It is this same idea that we use to begin to open communication with the realm of birds. The ability to sense what is being said to us does not need to be forced if we lay a solid foundation of knowledge. It simply involves relaxing into a deep awareness and a fuller sense of self. The exercises in this book will help you to develop that ability. Do not rush it. Let it unfold naturally.

Begin the first thing upon arising. Take a few moments, relax and quiet the mind. Visualize yourself stepping outside and being greeted by Nature through the encountering of a bird. Mentally ask that whatever bird has the most significant message for you for this day be the one you encounter. Mentally project the idea that the bird will reflect the kind of day it will be for you.

Visualize this in as much detail as possible. Do not worry that you may be imagining it or that you will become superstitious about it. This is just a door-opening exercise. It helps you to begin to see and respond to nature as a source of information for you about your life. Remember too that birds are associated with mental activities, so the thoughts will be picked up by those bird totems significant for you.

Develop a mindset for how you want Nature to respond to you. Take time in your meditation before going outdoors to outline how you want the message to come to you. If the bird appears on your right, what do you wish that to indicate? On the Left? The North? The South? The East? The West? Flying up? Flying down? Know ahead of time what you want these things to mean. You don't have to stay with them; as your relationship with the birds grows, so will the communication process.

Paying attention to the direction of flight is an age-old method of listening to Nature. One popular belief was that a bird which flew to the right before a trip would indicate that all would be well. To the left would indicate it would be best to stay home. I mentioned earlier that over the years I have developed the ability to recognize what certain hawk postures and activities usually indicate during my travels. This is something that you can begin developing now.

Take a few moments a day to establish this mindset and to send the message to Nature that you are ready to receive. You are programming yourself to deepen your response to Nature and her varied expressions. You are laying the ground-

---

3   Whitman, Walt. "There Was A Child Went Forth," *Two Ways of Seeing* (Boston: Little, Brown and Company, 1971), p. 15.

work for communication. You are inviting Nature to respond along very discernible and specific guidelines, so you will be able to understand her messages more effectively. Do this about five minutes every morning for about a week before taking the next step.

After a week of preparation meditations, it is time to take it further. Repeat your visualization, asking that nature send you a sign, through a bird, of how the day is going to go for you. Review in your mind what its possible appearances may indicate.

Then step outside and breathe deeply of the morning air. Take a seat and just relax. Listen and watch. What birds do you hear or see? Which—if more than one, stands out most strongly to you? How does it make you feel? What kind of day does that feeling seem to indicate as being before you? If you see the bird, is it flying or at rest? Is it, by its activity, indicating a day to fly high and sing or a day to get busy?

You do not even have to worry about the accuracy of what you encounter. Initially, the interpretation may not be very accurate, but, as you continue, you will find it becomes increasingly so. Remember that you have not been in the practice of listening to Nature for all of the time you've been alive. Because of this you may not establish immediate and accurate communications.

Note the basic qualities and characteristics of the bird. Examine its color. This alone will reflect much. When you see birds, are they alone or in groups? If in groups, what is the number? (Remember that numbers can be significant.) In what environment were they seen? Was it a nocturnal bird or a diurnal (daytime active) bird?

What do all these things seem to reflect about the day ahead? Trust your first impressions. This is just the first step. Then thank the bird and all of Nature for their presence within your life. This can be mental or some physical action, such as in a prayer or offering of seed.

Then go about your day's business. As you do, occasionally pause to look outside. Is that bird showing itself to you to reinforce the message. Are you able to see how what you experienced in the morning reflected what has occurred up to this time. At the end of the day, do a review. How did the bird reflect or not reflect what actually occurred? How could the message have been made more clear? As you continue, within a month you will find that the birds provide a wonderful barometer for the day ahead.

SYMBOLIC QUALITIES OF BIRDS

Blackbird = Omens and mysticism, color of fear and promise

Bluebird = Happiness and fulfillment, color of north or east

Canary = Healing power of sound, heightened sensitivity

Catbird = Communication potential, new lessons or opportunities

Chickadee = Sacred number is seven, seeker of truth and knowledge,

Crow = Intelligence, watchfulness, magical, past-life connections

Duck = Maternal, graceful and comforting, protective

Eagle = Capable of reaching zenith, great perception, bridging worlds

Finch = New experiences and encounters, wide range summer solstice

Goose = Story telling, fertility and fidelity, symbol of eight and infinity

Grosbeak = Heals old wounds, family values, past lives significance

Hawks - Primal life force, fulfillment, spring and fall equinoxes

Kingfisher - Halcyon days, peace and prosperity, linked to north, blue

Loon = Realizing dreams, haunting and eery song, imagination

Magpie = Occult knowledge, doorway to new realms, wily and willful

Meadowlark = Cheerfulness, sublimation, inner journey, linked to moon

Nuthatch = Applying wisdom to natural world, groundedness, ethereal

Oriole = Positive energy, reconnecting with inner sunshine, nature spirits

Owl = Silent wisdom and nocturnal vision, healing powers, magical

Peacock = Wisdom and vision, ostentatious, protective and powerful

Pelican = Self-sacrificing, non-competitive, buoyant, rising above trials

Pigeon = Love and security of home, fertility, archetypal energies

Raven = Shapeshifting, messenger or omen, blending human and animal

Robin = New growth, territorial, color link to throat center

Starling = Sociable, communicating diversity, forceful

Stork = Related to humanity, connected to emotions, water, birth process

Swan = Sensitive, emotional, dreamer and mystic, longevity

Swift = Feminine and psychic energies, speed and agility

Turkey = Spiritual connection to Earth Mother, shared blessings

Vulture = Purification, never-ending vigilance, guardian of mysteries

Woodpecker = Weather prophet, drumbeats into other dimensions

Exercise 2: The Power of Imitation

Everything in nature resonates with the force of the Divine spirit. Each animal, plant, bird, and stone reflects this spirit in its own way. The more you are able to align with it and create your own resonance, the easier it will be to understand what nature is saying.

Throughout time, one of the most common and effective means of attuning to nature was through imitation of it. Individuals would assume postures and movements of animals and incorporate them into sacred dances. Through the dance and a costume depicting the animal, the individual could take on the identity of the totem.

Every animal has its own movements and postures. Costumes and movements can be employed to awaken to the archetypal force behind various animals. An individual could crouch like a lion, creep like a turtle, hop like a bird. A barn owl will often rock side to side to assist itself in pinpointing location of prey through sight and sound. Great horned owls will clack their beaks together as warning. Vultures will, upon rising, face the sun and spread their wings outward.

Adopting the movements and guise of your animal is a way of reawakening yourself to the essence of it and the spirit manifesting through it. This helps you to shapeshift your normal consciousness to a stronger perception and consciousness of that particular expression of Nature. Examine some of the Eastern sciences such as yoga, taoism, and kung fu. They are filled with movements reflecting animals. They will stimulate ideas which you can imitate and use effectively to align with your animal totem.

Find books and videos on the behaviors of various birds and animals and study their basic postures and movements. Go to the zoo or nature center and observe how they move and stand. How do they hold their heads? How do they place their feet when they walk? Then when you are home, imitate them. See it as a form of dance that honors your totem and invokes its energy more dynamically into your life.

Make masks and costumes that reflect your totem. Masks have been used in most societies to assist in entering into other realms. They facilitate creating illusions, and in connecting with the supernatural. They can be a dynamic tool to assist in manifesting the energy associated with the mask. This book is not capable of covering this subject fully, but you may wish to consult the author's earlier work, *Magical Dance—An Introduction to Ritual Movement.*

Most of the ancient sacred animal dances were developed in this manner. It was simply a mimicking and imitation of animal forms and postures. Construct your own set of wings and practice your own flying. Have fun. All animals—including birds—love to play.

The Crane Stance

The crane is a dynamic symbol for poise and balance when working between the physical and spiritual realms. Working with its posture and movements will assist you in opening other dimensions and worlds with balance and strength. It can open the realms of the higher heavens or those of souls who have passed from physical life.

Exercise 3: Eggs, Nests, and Divination

One way of developing a more intuitive understanding of the language of birds has always been through divination. Eggs and nests were often tools for such work. Oomancia is the ancient science of divining the future through eggs. One branch of this, ooscopy, was used to determine the sex of an unborn child. A pregnant woman simply kept an egg between her breasts until it hatched. Then she would use the sex of the chicken to determine the sex of her child.[4]

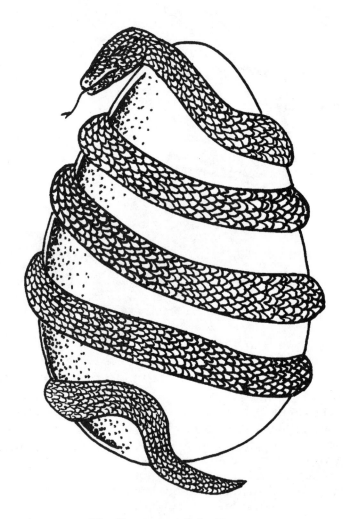

The Serpent and the Egg

Often considered a variation of the Orphic Egg, this symbol is one of the most ancient symbols for fertility and new birth. The egg is the female, the serpent, the male. Together they create new birth.

---

4   Baskin, Wade. *The Sorcerer's Handbook* (Secaucus: Citadel Press, 1974), p. 432.

There has always been a great mysticism about eggs. The Egyptian god Ra was born of an egg. In the Hindu tradition a golden world egg (Hiranyagarbha) hatched Brahma. In China P'an Ku, the first being, emerged from the cosmic egg. In the Greek tradition the Orphic egg was the form of the entire universe. The ancient symbol of the serpent and the egg has been found in many societies. (See the illustration on the following page.)

The egg is an ancient symbol for fertility and new birth. It is a symbol of resurrection, and it has even been used as a talisman against evil. In Egyptian hieroglyphics, the egg often represents potentiality. The egg of your bird totems can tell you much about the potentials and the time frame in which these potentials will begin to mature. The patterns, the colors and the shapes of eggs of your totem are clues to that which is about to be born into your life.

Examining the breeding habits of your bird should be one of the first things to do upon discovering your totem. It can reveal much information:

- The season in which it mates and most often lays eggs can tell you when your potentials are going to be more noticeable.

- The number of eggs usually laid by your bird will tell you how many avenues of expression your new potentials are most likely to take.

- The gestation period before hatching will give you an idea of how much preparation may be necessary to understand the language of your totem and its likely impact upon your life.

- The length of time it takes for your bird to mature from the time of hatching can tell you how long it may take before the full expression of energies associated with your totem manifest within your life.

The nesting habits of your totem can also reflect the most effective means for you to construct your new home. It can reflect the best manner to utilize the new energies associated with the bird. The size of the nest, its construction, and its usual location can have significance for you and your life.

Study the manner in which your bird constructs, develops, and utilizes its nests. Some birds, such as the crow, always build nests high up in the tallest trees, so that they have greater vision over the terrain. Some birds build a new nest every year. Others add on to that which they have already built. Your totem can help you in finding the ideal location and kind of home for you.

Exercise 4: Flights of Fancy

This exercise is a meditation to help awaken you to the power and majesty of birds and the archetypal forces that manifest through them. It can strengthen your connection to your own individual bird totem, and it can reveal to you which bird is truly your life totem. It can be used with any of the other exercises in this book without interfering or lessening their impact.

The symbolism used within it is designed to create a shift within your consciousness to that level of the mind which responds to and can understand the symbolic and actual power of birds and their primary medium, the element of air. The exercise will awaken within you the ability to call forth the archetypal force of birds and their actual physical manifestations. It is not unusual for those who have participated in this exercise to encounter shortly thereafter the actual bird that is their totem—in real life. This is always a wonderful confirmation.

With practice, this exercise can develop into a true shamanic journey. This exercise can be enhanced through creating and wearing bird masks and/or costumes. You will find, through this exercise, an increasing ability to leave the body and fly about the universe as a bird.

This ability is something common to most true shamans. Shamans of Siberia often wore bird costumes, and many shamanic societies used a staff with a bird's head carved on top to represent the pilgrimage, a soulful flight. This kind of staff, as a prayer stick and tool to assist in new travels of the spirit, will be explored in greater detail in the next chapter. It is something that you may wish to consider making for yourself at some point, as you continue to develop a deeper relationship with your bird totem.

1. Begin the exercise by making sure you will not be disturbed. Take the phone off the hook, and make yourself comfortable. You may either sit or lay down, whichever is more comfortable.

2. You may wish to don any bird mask or costume you may have made. If you have any feathers, place them about you, hold them in your hand or place them within your hair. Remember that any feather of any bird can be used to connect you with the essence of any other bird.

3. If you have a drum or rattle, you may wish to use it. The rhythm should be slow and steady. Five minutes of slow rhythmic drumming is beneficial to helping you shift gears and move into a level of mind that will facilitate the following visualization. Don't worry that you won't be able to keep up the rhythm throughout. If you stop in the middle, that is fine. It will have served its purpose by that point in the exercise.

4. Breathe deeply, and if you do not yet feel relaxed, perform a progressive relaxation. Send warm, soothing feelings to each part of your body. Take your time with this. The more relaxed you are, the more effective the energy will be experienced.

Bird Masks and Costumes An Eagle's Head Hat Mask

Making your own bird masks and costumes can be accomplished simply and inexpensively. It is a wonderful way of attuning to your bird totems. You can even create fun dances with them. It is empowering and it honors the essence of the bird, drawing it into your life more dynamically.

5. Allow your eyes to close and breathe deeply. Feel the breath filling your lungs and relaxing the body and mind. As you continue to relax and breathe, you feel a soft cool brush of air across your face. It is sweet and energizing, and in your mind you see an image beginning to form.

   You find you are in a green meadow. The grass beneath you is soft and lush, and the air itself seems to sparkle with sunlight. As you look about you, you see that the meadow you are in lies on a plateau on the side of a huge mountain. Above you, in the distance, is the crest, hidden from your view by soft mists of clouds. Below you see the town in which you live, and your home specifically.

   Again you feel the touch of a soft breeze, and then a shadow moves across you, momentarily blocking the sun. Then it disappears, and a moment later it returns. Across the meadow you see the shadow of what appears to be a large bird. And every time the shadow passes over you, there is a breeze, as if you are being fanned by powerful but gentle wings.

   You raise your eyes toward the sky and as you catch sight of this giant bird, it swoops, diving down and grasping you with its talons. It does not hurt, but you are held firm and strong.

You feel yourself being lifted up, as the mighty wings push and pull, sending gusts of wind past you. And as you look down toward that meadow, you see the grasses waving in response to the air currents caused by the wings of this bird, and for a moment you feel as if they are waving good-by to you.

You see yourself rising higher and higher as the bird carries you toward the top of the mountain. The air becomes cooler, but not uncomfortable. It has a vitalizing aspect. And then you find mists of clouds around you, as you continue to rise higher and higher, until even the clouds are left behind.

Then the flapping of the wings stops, and the bird begins to soar upon the air currents, gliding silent and soft. You see just below you a massive nest at the top of a huge tree at the very crest of the mountain. You are dizzied by the lightness of the air and the slow circular soaring of this magnificent bird. Slowly it circles down toward that nest.

You catch your breath as you draw closer, afraid that you will hit too hard. Then with a sudden and powerful flutter of its wings, it hovers just above the nest and gently lays you within it. With a powerful stroke of its wings, it rises once more and soars beyond your sight.

You stand in this nest at the top of this great mountain, and you are sure you are at the top of the world. You move to its edge and peer down, and the view is dizzying, causing you to step back. The air is clear and fresh, and a strong wind blows about you. You breathe deeply, and as you do you begin to hear the soft whispers of voices within the wind.

It is as if a soft chorus is speaking to you. With each breath you take, the voices become more distinct.

"Without air there could be no life. You could not exist—nor anything upon the planet. Where ever there is space, there is air. You breathe through air; you move through air. You use air every time you speak or think.

"You are affected by what air—what atmosphere—you are exposed to. You leave traces of your being within the air everywhere you go. The words you speak, the thoughts you think and the attitudes you assume affect the atmosphere.

"By learning to attune to the element of air—through those creatures most active within it—you will become more sensitive to all atmospheres you enter. You will learn to recognize which environments to avoid, which people may cause problems and who and what may be of benefit. You will learn to change the currents of your life through a word, a sound, a thought, or a breath for they all fly upon the wings."

You move once more to the edge and look out over the horizon. You breathe deeply and feel the air moving through your body and your organs. Every cell within you seems to be breathing, and with each breath, you feel yourself grow lighter and lighter. You begin to see the air as you breathe it, as crystalline spirals and waves of energy that strengthen and brighten your body. It is as if a million wings of light are flowing about you.

Each breath fills your mind and body with a new sense of joy and wonder, and soon you realize that you are not breathing, but rather you are being breathed. You stand on the edge of the cliff, feeling the currents breathing through you. You feel yourself growing lighter and lighter. You extend your arms out like an eagle spreading its wings to capture the air so that it can soar. You begin to understand how every bird has ever felt the moment it left the earth.

With your arms straight out, you step off the nest, and there is a soft drop and then the currents catch you and lift you, sending you up. You begin to glide and soar. See and feel yourself as a bird with great wings of light. Allow yourself to dip and dive and begin to get used to the currents. Ride the currents. Soar with them and not against them.

As you relax into the current, you see that you have begun a slow, gentle glide downward. You take in the whole world from this perspective. You see everything and everyone as new. Slowly and gently the currents carry you down. Through the clouds, you glide and soar. And then you spy the meadow beneath you. In the heart of the meadow is a tree that you seem to be gliding toward. Slowly, gently the currents lower you. Gently you reach out with your hand and touch the tree. It stabilizes you and helps you control yourself so that you can come to rest, landing solidly and gracefully in that lush grass.

You are filled with a sense of wonder, and you raise your eyes back up to the mountain again, searching the sky for that bird to raise you up once more. The sky is empty. Disappointed, you bring your focus back, and you see the tree is now gone.

Standing in its place is a wooden staff. Its head is carved in the shape of a bird, and it is festooned with the feathers of specific birds—birds that have always fascinated you and been around you your whole life. And you begin to understand. This is your journey staff. With it, you will learn to invite the birds into your life. It will become the tree from which you learn to fly. It will help you in all of your flights of fancy yet to come.

You take the staff in both hands and raise it to the sky and offer a thanks. And in response, a soft breeze flows across you and through you. You close your eyes and revel in its promise. You breathe deeply of its essence, and you make a vow to honor all of the winged beings.

Birds and the Faerie Realm
Many fairies and spirits of the air come to humans in the form of birds and other winged creatures. When seen in their true form, they are delicate and beautiful.

CHAPTER EIGHT

THE MYSTERY OF FEATHERS AND FLIGHT

Feathers fascinate humans. We love to hold them, wave them in the air, stroke our cheeks with them and even make bedding from them. Give a child a feather and the child will begin to play at being a bird in flight. We are all amazed by a bird's ability to fly with something so fragile and yet so powerful. Humans envy birds their ability to fly, and we know that ability is tied to feathers.

Feathers are symbols of the accomplishment of rising from the terrestrial world, of being free of the gravity of the mundane world. They are symbols of balance and of the wind. They are commonly used to symbolize all creator gods and goddesses—those who breathe life into humanity.

A feather is actually a specialized skin scale. It has a central shaft with hundreds of filaments held together by an intricate arrangement of barbs and scales. A single wing feather can be made up of more than a million parts. There are four kinds of feathers—flight/wing feathers, contours, down, and filoplume.[1]

The flight feathers are strong and vaned. They are stiffer and larger. Flight feathers usually fall into several categories: Primaries, secondaries, tertiaries, coverts, and tail feathers. (Refer to the illustration on the following page.) Primaries, secondaries, and tertiaries lift and propel. They also can help reduce drag. They link us to those archetypal forces that can help us to achieve new heights in meditation and move beyond elements in our life that are dragging upon us.

---

1   O'Connor, Karen. *The Feather Book* (Minneapolis, Dillon Press, 1990), pp. 4–5.

Examples of the Different Types of Feathers

Primary flight feathers usually fall out in pairs, one on each side. Only when one pair is replaced does a second pair begin to fall out. This prevents the bird from becoming grounded and thus endangered. In this way flight is always available. Flight feathers thus reflect a rhythm of two, a rhythm that helps connect you to the feminine energies of creative imagination, birth, and intuition. It is not unusual to find that feathers come to you in pairs. You may find one on one day and then two days later find another.

Coverts are smaller, and they grow along the forward edge of the wing, making the wing thicker in front. This causes air to flow faster over the top of the wing, reducing the air pressure and providing lift. They can help align us with those forces that facilitate out-of-body experiences. (Refer to "Experiments in How Flight Occurs" on the following page.) Tail feathers are used for steering and for braking. They can help us to align with those forces that can help us steer our life and put the brakes on in those areas needing it.

Contour feathers are large and fern-shaped. These are often the feathers most commonly found. It is what most people think of when they think of feathers. They hug the outer body, giving it a rounded appearance. This enables air to flow freely past the body, thus making flight easier. This is why any feather can be used to access those energies that will enable our own personal flights, be they flights of fancy, inspiration, or achievement.

Down feathers are found beneath the contour. These are bits of fluff and they are exquisitely soft. This is what provides insulation against changes in climate. Some contour feathers have the fluff or down attached. Down feathers grow continuously, and thus they are symbols of continual protection. Even when the tips of the down are worn away, they become a powder that helps oil the bird's skin. Down feathers can be wonderful tools for healing skin conditions, developing psychometry, and for stimulating the entire sense of touch.

They are also excellent for developing or controlling the gift of empathy. Empathy is an ancient healing gift with many variations. With empathy your body becomes an actual barometer for others. The aches, pains, emotions, and attitudes of others are felt within the empathic person's body as if they were his/her own. This can create expressions of hypochondria if not balanced, but it can also be developed to the point in which you can take another's illness into yourself. Then you heal it while it is within you. Empathic individuals need to be able to distinguish whether what they feel daily is from themselves or from those they have been around. Down feathers help in this discrimination process.

Down feathers also muffle the sound of flight, so down feathers can be used to help you accomplish and achieve without alerting others and thus encountering unwarranted resistance. They enhance secretiveness. They also help to quiet emotions, thoughts, and even pain.

The fourth kind of feathers are called filoplumes. These are usually clustered around the base of contour feathers. They often have a downlike appearance, and most experts are unsure exactly what purpose they serve. This mystery of purpose reveals their significance to us. Learning to meditate with these feathers and to align with the archetypal energies behind them will help you in discovering your own purpose in life. They can be used to link with those energies to help you uncover and explore the mysteries of your own life.

These four kinds of feathers serve three primary purposes: (1) they give great lifting surface without weight, (2) they can be fluffed by the bird to trap air and insulate against the cold, and (3) they provide a protective coat.

When a feather comes into your possession, it can help give lift to some area of your life. It can be used to help insulate and protect you against elements within your life. The kind of feather and the bird from which it comes can help you determine the specific elements in your life, from which it will help lift you and protect you against. For example, a dove is a bird that is often associated with peace. To the Hopi, it would lead them to sources of water. A dove feather can thus be used to protect your own sense of peace and help you to find that which will quench your greatest thirst at the time you encounter the feather.

EXPERIMENTS IN HOW FLIGHT OCCURS

Birds can move upward in two ways. By reducing the air pressure above the wings, the bird is pulled up. By increasing the pressure below its wings, it is pushed upward. Pushing and pulling are part of the aerodynamics of flight for birds. Movement is necessary. The bird must either move through the air with its flapping or the air must move past the bird.

Experiment #1: The Force of Gravity and Air Pressure

Fill a tin can with water, and then cover it with a piece of cardboard. Hold the cardboard tight against the top of the can, sealing the top, and then turn it upside down. Let go of the cardboard. The water will stay up in the can, held by the upward push (air pressure) beneath the can. The upward push of the air pressure is greater than the downward pull of gravity.

Experiment #2: Daniel Bernoulli's Principle (circa 1738)

Air flowing over the top of the wing lifts a bird into the air. Hold a paper in front of your face and blow on it. This is air pressure. As you blow, the paper moves away because the air pressure is greater on your side of the paper than on the other. It moves toward lower air pressure. A wing does the same thing. As air flows across the top of a wing, the pressure is reduced on top. If the lift is greater than the weight of the bird, it rises.

Next hold a sheet of paper by one end about two inches in front of your mouth. Allow the other end to lay limp over your hand. Blow gently on the top, and the loose end will start to move up. Blow harder and the paper will rise. This is what helps a bird to rise.

Feathers are, of course, necessary for flight, but every kind of flight requires a unique wing construction. The bone structure of a bird's wing is similar to the structure of the human arm, except in the hand section. In the bird, what would be fingers in a human are fused and longer. This gives the bird's wings greater strength, but it also reflects the idea that birds are the extended kin of humans.

Different birds have different styles of flight, and thus each bird is differently shaped. Fifty years ago, scientists could not understand how a bee could fly. Aerodynamically, its wings were too small for the size of its body. They now know that the bee moves its wings faster, giving it lift and flight. The penguin can't fly, but in water it uses its small wings as flippers. It actually appears to fly through the water, just as other birds do through the air. The ostrich uses its wings as a rudder to help it steer while it runs at speeds up to 40 miles per hour. This should remind us constantly that, regardless of appearance, we not only have the capability of flying to new heights, but we each need to do it in the manner that works best for us.

There are four common kinds of wing structures. You should examine the wing structure of your bird totem to see what kind of flight it will help you with in your life:

1. Big, long broad wings give maximum lift and great ability to soar and glide.

2. Small, swept-back wings give great speed and the ability to maneuver.

3. Long narrow wings usually reflect lots of energy to flap and also an easy ability to glide.

4. Short, broad and arched wings give great power with an ability for fast take-offs.

For any bird, take-off and landings are the two most dangerous moments in the flight. This has great mystical significance, especially when associated with mediumship and the movement into new dimensions within your life. Little or a lax preparation will create problems. Learning to leave the body and to re-enter takes much time and practice. To open to new dimensions in balance and control is important to avoid unnecessary problems. Individuals—like birds—that do not learn appropriately or try to rush it, usually end up injured in some way. Birds can teach us how to accomplish this safely and easily.

Several factors affect your ability to take off and land in any endeavor in your life, just as they do with birds. The speed, the size of the wings, and the angle of the wings all have an effect. The heavier and larger the bird, the greater its need for some outside help to get off the ground. A condor, because of its size, either needs a strong updraft from a cliff's edge, or it must find an upward-spiralling thermal to get enough lift. A loon can not take off from land. It must run across the top of the water to build enough lift. How does your bird totem successfully take off? This will tell you how best to initiate activities in your life. Do you, like the condor, need an outside source to give you the lift?

Landing is more difficult than the take-off. It has to do with ending stages and making transitions in your life. A fresh egg is safe while in flight until that flight is suddenly stopped by the ground. For a bird, the intended branch may sway, a gust of wind may roll the bird, and the legs must absorb the shock of the impact. This reminds us that no matter how good we are at flight we have to be able to bring that ability back and ground it. In the physical world, the environment often changes, and we must be able to adjust to those conditions. We must be flexible and strong enough to shift our energies accordingly.

In the next chapter, you will learn simple but powerful techniques for using feathers as a sacred fetish. These techniques will help you open your intuition and access the archetypal forces behind the bird and its feathers. It will help you to understand the language of birds. More importantly, they will help you to achieve new creative heights for yourself in any area of your life that you desire.

CONFIRMING THE FORCE OF FEATHERS

Before the exercises of the next chapter can work for you, you must first come to recognize how feathers are links, not only to birds but to the forces and energies of the air. Many traditions have spoken of the varied expressions of Nature. They have often described entire dimensions of life associated with the elements that are generally invisible to the human eye. These we know more commonly as members of the Faerie Realm—the fairies, elves, devas, and spirits that work with and around humans through specific elements.

Folklore and mythologies are filled with tales of beings associated with the element of air. These beings range in size from the tiniest of sylphs to great storm devas that move the winds and bring changes in the weather. They often appear delicate and those of the larger size may actually appear angelic. They are around when anything associated with the element of air is honored. Anyone who works with bird totems will have contact with them.

Fairies and spirits of the air often work through birds to assist humans in the initiation of air, the understanding of the workings and powers of the mind. Through birds, they help us in opening to wisdom and to everything discussed in chapter six.

Feathers are direct links to them. They call their forces into play. From the softest sigh to the strongest gale, the spirits of the air are found. Wherever birds live or are found, they are found as well. Many fairies and spirits of the air come to humans in the form of birds and other winged creatures.

Through them we can more easily connect with the archetypal energies of birds. Anyone who works with any element in nature has contact with the Faerie Realm of life—whether they are conscious of it or not. The more conscious of it that we become, the easier it is to work with any creature of their realm—in this case birds.

Many spirit totems that are birds are simply spirits of the air using the bird form to connect with humans more directly. Through feathers we can call forth birds or those fairy beings associated with the element of air. Through feathers, we can learn to make our wishes reality. They empower our thoughts, and through them we can invoke Nature to confirm this link for us. The confirmation process of a link with your bird totem or of an air spirit working through the bird is simple. Air makes possible the power of sound and the movement and activation of thought. When the connection with your bird totem is established or needs to be confirmed by you, simply perform the following five steps:

1. Choose a day on which the air is perfectly still. Take any feather, go outside and sit under a tree.

2. Allow yourself to relax and just breathe deeply.

3. Then slowly raise the feather above your head with both hands, and then lower it to just in front of your mouth.

4. Now slowly and gently blow upon the feather. As you do, move it with your hand as if it is being carried by your breath.

5. To enhance the effect, whistle a soft childhood tune that you remember upon your feather. If you have a penny whistle or flute, tie the feather to it and play the tune.

In just a few minutes, the air spirits and archetypal forces linked to the feather will become active. The tree leaves will rustle. You may see some leaves or dust swirl upon the ground. You will feel a breeze begin to pick up. Bird activity around you will increase.

This is a simple exercise, but it is one that helps awaken a realization of the force of air. It provides for you a quick confirmation that feathers are wonderful tools to connect with those forces and those spiritual beings that work with them. Having this confirmation makes the exercises in the next chapter more effective because you will have removed many doubts. You still may not understand exactly how it works, but you will *know* that it does.

Fetishes

A fetish is usually any natural object to whose energy you feel closely associated. It is a form and a focus to an expression of energy, be it an archetypal force or an actual spirit being, represented by the object. In the case of the latter, it is a symbol of the energy that the spirit being hopes to awaken within you. It is also a tool that facilitates a shift in consciousness so that you can more easily attune to the energy behind the object.

CHAPTER NINE

FEATHER MAGIC

Every feather is a fetish. It can become a sacred object. The use of fetishes and sacred objects has been employed by peoples from every part of the world. Their use is found in every religion, from the rosary and crucifix in Catholicism, to the feather fan of the Native Americans. The Tibetans used prayer bracelets and the Egyptians wore scarabs.

The word fetish comes from the Portuguese word "feitico" which first meant "charm." It was a word that applied to relics, rosaries and images thought to possess magical qualities. Portuguese explorers applied the word to objects worshiped by the natives of West Africa. This concept has taken many expressions throughout history—in reverencing of sacred places, trees, relics, and such. The essential idea behind fetishism is that spiritual powers reside within material objects.

A fetish is an object often believed to have mystical or magical powers. In point of fact, it is simply a reminder of that energy you are aligning with. It may be a carving, a figurine, a part of an animal, a stone, or an image. It may simply be an inscription on a piece of paper. Crystals, scarabs, shells, fur, feathers, clay figures and such are some of the most common forms.

Fetishes and sacred objects often are used as talismans and amulets. To the Golden Dawn, a talisman is "a magical figure charged with the Force which it is intended to represent."[1] In general, though, there is a difference between a talisman and an amulet. A talisman can be viewed as any object made to serve a specific end—usually to bring good fortune in some area of life or to help in the

---

1   Regardie, Israel. *How to Make and Use Talismans* (Wellingborough: The Aquarian Press, 1981), p. 11.

achievement of a goal. It has a suggestive effect upon the mind. An amulet is not much different, other than that it is usually worn for protection and for health. Both are usually consecrated or "charged" through some ritual or meditative act. This can be accomplished as simply as by applying concentrated focus while constructing them.

Feathers, fetishes, and other sacred objects are often used as tools. They can be used to help us connect with the more ethereal energies of life. They can be links to the archetypes of the natural world, or they can be antennae to the spirit realm. They can be a physical expression of reverence and prayer, or they can be a tool for protection and healing.

FETISH EXERCISES

When working with feathers, prayer sticks, and other fetishes and sacred objects, as you will learn to do in this chapter and elsewhere in the book, it is important to remember that the power and energy is not in the object itself—although there are exceptions (i.e. crystals, etc.). The object is a means by which we give form and focus to a particular expression of energy. The object expresses our relationship to that energy or force. By creating a sacred object, you help to establish and invoke a powerful connection to that force on physical, emotional, mental and spiritual levels simultaneously.

Exercise #1: Understanding What Your Feather is Saying

Anyone who has observed birds in the wild will notice that they do a lot of preening. This preening cleans and rearranges the filaments of the feathers. It distributes along them a natural oil that helps coat and insulate. When you find or are gifted with feathers, you should do some preening of them also. This preening will help you to get in touch with the essence and energy of the feathers. It will help distribute the natural oils from your hands to the feather, aligning you with it and its energies.

Birds usually preen in two ways. They do a nibbling action from the base of the feather to its tip, pecking at each strand. Then there is a drawing activity that is much like a zipper effect. Both are essential to the overall cleaning and insulating of feathers.

Handle your feathers gently, but do your own form of preening. Examine the filaments and gently run your fingers along as many of them as you can. Brush the filaments of the feather forward gently along the stem. If they overlap, you will find that it is easy to straighten them out by doing this. Then run the feather softly through your fingers, drawing upward along the stem. You enhance your sense of touch and you begin to imprint your energy into the feather as well.

This handling also helps you to pay more attention to it. Note the colors, the patterns, any striping, bars, or dots. All can have significance. They can help you to define the energy and the manner it is most likely to manifest in your life. Every aspect of the feather is important.

Exercise #2: Breathing on Feathers

We have already discussed the significance of breath and air in relation to birds and feathers. Breath is also essential to activating the energy of the feather, whether to help attunement or for healing purposes. There are, of course, many ways of breathing life into the feathers, but we are going to focus on two. In exercise #2 you will learn to activate the energy of the feather by breathing on it. In exercise #3 you will learn to heal with feathers by breathing through them.

The breathing on of feathers should be done throughout the time that you are getting acquainted with your feathers as described in exercise #1. It should always be performed before using the feather in meditation, healing, shapeshifting, or in any other endeavor. Your breath becomes the activating principal. It triggers the life and energy of the feather, awakening the archetypal forces reflected by it.

For this to work most effectively, you must have done some background work on the feather and the bird it came from. You should be aware of the kind of energies it is most likely connected to. Those qualities of the bird that you wish to have activated and breathed into new life within you are even more important.

1. Find a time in which you will not be disturbed.

2. Set the atmosphere with incense, sounds of nature music, or anything you find beneficial.

3. Set your feather(s) in front of you or upon your lap.

4. Begin slow, rhythmic breathing. Inhale for a count of four, hold for a count of four, and then exhale for a count of four. Keep your breath slow and steady. Feel yourself relaxing more deeply with each breath.

5. Bring to your mind the image of the bird. Mentally review all of its qualities and characteristics. Remember that air and breath are also associated with mental activity.

6. Now visualize your bird in flight, free and strong within your mind. As you observe its flight in your own mind, see it radiating the qualities you have come to associate with it.

7. Now pick up your feather. (If you have more than one, do this part one at a time.) Hold it by its stem with both hands several inches in front of your mouth. Keep your eyes closed and imagine its wing movement while in flight. As you focus on this, allow your breathing to follow that same rhythm. As the wings move down, you inhale. As they move up, you exhale. (This may seem strange at first, but remember that birds breathe opposite of humans.)

8. With each breath out, exhale on the feather. Envision this as a means of both honoring the power of flight and also of uniting your life breath with the life breath of your bird totem. Continue this breathing for a minute or two. Visualize this as a breathing of new life into the feather and the archetypal forces behind it.

9 As you do this you should begin to feel a slight vibration in the step of the feather. It may be a tingling, a sense of increased pressure, a warmth or some such feeling. This feeling will encompass both hands, as the energy of the feather comes to life and affects the air around it.

10. As you hold the feather, try to imagine the energy surrounding the feather moving up your arms and into your body. You may feel it, see it, sense it, or simply imagine it. As you focus on it, it will occur. Remember, all energy follows thought, and birds rule the realm of thought. Take a few moments and visualize the energy of the bird awakening in you, with all of its corresponding abilities. Envision yourself using those energies and abilities successfully in the week ahead.

Take a few moments and repeat this exercise as often as you use the feather(s). It awakens and empowers them. The energies around the feathers will increase each time you do this. It has an accumulative effect. It will enable you to fly higher or just go deeper within yourself. It will make manifesting the energies of the bird in your life much easier.

Keep your mind on the qualities of the bird. Know that with each breath you are aligning more completely with it. The more concentrated your thoughts during the breathing, the more powerful the energy of the feather becomes. It develops a dynamic link between you and those divine forces reflected by it in Nature.

Exercise #3: Breathing Through the Feathers

This is a powerful technique for activating the healing energies of the feather and its corresponding bird archetype. It facilitates sending specific healing energies into areas of the body. In essence, with your breath, you send the energies of your bird totem into the body and energy system to elicit specific effects.

It is important to know the specific qualities of your feather and its bird for the healing to be most effective. Certain birds are more effective for working on some conditions of the body than others. For example, a turkey vulture feather is wonderful for cleansing the aura, the bowels and the entire digestive tract. A cardinal feather can be used to breath new vitality into blood conditions. It is especially effective with anemia problems. A study of your bird totem will help you to identify specifically which body systems and organs are most easily affected by it.

Also keep in mind that any feather can be used to align with the energies of any bird. Even if you do not have a vulture feather, you can still align with its energies and use the feather you do have to breath through for alleviation of digestion and such. Simply remember that as you breathe on the feather you do have to activate its energies; hold within your mind the image and qualities of the bird whose energies you wish to invoke. Your feather then will take on the qualities and energies of the bird you are focused upon. The steps for healing with this technique are:

1. Make sure the environment in which you will be working is clean and prepared. Make sure there are no interruptions or disturbances.

2. Perform a relaxation exercise prior to working on the individual. This is more effective if it includes rhythmic breathing.

3. Perform the "Breathing On" exercise previously described. This can be done before the person to be healed even arrives. Make sure you concentrate on the specific healing quality of the appropriate bird.

4. If the exact health problem can not be determined, or the appropriate bird can not be determined, simply see this technique as a means of breathing new life into the person. Simply focus on your totem helping you to activate a more vital breath in the person who has come for a treatment.

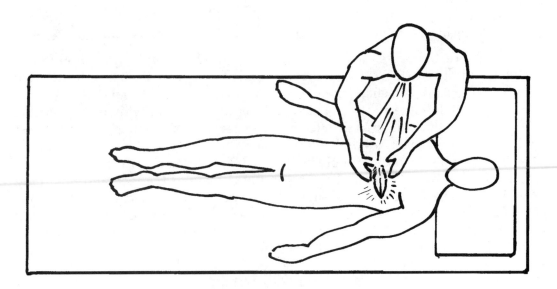

Healing by Breathing Through the Feather

Place the feather upon the troubled area. Then cup your mouth over the feather and breathe through it into the troubled area. Visualize your breathe activating and sending the archetypal energies associated with the feather into that part of the body. See it being healed and strengthened.

5. Have the individual take either a seated or standing position. Then cleanse the aura, sweeping it clean with a feather aura duster, as described in Exercise #4.

6. Now have the individual sit or lay down. He or she must be in a position in which you can place the feather directly upon the body. (This can be used with any feather other than owl feathers. When working with owl medicine, a touch of the feathers can push the problem deeper into the body, so owl feathers should not touch the body.)

7. Place the feather upon the area of the body needing help, and cup your hands on either side of it. Then lower your your head so that your mouth is cupped over your hands, directly over the feather. Begin slow rhythmic breathing.

8. See yourself blowing, activating the energy of the feather, and breathing new life into the unbalanced part of the body. See yourself sending the archetypal force of the bird into the body to heal and strengthen the unbalanced condition. The warmth of the breath, the visualization, and the feather work together to give form and focus to those healing energies most needed by the individual.

9. See and feel winds blowing through the body and taking with it any ill health conditions, to be scattered, dissipated and eliminated by the Divine winds of the world. Continue this until you feel or think it is complete.

10. End this by cleansing the aura again, using the your feather aura duster.

There are, of course, many variations of this which can be used. Sound is a powerful additive to this exercise. Breathing and toning certain chants through the feather to the body will elicit powerful results. Remember that sound is part of the element of air. Breathe and tone the vowel sounds of the individual's first name. This will make the healing more effective. The vowels and the first name are direct links to the primal energies of the individual.

You may also choose to begin by generally breathing into the body. Try placing the feather at the crown of the head, the chest, and the feet, and breathing through them in each of these positions before going to the specific problem area. Don't be afraid to experiment. Trust your intuition in this process. Every one you work on will be a little different. Remember that birds help us to use the intuitive faculties—with more creativity and flexibility.

Exercise #4: Cleansing the Aura with Feathers

One of the most common methods of using feathers is to cleanse or dust the aura. Most people today associate them with Native American and shamanic activities. Feathers used for this process are called by a variety of names, the two most common being an aura duster or a feather duster. They take a variety of forms, and on the following page, several of these are depicted.

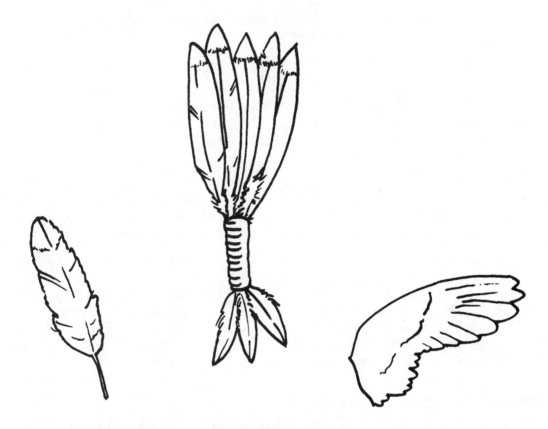

Feathered Aura Dusters

Aura dusters can be made up of many feathers or even just a single feather itself. Turkey vulture feathers make excellent dusters for cleaning out the aura.

The human aura is the energy field that surrounds the human body in all directions. It is comprised of many forms of energy, but it has a strong electromagnetic aspect. This means we are constantly giving off and absorbing energy. Everything and everyone we encounter has the capability of affecting our energy. Unless we are aware of this exchange, we can accumulate a lot of "energy debris" in the course of the day. In many ways it is like static electricity that has accumulated and has a detrimental effect.[2]

Aura dusters are effective to use before and after any healing activity. They are also beneficial to use every day to sweep out the energy debris you have accumulated in the course of the day's activities.

---

2   For more specific information on the characteristics of the human aura, consult the author's earlier work, *How to See and Read the Aura* (Llewellyn Publications).

1. Because the aura extends in all directions, you want to perform the dusting in the front, back, sides, head and feet.

2. Do not touch the body with the feathers, but simply use a soft, sweeping motion about 2-3 inches out from the body.

3. Start at the head and move down. Visualize as you do that you are literally sweeping and dusting all negativity away from the body. Remember all energy follows thought, and birds and feathers are linked to the thought process.

4. Also sweep the front and the back, and do extra dusting at any area of the body you feel inspired. Go under the arms, and have the individual raise his or her feet and dust them. You may even envision it as if you are creating an ethereal wind to sweep over and cleanse that area of the body.

5. To enhance the effect, smudging can also be used. This is a Native American process of brushing the fragrance and smoke of incense over the body, to further cleanse and purify. Often a bowl is used to burn the incense, and as the smoke rises, it is brushed with the feather(s) over and around the entire body of the individual. It is a means of bathing in the purifying fragrance. Sage, cedar, and sweetgrass are common herbs used for this. Frankincense and myrrh are also effective cleansing fragrances that can be used.

Exercise #5: Feather and Fetish Pots

Fetish pots and "medicine bags" are often used to house feathers and fetish figurines. One of the easiest to make is through coils of clay. These can be decorated and painted. Using such bowls or pots is more empowering to the fetish than to have it just sitting out.

All bowls, cups, and cauldrons are symbols of the divine feminine energies of the universe. It is the energy of the womb from which new life issues forth. The circular shape is dynamic, for it has no beginning and no end. It represents all that is unmanifest, along with all of the possibilities. The feathers and fetishes, when placed within the bowl, begin to accumulate energy reserves. When taken out and then used, that energy reserve is activated. A fetish that sits out will dissipate its force and may have to be recharged more often.

The bowls also have an inner and an outer expression—the unmanifest and the manifest. The bowl becomes a gateway through which the archetypal force behind the feather fetish enters and gathers. It leaves and is activated when the fetish is withdrawn and used.

The bowl is tied to the symbol and energies of the cornucopia. The original cornucopia was from the horn of the goat of Amaltheia who became the constellation of Capricorn. It is a symbol of infinite supply. It serves to remind us that we can use the fetish pot to multiply and increase the energies that are symbolized by and manifest through the fetish itself.

The bowl is the Great Mother. It is the symbol of the universe. It is the symbol of all forms of energy expression in the universe. When you place a fetish into a fetish pot or bowl, be it a simple feather or the figurine of an animal totem, the energies associated with that fetish begin to accumulate so they can eventually take form and expression more powerfully in your life.

Using fetishes and fetish pots is a way of honoring and attuning to your animal totems. Animal envoys no longer serve and guide humans the way they used to, but there is still within us the unconscious memory of them. This memory is often awakened in people who are out in the wild. It can awaken in storms and it often awakens in dreams. If we wish to begin the process of more conscious reawakening that ancient relationship with the animal world, we can use the fetish pot and the fetish to assist us:

1. Use a clay pot or make one. Using one of natural materials, such as clay, facilitates and symbolizes our connection to Mother Earth.

2. Once you have chosen your bowl, you may leave it plain or decorate in the manner that is sacred to you. You may wish to have inscriptions or other symbols on the outside, or even on the inside of the bowl. The inscriptions should reflect the energies of the totem. For a fetish bowl for feathers, you may wish to decorate it outside and inside with pictures of wings, etc.

Sample Fetish Pots With a Prayer Stick

These fetish pots are filled with quartz crystal points. They strengthen the energy of the fetish and provide a support base for prayer sticks.

3. I recommend that for all work with animal totems you use the fetish pot only for specific kinds of fetishes. If you have religious fetishes, have a separate bowl for them. Keep one bowl, though, as an animal spirit fetish bowl and keep another as a fetish bowl for your bird totems.

4. You may also wish to place various stones and crystals at the bottom of the bowl. This will further amplify the energies symbolized by your fetish. It will also remind you that the fetish grounds the spiritual force behind it into your life.

5. Smudge or cleanse your totem fetish. Meditate with it. Even perform the previous exercises to help bless and charge it. It is important to visualize, imagine, and feel the energy of the animal as you do this. Know that each time you hold your fetish it is an awakening call to the energy of your animal spirit. Remember that the fetish gives form and focus to the archetypal force behind it.

6. Keep your totem fetish in the bowl until you need to use it. You may also choose to keep it covered with a dark cloth, reflecting the womb of life in which the energies of your totem become fertile. As you uncover the fetish bowl and draw out your totem fetish, do so with reverence. Remember that this is symbolic of the womb of life, and each time you bring forth your fetish, you draw its energies out of the *unmanifest* into the manifested world. Refer to Exercise #8 for specific ways of enhancing the effects of feather fetishes in pots or bowls.

7. When finished with the work of the fetish, replace it back within your animal spirit fetish bowl, until time to bring it forth once more.

Exercise #6: Prayer Sticks

One of the most powerful and magical ways of using feathers is with prayer sticks, staffs and wands. Sticks, staffs, and wands have long been used as tools and symbols of higher forms of communication. A stick, staff, or wand is an antennae. They direct, receive, and channel energies. They are used to draw forth and give expression to the feminine life force, for healing, protection and creation.

"This man wandered through the darkness until he began to think; then he knew himself and that he was a man; he knew that he was there for some purpose. He put his hand over his heart and drew forth a large stick. He used the stick to help him through the darkness, and when he was weary he rested upon it." [3]

The stick, staff, and/or wand is the second half of the creative principle. It is the assertive, masculine aspect. Almost any staff or prayer stick can be considered

---

3   Russell, Frank. "The Pima Indians," in *26th Annual Report of the American Ethnology*, 1904–1905 (Washington, D.C.: Government Printing Office, 1908), pp. 206–230.

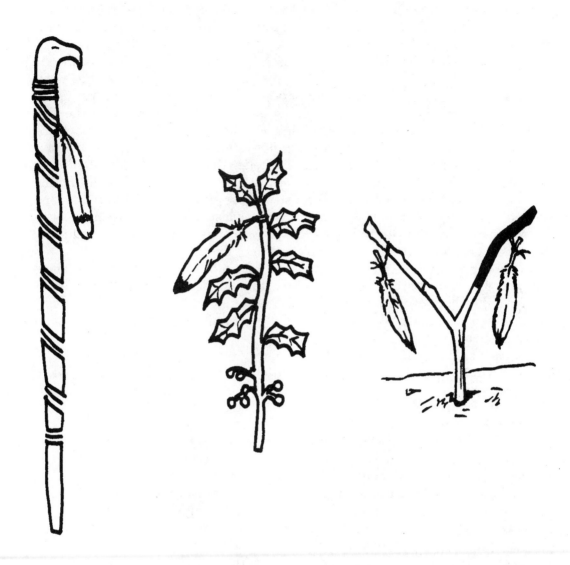

Prayer Sticks, Staffs, and Wands

Above are three examples of prayers sticks and staffs: (left to right) a Journey Staff with Hawk feathers, a Faerie Realm Prayer Stick made of Holly and a Griffin feather,[4] and a more traditional prayer stick. This latter prayer stick, made from a forked branch, has feathers from an oriole. One fork of the branch is painted black, the other orange—the colors of the oriole. A forked branch is used because the oriole will build its hanging nest from a forked branch of a tree.

---

4   Holly is protective to the fairies and elves, and the griffin is also their guardian. Whenever a griffin appears, it often leaves a gift of a feather. Such a feather came into my hands after such an appearance, and is described in my book *Enchantment of the Faerie Realm*.

a magical wand. The stick or wand is the Father. It is what brings forth those things desired out of the unmanifest. Such tools help us to magnify and select the creative process.

Sticks, staffs and wands have been used in many societies. Most people are familiar with the magic wand of the stage magician. This is but a prop, but a true wand serves a creative function in the process of transformation and manifestation. When used with fetishes and such, we are using it to connect with the Natural world and the spirits and energies of it.

Prayer sticks, staffs, and wands are most effective for working with spirit totems when made from natural elements. Wooden dowels are effective, but so are branches from various trees. Every tree has its own unique energy and keeping this in mind will help make your prayer stick more effective. (For information on some of the energies of trees, you may wish to consult one of my earlier works, *The Magical Name*.) Copper tubing, capped at both ends, can also make wonderful prayer sticks and wands. Copper is an element of the earth.

The copper and the wooden prayer sticks can be decorated to imbue them with greater significance. Different colored cloth and leather wraps can be made for them. Feathers of your totem can be attached so that the wand becomes a direct line to your totem. Wood sticks, staffs, and wands can be carved with symbols and such.

Crystals, shells, and stones can be attached. Remember that it is important to research your totem. And everything you attach to your stick, staff, or wand should reflect some aspect of that totem. For those who are working with the Native American tradition, the colors of the directions of the world can be painted on them. For example, some birds came to be associated with various directions. A vulture is a totem of the South, and a hawk is often considered a totem of the East. If your prayer stick, staff, or wand is to connect with a specific bird, you might want to paint it or wrap it in its appropriate color.

Different tribes and traditions used different colors for the directions. What is most important when using colors is that you find the significance for the specific color. Don't just use it because it is in a chart somewhere. The more significance you can find for the color of your prayer stick, the better it will work for you. On my personal journey staff, described a little further on, I use a paint that I can wash off. On each pathworking journey I use colors, feathers, and symbols specific to that magical journey. At the end of my magical journey, as I wash off the paint, I imagine the washing as the final act in releasing my prayers and actions to be fulfilled.

Prayer sticks, staffs, and wands are extensions of your own energy and purpose in working with your animal totems. These tools are channels of energy, and as much care should be given them as to other fetishes and the fetish bowl. These tools are the symbols of the great fertilizing activity. Variations of them in art and totem activity also include scepters, thunderbolts, clubs, and the phallus.

The use of prayer sticks, staffs, and wands is most effective when used to connect with an animal totem that is a bird. Almost all people have some bird that is a totem for them. Discovering it and then using prayer sticks to communicate and work with it is a dynamic means of empowering your life. It can help you to truly understand the language of animals, and more importantly, get them to understand you.

The most effective prayer sticks, staffs, and wands are those which have feather fetishes attached to them. It is very beneficial if you can use a feather of your actual bird totem, but it is not essential. Every feather is a link to any member of the bird kingdom. It may take a little extra persistence, but they can still be used.

1. Prayer Sticks and Wands

To the Hopi and Pueblo Indians there were many ways of making offerings to Spirit. Corn meal could be cast to the various directions. Turquoise was often offered, and water contained within a shell was also a common offering. By far the most important tool for connecting with and making offering and petitions to the spirit world was the prayer stick.

Prayer sticks can be shorter than your fingers, or as long as your forearm. There are no set rules as to their length. To the Pueblo of Acoma there were 17 common types of prayer sticks, and the people would make offerings of 16-80 prayer sticks a year.[5]

The most common stick was that of a peeled willow branch. These were often painted and had carved notches and grooves. Once the painting and carving was completed, then the feather(s) would be attached. The feather(s) are either tied or stuck into one end of the stick. The colors, the notches, the feather, and the kind of stick all had significance and were combined into a prayer stick to serve as a petition to a spirit.

The stick is the message, and the feather the call to the spirit bird or totem to carry the message to the heavens. One end of the prayer stick is then planted in the earth. As the breeze catches the feather, it activates its energies and links the earth request with the heavens.

Ideally, the stick and the feather should be compatible. The qualities of the bird should harmonize with the qualities and energies of the stick. One of the easiest ways to determine this is to examine the kind of tree the bird usually builds its nest in. For example, grouse love oak forests and areas where wild grapes grow. If you had a grouse feather, you could use an oak stick or the stick from a wild grape bush. An oriole will build its hanging nest from a forked twig, so using a forked stick with the oriole feather would add to your ability to link with this totem. You could add to its effectiveness by painting one fork of the stick yellow or orange and the other black—the traditional colors of the oriole.

Remember that all feathers relate to spirit and the gods. They are symbols for the breath of life. Learning to breathe your intentions onto the feather is very

---

5   Tyler, Hamilton A. *Pueblo Birds and Myths* (Flagstaff: Northland Publishing, 1990), p. 2–3.

important. While constructing your prayer stick, occasionally hold your feather over it and breathe gently through the feather and onto the stick. This helps activate its energy and implant it in the stick.

Most of us don't have access to the quantity of feathers that those who live in the country may have, but even those in the city can find feathers. Take regular walks. Aside from its health benefits, as you walk pay attention to the ground. I rarely take walks or runs without coming back with some feathers I have found.

We also don't have the luxury of planting our prayer sticks. I recommend making some general, all-purpose prayer sticks that you can use over. You may have one for healing, one for protection, one for abundance, etc. One that I have seen is made of a combination of vulture feathers and the wood of a crabapple tree. This is very beneficial for purification.

You do not have to plant the prayer sticks outside. You may simply hold them and meditate with them in much the same manner as you would a wand. Wave it around. As the feather moves and dances, the energy comes alive. Spiral it up and down in front of you, and see and feel the energy rise. Feel the presence of your spirit totem arriving. Imagine and feel the energy of your petition being activated.

Rather than make them and plant them outside in the traditional manner, you can keep them and use them over again. Make sure that you smudge or cleanse them after each use, and then recharge them with your new, more specific intention. There are a number of very effective ways of doing this, but by far the most powerful and most effective means is to combine the use of the prayer stick with the use of the fetish pot as depicted on page 108.

A very ancient pagan ritual involves placing a knife into a cup, symbolizing the union of the Father and the Mother. This is the act of creation.

Every time you place a prayer stick into the fetish pot or bowl, you are symbolically doing the same thing. Anytime the male and female unite, whether sexually or symbolically, there is a birth of new energy expressions. This energy expression is greatly determined by the focus of one's thoughts and the manner in which the prayer stick is created.

The prayer stick and the fetish pot become an extension of your own energies. They amplify, empower, and ground. They represent the renewal of life, the union of the sun and the moon on earth so that the new can be born.

The fetish pot and the prayer stick together are the symbols of birth and initiation. It is the joining of the scepter and crown. It is the marriage of opposites to bring new expression and harmony. This symbolic sacred marriage between god and goddess, sun and moon, heaven, and earth is reflected in the combination of prayer stick and fetish bowl. And this creates a new state, a new life and a new completeness.

One of my fetish bowls is filled with crystal points and pieces. Whenever I use a new or old prayer stick, I take it out and I plant it in the heart of that fetish pot of crystals.

2. The Staff

The staff is a symbol of the tree of life, the axis between heaven and earth. It is a tool to take messages skyward. It provides support, and it gives direction and intensity to energy. The staff is a symbol of the link to your most spiritual energies.

Magic and power have long been associated with staffs. In Biblical lore, the staff of Moses turned into a snake and swallowed the staff/snakes of the Egyptian priests. The great magician and shapeshifter Merlin is often depicted with a staff.

The staff provides support in our life journeys. It also reminds us to keep our own magic alive while journeying through life. Birds often decorated the tops of staffs, reflecting shamanic journeys.

A powerful application of the creative imagination is employed in a technique called pathworking. This is often used in the ancient Hebrew form of mysticism known as the Qabala. The paths depicted in the Qabalistic Tree of Life are symbolic pathways to various levels of the mind and the universe. They link different levels of the mind (called Sephiroth in traditional Qabalism) and the energies available to us at those levels. They can be used for astral travel and for skrying in the spirit. They employ powerful symbols in imaginative scenarios to invoke and manifest specific energies into your life.

In one of my previous works, *Imagick: Qabalistic Pathworking for Imaginative Magicians,* I describe how movement and playacting can be used in pathworking to open to deeper levels of the mind and the more dynamic energies of the universe. I have made and use a journey staff in my pathworking exercises, employing it within dance movements and in performing various scenarios to activate the energies within the Qabalistic Tree of Life.

It has become a powerful tool. It is a reminder that the Tree of Life and all of its energies are within me. On my pathworking staff, I will often paint the symbols and words of the path and the two Sephiroth in the Tree of Life that path connects. This gives even greater form and focus to the energies I am working to activate.

Decorate your staff the same way you would your prayer stick or wand. Attach appropriate feathers. If you are using the staff to represent your life's journey, you may wish to attach feathers painted to represent feathers of birds that are migratory. You will want to have the feathers of your individual bird totem as well. Paint it with colors symbolic and significant to your purpose. You may wish to use some of the ancient alphabets and carve names and words important to you and your life goals.

You can have more than one staff. You may wish to have a healing staff, a journey staff, one of protection, and a staff to represent your life growth. Don't be afraid to change and add to the staff. I mentioned earlier that I have a staff that I use for dancing my Qabalistic pathworkings. On this staff I use water soluble paints, so I can reuse it over and over again. I also attach different feathers—those which correspond to the energies I am trying to invoke. Don't worry if you do not have the feathers to do this with. You can always paint the bird image or use generic feathers.

At some point, I have had all of the traditional symbols of the Qabalistic Tree of Life and its various paths painted upon my staff. In performing this activity, the staff has become my individual tree of life. Each time I use it, it becomes more charged, and it becomes easier to access the energies.

Don't be afraid to experiment. You don't have to dance with your staff. Simply holding it once it is prepared will activate the energies. Remember it is an antennae. It will channel and direct energies accordingly. It will lift your intentions and they will fly to the heavens to begin to manifest for you.

Exercise #7: Wearing Your Feathers

One of the easiest ways of activating the energies of your bird totem and aligning yourself with it is by wearing feathers. It is a direct way of honoring it. It also serves as a constant reminder to you of its play of energy within your life. it also serves to strengthen your thought processes throughout the day. There are many ways of wearing the feathers, and none is more correct than any other. What works for you is what you should keep in mind. The following list provides just a few of the many decorative and creative ways in which feathers can be worn by you. Experiment. Be creative. Feel how much lighter you are throughout the day when you are wearing feathers.

1. Tie them into the hair.

2. Attach them to bracelets.

3. Fasten them to buttons on your shirt or blouse.

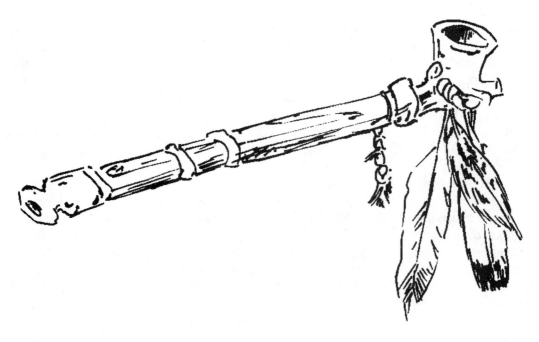

4. Wear them on your ankles. (This is most effective with small pin feathers. Be sure not to allow them to dangle too much, or you may step on them. When performing various dances, I will often attach specific feathers to my ankles.

5. Make necklaces of them.

6. Fasten to belt loops.

7. Attach to purses and bags.

8. Fasten them to ear rings or fashion your own ear rings from feathers.

9. Pin them to clothing.

10. Attach them to personal articles you use or carry with you.

Exercise #8: Enhancing and Protecting Your Feathers

Feathers can be quite fragile, and it is important to handle them gently. There are ways to protect them and to strengthen their energies:

1. Wrapping feathers not being used in silk or cloth will help protect them, especially if they are not kept in a fetish pot. Some feathers I keep in a pot, while others I keep stored.

2. It is beneficial to the feathers to be stored with sprigs of sage. Sage helps keep them more vibrant and fends off deterioration. it keeps the feathers more vibrant.

3. Occasionally taking out all of your feathers and energizing them through the "Breathing On" exercise is essential for their life and vitality. Depending upon the quantity of feathers, you should do this at least several times a year, even if you are not using them. I try to do this at least four times a year around the equinoxes and solstices.

4. Occasionally smudge all of your feathers. A sage or sage combination smudge is beneficial. As the herb smokes, simply run the feather through it, turning it every which way. This keeps the feathers cleansed and more ready to be used.

5. Learn to use sound with your feathers. Sing with them. Hum, chant, and tone with them. Sound is part of the power of air. It is a dynamic means of strengthening the energy of the feather. Know that as you sing or chant, the feather helps carry its sounds forth, while also being honored by it. It always blesses.

CHAPTER TEN

DICTIONARY OF BIRD TOTEMS

When you start to work with bird and other animal totems, it is important to examine them carefully. A casual look will not do. To look at their qualities and behaviors casually will lead you to miss aspects important to you and your life. It is too easy to be wrong about their role, especially in the beginning.

Begin by asking yourself some basic questions:

- What is its color? (Remember that colors are significant and symbolic. Some birds and animals change colors with the seasons. Ask yourself what this should tell you about your own life.)

- What is its size? (Do not compare the size of the bird to the power that it can reflect. A ruby-throated hummingbird is one of the tiniest birds upon the planet, but it has the ability to make great migrations of over 500 miles. Bigger birds and totems do *not* reflect greater power.)

- What is its shape? (Shapes of the bird and its nests can reveal much about its character and activities. WIth some birds, characteristics may stand out. Does the bird have an unusual neck? Beak? Legs? These aspects can be very symbolic.

- How does it act? (We have already discussed the importance of looking at its behavior. Every bird and animal has something unique and characteristic about its behavior. This is one of the primary clues as to the significance of this totem in your life.)

- How does it fly? (Not only how it flies is important, but where. If it migrates, is it to a specific part of the world. This can tell you much. Remember directions are also symbolic. Sometimes, the place it migrates to can reflect a past life that is affecting you and which you may be drawing upon more within your present life.)

- Where is it from? (Places are just as symbolic as other aspects of the totem. Some birds and animals are actually imports from other countries. If such an animal comes into your life as your totem, it can reflect past-life connections to that area or time. For example, the kingfisher has a mythological link to ancient Greece, and the legend of Halcyone. If this is your totem, it can reflect that there are past-life connections to this time and place in Greece or even that current events and situations in your life have ancient ties to this area.)

- When is it most often seen? (The time of day at which it is most visible and active will tell you when its energies are more likely to become active and be experienced in your own life.)

- What kind of sounds does it make? (When and how sounds are most often made can reflect much about the energy of this totem. Sound is an expression of energy. A crow's constant "cawing" out is significant.)

- What is its favorite food? (Remember there is always a balance of predator and prey. Its primary food source will often be a totem as well.)

- When does it breed? (Usually the breeding time will also reflect the time in which its archetypal energies are most powerful, fertile, and recognizable.)

- What environment does it live in? (Remember that the kind of environment it lives in will reveal much about the energy coming into your life. Is it forested? Marsh? Open fields? Just where does it live?)

The following dictionary will help you get started. It is not complete by any means. It will simply give you a starting point at beginning to understand the energy and force associated with your totems. If there are myths associated with them, I heartily recommend studying them as well. Myths and tales have long been a source of spiritual insight and they can help you in understanding the spiritual significance of the totem.

The keynote and its cycle of power are guidelines. The keynote is a synthesis of the bird's energies based upon my own studies and observations. The cycle of power reflects several possibilities. It can indicate the time of the year, month, or day it is most active, or it can reflect its most fertile time, based upon its mating season. In your own, more in-depth studies, you may find that other times are more fertile and powerful. Use those. Remember that these are guidelines, just to get you started.

This list is also not complete. There are many more birds and variations of species than are listed within this text, but this will show you how to begin to read the significance into your own totem. Some birds are listed generically, grouped under common headings. For example, all species of hummingbirds are listed under "Hummingbirds" and the description is based on general characteristics that they all exhibit.

BLACKBIRD

KEYNOTE: *Understanding of the Energies of Mother Nature*

CYCLE OF POWER: *Summer*

The blackbird has long been associated with omens and mysticism. Its color, alone, has evoked both fear and promise. Although called a blackbird, only the males are black. Females usually have a streaky, brown plumage.

Not all blackbirds are black. One variety has a yellow head and throat which stands out strongly against the black plumage. The yellow and black coloring has long been associated with the Archangel Auriel. Auriel is considered the tallest of the angels, with eyes that can see across eternity. This being oversees all of nature and all of the nature spirits. Auriel has traditionally been associated with the summer season.

Another variation of the blackbird is the red-winged blackbird. This bird has a red path on its wings, with a dash of yellow as well. These colors connect this bird to the level known as Binah in the Qabalistic Tree of Life. This is the level associated with the Dark Mother and the primal feminine energies. This bird has ties to all of the creative forces of Nature.

On the Tree of Life, black is the color for Binah and red is the color for Geburah (Mars type of energy). Yellow or amber is the color of the path that connects the two, and it is the path of Cancer, the mother sign of the zodiac. The red-winged blackbird is thus a totem associated with the stellar energies of Cancer.

The male red-winged blackbird will lose its luster during the winter. This reflects how the summer is the time of vibrancy and vitality for those with this bird as a totem. It indicates the need to use the winter to go back into the great womb of life in order to be able to bring forth new energy and expressions of energy the following summer.

Blackbirds nest in swamps, marshes, and low brush—usually just a few feet from water. Again this reflects a tie to water, an ancient symbol for the feminine force and for Nature. They often use cattails as perches. A study of the herbal qualities and characteristics of cattail will also provide further insight.

Blackbirds are known for fiercely staking out their own territory, and they will often drive off any other of their kind that are in the vicinity. Because of this, the sight of two blackbirds sitting together is often considered a good omen. In Europe, blackbirds came to be associated with St. Kevin, and one story tells of how they nested in his hand. Again because of this association, to have blackbirds nesting in your environment is usually a beneficial sign. St. Kevin was known as a person of tremendous gentleness and love.

Europeans used to eat blackbirds in a pie, as reflected in the nursery rhyme. Most of the time though, live blackbirds were hidden in empty pie shells to provide amusement at gatherings. If the blackbird has come into your life as a totem, you will open to new surprises and to a new understanding of the forces of Nature as they begin to migrate into your life.

BLUEBIRD

KEYNOTE: *Modesty, Unassuming Confidence and Happiness*

CYCLE OF POWER: *Winter and Summer* **(changes of seasons)**

The bluebird is a native bird of North America. Although once common, they are now quite rare. This often is a reminder that we are born to happiness and fulfillment, but we sometimes get so lost and wrapped up in the everyday events of our lives that our happiness and fulfillment seem rare. When bluebirds show up as a totem, it should first of all remind you to take time to enjoy yourself.

Bluebirds are part of the thrush family, and you may wish to read about thrushes to learn more of the bluebird. The males are entirely blue, while the females are blue only in the wings. Occasionally there will be some warm reddish tones on the chest as well. Pay attention to the colors and where they are located. This will provide some insight.

To the Cherokees, blue is the color of the North, while in many magical traditions, it is the color of the East. The edges of many Jewish prayer shawls were often the color of blue. Blue is associated with the throat chakra and creative expression. Blue is symbolic, so ask yourself what blue means to you personally.

The idea of the bluebird being symbolic of happiness is fairly recent. This concept has developed more within this century than any other time. As far as I have been able to discover, the bluebird did not play any major role in Indian myths or tales.

This bird always has a plaintive song and a modest, unassuming appearance. Its shoulders are hunched up when perched, giving an impression as if ready to dive. This can be symbolic of a need to work hard and play hard. Are you trying to shoulder too much responsibility?

To the Pueblo, bluebirds are considered winter birds because they descend to the lowlands with the snow and cold during that season. This transition from winter to summer is dramatic in the area of the western home of the Pueblo. It is a transition from great coldness to summer heat.

This is symbolic of a passage, a time of movement into another level of being. Specifically, it is connected to the transformation of a girl into a woman, and thus the bluebird is also sometimes connected to puberty rites.[1] This, of course, has connection to human fertility and a new confidence and happiness in coming into your own.

Other Pueblo rites revolved around the use of bluebird feathers as prayer sticks. They were considered beneficial for snow and ice, and for bringing the summer rainy season. There are also rites in the Pueblo tradition that tie them to the fertility of the land.

Bluebirds are gentle and unaggressive. They do not push or bully other birds, but they are very scrappy when threatened. They have been known to put to flight jays and even larger birds. Their homes usually have an entrance facing South, the direction for awakening the inner child. If a bluebird has come into your life, look for opportunities to touch the joyful and intrinsically native aspects of yourself that you may have lost touch with.

BLUE JAY

KEYNOTE: *The Proper Use of Power*

CYCLE OF POWER: *Year-round*

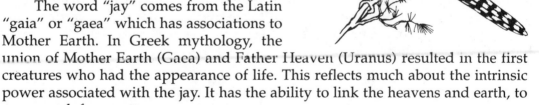

The blue jay has long been thought of as a bully and a robber, and although it can have those tendencies, it has other qualities that make it stand out positively. For those to whom the jay comes as a totem, it can reflect lessons in using your own power properly. It can also reflect lessons in not allowing yourself to be placed in a position in which power is misused against you.

The word "jay" comes from the Latin "gaia" or "gaea" which has associations to Mother Earth. In Greek mythology, the union of Mother Earth (Gaea) and Father Heaven (Uranus) resulted in the first creatures who had the appearance of life. This reflects much about the intrinsic power associated with the jay. It has the ability to link the heavens and earth, to access each for greater power.

The black and white markings found on its blue wings also reflect this same ability. The sky (blue) separates the Heavens (white) and the earth (black). This is a totem that can move between both and tap the primal energies at either level. The jay is aware of this innate ability, and this is reflected in its blue crest—higher knowledge that can be used.

---

1   Tyler, Hamilton A. *Pueblo Birds and Myths* (Flagstaff: Northland Publishing, 1979), p. 141.

The main problem will be in dabbling in both worlds, rather than becoming a true master of both. Those with a jay as a totem usually have a tremendous amount of ability, but it can be scattered or it is often not developed any more than is necessary to get by. It is not unusual to find individuals with blue jays as totems being dabblers—especially in the psychic and metaphysical field. They know a little bit about a lot of things, and they use that knowledge sometimes to give the impression they know more, or that they are true masters.

The bright blue crest of the jay should always be a reminder that to wear the crown of true mastership requires dedication, responsibility, and committed development in all things in the physical and the spiritual. The blue jay is a reminder to follow through on all things—to not start something and then leave it dangling.

The blue jay reflects that a time of greater resourcefulness and adaptability is about to unfold. You are going to have ample opportunities to develop and use your abilities. The jay does not usually migrate, staying around all winter, so look for there to be ample time to develop and use your energies to access new levels. It will stay around and work with you as long as you need it.

The blue jay is actually a member of the crow family, and most crows have no fear. Crows and jays alike will gang up to harass and drive off owls and hawks. The jay is fearless, and it is because of this that it can help you to connect with the deepest mysteries of the earth and the greatest of the heavens.

The blue jay is an excellent mimic, with a sharp eye and voice. It especially has a wonderful knack for imitating red-shouldered hawks. Old-time naturalists were convinced that the blue jay derived pleasure from this activity. As with all members of its family, this sense of seeking pleasure—often at the expense of others—can reflect an imbalance. Sometimes jays show up when this is occurring in your own life.

Blue jays have a tremendous ability for survival with the least amount of effort. They reflect great talent, but that talent must be developed and utilized properly. If the jay has flown into your life, it indicates that you are moving into a time where you can begin to develop the innate royalty that is within you, or simply be a pretender to the throne. It all depends upon you. The jay has no qualms. It will teach you either direction.

CANARY

KEYNOTE: *Power of Song and Voice*
CYCLE OF POWER: *Year-round*

The canary is not native to America. It originally came from what we now call the Canary Islands (Insulae Canariae). It is a member of the finch family, and a study of the basic qualities of the finch family should be studied as well.

Originally canaries were a dull, olive green or a greenish yellow, streaked with black and yellow, but centuries of breeding have produced the completely yellow canary. This breeding also improved its singing voice.

In Germany there was a center for breeding canaries and for training them to sing. Those involved were the people of Hartz Mountain. This is one of the most familiar brand names for many pet products today—especially bird supplies. This links the canaries and those with it as a totem to the ancient schools of the meistersingers. Minstrel brotherhoods existed in Europe during the Middle Ages. One was the Strasburg Brotherhood of the Crown, and another was formed by St. Nicholas of Vienna in 1288. In Germany, specifically, there existed a guild of meistersingers at Nuremburg. This schooling was to teach the power of sound, music, and voice—physical and spiritual. It was part of the bardic tradition as we now know it today.[2]

Those who have a canary as a totem may have past-life connections to this guild. It can also reflect that you are going to learn more about the mysteries of sound, music, and voice to heal and bless your life and that of others.

The power of your own voice is going to be awakened. This doesn't necessarily indicate musical training. Sound, whether spoken or sung, is one of the most powerful forces in the universe. With it you can heal, enlighten, excite, stimulate, awaken intuition, and manifest joy. When the canary shows up as a totem, it is time to ask yourself what song you have been singing. Are there sour notes echoing within your life? Where are they coming from? You may find that those things you say more lovingly will be felt more lovingly. Those things you say more sharply will cut more deeply. What you say is going to have a much greater impact, as the canary awakens the power of sound, music, and voice in you.

Canaries usually reflect an awakening and stimulation of the throat and heart centers of the body. This gives increased ability to feel and to express feelings. Learning to use your voice to bring sunshine into the lives of others will be part of the process.

Canaries used to be taken into coal mines to detect gases. They were so sensitive that if there were gases present, they would soon die. Again, this reflects connections to heightened sensitivity of the throat and heart centers or chakras of the body. It also can reflect that you will need to be careful as to the kind of atmosphere you create with your words, as well as what you expose yourself to in others.

Fresh air is essential to the song of the canary, and it will become increasing so for you as well. Observe the atmospheres you expose yourself to. With time and practice you will find your life begins to take on new tones, and the sour notes are eliminated.

---

2   You may consult my earlier text, *Sacred Sounds—Transformations Through Music and Voice* (Llewellyn Publications) for more information on this.

CARDINAL

KEYNOTE: *Renewed Vitality through Recognizing Self-Importance*

CYCLE OF POWER: *Year-round* **(often with a rhythm of 12—hours, days, months, years)**

Most people have no trouble recognizing these redbirds. They also are part of the finch family, and a general study of finches is beneficial for those with this totem. Unlike many other birds, they are usually year-round residents, and their influence and the archetypal energies associated with them can be accessed all year long. They remind us that regardless of the time of day or year, we always have opportunity to renew our own vitality and recognize the importance of our own life roles.

The cardinal has a loud and clear whistle. Whistles are often reminders to listen closely—to pay attention to what is blowing on the winds. In the case of the cardinal, the female joins in on the whistling, which is unusual among birds. This reflects that we should be listening to the inner voice (the feminine) more closely for our own health and well-being. Since most female birds usually are quiet and camouflaged, a cardinal totem almost always reflects a need to assert the feminine aspects of creativity and intuition more strongly.

The Cardinal

The cardinal's presence reflects a time to renew our vitality. It reflects lessons in developing and accepting a new sense of our own true self-importance.

All cardinals are beneficial and friendly. They eat many weed seeds and injurious insects. The seventeen-year locust (cicada) is one of these. Cardinals can reflect a need to be more careful about your diet, that what you are eating may be injurious to yourself and affecting your overall vitality.

Cardinals lay three to four eggs, and they hatch in about twelve days. This, along with it being a 12-month resident, reflects the rhythm of twelve that is going to become more prominent within your own life.

The male cardinal makes a good parent, and often shares with the female the task of egg incubation. The male, though, will always feed the female while she is in the nest, and the baby cardinals as well. Although the male normally has the brighter color, when it shares the task of incubation, its colors remain much the same as the females, all for the sake of camouflage. This often reflects lessons associated with responsibility and the recognition of the importance of the task at hand.

The males usually have a bright head, although their coloring will often be duller on the back and wings. The bright-colored crest is a warning to rivals, while the duller colors can help shield it.

These birds are named for the cardinals of the Roman Catholic Church, with their bright red robes. If it is your totem, it may reflect past-life connections with the church, or even a reviving of more traditional religious beliefs, regardless of denomination.

Cardinals brighten the environment. They catch the eye and add color to our lives. When they appear as a totem, they do so to remind us to become like them. Add color to your life, and remember that everything you do is of importance.

CATBIRD

KEYNOTE: *Language and Communication*
CYCLE OF POWER: *Spring and Early Summer*

This dark, slate-gray bird with the black cap is named because of the catlike sound it makes. This bird is a talented and tireless singer with the capability of making a variety of sounds. Its ability along this line, especially in its catlike mewing, hints at a facility with foreign languages.

Those to whom the catbird appears as a totem will find that some new form of communication is going to be learned. This may have to do with the actual learning of another language, although a facility with foreign languages is usually what mockingbirds can teach most effectively. The catbird may simply reflect being able to read people more easily.

The catbird is a bit of a busybody. Its presence should caution you to be extra careful about what you say and to whom. Things will have a greater potential of being made public or being distorted. Its presence can hint at others being overly inquisitive about your own affairs or that you are being so about others.

The catbird usually has two broods in its season. It is also a migratory bird. Its presence can indicate a brief but very fertile period in your life while it is within your environment.

The presence of a catbird as a totem indicates you will be encountering a wider range of people than you are normally in contact with. The catbird usually takes up residence in the vicinity of humans and their homes. With the catbird as a totem, look for new people coming into your life that will teach you lessons in your ability to communicate.

CHICKADEE

KEYNOTE: *Cheerful and Truthful Expression*
CYCLE OF POWER: *Spring*

The chickadee is part of the titmouse family. "Tit" is a folksy 14th-century English name for anything little. The "mouse" part of titmouse comes from "mose," a general name that was applied to any small, dull-colored bird in that same period. It is known for its cheery call, and to many people its mating song is the first true sign of spring.

The chickadee usually has a black cap on its head. Many birds have caps, and this has great significance. Anything associated with the head has applications to the thinking process, higher mind, and higher perceptions. Black is associated with mystery, the feminine, and the great womb of life. As to the color of the cap, it reflects that the chickadee can help you with the uncovering of mysteries of the mind. It can awaken understanding and higher truth. It can help you to perceive more clearly in the dark.

To the Cherokee Indians, the chickadee is the bird of truth. It helps us to pinpoint truth and knowledge. One tale speaks of a witch by the name of Spearfinger who terrorized the entire tribe. She would wait in hiding to kill any passer-by. After killing them, she would stab the liver of the individual with her spearfinger and eat it. Nothing seemed to be able to stop the witch as she was made mostly of stone. Then a chickadee landed on her, showing the tribe warriors exactly where she was vulnerable to attack.

Chickadees usually travel in groups, reflecting a cheerful sociableness about them. For such a small bird, it is also fearless, with no qualms of taking on larger birds that may threaten it.

There are seven kinds of chickadees and this is most significant to those with this totem. Seven has an ancient mysticism associated with it throughout the world. It is a sacred number. It is a symbol of the individual rising from the material plane of life, as depicted in the ancient image of the triangle (3) upon the square (4). It has association with the seven rays of power, the seven major planets, the seven bodies of the human being, and the seven chakra centers.

It is this last correspondence that is reflected most strongly with the chickadee. When the seven chakras or energy centers of humans are balanced, there is a greater realization of truth in the world around us. It also enables us to express the truth more joyfully within our life. Some people say, "The truth hurts." Those who have a chickadee as a totem will learn to express the truth in a manner that heals, balances, and opens the perceptions. Truth is shared in a manner that adds cheer and joy to your own life and the lives of others.

CHICKEN

KEYNOTE: *Fertility and Sacrifice*
CYCLE OF POWER: *Year-round/Daybreak*

The chicken is one of the first birds ever to be domesticated, and even though it is a domesticated bird, it still has a great deal of symbolism and significance to it. The word "chicken" comes from the Anglo-saxon word "cicen," referring to a young domestic fowl. It is a descendent of pheasants or galliformes (fowl-shaped birds). Examining the significance of wild pheasants may provide even further insight.

Because of their egg-laying ability, chickens are always associated with fertility. The feathers of chickens were used to stuff bedding, the primary place of sexual activity. They have also been, throughout history, a common animal used in sacrificial rites. This explains only partially half of its keynote. Sacrifice has ties to the ancient mystery of sexuality. In the fertilization process, the male seed is sacrificed to impregnate the female egg. Because ejaculation occurs outside of the body, it has correspondences to an act of sacrifice. Even in Shakespearean times this was common knowledge. The word "die" in many of his plays had a slangy, punnish double meaning that corresponded to orgasm or ejaculation. This was known to the common folk audiences of that time.

Forms of divination surrounded the use of eggs and chickens. It was considered unlucky if a hen laid an even number of eggs. Eggs laid on Good Friday were an assurance of fertility in all areas of your life. Deities were invoked through the simple act of throwing grains to chickens. If the chickens were listless in their eating, then it indicated that the gods must be angry.

COCK

> **KEYNOTE:** *Sexuality, Watchfulness and Resurrection*
> **CYCLE OF POWER:** *Daybreak*

The cock or rooster has a long history of symbolism associated with it. Its primary symbolism is that of sexuality, because one rooster will fertilize and serve an entire brood of hens. Because of its early morning crowing, it is often considered a solar symbol. Every morning the sun resurrects itself, and the cock heralds this resurrection. It is because of this same activity that it is considered the enemy of ghosts and evil spirits which roam free at night and are bound during the day. Another reason for its association with resurrection is the old tale of how a cock heralded Christ's birth.

The cock is extremely vigilant in its activities with the hens in its yard. It is very active, moving often among them, and many believe that this is a reminder to be vigilant in keeping things of the spirit first. This was reflected in Biblical scripture when the cock crowed after Peter denied Jesus three times. This idea of spiritual vigilance was expanded upon in the 4th century as the belief arose that a cock would sing out when Judgment day arrived.

A cock as a totem may even reflect past lives associated with early Christianity, or it may even go back further to ancient Greece. In Greek mythology, the cock is associated with a story of love between Ares and Aphrodite. In this story Ares commissions Alektraon (cock) to keep watch over Aphrodite. It was also a symbol for Cadmillu in the Samothracian mysteries.

To the early gnostics, the cock was a major form of the god Abraxas. Abraxas was "the rooster-headed god with serpent feet, in whom light and darkness are both united and transcended."[3] The cock will always be a totem of great power and mystery. It has ties to the ancient past and clues to your own powers in the future.

The rooster is also one of the twelve signs of the zodiac in traditional Chinese Astrology. It is a sign of enthusiasm and humor. Roosters are considered very eccentric and colorful, but they do have a direct approach to life. If the rooster is your totem, it may be telling you the same thing, or it may have shown up to teach you how to be more direct. A rooster can stimulate a new sense of optimism, and it will help you to come to terms with your own wonderful eccentricities.

COWBIRD

> **KEYNOTE:** *Parent and Child Relationships*
>
> **CYCLE OF POWER:** *No Specific Period*

The cowbird is one of the smallest of blackbirds, but it is not entirely black. It is black with a rich brown head. This combination of colors can serve as a reminder to keep ourselves grounded and take care of responsibilities.

The cowbird is often thought of as a cruel bird because it has a habit of depositing its eggs in the nests of another bird. Its favorite victims are warblers, sparrows, and robins. It then departs, leaving the egg to be hatched and reared by the real owner of the nest. The cowbird hatchling will usually be the biggest bird in the nest and soon overwhelms the others; therefore it is often reared at the cost of the whole brood.

This activity has great significance for those with this totem. It can reflect a time of resolving old childhood issues of abandonment. It can reflect a time of renewed opportunity for new parenthood. The appearance of the cowbird can also reflect that you may be doting on or interfering too much in the lives of your children. They may also reflect that you are not paying enough attention—or enough of the proper attention. If cowbirds are making themselves known to you, examine the expression of balanced responsibility in parent and child relationships.

I have also encountered a number of adopted individuals who have had cowbirds show up as totems about the time they begin the search for their biological parents. Cowbirds can help in resolving many issues surrounding adoption.

---

3   Hoeller, Stephan A. *The Gnostic Jung* (Wheaton: Theosophical Publishing House, 1982), p. 85.

CRANE

KEYNOTE: *Longevity and Creation through Focus*
CYCLE OF POWER: *Year-round—During Daylight*

The crane was a powerful symbol to the ancient Chinese. It is a symbol of justice and longevity, and it is one of many solar symbols. The crane is a bird of the waters, and so is one that will often help teach you how to express your own feminine energies.

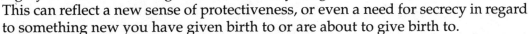

The whooping crane, since the early part of this century, has been a symbol of the wildlife conservation movement. At one point, due to overhunting, they almost became extinct. If the crane has shown up in your life as a totem, it could very well reflect that you are about to recover what had almost become extinct within you.

Most photos of cranes only reveal the adult birds. This is partly due to the fact that the young are very scarce and also because the parents are highly secretive in rearing their vulnerable young. This can reflect a new sense of protectiveness, or even a need for secrecy in regard to something new you have given birth to or are about to give birth to.

Although the crane lays two eggs but usually only raises one, it will also reflect the importance of not dividing your attention—especially in rearing your children, be they your actual children or symbolic children, as in the case of special projects. Women who have cranes as totems do better to stay at home with the children rather than to divide their time between work and motherhood. If this is impossible, as is often the case in today's world, the crane can teach you how best to accomplish both.

The crane can also provide possible clues to past life experiences. "In China it is 'The patriarch of the Feathered Tribe' and in Japan it is 'Honorable Lord Crane'. It is usually depicted with the sun and the pine trees in oriental art. In direct contrast, in Celtic mythology, it is sacred to the king of the underworld and heralds war and death."[4]

One of the most remarkable aspects of this bird is its loud whooping sound. Its haunting tone is reminiscent of a primal celebration over birth. The crane can teach you how to celebrate your creative resources and keep them alive, regardless of the conditions in which they are manifest, both by simply having the proper focus in your life.

---

4   Cooper, J. C. *Symbolism—The Universal Language* (Wellingborough: The Aquarian Press, 1982), p. 67.

CROW

> **KEYNOTE:** *The Secret Magic of Creation is Calling*
> **CYCLE OF POWER:** *All Day—All Year*

My grandfather once told me that the crow was the smartest of all birds. What's more, it even knew it was the smartest of birds and enjoyed it to the fullest. In fact, it was so smart that it chose to stay a crow, rather than move on to some other area of evolution. It has a unique ability to outwit most birds, animals, and even humans at times, and they make for themselves a wonderful living. It can be thought of as another being who felt it was better to rule in hell than serve in heaven. Crows seem to have mastered it well.

Crows intrigue us and they aggravate us. They and their other family member, the raven, have a great mysticism and mythology about them. There are actually five species of crows, one of which is the raven. Because they are of the same family (the only real difference being in size) it would be beneficial for those with crow as a totem to also study the qualities and mystical aspects of the raven.

The first noticeable characteristic about this bird is its striking black color. Sometimes it will have hints of deep blue and purple on the feathers as well. Black is the color of creation. It is the womb out of which the new is born. It is also the color of the night. Black is the maternal color and thus the black night gives birth to a new day. Although the crow is a diurnal or daytime bird, it reminds us that magic and creation are potentials very much alive during the day. The crow, because of its color, was a common symbol in medieval alchemy. It represented "nigredo," the initial state of substance—unformed but full of potential.

In Roman mythology raven and crows used to be as white as swans. In fact a white crow watched over Apollo's pregnant lover at Delphos. One day the crow brought bad news to Apollo and was turned black.

This connection to watchfulness is still strong today. Crows always have a sentinel posted. They build their nests high in the treetops so that they can see the entire area in which they are living and feeding. Occasionally crows have been seen attacking and killing one of their own. There arose an old belief that the crow being attacked was a sentinel who failed. It may also be a reminder of what can happen if we are not watching for magic and creation every day.

Watchfulness warns other crows and other animals of intruders and threats—human and animal. They have been observed raising a ruckus when hunters are around, warning deer and other birds. They recognize possible dangers and they always post lookouts when feeding—their most vulnerable time.

This ability to warn is connected to the crow's second, most-noticeable characteristic—its voice. The crow is actually a member of the songbird family because of its voice box structure. Although few think of the crow as a songbird, there have been many claims (unsubstantiated) over the years that when it is alone, it will sing in a soft musical voice.

Crows have a complex language. They have a remarkable voice range, but they actually do not sing. They can caw in many different ways, each with its own meaning. Learning to understand the language of crows is something we all can do with practice. Although it has a tongue, it does not use the tongue to make any sounds. Pliny once wrote that if the tongue of a crow were split, it would learn to speak like humans. This, of course, was not true. All that would happen is that the crow bleeds to death. The cawing out of the crow should remind us that magic and creation are cawing out to us every day.

The great horned owl is probably the most deadly enemy of the crow. If an owl comes into the area of a crow it will mob the owl and chase it off. Crows know that if the owl discovers its nests, the night could bring death. Many crows have lost their life to the silent night hunts of owls.

The crow has great intelligence. It is adaptable to its environment. It will eat almost anything. Part of their ability to survive is their being omnivorous. They have a unique ability to communicate with each other and to work together.

Their ability for watching and their intelligence has given them a reputation for thievery. They will rob food from other birds or whatever source is around— including human food supplies.

Crows and all corvines are easily imprinted with the image of their keeper. Those who have had crows as pets have found them extremely trainable, with an ability to count and develop a complex communication with their owner. And yet in the wild, even though they are constantly seen and heard, it is hard to get near them. Again I have found that it reflects for most people little awareness or realization of the magic necessary to create or recreate their life.

The courtship and mating procedures also reflect much about the crow's association with magic. The male crow sets out to make itself as handsome as possible, and it is during this time that its voice takes on a singing quality. (Love makes the whole world sing.) The male and female build the nest together. The nest is built high up for protection and it is kept very clean. Even young crows do not foul their own nest. A little meditation on this will reveal much about health, home and respect.

Crows have a great mythology about them. This can reflect not only past-life connections to those times and cultures but it also reflects some of the archetypal forces that it can connect with us. As with many animals, crows also have been known to predict tornadoes, rain, and other changes in weather by the way they fly. Working with crows can help you to see how the winds are going to blow into your life and how to adjust your own life flights. Crows have long been considered magical, and my grandfather once told me how even finding a dead crow was a sign of good luck.

We have spoken of crows and their link to Greek/Roman mythology, but they have appeared in others as well. In China a three-legged sun crow was worshiped. It was a symbol of solitude. To the Athapaskan Indians of Alaska, a crow (in the form of raven) was the creator of the world. To the Celts, the crow was also associated with creation. In Biblical lore, the prophet Elijah was fed by ravens and crows while hiding in the wilderness. In the Norse tradition, the god Odin had two ravens who were his messengers.

Wherever crows are, there is magic. They are symbols of creation and spiritual strength. They remind us to look for opportunities to create and manifest the magic of life. They are messengers calling to us about the creation and magic that is alive within our world everyday and available to us.

CUCKOO

KEYNOTE: *Heralding of New Fate*

CYCLE OF POWER: *Spring*

In every European language, the name of this bird was chosen because of the sound it makes. Its call is the spring mating song of the male. As you will see, its song has always been associated with a heralding of new fate.

On yet another level, its song indicates that you should hone your listening skills. There will be things unsaid by those around you that, if you listen, you will learn about them. Listen to what is not being said. Trust your hearing.

The cuckoo is a relative of the road runner, and you may wish to study it to find even more connections to your own life. A study of the colors of the cuckoo that has come into your life will also provide insight into the role or the new fate about to unfold. Usually it is the color of the bill that stands out most strongly. The bill is usually either yellow or black. It reflects how your own communications should be. If it is a black-billed cuckoo, you may want to be extra cautious about what you say and to whom. If it is a yellow, it may reflect a time of sharing knowledge that is about to approach.

The cuckoo no longer builds its own nest. In Europe, the cuckoo acts much like the cowbird in that it will lay its eggs in the nests of other birds. It will usually choose a nest with eggs that match its own in color. The American cuckoo does not do this. Anytime a cuckoo shows up, though, it will reflect a change in home or family. Something new will be heralded within that environment.

The cuckoo is one of the few birds that will touch the fuzzy/hairy caterpillar. It is not bothered by the outer covering. For those with this totem, this reflects opportunity to develop the ability to assimilate that which could not before. It can reflect less sensitivity to others, and an increased ability to get beneath the surface. It reflects opportunities to experience the real person—regardless of outer appearances.

The cuckoo will also eat the very destructive tent caterpillars. It thus can often reflect lessons associated with eliminating what has been eating at us, so that we can experience new life. It can reflect a time of eliminating the negative in our life, again heralding a new spring—if only symbolically.

The cuckoo is a slow and deliberate bird. It has a gracefully curved bill and a unique arrangement of toes on its feet. It has two toes in front and two in back. It provides balance and stability. Together these qualities reflect a need not to look for the quick and the easy. It reflects a new spring arising, but to move with its energies slowly and deliberately. The cuckoo is a bird that can teach us how to allow the flow of life and all of its rhythms to unfold easily and gracefully. It teaches how not to suffer in our growth. By approaching life slowly and deliberately, everything unfolds in the time, manner, and means most beneficial for us.

The cuckoo has long been a symbol of new fate and conditions within the lives of humans. Most of the old beliefs center around its song and when it is heard. It was considered good luck to have money on you when its first call of the spring is heard. It is still believed by many that if you make a wish on its song it will be fulfilled. Whatever you are doing when you first hear its song, you should do frequently throughout the year for good luck. The call was considered a sign that activity would be beneficial to you. For single people, the number of calls or notes would often indicate the number of years the person would be unmarried or have to wait to be married.

If the cuckoo sound came from the right, it could reflect good luck, but if it came from the left, many believed it indicated an ill fate. Even today, especially in Europe, many believe you can predict rain accurately by its call. At one time it was even called the "rain crow."

In Sweden, the direction from which it was heard would reflect specifically the kind of fate that would likely ensue. If the cuckoo was heard in the north, it would indicate sorrow. If heard in the East, it would reflect consolation. If it came from the south, death, and from the west, good luck.

Usually if a bird or animal has this much folklore and mythology about it, it is worth examining. It usually reflects dynamic archetypal energies, that even if not fully understood, are definitely felt. Working with the cuckoo can help you to use it and its song to help you understand what new fate is coming into your life. It is a bird that can teach the gift of intuitive heraldry.

DOVES

KEYNOTE: *Feminine Energies of Peace, Maternity, and Prophecy*
CYCLE OF POWER: *Dawn and Dusk*

The dove has a tremendous wealth of lore and legend surrounding it. Most of it centers around all of the traditional feminine and mother symbols. In the Greek tradition, Aphrodite was born from an egg brooded by a dove. The Oracles of Dodona which Alexander sought were founded by a dove. To the Slavs, the soul would become a dove at death. To the alchemist, it was a symbol of sublimation. To the Christians, it is a symbol of peace, while to early pagans it was a symbol for the yoni or female sexual organs. It has been associated with female sexuality through such goddesses as Astarte and Isis. Because of its association with many goddesses, it was considered the embodiment of the maternal instinct. "The name dove has been given to oracles and to prophets . . . The prophet sent to Ninevah as God's messenger was called Jonah or the Dove . . ."[5]

---

5   From *The Secret Teachings of All Ages* by Hall, Manly P (Los Angeles: The Philosophical Research Society, Inc., 1977), LXXIX–XC.

To the Pueblo Indians it was also honored. Its feathers were often worn and used in prayer sticks. The mournful song of the dove was considered an invocation to water and an indication to men where the water could be found. (Again we have the ancient symbol for the maternal in the connection to water.) Its song would signify waterholes or springs to which the dove must return at dusk to drink.

The song of the dove speaks to all who hear it. Its mournful tones stir the emotions, the internal waters. During the summers, as a child, I loved being up before others had arisen. I remember stepping out the front door, the morning sun soft, and from the woods surrounding the house would come the sweet-sad song of the mourning dove. It always seemed to stir a sense of promise.

The dove is actually a smaller copy of the now-extinct passenger pigeon. A study of its qualities will help you in understanding the significance of the dove in your own life.

The dove is also a ground feeder, reflective of keeping contact with Mother Earth and the creative possibilities of the feminine energies on earth. Its diet is mostly seeds, but it will eat stones that accumulate in the gizzard to help with digestion. Those with a dove as a totem will find it beneficial that they eat bulk to aid their own digestive and creative processes.

The brood of the dove consists of two eggs. Two is a traditional number for the feminine and creative energies. A study of numerology, as applied to doves, will add even more insight for you.

The dove's song is its most distinctive characteristic. The voice of the dove is the rain song. Out of its mourning, it invokes new waters of life. Its song should remind us that no matter what our life conditions, new waters and new life are still possible. The Earth is a female planet, and this should remind us that creation and new birth is available to all of us upon it. The mourning dove helps us to remember that.

Although its song is heard throughout the day, it seems more distinct at dawn and dusk. These are the "Between Times"—a time in which there is a thinning of the veils between the physical and the spiritual, the past and the future. The dove can help you to use these times to see the creation process active within your own life.

The song of this totem tells you to mourn what has passed, but awaken to the promise of the future. It is a bird of prophecy and can help you to see what you can give birth to in your life.

DUCKS

KEYNOTE: *Emotional Comfort and Protection*
CYCLE OF POWER: *Spring and Summer*

The duck is probably the most common waterfowl. Because of its connection to water, it is linked to the feminine energies, the astral plane, and to the emotional state of humans. Water is necessary for all life on earth. Nothing can live without it. Ducks can remind us to drink of the waters of life as well as to nurture our own emotional natures.

The Wood Duck

Wood ducks are unique among all ducks in that they can climb trees and actually will live in them. As with all ducks though, they can help us connect with the archetypal energies that can help us develop a greater sense of emotional comfort and protection in our lives.

(Photo courtesy of Brukner Nature Center, Troy, Ohio.)

All breeds of ducks swim. Some can dive as deep as 100 feet. Others eat by dipping under the water, reminding us we can find sustenance in our emotions. All ducks live near or on the water, except the wood duck. On land they do not move as well. For those with a duck as a totem it may reflect an inability to feel comfortable with most people in your life. It may reflect a need to find comfort in your own element and with those of life mind and spirit. Ducks can remind us that we are going to have such an opportunity.

Ducks have played important roles in other countries and cultures, and this may reflect past-life connections. The Egyptians were the first to domesticate ducks. The Chinese pioneered the art of duck raising. These are but two simple examples that could be explored.

The colors of the duck can help you in determining specifically the role it will play in your life. Most ducks are a variety of colors, ranging from white to the rich blue-green iridescence of mallards and wood ducks.

The mallard is one of the most prolific ducks. It is probably good that it is so because it is also one of the most widely hunted. They can be very amiable and display a wide variety of emotions. They are also easily imprinted. For several years I participated in an adopt-a-duck program run by the Dayton Museum of Natural History every Easter. The mallards would be raised until old enough to be released into the wild to help repopulate certain areas.

They would follow me around the house and yard. I was, to all purposes, their father and mother. They have a great ability to show affection, and they are very community oriented. They like having others around. They will also return to wherever they feel safe and comfortable. Ducks can sometimes remind us to return to those parts of ourself or those activities that we feel safe and comfortable in as well.

During the summer, most male mallards go through an "eclipse" phase—a period in which they are flightless. During this time, they wear the drab plumage of the female for extra protection in the rearing of the young. Even the young take to the water easily, and it reminds us not to close off our emotional sides. We should be as willing to explore our emotions as every other aspect of our life.

The wood duck is also a colored wild duck. It has an iridescence to its feathers that reflects a kind of spirituality that will open up to you as you begin to come into your own element. Wood ducks all perch in trees to some extent, and they have toes on their webbed feet to help them in climbing. The wood ducks nest in hollow branches and large woodpecker-type holes above and away from the water.

How the young get out of the nest and into the water is difficult to say, although it is generally accepted that ducklings can and do jump down from the trees alone. Wood ducks, in general, have many intriguing habits—more than can be covered in this work. As you study them, you will find ways of applying their habits to your own life.

All ducks have a grace upon water, and as a totem they can help you to handle your own emotions with greater grace and comfort. They serve to teach you how to maneuver through various waters of life. Many psychologist and therapists could do no better than to have a duck as a totem to assist them in helping others move through their emotional tangles.

EAGLES

KEYNOTE: *Illumination of Spirit, Healing, and Creation*
CYCLE OF POWER: *All Seasons and during Daylight*

The eagle is one of the greatest and most admired birds of prey. It has served as inspiration to many societies. Their ability to soar and hunt amazes and thrills those who are witness. Eagles, in fact, are so good at getting food they spend very little time hunting. The fact that they are good at feeding themselves from the land and still soar to great heights in the sky reflects much about the hidden significance of the eagle who comes as a totem. They will teach a balance of being of the Earth but not in it.

Every society which has had contact with eagles has developed a mythology and/or mysticism about them. In the ancient Aztec tradition, the chief god told the people to settle at a place where they find an eagle perched on a cactus eating a snake. This place would become Mexico City.

The eagle was sacred to Zeus, who often changed into the form of an eagle to help himself control thunder and lightning. The Sumerians worshiped an eagle god, and the Hittites used a doubleheaded eagle as a symbolic emblem so they would never be surprised. The eagle has also been associated with Jupiter, and it was a strong emblem for the Roman Empire. In Egyptian hieroglyphics, the eagle is a symbol for the vowel "A"; and also a symbol for the soul, the spirit, and the warmth of life. In early Christian mysticism, the eagle was a symbol of resurrection.

The Thunderbird, to the Native Americans, is most often depicted in the form of an eagle. This was

The Bald Eagle

Long a symbol of spiritual power and illumination, eagles inspire people of all societies. Their energy is healing and aids in creation.

(Photo courtesy of Brukner Nature Center, Troy, Ohio.)

the great spirit who controlled lightning and rain, punishment and reward. To the Plains Cree all eagles had mystical power, and these powers could be shared by anyone who possessed part of the bird.

To the Pueblo Indians the eagle was a bird of the sky with the ability to spiral upward until it passed through a hole in the sky to the home of the sun. It was associated with all the energies of the sun—physical and spiritual. The Pueblo Indians honored six directions—north, south, east, west, zenith (above), and nadir (below). The eagle was the symbol of the zenith because of its ability to soar to great heights. From these heights it could survey all four directions. They became symbols of greater sight and perception.

To the Hopis, the golden and the bald eagles were the greatest of all the birds of the sky, but these are the only two eagles that live upon our continent. Some groups of Hopis also included the red-tailed hawk as an eagle, referring to it as the Red Eagle.

There are 59 species of eagle, and they are often divided into one of four categories: (1) Fish and Sea eagles, (2) Snake eagles, (3) Harpy or Giant Forested Eagles and (4) Booted Eagles; but there is always a great deal of variety within these four groups. When it comes to coloring and feather patterns, every eagle is unique and beautiful in its own way.

Fish and sea eagles are those who live primarily upon a diet from the sea (fishes, etc.). Upon the North American continent, the bald eagle is part of this category. Those who have a bald eagle as a totem need to look at the symbolic associations of water. Water and fish are often symbolic of the psychic aspects of life and the creative energies. Water is also an area that separates land from the heavens. Thus a bird of the water, such as a fish or sea eagle, reflects an awakening ability or need to learn to walk between worlds.

Water is the creative source of life, and living near natural water sources may be important to the health of those who have a bald eagle as a totem. An eagle hunting in the waters must be able to penetrate the waters, grasp what it requires and then rise out of them. All this reflects increased ability and need to learn to work with emotions, psychism, and all aspects of spirituality with greater control. It reflects teachings about true mediatorship being able to enter and exit the more ethereal realms at will.

Snake eagles often have crests of feathers upon their head. Their toes are short and strong to enable them to grasp and hold onto wiggling snakes. Those who have a snake eagle as a totem would do well to study the section on snakes within this text. The snake eagles swallow the snakes whole, reflecting the swallowing and digesting of higher wisdom—the serpent knowledge.

The Harpy Eagles are the largest and most powerful. None of these are found upon our continent. They have huge claws that can be used for grabbing larger prey, including deer. An examination of the particular food preference of the individual harpy eagle will provide further insight.

The other type of eagle found upon this continent is the golden eagle. It is part of the Booted Eagle group. Booted eagles, in general, usually have a majestic mantle of feathers on their head and neck, and their legs have a heavy covering of feathers so that they look as if they are wearing boots.

The two that are most important to those upon this continent are the bald eagle and the golden. The bald eagle is larger than the golden, but it cannot fly as high nor is it considered as graceful. The bald eagle is often a symbol of the feminine, while the golden symbolizes the masculine. The white feathers of the bald eagle especially are often treasured as they are links to Grandmother Medicine—tremendous wisdom, healing, and creation.

The feathers of eagles are sacred to the Native Americans, and since the eagle is protected by the United States government, it is a felony for anyone to possess such who is not of Native American blood. The feathers, though, are used in powerful healing ceremonies (cleansing the aura) and even for shapeshifting. White and black tipped feathers were often used on the masks of the Pueblo Indians to give the appearance of white and black clouds. Again we see the ancient connection to the mysteries of the sky and all of its phenomena.

Both the bald and the golden eagle have come to symbolize heroic nobility and divine spirit. These eagles are the messengers from heaven and are the embodiment of the spirit of the sun.

They are also symbols of the rediscovery of the inner child. There once was a belief that as old age approached, the eagle's eye would grow dim, and the eagle would then fly so near the sun that it would become scorched. It would then seek out a pure water source and dip itself three times into the clear water and its youth would be destroyed.

This reflects much from a mystical point of view. It hints of resurrection, but it also hints of alchemy. The fire of the sun and the clear water are opposite elements brought into harmony in a manner that elicits a change. It reflects several needs for those with an eagle totem:

1. There must be involvement with creativity. Three is the number of new birth and creativity.

2. A willingness to experience extremes in a controlled condition and thus facilitate the alchemical process within your life.

3. A willingness to use your passions to purify (flying into the sun) and to use your abilities even if it means being scorched a little.

4. A willingness to seek out the true emotional aspects of oneself and immerse yourself within them, and by doing so rediscover the lost child and awaken a higher sense of purity, passion, creativity, healing, and spirituality.

An examination of the individual characteristics and behaviors of the eagle will reveal even more of the medicine and power attunement will bring to you.

The feet of the eagle have four toes. Four is a traditional symbol for keeping oneself grounded and laying a solid foundation for oneself. Even with the eagle's magnificent ability to fly, it stays connected to the earth. The talons of the eagle are meant to grasp and to hunt. This reflects the need to stay connected to grasp and utilize the things of the earth. Without an ability to grasp powerfully and utilize what it grasps, it will not survive.

The sharp beak is designed to cut, tear, and crush. Eagle has strong jaw muscles. The jaw is important to digestion and speech with humans, but there is a difference with eagles. Although vocally the eagle is weak, its jaws are one of its most powerful muscles. For those with eagle totems, it will be important to know when to speak, how much, and how strongly. It will be important to remember that unless this is controlled, it will be very easy to inadvertently hurt someone with words (cutting, tearing, and crushing).

For those with eagle totems, new vision will open. This vision will be far reaching to the past, within the present and to the future as well. The eyes of the eagle are set closer to the front of the head, and they have a 3-D or binocular vision, just like humans. They can see forward and sideways, and their vision is eight times greater than humans. Meditation on the number 8, especially its figure (or the symbol of infinity) will reveal much about the kind of vision that eagle can awaken.

The ears of the eagle are not visible, but it hears very well. It can hunt as much by ear as by sight. To those to whom eagle comes, the ability to hear—spiritually and physically—will also increase.

Many eagles mate for life. The male will collect the material for the nests, but the female will be the architect. These roles should be considered by anyone working with eagle medicine. The nests are always large and built high up for safety. Although the roles in the construction of the nests are separate, the task of feeding the young is shared by both, teaching the lesson of cooperative responsibility.

The mating ritual of the bald eagle is one of its most mystical and intriguing aspects. A powerful form of sky dancing occurs. The birds soar, loop, and plunge into deep dives. At a certain point, they grab each other's feet and lock talons, rolling and falling, until the mating is completed. Then they separate and soar upwards to repeat the process over and over again. This reflects some of the mystical joy, danger, excitement, and power of the sexual energy experienced by those with eagle medicine. It can open them to new heights and thrills.

The eagle is a true predator, and as with all predators, it helps to keep the world in balance. Predators capture the weak and the sick, helping to keep the natural world healthy by preventing the spread of disease. This healing role is one that will awaken in many forms for those working with eagle totems.

They have a powerful sense of energy conservation in their hunting. They will often perch and wait, biding their time through joyful soaring and aerial acrobatics—all the time using their great vision to let them know when to take flight and capture their prey. This sense of confident energy conservation will be necessary for those with eagle medicine to develop.

They also are opportunists, and they will let other birds do the hunting for them, often stealing the food from other birds or predators. Whenever eagle flies into one's life, opportunities (even those thought long lost) always arise. Those with eagle totems must learn to see their opportunities and snatch them as they arise.

Eagles don't always swoop down to kill. They have tremendous control over their powerful wings and they can glide slowly and silently down so that the prey does not hear them coming. They are also known to be able to stop their movement and just hover in the air for brief moments to make the strike more accurate. A new sense of timing and movement will begin to develop with those of eagle totems. You will learn to swoop, to soar, to dive, and to hover—to use the winds within your life and your own developing wings to ride them to your own benefit.

Large eagles don't just kill with their beaks or talons. Some can hit their prey with great force—this alone being enough to stun or kill their prey. A bald eagle can strike with twice the force of a rifle bullet.[6] This reflects the primal force inherent and easily awakened in those with eagle medicine.

Eagles are symbols of great power, a power that goes beyond their actual size. An average bald eagle will weigh 8-10 pounds, about two pounds less than the average house cat.

To align oneself with eagle medicine is to take on the responsibility and the power of becoming so much more than you now appear to be. From a karmic aspect, it reflects that the events will now fly faster, and the repercussions for everything you think, do or say (or fail to think do or say)—positive and negative—will be both stronger and quicker. To accept the eagle as a totem is to accept a powerful new dimension to life, and a heightened responsibility for your spiritual growth. But only through doing so do you learn how to move between worlds, touch all life with healing, and become the mediator and the bearer of new creative force within the world.

FINCH

KEYNOTE: *Energy of Variety and Multiplicity*

CYCLE OF POWER: *Varies according to the Species*

The finch is one of the most abundant types of birds in North America. A finch that becomes a totem will always increase opportunities to experience a variety of activities. Everything is going to be amplified. The specific species of finch is important to determine for the greatest understanding of its role in your life.

There are over 300 kinds of finches. Some of these are described specifically in this dictionary; others you will have to examine for yourself. This great number of varieties does reflect an ability to multiply and intermingle with a wide variety of environments and people. If a finch has flown into your life look for new kinds of experiences and encounters with people from all walks of life.

Pay particular attention to the color of the finch. Do not go solely by the name. The purple finch usually has little or no purple at all. The color is more of an old rose. Study the location of the finch and where it originated if possible. Folklore of that area may reveal much. For example, the thistle finch was a legendary bird of happiness to the Pennsylvania Dutch.

Finches have a wonderful ability to sing. Some have even been trained to sing like canaries. Again this reflects a generally increase and variety of potentials that are likely to unfold within your life. Anytime a finch arrives, life is going to become more active.

---

6   Wexo, John Bonnett. *Eagles—Zoo Books* (San Diego: Wildlife Education, Ltd., 1988), p. 12.

FLICKER

KEYNOTE: *New Rhythm of Growth and Healing Love*

CYCLE OF POWER: *Summer* **(especially around the Summer Solstice)**

The flicker is a member of the woodpecker family. A study of woodpeckers and their characteristics in general will add to your own insight. Flickers are woodpeckers in the process of changing from life in the trees to life on the ground. Because of the tapping and drumming that all woodpeckers do in their search for food, they have connections to new rhythms coming into your life.

The Chippewa medicine man Sun Bear speaks of the flicker as the totem for the Strong Sun Moon in Medicine Wheel astrology. This corresponds to the period between June 21 to July 22, or the sign of Cancer in traditional astrology. To the Native Americans it is an especially courageous bird.[7]

The flicker is a golden-winged woodpecker. It often has a red patch on the back of its head and a black crescent on its breast, all of which are very symbolic. When it flies up from the grass, it takes off in a strong, bounding flight, flashing the gold of its wings. When a flicker comes into your life, it will reflect new bounding leaps of spiritual growth.

The red on the back of its head reflects a stimulation of the chakra centers of the head—the throat, brow, and crown centers. These centers will be stimulated into new activity. This reflects that latent talents and intuition are going to be activated to a greater degree. It usually reflects , especially when it is a red shafted flicker, that the stimulation of the latent talents is going to be a catalyst for major creative changes in your life. Your physical and material life is going to change. When it is a yellow-shafted flicker, the changes will occur more in your own perception than in the outer world.

The black crescent is also significant, more so because it is over the breast area. The moon is a symbol of sensitivity and emotions. The black color of the moon often reflects the phase known as the New Moon. The flicker thus symbolizes a new sensitivity of the heart that is about to be awakened. This will stimulate new healing energies, and it can reflect that you will experience emotions more intensely.

The woodpecker has ties to Roman Mythology as well. The Roman god Picus, with whom Circe fell in love, refused to accept the sun as a father-in-law. Because of this Circe turned him into a woodpecker. Meditating and studying this tale, as well as some of the Native American tales of the flicker, will provide insight into the role it will play in your life.

The name of the flicker actually comes from one of the sounds it makes. It can make a variety of sounds, and during the mating season it displays great musical talents. Of course, the drumming it makes is also tied to the mysteries of

---

7   Sun Bear and Wabun. *The Medicine Wheel* (Englewood Cliffs: Prentice-Hall, Inc., 1980), pp. 71–78.

music and rhythm, and anyone with a flicker as a totem should begin to study the use of percussion instruments. Drums and rattles are inexpensive and can even be easily made. They are powerful tools for healing and for inducing altered states of consciousness.

Flickers and other woodpeckers are the master drummers. They can link you to any other rhythm in the world. They can help teach you to align with the heart-beat of the planet or the heartbeat of other animals. Its drumming is a reminder of the natural rhythms of the universe and that when we are not in synchronicity with them, things do not work for us.

The flicker is the most numerous member of the woodpecker family. They live in a variety of woods and other environments across the country. They build their nests in holes and they are very particular about the cleanliness of the home. They make excellent parents, both sharing in the responsibility. This is especially important as flicker babies are very demanding.

The flicker has a stout, sharp bill with which it does its drumming on trees in a search for insects and other food. It has a long tongue, giving it an ability to extract nutrition from the holes it creates with the bill. The mouth and any part of it is the beginning point for digestion and nurturing—through food or words. This reflects the role a flicker can play in your life.

The flicker also has two toes in front and two toes in back on its feet. This is different from most birds, but this balance also reflects their ability to maintain balance on the side of trees. It facilitates their climbing ability. For those with this totem, it can reflect a new balance coming into your life, regardless of the conditions. Anytime there is balance, there is greater health.

To the Pueblo peoples and other Native Americans, the feathers were considered religious articles. A red feather on a prayer stick usually reflected war against some enemy—physical or spiritual. When the feathers were worn in the hair, it indicated the individual was a member of the medicine society. The same energy that can be used for war can also be used for healing. This is what flicker teaches.

If flicker has come into your life, it indicates a time of rapid growth and trust. Flicker will awaken a new rhythm and the ability and opportunity to manifest all-healing love.

GOLDFINCH

KEYNOTE: *Awakening to the Nature Spirits*

CYCLE OF POWER: *Summer Solstice and Summer Season*

The gold finch is named for its summer costume of shiny yellow feathers on its body. It also has black wings and a black cap on its head. This color combination is very symbolic.

Black and yellow are the colors of the archangel Auriel. These colors in meditation and ritual are used to invoke that aspect of this being that oversees the activity of nature spirits—the fairies, elves, and devas. The high point of activity of nature is during the summer, its highest point being at the solstice itself.

The presence of goldfinches usually indicates an awakening to the activities of those beings that are normally relegated to the realm of fiction. Goldfinch can help you to deepen your perceptions so that you can begin to see and experience the activities of the nature spirits yourself. This deepening of perceptions is reflected in the black cap—awakening to that which is normally hidden from view.

Goldfinches are usually permanent residents, and in those areas where they are found, you can also find the fairies and the elves. Goldfinches like border areas and young brush growth found at edges and borders. Edges and borders are intersections where there are natural doorways to that other realm of life.

Even their nesting habits reflects this link to the border areas, the 'Tween Places. They build their nests in a fork on an outer branch high in a tree. It is usually made of thistledown. Thistle has a long association with nature spirits and the healing aspects of animals. Blessed thistle was once used to invoke the god Pan. Thistle has been a symbol of endurance. It is through endurance and persistence that we can open to the Realm of Faerie once more. Goldfinches are birds that can help us connect with those nature spirits that can show us how to heal animals— wild and domestic.

Goldfinches are rarely silent. This in itself is a reminder that Nature is speaking to us constantly and that we should learn to listen and communicate with it from all levels. It reflects that the nature spirits are around us at all times.

In the winter, the male loses its black cap, and the bright yellow turns to an olive yellow. This also reflects the connection of goldfinch to the world of the nature spirits. In the winter, they withdraw, working more within the earth, rather than in the outward expressions which are more evident in the spring and summer. It does not mean they are not there, but rather that they may not be as easily perceived.

The goldfinch also has an undulating (an up and down movement) flight pattern. This rhythm and pattern can be used in visualization to help loosen the subtle energies of the aura and facilitate leaving the body. The wave pattern also reflects the ability of a goldfinch to lead us to the inner and to the outer realms, from the human to the Faerie, from the physical to the spiritual.

GOOSE

> KEYNOTE: *The Call of the Quest and Travels to Legendary Places*
> CYCLE OF POWER: *Autumn (For snow geese—*
>   *Winter Solstice and Full Moons)*

The goose is a bird with an ancient mythology and a mixture of symbolism. It was a sacred bird in Rome's temple of Juno. The snow goose is also associated with Boreas, the North Wind in Greek mythology. The snow goose is also the totem for the winter solstice in the Native American medicine wheel.

Most people have heard of the legendary Mother Goose whose stories and rhymes were designed to quiet children. Myths, fairy tales, and other stories capture the imagination of children and adults alike. The goose is thus a totem reflect-

ing a stimulation of the childhood thrill and belief in stories and legendary places. The story(s) we most loved in childhood often reflect the life quest we have come to take upon us in this lifetime. That is why it resonated with us so strongly. Going back and rereading the one or two stories you most loved will often help you to see the patterns in your life.

These stories either reflected an imprint for this life or they may have even imprinted you with certain seed ideas. This is reflected in the early life of a gosling. A baby goose is imprinted usually by the first moving thing it sees.

The goose can also be a totem to aid you in communication especially through the use of stories. Its feather for a long time was the standard writing instrument. Individuals wishing to write—be it stories or anything—can facilitate the process by working with the goose as a totem. It will stimulate the imagination and help move you through creative blocks. Writing with a goose quill pen will help this even more. Many arts and crafts shops can help you in finding or making your own quill pens.

Because its feathers are the most commonly used in making bedding, it is also a symbol of fertility and marital fidelity. To many people sleeping on bedding made of goose feathers will help insure both fertility and fidelity.

The breast bones of a roasted goose also had superstitions in relationship to the weather. If the bones were brown, it would indicate a mild winter. If they were white or bluish, they would indicate a severe winter.

Geese are related to ducks and swans. They are more terrestrial than ducks, and they are vegetarians. To those to whom the goose comes as a totem, it may well reflect a need for more vegetables in the diet, and maybe even becoming vegetarian for a while.

Geese mate for life and they both share in the raising of the young. The fact that they mate for life often reflects again that innate belief that there is one special person for us in the world. This has ties to many of the fairy tales that we are often imprinted with as well.

There are eight species of geese in North America. This is very symbolic in that the number eight is so similar to the symbol for infinity. It reflects an ability to move forward or backward. It reflects movement, and in the case of the goose, a call to the spiritual quest.

This is further exemplified by its migration patterns and behaviors. Their leaving in the autumn stirs our imagination and makes us want to search out new worlds and dimensions. Their incessant honking seems to be calling us to follow them on the great spiritual quest. Their return is a harbinger of spring second only to the robin. It speaks of the fulfilled promises that great quests bring.

The goose epitomizes the mystery of migration. They constantly shift formation, creating wind drafts and easier flights for those behind them in the formation. This reminds us that as any one individual makes his or her quest, it becomes easier for others to do so as well. They never fly directly behind one another. Each goose's view is unobstructed, reminding us that we should not undertake any quest in life without having a full view of what it entails. In this way the journey is facilitated for others.

The V-formation is very symbolic in itself. It reflects by its shape an opening to new possibilities. It is like an arrowhead, pointing to new directions and new possibilities, and with one end open, it also reflects an openness to new ideas. The "v" as a letter comes from the Hebrew "vau" meaning "nail." This formation usually indicates we are about to affix ourselves to a new path. It is a letter and symbol that reflects great fertility that should be acted upon if growth is desired.

The Canada Goose is the most abundant in North America. It has a powerful voice and great strength in migration. The snow goose is predominantly white with black wing tips. Both species have a very keen vision. For anyone with a goose as a totem, greater vision, physical and spiritual, will occur.

As mentioned, the male and female mate for life. Both share in the raising of the young, alternating staying with the nest. Goslings are very quiet, especially in the first part of life, and then they learn to break free. A goose as a totem can reflect that you are about to break free of old childhood restraints and begin to come into your own. Anytime the goose comes in as a totem, you can expect to have the imagination stirred toward new travels to distant places—whether in the body or in the mind.

GRACKLE

KEYNOTE: *Overcoming Excess and Emotional Life Congestion*

CYCLE OF POWER: *Early spring*

Although the grackle is often considered part of the blackbird family, along with crows and starlings, it actually is not. It is part of the meadowlark and oriole family of birds. It is a large black bird with an extra-long tail. About its head and shoulders are iridescent feathers that change from blue to green to purple or bronze, depending on the light.

This coloring often reflects a need for those to whom the grackle comes to look at what is going on in their life differently. It says that situations are not what they appear to be and you may not be looking at them correctly—particularly anything dealing with the emotions.

Keep in mind that black is the color of the inner and the feminine. The purple and bronze coloring about the head especially usually indicates that emotions are coloring our thinking process. The grackle can help us to correct this.

During courting season, the male grackle will fold its tail, creating a diamond-like trough. This diamond shape is often reflective of activation. It hints at a need to become active in regards to emotional situations. Have we been too passive in our emotions? Are we simply rehashing and talking about them without doing anything to correct the emotional situations of our life? The grackle is a noisy, chattering bird and may be a reminder to quit talking and *do* something.

Grackles are very sociable birds as well. It is not unusual to find people that are in the midst of unbalanced emotional states constantly narrating and rehashing the conditions in every social situation. It can be therapeutic to speak of problems, but many social occasions do nothing but aggravate the conditions and feelings surrounding them. Again it can reflect we may be talking about things too much and not doing something about them.

Grackles have inside their mouths on the hard palate a keel which helps them cut open acorns and eat them. We have often heard the expression, "It's a tough nut to crack." Well, this reflects the role a grackle can serve as a totem. Dealing constructively with our emotions and those people and things in our life which aggravate them can be a tough nut to crack. The grackle can show us how best to do this.

Grackles love to live in pine trees. Pine trees are very therapeutic to emotional states. In a form of homeopathic medicine known as flower essences, the essence of pine can be used to help alleviate strong emotional states, particularly feelings of guilt. Again this reflects the grackle showing up as a sign to help you clear the emotions.

Emotions that are not dealt with can congest our life, aggravating or even creating congestion in the body at some level. The grackle can serve as a warning to be careful of this possibility, but it can also help show us how to prevent it from occurring. The droppings of grackles can serve to culture fungi which, if the wind blows, can cause a pneumonia-like infection.[8]

Most illness is symbolic. Congestion, especially pneumonia-like in appearance, can tell us that we are holding in our emotions. It can reflect a suppressed crying or a refusal to deal with certain long-standing problems and issues. (Have we neglected situations, giving them time to be cultured?) It can reflect a refusal to take in new life and new approaches to life, and so we become congested with old emotions.

The grackle shows us how to handle this. It can teach the proper expression of emotions. They can show us where excesses are dissipating our life force and facilitating a congestion of growth and movement. They can teach how to get back to creative and beneficial experiences and expressions of emotion.

---

8   Clement, Roland C. *The Living World of Audubon* (New York: Grosset & Dunlap, Publishers, 1974), p. 254.

GROSBEAK

KEYNOTE: *Healing of the Family Heart*
CYCLE OF POWER: *Spring and Summer*

The rose-breasted grosbeak is a wonderful little bird. It has on its chest a rose-colored triangle that looks like a bleeding heart. This totem can help teach us to heal all of the old wounds and hurts of family origin.

A grosbeak has a beautiful melodious voice. This is significant. A melody is formed by a relationship between notes. A single note does not make a melody. The grosbeak can help us to see our family relationships as a true melody—each note separate but part of a larger whole. They can help us to see how our family has affected many of our life patterns.

Grosbeaks are good to their family. The male is an affectionate mate and a good parent. It takes time sitting on the eggs. It is a good provider. The grosbeak awakens a new pride and nobleness in the parenting process.

The grosbeak is a migratory bird, and it winters in Central and South America. For those to whom the grosbeak comes as a totem, you may wish to explore the possibilities of past lives associated with this part of the

The Rose-Breasted Grosbeak

This beautiful little bird can teach us much about proper family relationships. It can help us in healing family hurts and restoring family love.

(Photo courtesy of Brukner Nature Center, Troy, Ohio.)

world. They will probably be lives in which your present family also played a significant role. It can help you in seeing family patterns that you have brought over into your present life, along with your present family members.

GROUSE:

KEYNOTE: *Sacred Dancing and Drumming*
CYCLE OF POWER: *Spring*

The grouse is a pheasant-like bird of field and brush. It is an extremely hardy bird. During cold weather its toes will sprout a fringe to help it walk about in the snow.

Dancing and drumming are both powerful ways in their own right to invoke energies. When combined, they create opportunities to be drawn into higher states of consciousness. Movement is a part of life. Rhythmic movement creates life. All human activity is a kind of dance and ritual. The grouse is a dynamic symbol of this.

Religious and sacred dance has been a functional part of every society throughout the world. Shamans and priests used drumming and dance to induce trance states. Circle dances imitated the path of the sun, and chain and spiral dances were used to link the male and female energies. True sacred dance is very ancient; it is an outer expression of an inner spirit.

Sacred dance and drumming was a means of transcending humanity. The dancer can gain control over normally automatic responses by evoking emotions and energies, and then channeling them through the dance. In this manner, transcendence over these lower energies could be achieved. This is what grouse can teach.

My first encounter with a grouse dance occurred four to five years ago in Superior National Forest. I came over a rise and a grouse stepped out of the woods into the middle of the road. There it began to perform its spiral movement. As I moved closer, it continued its dance, carrying it back off the road toward the brush along the tree line. It was an amazing performance. Since then in my travels I have had a number of other encounters, and they always remind me not to force my movements, but to follow the natural rhythm and spiral of life.

The two most common forms of grouse are the ruffed and the sage. The ruffed grouse is called such because of a ruff of black feathers about the neck and shoulders. This is very symbolic. The neck and shoulder area is the point of connection between the head and trunk, the upper and lower. It is the bridge between the two. All bridges enable a crossing over and an opening to new realms.

The ruffed grouse reflects that working with new rhythms and new movement will be beneficial to opening a new flow of energy into your life. Dance and drumming would become wonderful tools to open new realms for you. This doesn't mean you have to go out and take dance lessons, but simply practice and develop your freeform expressions. You will be surprised at the changes in your own energy. See yourself dancing into new patterns and realms within your life

If the grouse has come into your life use the dance. Focus on something you want to change, manifest, or desire, and create your own movements that reflect it. Perform it to some drum music. Then watch how quickly the energy begins to flow for you. If performed with the right intention, you will see results in less than a week.

The sage grouse is the largest of the American grouse. It is a very territorial animal with a lavish display of its great air sacs, spiked tail, and a flaring mane of stiff, white feathers. It has its own dance to create its sacred space. One way of looking at territoriality is from the view of sacred space.

Dancing a circle is an act of creation. It is the marking off of sacred space. When a circle dance is performed, the individual creates a sacred space within the mind—a place between the worlds, a point in which the worlds intersect. The creation and marking off of a circle in Wiccan beliefs is often referred to as raising a cone of power. The circling creates a vortex of energy that is amplified by the will of the participants and the ritualinstruments of the participants. When a grouse displays itself and moves in its circular pattern it is marking off its sacred space.

To those to whom grouse comes there should be a marking off of sacred space in your life. Make sure there are territories and areas you do not allow others. This enables your own natural rhythms and movements to create for you without too much outside influence.

For a long time there was confusion on how the grouse accomplished its muffled drumming in the spring. Today ornithologists know that it is created with rapidly beating wings. The grouse wings beat the air. They set the drumming vibration in motion, setting its power loose on the winds.

Grouse are protective parents. If its young are threatened, the mother will rush at you with feathers ruffed, or it may feign an injury to lead the predator away from the young. Hidden within this act is the ability to perform as is needed, to change the rhythm for appearances.

A whirring flight sound is often associated with the grouse, along with pheasants and other similar species. Often a grouse will use this take-off as if to indicate it has no fear. In reality it is most likely a warning to others in the area. The grouse does have an ability to fly softly if it chooses. Rhythm does not have to be audible to be effective. If grouse has come into your life, expect new rhythms and new teachings on dancing and drumming your life to new dimensions.

GULLS (HERRING/SEA)

KEYNOTE: *Responsible Behavior and Communication*
CYCLE OF POWER: *Year-round*

Gulls are wonderful birds. Most people, especially in seashore resort areas, have a tendency to look upon them as pests. In their communities, away from human contact, their behavior is much different.

Sea gulls—or herring gulls as they are rightly called—are actually shore birds, and they seldom venture far from land. Shorelines are places of great mystery and magic. It is a place neither of land nor of the sea; it is between the two. It is one of those regions often associated with fairy contact. Because of this, gulls can help teach how to open communication with the Faerie Realm of life—especially the water sprites and spirits.

This idea is further reinforced by the fact that the gull is associated with the element of water, as well as the air. It is a bird which can combine the gifts of swimming and flying. It is very buoyant in the water. It knows how to work in both kingdoms; it knows the behaviors appropriate to both. This reflects the ability to teach you how to behave and work in other dimensions than that which is normal.

The appearance of a gull usually indicates lessons or abilities in proper behavior, courtesy, and communication. It may reflect you need the lessons, or that you may become the teacher of such. It may also reflect new learning in the subtleties of communication.

Gulls have developed an intricate code of behavior. They have developed a regular signal code for all of their ritual activities. They use a combination of calls and gestures. Because of this they can teach you how to read people more effectively. They can help you to understand the subtleties of communication—what is not being ostensibly expressed. They can help you to read between the lines and understand the body language of others. They hold knowledge of the techniques of psychological communication.

Gulls also help to keep the beaches and shores clean. They are ecological birds. Their appearance as a totem may reflect opportunities to work on ecology in general or to work on cleaning up the shore areas of your own life.

The young are fussy eaters. They have to be stimulated to eat, and the color red is their eating stimulus. Adult mother gulls have a red spot on their beak. The baby gulls know that only by poking at it will they get something to eat. This process reflects many subtle lessons. It has ties to proper eating behaviors, stimulation of diet (physical and otherwise), and more. Meditation on this will elicit some wonderful insight into your own life patterns and stimuli.

HAWKS

KEYNOTE: *Visionary Power and Guardianship*

CYCLE OF POWER: *Spring and Fall Equinoxes—New Moon*

Hawks are one of the most intriguing and mystical of the birds of prey. They are the messengers, the protectors, and the visionaries of the air. Hawks and owls have the keenest eyes of all raptors.

Hawks vary in size, appearance, and environments. There are so many different species that it is sometimes difficult to tell them apart. There are marsh hawks, forest hawks, sea hawks, and prairie hawks. The environment in which your hawk is found will tell you much about how its energies are likely to manifest within your life.

Even when people cannot tell one hawk from another, they can recognize it is a member of the hawk family. All hawks are impressive and stir the imagination. Their hunting ability, their eyesight, and their powerful flights and other behaviors are dynamic symbols.

In most raptors, the colors of the male and female of the same species are very similar. It is almost always the female who is larger though. This has much to do with the fact that the mother guards the nest. Many hawks mate for life, the red-tailed hawk being one example. The length of time that mated birds stay together is often determined by the number of seasons they spend raising the young.

An examination of the specific species of hawk and its behaviors will reveal much. For example, an osprey is sometimes referred to as a "fish hawk," based upon its primary diet. This magnificent bird is often mistaken for an eagle because of its nearly all white head, but it is the only large hawk that is clear white underneath. It is most numerous in coastal regions, as if its white breast reflects the white foam of the waters in which it hunts. Other examples are the Cooper's

The Red-Tailed Hawk

This powerful bird can awaken visionary power and lead you to your life purpose. It is the messenger bird, and wherever it shows up, pay attention. There is a message coming.

(Photo courtesy of Brukner Nature Center, Troy, Ohio)

hawk, the goshawk and the sharp-shinned hawk who feed frequently on other birds. Although they eat rodents and such, most of their food is feathered. This reflects the old idea that what you eat, you become.

We do not have the space to explore all the characteristics of every hawk, but we will examine one species more closely. That species is the most numerous member of the hawk family, the red-tailed. It is named for the distinctive coloring on its tail feathers. Only the mature red-tails have this coloring. The immature also have lighter colored eyes, distinguishing them from their more mature relatives.

The red tail is very symbolic. It has ties to the kundalini, the seat of the primal life force. In the human body it is associated with the base chakra, located at the base of the spine the coccyx or tail bone. Those who have a red-tailed hawk as a totem will be working with the kundalini. It can also reflect that this bird becomes a totem in your life only after the kundalini has been activated. It can also reflect that the childhood visions are becoming empowered and fulfilled. It may pop up as a totem at that point in your life where you begin to move toward your soul purpose more dynamically.

The red-tailed hawk is a member of the buteo family or the group of soaring hawks. The ability to soar and glide upon the currents is part of what hawk can teach. Although it is a part of this species, it is most often seen perched on treetops and utility posts, using its phenomenal eyesight to locate prey. It teaches how to fly to great heights while still keeping your feet on the ground.

Hawks are occasionally harassed and attacked by smaller birds. This is very significant for those of you who have a hawk as a totem. It indicates that there are likely to be attacks by people who won't understand you or the varied and different uses of your creative energy. They may attack your ability to soar.

The red-tailed hawk is usually a permanent resident in an area, although occasionally it may migrate. This permanency reflects that as a totem, this hawk will be with you permanently once it shows up.

Although incorrectly called a "chicken hawk," the red-tail feeds mostly on rabbits, rodents, and snakes. It has an adaptable diet which has helped it to survive. The red-tail was often accused of and shot for killing chickens when in reality it was one of the bird hawks, such as a cooper's hawk.

It is generally accepted that red-tails mate for life. Both the male and female help care for the young. Two to three eggs are laid in the spring. They vigorously defend their nests against any intruders. They cling to their home territories for years. And they can live up to 14 years in the wild.

This "14" is significant. The 14th card in the tarot deck is the card for Temperance. This is the card that represents the teaching of higher expressions of psychism and vision. It can be used in the development of astral projection—new flights out of the body. It has ties to the activation of your vital energies (kundalini), and the bold expression of it. It is tied to the archetypal forces that teach beauty and harmony in moderation. It holds the keys to higher levels of consciousness.

Rising to a higher level can bring a rapid development of the psychic energies. The red-tailed hawk helps us in balancing and using those senses appropriately. It teaches the balance necessary to discover our true purpose in life. If you have a red-tailed hawk as a totem, meditation on the 14th tarot card will help you to see how this hawk will lead you to use your creative energy in manifesting your soul purpose.

The red of the red-tail reflects a greater intensity of energy at play within your life. It reflects an intensity of physical, emotional, mental, and spiritual forces. This bird is the catalyst, stimulating hope and new ideas. It reflects a need to be open to the new or shows you ways that you may help teach others to be open to the new.

To the Pueblo, the red-tailed hawk was known as red eagle. Its feathers and energies were used in healing ceremonies and for bringing the rains and waters necessary for life. To the Ojibwa, the red-tailed hawk represented leadership, deliberation, and foresight. "Hawk is akin to Mercury, the messenger of the gods. Hawk medicine teaches you to be observant . . . Life is sending you signals."[9] The red-tail can spread its wings to a great width, and it can teach you to use your creative energies in the same way. It can extend the vision of your life.

The beak and the talons are always commented upon by observers. They are the most striking features of any hawk, especially the red-tail. It is a fearless bird. It will even take on poisonous snakes. It has a scaled leg to help protect it against poisonous bites, and immediately upon grasping its snake prey, it tears off the head. On one of my trips to Colorado, while traveling through Kansas, I was fortunate enough to see a red-tail swoop down upon a snake. Within seconds it had taken flight again, cutting across my path. I could see the head of the snake dangling by just a few threads of skin. It happened so quickly, that by the time I realized exactly what I had observed, the red-tail had disappeared.

Because of the strong energy (the intensified life-force) activated by this totem, an individuals with it must be careful in how they express themselves. There will unfold within you the ability to tear off the heads of any snakes in your life, or anyone or anything seen as an enemy. Your comments and actions will be like the hawk's beak and talons—strong and powerful, but with a capability to tear and/or kill.

The feathering of the red-tail actually has two phases. Both of these are significant to anyone with this totem. Its feathering is a little lighter during the summer and darker during the winter. The lighter is often symbolic of more joyful and sociable kinds of energies. The darker phases can reflect a time to be alone or to withdraw a little. The red-tail and its color phases also help us to guard against blazing so brightly and intensely that we get burnt out.

The sky is the realm of the hawk. Through its flight it communicates with humans and with the great creator spirit. It awakens our vision and inspires us to a creative life purpose.

---

9 Reprinted from *Medicine Cards* by Jamie Sams and David Carson, copyright 1988, Bear and Company, Inc., P.O. Drawer 2860, Santa Fe, NM 87504.

HERON

KEYNOTE: *Aggressive Self-Determination and Self-Reliance*
CYCLE OF POWER: *Spring*

There are many variations of herons, including bitterns and egrets. Storks and cranes should not be confused with them. Herons are part of a group of birds called "waders." It is a bird of the marshlands and shallow waters. All waders have similar physical characteristics—long, thin legs, long necks, and sharp bills. These physical characteristics are important to understand for those who have a heron as a totem.

Legs enable animals and people to move about on the earth. They are symbols of balance, and they represent an ability to progress and evolve. Also the longer the legs, the deeper the water the heron will feed in. The deeper life can be explored. The long thin legs of the heron reflect that you don't need great massive pillars to remain stable, but you must be able to stand on your own. This is especially significant for those with a totem of the great blue heron, as it is a lone hunter.

When it feeds, it stands in the water, reflecting a connection to the earth—while implying the exploration of other dimensions on the earth (water element). It is important for anyone with a heron totem to explore various activities and dimensions of earth life. On the surface, this may seem a form of dabbling, but those with heron totems are wonderfully successful at being the traditional "jack of all trades."

This ability enables them to follow their own path. Most people will never be able to live the way heron people do. It is not a structured way, and does not seem to have a stability and security to it. It is, though, just a matter of perspective. There is security in heron medicine, for it gives the ability to do a variety of tasks. If one way doesn't work, then another will. This heron people seem to inherently know.

Heron do not seem to need a lot of people in their life, nor do they feel pressure to "keep up with the Joneses" or be traditional in their life roles. The only time they gather in colonies is during the breeding season. They stand out in their uniqueness, and they know how to snatch and take advantage of things and events that the average person would not even bother with.

The great blue heron is considered the king of the marsh, although the short-eared owl has been known to readjust a heron's viewpoint. It is the tallest of the herons, and when it flies, its head is folded back in a flat S-shaped loop. This reflects the innate wisdom of being able to maneuver through life and control its life circumstances. It reflects a need for those with this totem to follow their own innate wisdom and path of self-determination. You know what is best for you and should follow it, rather than the promptings of others.

The great blue heron in flight is powerful, and its legs and head are held in a straight line. It uses a slow stalking stride when hunting. When it spies a fish, it spears its prey with its sharp beak and with quick speed. Again it reflects an aggressive movement toward opportunities that present themselves.

The green heron is actually more of a slate blue, and it has orange legs which are distinctive. This color combination reflects an innate balance at living life in its own unique style. It flies silently, and is most often seen in flight at night and at dusk. Like all herons, it is a marsh bird.

There are distinctive seasonal changes in the color of this bird. The irises of the eyes will turn from yellowish to bright orange, as will the legs. Meditation on this color will provide a lot of insight as to its role in your life.

HUMMINGBIRD

> **KEYNOTE:** *Tireless Joy and the Nectar of Life*
>
> **CYCLE OF POWER:** *Daytime*

The hummingbird may be the smallest of birds, but it is also the most fascinating. Anyone who has ever seen this tiny bird is filled with a sense of wonder and joy. Its name comes from the vibration of its wings as it flies or hovers. We have all heard how good it is to whistle while we work, but humming is much more effective. It creates an internal massage, restoring health and balance. This the hummingbird reminds us to do. It reminds us to find joy in what we do and to sing it out.

There are over 300 species of hummingbirds.[10] This is very significant. In the Hebrew alphabet, the letter "shin" is given the numerical value of 300. This has associations with fire and relationships, the past and the future. As we will see later, this is even reflected in the wing movement of the hummingbird. It has the ability to move its wings in a figure 8 pattern—a symbol for infinity and links to the past and future and the laws of cause and effect.

Hummingbirds have long bills and tongues that enable them to extract nectar from flowers. In fact, they could not live without flowers, and many flowers could not live without pollination by hummingbirds. Again this reflects the mysteries of cause and effect that the hummingbird can teach so that you can extract your own nectar.

Hummingbirds have knowledge of how to use flowers for healing. This includes their fragrance, their color, and herbal qualities as well. They can teach you how to draw the life essence from them and create your own medicines—as

---

10 Biel, Timothy. *Zoobooks 2: Hummingbirds* (San Diego: Wildlife Education, Ltd., 1987), p. 6.

in the case of Bach flower remedies and other flower elixirs. They can teach you how to use flowers to heal and win hearts in love.

The hummingbird is the most skillful flyer of all birds. It can hover in the air. It can fly backward, forward and sideways. In fact, it cannot walk; it flies everywhere. It reminds us that if we truly enjoy what we are doing, we become light as a feather, and life is rich with nectar.

The hummingbird can reach high speed at its take off. It can also stop immediately in flight from a high speed. It is such a skillful flyer and is not afraid of any predator. Hummingbirds have even been known to chase off eagles.

No other bird can fly backwards. This reflects the hummingbird's ability to explore the past and to draw from it the nectars of joy. The hummingbird can help you to find joy and sweetness in any situation. Its swiftness is always a reminder to grab joy while you can—as quickly as you can.

Because of its iridescent colors, the hummingbird has been named for jewels and glittering stones—i.e., the ruby-throated hummingbird. It has also come to be associated with the Faerie Realm. One species has been called the wood-nymph hummingbird and another the purple-crowned fairy.

The iridescent colors have also caused it to be associated with rain. More specifically, it is associated often with the rainbow of promise that follows the rain. To the Pueblo Indians, the hummingbird's rainbow coloring, its great strength in flying, and its hovering about flowers, has associated it with various ritual practices. Prayer sticks and ceremonies were used to bring the rain and to help with endurance.[11]

Hummingbirds are big eaters, and most of their food is comprised of the nectars (sugars) of flowers, although they will also eat tiny insects. The hummingbird may eat 50-60 meals a day. Because of its small size and its high degree of activity, it loses body heat quickly, so it must digest food quickly. Individuals with hummingbird totems should watch their own sugar levels. Are you getting too much or too little? Are you hypoglycemic or hyperglycemic? Are you not getting enough sweetness in your life? Are you not savoring the sweet things of life?

Hummingbirds are very playful. Even when bathing—and they bathe often—they play in the water. They also seem to fight with each other, although no one seems to get hurt. Now scientists pretty much agree that these are only mock fights for exercise and fun.

Hummingbirds are fiercely independent. Except when mating, they like to be alone and free, seeming to revel in that freedom. During the mating ritual, the male does anything he can to gain the attention and affection of the female. If the female chooses to mate, she returns the attention, otherwise she just flies off.

Mother hummingbirds are hard workers. This is necessary, for they receive no help from their mate. She will usually lay two eggs, again very symbolic. Two is the number of the inner self, the feminine to which we must give birth and expression to find our own joy.

---

11 Tyler, Hamilton A. *Pueblo Birds and Myths* (Flagstaff: Northland Publishing, 1991), pp. 98–104.

Hummingbirds are master architects. They build their homes with great care and design. Some are very intricate, but each is unique to itself. If the hummingbird has taken up residence in you, you may wish to redecorate. It may be telling you to do something to create joy in the home.

Hummingbirds can also hibernate overnight. The body temperature will lower, its feathers will ruffle up as insulation and it will assume a state of torpidity. It will appear to have died on its perch. This is done to prevent exhausting the energy supplies necessary for it to live—while allowing it to rest. For those with the hummingbird as a totem, it is important to get regular and deep sleep and rest. It will be necessary so that you do not burn yourself out.

The ruby-throated hummingbird is a wonder of migration. Every winter it makes an amazing journey. For several days it will eat and eat, storing up food and energy in its tiny body. Then it will fly for days and days to get to a warm climate. Some have been known to make a journey of 2500 miles or more, from Alaska to Central America. Scientists still are unsure how it is able to store up enough energy to accomplish such a journey.

But it does, and because of it the hummingbird is a symbol for accomplishing that which seems impossible. It will teach you how to find the miracle of joyful living from your own life circumstances.

KESTREL

KEYNOTE: *Mental Speed, Agility and Grace*

CYCLE OF POWER: *Year-round*

The kestrel is the most common member of the falcon family found in the United States. Among American birds of prey, only the great horned owl is as widely distributed. It is also the smallest member of the falcon family. The peregrine and gyrfalcon are larger and faster, but they are also endangered. Efforts to help the peregrine recover are just beginning to succeed.

Falcons have an ancient history and an aura of mystery in regard to their speed and grace in hunting. Falconry has survived for thousands of years and is still practiced today. If the kestrel or any other member of the falcon family has come into your life as a totem, you may want to explore past-life connections. Falconry was practiced in China as long ago as 2000 B.C.[12] Kings handled eagles, and falconry found great popularity in medieval Europe and Scandinavia. The Vikings often used falcons and birds of prey for hunting.

The American kestrel is sometimes called the "sparrow hawk," although this is really a misnomer. While most falcons do live on feathered prey, the kestrel will feed primarily on grasshoppers, beetles, mice, and other small rodents. It does occasionally take smaller birds as prey, and some people credit the kestrel with keeping the population of house sparrows down, but it has never been truly veri-

---

12 Mackenzie, John P. S. *Birds of Prey* (Toronto: Key Porter Books, 1986), p. 13.

fied. It is an excellent hunter, with eyes that can detect the movement of a beetle at a great distance. It usually hunts from a perch. It will move from one vantage point to another, watching and listening.

The kestrel will usually plunge down upon its prey from a perch, or hover above it about twenty feet up before the plunge. This is unique among birds of prey, but also among most birds. Few birds can actually hover in their flying. For those with a kestrel as a totem, this is very significant. It allows the movement to be performed with great speed and precision. It gives the kestrel a gracefulness. It implies the ability to stop and use the flight to its fullest advantage.

The kestrel teaches control of speed and movement. It teaches patience. The kestrel is often a symbol for recognizing opportunities and acting upon them at only the correct moment. It teaches speed and accuracy of action. Most falcons use the flight and the plunge to kill their prey, striking it hard. The kestrel and any falcon can teach us to know when to act but to fully commit to our actions for the greatest success.

The kestrel is found in both the country and the city. Those in the city often find their food in the mice around garbage areas or around open, grassy areas where larger insects can be found. I often see kestrels sitting upon power and phone lines along the major streets or highways, studying the grassy areas

The American Kestrel
This amazing falcon has a unique ability to hover in flight over its prey. Its speed and gracefulness can awaken, within those who have it as a totem, a quick and agile mind.

160

below them. The kestrel will nest and winter in the city, making it a year-round totem. The kestrel prefers open grass areas for hunting, but it always does its hunting from a perch. It is not unusual for individuals with kestrels as totems to want to always sit or be placed in a position where they have a wide vision of everything around them.

All flying falcons are usually detected by their long wings, their swift flight, and their narrow tails. The shape of the wings is usually broad at the base and then swept back, tapering to points. As mentioned, they kill with speed and hard strikes while in flight.

The male kestrel usually has a bluish wing and plain, reddish feathers on the tail. The females usually have a barring on their wings and it takes more of a rust or reddish color. Both the male and female have black facial feathers, swept back like sideburns.

Its overall head shape is squarish, indicating a solidity and control of the thinking process and the element of air. It is this feature which usually distinguishes them from other birds perched on wires. They are also usually perched alone.

The kestrel is a bird that can stimulate a quick, graceful and agile mind. It will teach you how to use your mental faculties more effectively and more patiently to capture what you most need and desire.

KINGFISHER

> **KEYNOTE:** *New Warmth, Sunshine, Prosperity, and Love*
>
> **CYCLE OF POWER:** *Winter Solstice and Season*

In Greek mythology there is a legend of a woman by the name of Halcyone and her husband Ceyx. Shortly after their wedding, Ceyx had to make a voyage. A storm arose during the voyage, and Ceyx was drowned. Everyday that he was gone, Halcyone walked the shores of the beaches, longing for her husband. After several months, the body of her husband washed ashore.

Halcyone was so filled with grief that she threw herself into the ocean. The gods were moved by her love and grief, and she and her husband were turned into kingfishers. They rose out of the ocean and flew off happily into the blue skies. It was declared that the seas would be calm and the sun would shine for seven days before and seven days after the shortest day of the year. This time came to be known as the halcyon days. Today, all sunlit days upon the water are considered halcyon days.

The kingfisher is a long-time symbol of peace and prosperity. It has many legends and superstitions about it. Most originate in ancient Greece from the above myth. The body of the kingfisher if dried—could ward off thunderbolts and storms. If hung in a closet, it would keep moths away—keeping things as fresh as the love found within the tale.

The kingfisher is a beautiful bird with a dull, blue-gray feathering with a white underside, in America. In other parts of the world, most kingfishers are bright blue and greens. An old legend tells how all kingfishers used to be a dull gray. When

Noah released it from the ark, it flew toward the sun and the blue sky. As it rose up toward the sun, it was burnt and changed into a brighter new color.

Blue is a color often associated with the planet Jupiter in astrology, the planet of abundance. The kingfisher is the promise of abundance—of new warmth, prosperity, and love about to unfold within your life. It also has a dark crest—reflecting an abundance often associated with royalty.

The coloring of the kingfisher is unique among most birds. The female of the species has more color than the male. Some people attribute this to the legend of Halcyone and how her greater love touched the gods and restored the life of her husband. It can reflect that as we bring out a self-sacrificing love and manifest it, it will bring new life to us and those closest to us.

The kingfisher is different from other birds in yet another way. Kingfishers build their nests in holes in the banks along water, or as near to water as possible. Sometimes they tunnel into the bank as much as ten feet. They lay five to eight eggs, usually at the inner end of the tunnel. Usually by the time the babies come out of the tunnel, they are ready to make a life for themselves. Parents with totems have a knack for teaching their children how to enjoy life, but also how to prosper at life as well.

Individuals with kingfishers as a totem need to be close to the water, preferably as far north as possible. The kingfisher prefers northern climates. (You may wish to examine the kingfisher in relationship to the symbolism of the direction North as we discussed earlier in the book.) It will go as far north as it can, as long as there are open water sources in which it can hunt.

The kingfisher is a bold bird that fishes for its living. It is often seen flying along ponds, streams, and rivers. It will dive headlong into the water for small fish. Its ability to draw life out of the waters to feed itself reflects the kingfisher's ability to stimulate new opportunities for prosperity. Often it requires that you dive headlong into some activity, but it usually proves to be very beneficial.

If a kingfisher has come to you, prepare yourself to dive into something new. Have you been avoiding the new? Have you been afraid to take the plunge? Are you needing new warmth? Don't worry. If a kingfisher is around, you won't drown. In fact, you will find that, as a result, you will have new sunshine and prosperity unfolding within your life.

LOON

KEYNOTE: *Lucid Dreaming and Re-awakening of Old Hopes, Wishes and Dreams*

CYCLE OF POWER: *Dusk and Dawn*

The loon is an unusual bird. Even when compared to other water birds, it stands out as unique. It is the best swimmer of all birds in North America, and it may even be a better swimmer than the penguin.

The loon is always around water. Water, of course, is the ancient symbol for the astral plane, dreams, and other levels of consciousness. Many myths and stories symbolize a move to a new state of consciousness by describing trips across the seas.

Though it is awkward and clumsy on land, it is a powerful swimmer. Its wings steer, and its feet act like a diver's fins. The loon can swim underwater up to five minutes. Loons can dive deeper and swim faster than any other birds. They are like miniature submarines.

Unlike most birds whose bones are filled with air, the loon's are solid. To sink and dive, the loon empties its lungs. It retains enough air to sustain itself. It is this ability which enables it to escape many predators and to be such a masterful swimmer. Many trance-like states require an adjustment of the breathing, often slowing down to a slow, barely perceptible rhythm. The loon can teach this so that it is easier to enter into varying degrees of consciousness—while maintaining control.

This ability also reflects the potential for an individual to become more conscious in the dream state. Lucid dreaming is when you become aware in your dream that you are dreaming. Then you can change the dream scenario. Lucid dreaming is only a half step away from fully conscious out-of-body experiences.

Anytime the loon shows up as a totem, it is calling to you to pay attention to your dreams. It indicates that they will be of greater importance, along with becoming more vibrant and colorful. The haunting call of the loon may also be telling you that all of those hopes, wishes, and dreams that you have tucked to the back of the heart are about to come to the surface. The loon may be signalling you not to compromise them again, or you may truly find yourself haunted.

The loon will teach new states of consciousness. It will also help you to deepen those you have already awakened. Because it lives close to the water—at the shore line—it can teach you to use these various states of consciousness to open to new dimensions and other life forms—such as those found within the Faerie realm of life. The call of the loon can be an invitation to enter the Faerie realm. It is likened to the distant call of the sirens.

To most people, the call of the loon is its most distinguishing feature. It is haunting and touches the soul in a primal way. The loon is actually very talkative, and it has a whole repertory of calls—each different in sound and meaning. One of its calls is similar to the sound of a wolf howl. One is like a trilling laugh. It will often use the call to distract predators away from the nest. To many outdoors people, the loon call is the true call of the wild. It stirs the primal embers within all who hear it—no matter how long those embers have lain cool. It is as if the sound is calling forth all that we have ignored or shoved to the back of the closet in our minds.

The loon is also a good flyer, but unlike other birds it cannot take off from land. It will run across the water to build up lift. Again this reflects its ability to use altered states of consciousness through greater expression of the will force.

On land, the loon can not walk or waddle very well, and an individual with a loon totem often finds that he/she is only truly comfortable in one—or maybe two—environments. Such people are often not comfortable in the traditional behaviors and social mores of the times. They also have a hard time landing, and so the loon that comes to you as a totem may be coming because it may help you to learn how to become more comfortable in different environments.

For those with the loon as a totem, the imagination and dreaming abilities (while awake or asleep) are powerful. Images and visions will always be very life-like, and the individual may have difficulty separating the real from the unreal. This the loon can help us to do. If you are one of those who has a loon totem, you must ask yourself some questions. Are you looking at something through rose-colored glasses? Are you allowing your imagination to run away with you? Are you not allowing your imagination and dream life to work for you? Is it calling to you to distract you from that which could create problems?

Many superstitions have arisen concerning the loon. To the Norwegians, its eerie call is the sound of the spirit of one who is drowning or soon will. Many northern Indian tribes believed its call signaled that rain was coming or even caused the rain. To the Algonquin Indians the loon is the messenger of Glooskap, a superhuman hero. In Siberia it was believed that when it took to the air, it was escorting the soul of the dead to heaven.

One Eskimo story of the loon speaks of how it was not always a bird. Once two men were fishing, but only one man was catching the fish. The man who had caught nothing all day knocked the other man out and stole his fish. He then proceeded to cut out the tongue of the second man so he could not tell others. He was then pushed out of the boat into the sea. As he wailed in pain, the Great Spirit heard him, and turned him into a loon. Many believe that the eerie cry of the loon is the spirit of this man crying out for justice.

All of these reflect the mystery of this bird. Its haunting and eerie call, its iridescent colors, and its wonderful ability to swim are all reminders of the possibilities that open to us through learning to shift into altered states of consciousness. The loon awakens the imagination, and it reminds us that we are never given a hope, wish, or dream without also being given opportunities to make them a reality. And the only thing that can shatter that possibility is compromise. The loon can lead you back to your greatest dreams and imaginings.

MAGPIE

> KEYNOTE: *The Proper Use of Intelligence, Familiars, and Occult Knowledge*

> CYCLE OF POWER: *Winter and Summer*

The magpie is a cousin to the crow. It is a large bird with a glistening black head. Magpies are curious and somewhat impudent, and they have a reputation for stealing anything they can carry off. This reflects their skill at using whatever they can find. The magpie as a totem can help you to use whatever metaphysical or occult knowledge that you do have—no matter how incomplete it may be. The only thing that you must be careful of is that of thinking and acting as if it will do more for you than it can.

Many consider the magpie the most intelligent member of its family of crows. They have great intelligence, adaptability, and social organization. It is found most predominantly in the northwest, and a study of the directions will help you to define its specific role in your life.

They are scavengers and opportunists, reflecting their great intelligence. Because of this, they can teach you to use what is at hand or they may reflect a "dabbling" pattern in your life. They can help you to advance your knowledge or your life. Their appearance most often reflects opportunities for advancement through proper use of intelligence.

The magpie has often been considered unlucky or lucky depending upon the times and the quantities in which they are seen. One reason for this mixed response to the magpie comes from an old story of how it was the only bird which refused to enter the inside of Noah's ark, preferring to perch on the roof.

From this story and the magpie's own home construction comes an old idea that if a magpie perches on the roof of a house, the house will never come down. Magpies make their nests of mud and twigs. The nests are usually large, and often they are anchored in the forks of a tree or in a thorn bush. This makes the homes strong, and it also links the magpie to being able to open up an individual to new realms as simply and quickly as possible. (Thorn bushes often guard doorways to the spirit and fairy realm. Forked branches are intersections between worlds— again a doorway.) These homes are usually along a watercourse, and they can be used winter and summer.

Their homes are often messy, and this can be a warning not to look for quick and easy methods of attainment through occult knowledge. Their homes usually have a roof and are entered in through the sides. A magpie as a totem usually indicates that you are going to encounter the spirit realm and the metaphysical world in a different manner. You will enter into it and experience it in a way different from most—and often it is in an unusual manner.

The Scots had a fortune-telling rhyme about the number of magpies you might meet while out walking:

> One's sorrow, two's mirth,
> Three's a wedding, four's a birth.
> Five's a Christening, six a dearth,
> Seven's heaven, eight is hell,
> And nine's the devil his ain sel'.[13]

A similar kind of association has been passed on in the United States in the folk tradition. One magpie is unlucky and can indicate anger. Two is merriment and marriage, like the "mirth" in the Scot's rhyme. Three magpies indicates a suc-

---

13 Limburg, Peter. *What's in the Names of Birds* (New York: Coward, McCann and Geoghegan, Inc., 1975), p. 4.

cessful journey. (Weddings can be a journey.) Four magpies indicate good news, and five company or parties.

The magpie has an association with witchcraft. It was once believed that magpies were the familiars of witches and magicians. They were spirits in animal form. Part of this belief comes from their intelligence and their keen observation of human activity. It also, I'm sure, has connections to their thievery—as witches and magicians were not often looked upon kindly.

Its intelligence and wily character makes it an interesting totem, but one not easily controlled. It is a bird with a will of its own. It does have knowledge of how to use animals as familiars. It can also teach how to use occult knowledge for quick effects. Part of the problem with this bird as a totem is that the knowledge is usually incomplete. You may gain what you desire from the use of the knowledge, but it may come in an obtuse or unusual way. It may have other repercussions that you may not have considered.

If magpie has shown up in your life, you need to ask yourself some serious questions? Do you have knowledge and are not using it? Are you employing whatever skills you have to get what you most need? Are you using your knowledge and skills inappropriately? Magpie can help you to define these answers. It can help you to learn to use occult knowledge in responsible but effective ways. The magpie will show you what you can do for your life with just a little occult knowledge.

MARTIN

KEYNOTE: *Good Luck and Community Peace*

CYCLE OF POWER: *Late Spring and Summer*

The martin is the largest of the swallows, and you may want to study swallows in general to help you define the role the martin will play within your life.

The color of the martin is most significant. Of these, the purple martin is the most outstanding and the most familiar. Its color has caused it to be associated with the divine. Its color and its aerial ability have caused it to be called God's bow and arrow. The martin is a good-luck bird. It has long been considered fortunate to any home where it nests, lays its eggs, and rears its young.

In more primitive times, dried gourds were hung out as homes for the martins. They take naturally to community life. Many martin birdhouses, made by humans, look like huge apartment complexes. They are at peace with others in the complex and get along well with all.

When the martin arrives as a totem, look for a positive change in your fortune. It is a bird that brings peaceful living energies with it. It can help solve many of the problems associated with community life. It is a wonderful totem to meditate upon whenever you move into a new environment and community. It will help you to make the move positive. It will help make your integration into the new neighborhood more enjoyable.

MEADOWLARK

KEYNOTE: *Cheerful Journey Inward*

CYCLE OF POWER: *Summer*

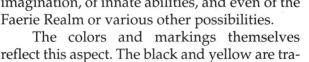

The meadowlark is actually a blackbird. It has a bright yellow breast, usually with a black crescent across it. It is a bird that usually indicates that you are about to experience a cheerful journey into the inner you. Many of its behaviors reflect the inward journey and movement often associated with self-discovery. This can be discovery of the intuition, the imagination, of innate abilities, and even of the Faerie Realm or various other possibilities.

The colors and markings themselves reflect this aspect. The black and yellow are traditional colors associated with the archangel Auriel, who oversees the summer season and the activity of the nature realm. The crescent is reflective of lunar significances—the moon long being associated with the inner self.

Its behaviors and activities also reflect the inner journey. It builds a dome-shaped nest, or it uses depressions in the ground in which it lays its eggs. The shapes indicate a drawing in. The bird rarely leaves the ground (staying close to the self) except when disturbed or when perching to sing. Unlike most birds, it walks when feeding upon the ground, rather than hopping. This reflects a comfortableness with the inner environment, which the earth is in relation to the air.

So what of the cheerfulness? Well, the meadowlark has a cheery song. It also sings as it flies—not like most birds which sing only when perched. It also lives in open meadows, and meadows are places of positive growth and fertility.

The meadowlark also has an unusual flight. It flies with very stiff wings and a fluttering motion. It alternately sails and flaps, giving it the appearance of a playful flight.

To the ancient alchemists, the lark was a symbol of sublimation. According to the *Random House Dictionary of the English Language,* sublimation is the "act of diverting energy from its immediate goal to one of a higher social, moral or aesthetic nature or use . . . the act of making nobler or purer."[14] The meadowlark teaches us to find joy in going within ourselves. It helps us to find ways to sing within our life conditions by helping us recognize that every individual event is part of a greater journey. It can teach you that the joy of the quest is not in reaching the destination but rather in the journey itself.

---

14 Stein, Jess. *The Random House Dictionary of the English Language* (New York: Random House, 1970), p. 1415.

MOCKINGBIRD

> KEYNOTE: *Finding Your Sacred Song* (Soul Purpose) *and Recognition of Your Innate Abilities*
>
> CYCLE OF POWER: *Year-round—Day and Night*

The mockingbird is famous in song and story. It is a traditional symbol of the South, and anyone who has a mockingbird for a totem should study the symbolism of this direction. It is a plain woodland bird, but has a magnificent song.

In spite of its plain appearance, the beauty of the mockingbird is recognized by all. This beauty lies in its song. It has one of the best singing voices of all birds, equal to that of the nightingale. It also has a talent for mimicry. Mockingbirds can imitate other birds, cats, and even dogs. Some mockingbirds have a repertory of over 30 songs and calls of other birds. Impressionist comedians, such as Rich Little, have to have a mockingbird as one of their totems.

Mockingbirds will live close to humans because they are not afraid. They also like company, reflecting the idea that songs should be shared. They sing throughout the entire year, and will even sing while flying, which is rare among birds. They have also been known to sing by moonlight.

The mockingbird can teach you about the power of song and voice. It can help you to learn new languages and sing them just as naturally as one born to them. Anytime the mockingbird shows up as a totem, it is a time to learn to sing out your talents. Regardless of how others may see you, expect people to notice your actions—not your appearance.

The mockingbird can help you to realize your inner talents and sing them forth. It can help you to find your own sacred song in life. By singing that sacred song, you will find your life more rewarding and more significant. Most people, even if they know their inner sacred song (life purpose), are afraid to act upon it. The mockingbird can assist with this.

The mockingbird is a courageous bird. During breeding season (the development of your inner song and abilities), it will attack cats and any other raiders. It tolerates no impudence. It fiercely defends its nest. It takes the fight to the intruder, confident in its abilities.

Unlike many birds, the mockingbird may lay eggs two to three times a year. This reflects that opportunities to follow the inner song are never lost. They always come back around.

The mockingbird is the master of languages—spoken and unspoken, sung and unsung. It can read the language of the body and teach this ability to you. It can teach the secrets of all communication so that you can become more successful in life. This is reflected in the manner in which it finds its own food.

On its shoulders are prominent white patches. As it walks along, it occasionally opens its wings, flashing the white patches. They reflect the sunlight, alarming insects in the area. When they react, the mockingbird sees them and snatches them for dinner.

This ability to subtly stimulate responses in others is part of what the mockingbird can teach you. It can help you to flush out injurious insects around you in your life and see where and who they are. The mockingbird will help you to recognize the subtle clues that others may miss. You hear the true song of others.

Whenever the mockingbird arrives, look for opportunities to sing forth your own song. Follow your own path. Learn to take what you can and apply your own creative imagination and intuition to i, so that you sing it forth in the manner and tone that is most harmonious for you and your life.

NUTHATCH

KEYNOTE: *Grounding of Faith and Higher Wisdom*

CYCLE OF POWER: *Year-round*

This small bird is one of many that may seem insignificant, but which, when examined, have unique characteristics. It is a bird that reflects the need to stay grounded and apply the spiritual energies you invoke within your everyday life.

This is most reflected through the fact that it descends down a tree head first. This reflects the need to learn to bring down the Tree of Life the wisdom and apply it within the natural world. The spiritual realm is not a realm in which all of our troubles are dissolved into some blinding light. The true path to realization is learning to manifest the spiritual within the physical. This is what the nuthatch teaches.

A number of psychics and healers I have encountered over the years could use the nuthatch as a totem. They become so lost in the spiritual and "ethereal" realms that they have difficulty in the real world. They are out of touch and often unhealthy. They ignore the physical while they focus on the spiritual. They forget that we are physical, and we must give it as much care and attention as we do the spiritual.

As we learn to release our preconceptions about the spiritual and physical realms, we begin to see the world from a different perspective. For anyone with a nuthatch as a totem, it would be beneficial to meditate upon the Hanged Man card of the tarot deck. The figure is depicted upside down. The nuthatch teaches you to have faith in your abilities and to trust in what you have learned about applying spiritual rhythms and vibrations within the physical world.

This is further amplified by the fact that the nuthatch is the traveling companion to the woodpecker. As new rhythms are sounded out (woodpecker), the nuthatch works to bring them down out of the ethereal realms and ground them into physical life. Anyone with a nuthatch as a totem should also study the woodpecker, and vice versa.

The breast of the nuthatch is white. White in the heart is the white of faith and truth. The nuthatch can show you where the truth is and how to act upon it most effectively in faith. The nuthatch teaches us not to have blind faith. It teaches us that one who speaks the truth is not necessarily the Truth itself. It teaches us that one who points at the sun is not the sun. Rather it teaches proper strength and action through faith in yourself.

ORIOLE

KEYNOTE: *The Weaving of New Sunshine*

CYCLE OF POWER: *Summer*

This beautiful yellow/orange and black bird is considered the first sign of summer in many northern areas. Its clear, cheery song and bright colors are signs of new golden sunshine about to enter into your life. The name of this bird comes from the word *aureolus* which means "little golden one" in Latin. This reflects its keynote symbolism.

Whenever the oriole shows up, look for sunshine to show up within a two week period. This may occur in any area of your life. Doing prayers and meditations with the oriole in connection to any project will help it to work out or move forward wonderfully within a two week period. All of this is because the eggs (usually 4 to 6) hatch in two weeks.

The male is usually always close to the female oriole. This has many connotations, especially in connection to new sunshine. Look for positive changes or even new sunshine in the area of relationships. It also reflects that the bird is a harbinger of positive energy, blessing unions.

As mentioned in conjunction with several other birds, the colors of orange/yellow and black are colors associated with the nature spirits in traditional metaphysics. Specifically, they are the colors of the archangel Auriel who oversees all nature spirit activity upon the planet. The oriole can open doorways to positive relationships with all members of the nature realm.

The presence of an oriole or its nest in your home environment often indicates that the fairies and elves have drawn close or even moved into your home. The oriole weaves its nest from plant fibers to form a hanging nest, suspended from forked branches. The suspension reflects its ability to help you suspend time and space and reconnect with the inner sunshine of your soul. Forks and intersections are always places in which realms and dimensions intersect, creating doorways.

The oriole is a weaver. Its nests are intricately woven, and it reflects an increasing ability to weave your life along new lines—ones that bring greater joy. Earlier in the text, I mentioned a prayer stick that is effective for working with orioles. The prayer stick is forked, and one fork is painted black and the other is painted orange. It is a powerful tool to construct when you are starting any new endeavor and project.

The oriole will help you to weave new sunshine into any area of life you desire. It will help you to rediscover your own inner child and a renewed sense of joy in life.

OSTRICH

KEYNOTE: *Becoming Grounded*

CYCLE OF POWER: *Year-round*

If you find yourself becoming a little flaky and flighty, if friends and others are accusing you of being out of touch, then it could be beneficial to work with ostrich medicine. The ostrich is the largest bird, but unlike most, it cannot fly. This is very symbolic.

Remember that flight has to do with opening to new wisdom. Birds are symbols of connecting with the more ethereal realms of life and with higher knowledge. A bird that cannot fly can still connect us with these same energies. It also helps us in using them within the physical life. The ostrich is a bird that can help you to take new knowledge out of that ethereal mental realm and apply it practically.

The ostrich can still help us link to those realms and prevent us from getting lost in them. This is reflected in its long neck and legs, its height giving us a link. The symbolism of the neck and the legs should be explored as well. In my forthcoming book *The Healer's Manual*, I discuss the symbolism and metaphysical correspondences of the major parts of the body—human or animal.

The ostrich is very fast moving on land with great strength in its feet. Its kicking ability is its defense, and it can kill with its feet. The feet is how humans stay connected to the earth, again reflecting the idea of staying grounded. If an ostrich shows up as a totem, ask yourself some pertinent questions. Are you not staying grounded? Are you afraid to use your knowledge and fly to new heights and realms? Are you using your knowledge to move forward? Are you not using your knowledge? Are you getting becoming flighty, or are others around you becoming so?

There is an old myth that says when an ostrich is frightened or scared it buries its head in the sand, refusing to see or acknowledge what is going on. This really does not apply. The ostrich does not bury its head. It will lower its head as a protective gesture. Because of its height, this makes itself and its eggs less visible. Maybe if an ostrich assumes this posture with you, you might want to consider being more protective of yourself and less visible. Make sure you are not placing yourself in a vulnerable position.

The ostrich is often seen walking among zebras and antelope. The animals stir up insects and other food for the ostrich. They both serve to warn each other of predators as well. If you have an ostrich as a totem, it would be beneficial to study the zebra and antelope as well, as they are often companion animals.

The ostrich has a healthy appetite—reflecting an appetite for greater knowledge. They often swallow stones to help assist in the digestive process. This is very significant. Any bird that does this usually indicates a need for you to assimilate knowledge before acting on it. It has to be digested and assimilated or you are likely to become flighty and use it inappropriately. The ostrich is a bird that can help us in assimilating new knowledge and in staying grounded as we open to it as well.

OWL

> **KEYNOTE:** *The Mystery of Magic, Omens, Silent Wisdom, and Vision in the Night.*

> **CYCLE OF POWER:** *Nocturnal—Year-round*

No bird has as much myth and mystery surrounding it than the owl. Most perceptions of it are confused. It is not unusual to get contrary opinions of the owl. It has an ancient aura of mystery about it. Part of this is because it is a nocturnal bird, and night time has always seemed mysterious to humans.

The owl is a symbol of the feminine, the moon, and the night. It has been called a cat with wings. It has been worshiped as an idol and hated as the reincarnation of the devil. It has been believed to have great healing powers, both in North America and on other continents. Because of its association with the moon, it has ties to fertility and seduction, for the moon is the arouser of men and owls. The owl is the bird of magic and darkness, of prophecy and wisdom.

To the ancient Greeks, the owl was associated with the goddess Athena, and it

The Mystery of Owls

The short-eared owl (above) is one of the most gifted and courageous flyers among birds of prey—able to outfly even the harrier hawk.

(Photo courtesy of Brukner Nature Center Troy, Ohio.)

was a symbol of higher wisdom. It was the guardian of the Acropolis. To the early Christian Gnostics, it is associated with Lilith, the first wife of Adam who refused to be submissive to him. To the Pawnee, it was a symbol of protection. To the Ojibwa, it was a symbol of evil and death. To the Pueblo, it was associated with the Skeleton Man, the god of death, but who was also a spirit of fertility. "Owl medicine is symbolically associated with clairvoyance, astral projection and magic, both black and white."[15]

Many superstitions and beliefs have come to be associated with it. Owls have been thought of as the reincarnation of the dead. In Wales, the owl has come to be associated with fertility. If heard near a pregnant girl, it indicates an easy birth.[16] The most predominant is that of the owl being able to extract secrets. It was believed in ancient Rome that to place a feather or part of an owl on a sleeping person would enable you to discover his/her

The barred owl is the champion vocalist among owls. While great horned owls are majestic, aloof and dangerous, barred owls are quite harmless, though they may try to look menacing.
(Photo courtesy of Brukner Nature Center, Troy, Ohio.)

secrets. This is all tied to one of its keynotes, especially when we look at its acute vision and hearing.

The owl is a bird of the night, and the night has long been a symbol of the darkness within—the place in which humans hide their secrets. The owl has great vision and hearing. They can adjust in an instant from a telescopic to a microscopic focus. The pupils respond in a fraction of a second to very minute changes in light intensity. The owl's eyes are specially adapted to detect subtle movements. They also have extra light-sensitive cones and rods in the retina to help with this.

---

15 Sams, Jamie and Carson, David. *Medicine Cards* (Santa Fe: Bear & Company, 1988), p. 121.
16 de la Torre, Julio. *Owls—Their Life and Behaviors* (New York: Crown Publishers, 1990), p. 8.

The Mystery of Owls

The great horned owl (above) and the screech owls (left) are two of the most common. Both have the tufts of feathers that look like ears, but are not. These ears that are not ears have made them symbolic of being able to hear what is not being said. The barn owl (facing page) is sometimes called the ghost owl because of its color and its silent flight. It is an old symbol of spirit and ghostly contact. (Photos courtesy of Brukner Nature Center, Troy, Ohio.)

The yellow coloring of the eyes is very symbolic. It makes the eyes much more expressive, but it hints of the light of the sun, alive in the dark of the night. The sun lives through the owl at night. Meditation on this alone will reveal much about the magic of the owl within your life. Contrary to popular belief, the owl can see very well during the daylight. It is just more effective and more acute at night.

Even in the darkest night, with its acute eyesight an owl can pinpoint the exact location of its prey. Its hearing is just as keen as its eyesight. The ears of the owl are asymmetrical, and one ear is usually larger than the other. They are also located in different positions on the head. This enables it to sort out the auditory signals it picks up, facilitating it being able to locate its prey more easily.

The barn owl can locate its prey as easily or even easier with its ears than its eyes. It will swivel its head and rock back and forth to pinpoint noises of prey with great accuracy. It will also make period clicks as a form of echo location.

One who works with owl medicine will be able to see and hear what others try to hide. You will hear what is not being said, and you will see what is hidden or in the shadows. You can detect and pinpoint the subtleties. This can make others uncomfortable because they will not be able to deceive you about their motives or actions. Owl people have a unique ability to see into the darkness of others' souls and life. This is very scary to most people. This vision and hearing capabilities has metaphysical links to the gifts of clairvoyance and clairaudience as well.

The owl, as a bird of the night, can teach all of the secrets of the night. These secrets involve everything that transpires when the Sun is gone. Owls are the eyes of the night, and they see what is not in the open. They have secret knowledge that they can share. Their medicine can extract secrets.

There are over 100 species of owls, and they have always had an intimate link to humans. Wherever humans live, so do rodents the primary food of owls. Because of this, owls live wherever humans live. The unfortunate part is that many hunters and farmers kill owls frequently, believing cats will do better with rodent control. Nothing is further from the truth. A barn owl can kill ten times the amount of mice than a cat in a single night and more if there are young to be fed.

Like humans, they blink by closing the upper eyelids, giving them a human expression which has added to the mysticism of owls. Unlike humans though, their eyes cannot move. Their neck is flexible, giving them a wide range of peripheral vision. They cannot turn their heads completely around, but they do move it so quickly that it gives that appearance. The symbolism of the neck and its flexibility should be meditated upon for those with owl medicine. If your neck is stiff and inflexible, you are hindering your perceptions to a great degree. Neck massages would be very beneficial for anyone working with owl totems.

The owl, like hawks and other birds of prey, has a third eyelid. This nictitating eyelid moves from side to side. It cleanses the eye, clearing its vision. Again this symbolizes so much about new vision opening to you. It often reflects that you were born very perceptive—with a vision of others that you may or may not have recognized or acknowledged. Often those with an owl as a power totem have a unique ability for seeing into the eyes and souls of others. Often these perceptions are discarded as wild imaginings or with such phrases as "Why in the world would I think *that* about this person?" These kinds of imaginings, positive and negative, should be trusted.

The mating habits of owls follow similar patterns to other birds. The male will often increase its hooting and dance to get the attention of the female. Many owls like living alone and only come together to breed. So the female, especially of the great horned species, only mates when she truly trusts the male. Some owls mate for life, such as the barn owl. Others mate and stay together only until the owlettes leave the nest.

Many owls do not build nests. They will lay eggs in the forks of trees or use abandoned nests of other birds. Because they often have unusual nesting procedures, it is not uncommon to find owlettes and fledglings at the base of trees where they have fallen. Many people pick them up, believing them to be abandoned. This is rarely so. If left alone, the mother will take care of them.

Usually only the female will brood, but the male will keep the mates and the owlettes in a steady supply of mice. A male feeding the female and her brood can kill dozens of mice or its equivalent in a single night. This attests to the great hunting ability and rodent control that an owl can bring to an environment.

Owls fly silently. The front edge of the wing has a fringe that silences the flight. Most owls have wings that are great for the size of the owl. This also enables the owl to fly slowly and smoothly, facilitating its silent hunt. This silence is something that all with an owl totem should practice. Keep silent and go about your business. This will bring you the greatest success.

Some owls are endangered. This is partly due to destruction of habitat and partly due to unthinking hunting. The spotted owl is an example of an owl in danger because of loss of habitat. The barn owl is threatened or endangered in many states. This is due predominantly to hunting and the perception of owls as pests.

Much study has been done on owls in regards to their prey. This is possible predominantly due to "owl pellets." An owl will usually swallow its prey whole and head first. The parts of the prey that are indigestible (bones, fur, teeth, claws, and such) are then regurgitated in the form of pellets. This is a very symbolic act in which much significance can be found. In the swallowing of the prey head first, the owl takes into itself the wisdom and energy of the prey. The regurgitation reflects its ability to eliminate those aspects that are unbeneficial and unhealthy for it.

It is important to study the individual characteristics of each species of owl, as well as those for all owls in general. This will help you to define exactly how the owl is going to affect you and your life. In the context of this book, we are only going to examine six particular owls, but this will be enough to provide you with an idea as to how best to relate your owl totem to your individual life.

Some owls have a balancing raptor. The owl is lunar and nocturnal, while some raptors are diurnal and solar. Owls and some hawks will share the same territory, one hunting and using it by day, and the other by night. They don't necessarily get along, but they do tolerate each other in varying degrees. These can be seen as balancing medicines, and rituals and meditations can be used with the owl and its solar equivalent. They can be used to balance the male and female.

One example is using owl and hawk feathers together as part of a dream bundle to help stimulate lucid dreaming. For example, a red-tailed hawk feather tied between two great horned owl feathers and hung over the bed may help you assert your will over the dream state. This can be used to develop astral projection or just for conscious control of the dream scenario during sleep.

The most common examples of owls and their daytime hawk equivalents are found in the chart below:

OWL		HAWK
(Lunar/Nighttime)		(Solar/Daytime)
Great Horned Owls	=	Red-Tailed Hawks
Barred Owls	=	Red-Shouldered Hawks
Screech Owls	=	Kestrels
Short-Eared Owls	=	Harrier Hawks
Snowy Owls	=	White Phase Gyrfalcons

The first owl we will examine is the great horned owl. This is the most ferocious and the most successful predator in the owl family in America. It is powerful and swift. It can easily snap the neck of a woodchuck. It will not hesitate to take whatever prey presents itself. The great horned owl will even take on all other birds of prey. Most are in awe of its formidable talons and strong beak.

The red-tailed hawk is most often considered the solar or daytime equivalent to the lunar and nocturnal great horned. This is because they may nest in the same tract of land. This does not mean they get along though. In fact great horneds will harass red-tails to the degree that if the opportunity presents itself the hawk will try to eliminate the owl. Truly only the golden eagle is the one raptor unafraid and unintimidated by it.

This ferocity has enabled the owl to survive and adapt to constantly changing environments. It attacks life with a fervor. Unfortunately, this same ferocity has interfered with the reintroduction of the peregrine falcon into its former habitats. In the peregrine's absence, the great horned owl has taken up residence and will not share either its habitat or its food sources.

To many the hooting of the great horned owl, especially strong and frequent during mating, is a harbinger of spring. Its favorite habitat is in dense wooded areas of hardwoods and conifers. But it can live almost anywhere there is a food source.

The favorite food of the great horned is the skunk, and anyone with this owl as a totem should also study the significance of the skunk. This owl does not have a great sense of smell, which is probably why it is the skunk's most fearsome predator. It would also be good to study crows as they will often gang up and mob owls in their environment. Crows know that if the owl finds their home during the day, it is likely to visit at night when the crows can neither see nor hear it approach.

The tufts on the top of its head are not its ears. They are simply tufts of feathers. The ears are located lower in the head, and as with all owls are extremely acute. They can hear as well or better than they see.

Next is the common barn owl. This owl has a heart shaped facial disc which is unique among owls. This reflects the ability to link the heart and the mind. It is part of what this owl teaches. It also has darker eyes. It has a golden buff feathering on top, and white feathering beneath.

The common barn owl has a variety of names. When seen at night from below it has a ghostly appearance due to its white feathering. It is this aspect which has earned it the name of ghost owl. It is an owl whose medicine can connect you to old haunts and spirits of properties and homes that may still be lingering about. Its medicine can be used to help develop mediumship and spirit contact.

The barn owl is the master hunter. Many farmers have shot barn owls and tried to replace them with cats. Unfortunately, the farmers often do not realize that "one pair of nesting barn owls can eliminate more mice per night than ten cats put together."[17]

---

17 de la Torre, Julio. *Owls—Their Life and Behavior* (New York: Crown Publishers, 1990), p. 26

It is the barn owl's hearing ability which makes it stand out as a hunter. In fact, a large portion of the barn owl's brain is devoted to sorting out the auditory signals that it picks up. It has the ability to use echo location, a kind of sonar in locating prey. For those with this bird as a totem, the ability to hear the inner voice and even spirit (clairaudience) will definitely begin to develop.

Barn owls are inventive opportunists. They are adaptable and will take their food wherever they can find it. Their most common prey is the mouse, and those with barn owl medicine should study the qualities of the mouse as well.

Another marvelous owl is the barred. They are master vocalists and they have charming personalities. They are large and round, with dark eyes. They have a barred marking on their feathers, especially crosswise on the upper chest. It is almost as if this barring is an outer signal that it has much of its ferocity in check.

The barred owl is often found in dense deciduous forests and swamps. Because of loss of environment, it has invaded the haunts of the spotted owl. In the owl kingdom, the larger will also hunt the smaller. Since the spotted owl is smaller, it is somewhat threatened, even though many believe the spotted owl is just a close relative. Both share a love for the primeval forests.

The daytime equivalent of the barred owl is the red-shouldered hawk. These two share the same territory amicably—unlike the great horned and the red-tailed hawk. Both the barred owl and the red-shouldered hawk are at home in moist woodlands. They even share the same nesting space on occasion.

The barred owl has a benign nature, and this is what is most outstanding about it. Although they may try to appear threatening, they are harmless. It is a great actor and can put on quite a show. Many believe its vocal performances are designed to put other animals and people off. It reflects the ability of this owl to teach us how to use the voice for greater effects.

Screech owls are much smaller than those we have discussed so far. Like the great horned, they have tufts of feathers on their head that look like ears. They are usually reddish or gray in color and they are only 6-10 inches tall.

Contrary to their name, screech owls do not really screech. Their sounds are more like a soft whinny. During mating season, the male and female screech owls will sing duets. The males have a lower pitch. If the young are threatened, this is when the "screech" is usually heard.

In spite of their small size, the courage and ferocity of the screech owl is often compared to that of the great horned. It is thought by many to be a miniature of the great horned in this aspect.

The daytime equivalent of the screech owl is the kestrel. They both share the same territory. They both have a fondness for woodland borders and the use of tree holes for nesting. They both have a fondness for crickets and mice.

Screech owls are excellent hunters. They also occasionally use cooperative hunting. This ability to cooperate to survive is part of what the screech owl can teach. It can show you how to be a fierce individual with an ability to cooperate with others—maintaining that individuality throughout.

The short-eared owl is one of the few owls that will hunt day or night. This in itself reflects that its medicine is powerful day and night. It is also unique in that it will meticulously build its home. It will also migrate. The markings on it are flame-like, reflecting its scientific name (Asio flammeus). This fiery aspect is reflected in its personality.

Earlier in the book I spoke of how the short-eared owl has a unique ability to show up overnight wherever there is an eruption of field mice populations. This sixth sense, of being in opportune places at opportune times, is what this owl can teach.

This owl is courageous and playful. While crows can mob and chase off hawks and other owls, the short-eared will turn the tables on its assailants. The crows often become the victims when they try the mobbing with short-eared owls. Though small, they are strong and fast—and they have no fears. And they shouldn't. Few birds can compare to them in aerial ability. Even the great blue heron, who thinks it is the king of the marshes, has fallen to the short-eared owl on more than one occasion.[18]

Even its counterpart, the harrier hawk (the most agile of hawks) cannot outfly it. These two though will often share the same territory and have mock "dogfights." This owl and this hawk nest close to each other and rarely do they ever fight.

The short-eared owl is a versatile and curious bird. Its abilities are second to none, and it has no fear. It reflects a blending of fire and air. They have a stimulating effect upon all energies. They stir passion for life and fire the inspiration. They awaken the imagination.

The last example I will use is that of the magnificent snowy owl. It is larger than the great horned, but it is most noted for its white coloring. It is found in the open tundra of the arctic, but it will migrate as far south as is necessary to find food.

Most owls hunt by night, but like the short-eared owl, the snowy is at home both night and day. It can hunt in full sunlight or total darkness. It has the unique ability to open and close its iris to adjust to whatever light intensities (or lack of) there may be.

The snowy owl hunts predominantly by sitting and waiting. They seem to hunt lazily and often appear to be resting. This is far from true. They conserve their energy, and they are continually observant, going into action when the opportunity presents itself. This sense of timing is part of what the snowy owl can teach.

Its primary prey are lemmings and arctic hares. These should be studied by anyone with this bird as a totem. It will usually eat its weight in food everyday, and like the short-eared owl, it has a knack for moving to areas where food supplies will more likely be found. It seems to instinctually detect possible famine periods and thus is able to move at the opportune times and return as well. This kind of prophetic instinct is part of what this bird can teach. It has the power of prophecy and spirit.

18 Ibid, p. 178.

When the snowy moves into a new area, it does not proclaim its presence. It enters quietly and goes about its own business. This is part of what makes it successful. It can teach us this same ability. When it walks, its talons are withdrawn into its well-padded feet. Again this reflects its ability to be non-threatening in spite of its power and ability. It accomplishes its tasks with timing and skill, not through intimidation. True strength is gentle and this is what the snowy teaches.

This is a very skillful bird at the game of survival. Even the young can sprint, swim, and even play dead if it is necessary, assuming an almost torpid state. This bird seems to embody the strength and power of the great horned, while having the temperament of the barred. And on top of it all it has the skill, courage, and talents of the short-eared.

PARROT

KEYNOTE: *Sunshine and Color Healing*

CYCLE OF POWER: *Year-round*

The parrot is a bird of the sun. Its bright colors and sunshine aspect are what gives it its magic. Its feathers can be used in prayer sticks for powerful healing rites and to invoke the energies of the sun at any time of the year.

In the Pueblo tradition, it is a bird associated with the gathering of salt. The places where salt was found were considered a gift of the sun. Since the parrot was to the Pueblo a bird of the sun, there is the correspondence. Parrots come in a variety of colors. Anyone with a parrot as a totem should do some study of colors and their effects. The parrot is a wonderful teacher of the power of light and colors.

Some parrots have been taught to mimic humans. Because of this ability, the parrot has been considered a link between the human kingdom and the bird kingdom. Parrots, in this sense, could be likened to ambassadors, diplomats, and interpreters for the bird realm. They have a magic that will enable you to understand others more effectively. They can help you awaken a sense of diplomacy.

PEACOCK

KEYNOTE: *Resurrection and Wise Vision (Watchfulness)*

CYCLE OF POWER: *Spring and Autumn*

The peacock is a bird which has stirred much lore and myth in every society. This bird with its beautiful plumage fascinates all who encounter it. As with many birds, the male has the brighter feathers and is more ostentatious. The peahen is no less magnificent in its own right. It is a protective and powerful bird.

Probably the peacock's two most outstanding features are the feathers and its eerie and raucous calls. The call has a kind of laughter quality to it, as if the peacock is a reminder to laugh at life. One story I have heard in connection to its vocalizations is tied to the appearance of its feet. The peacock has ugly feet, and there is a story that it screeches every time it catches sight of them.

For anyone with a peacock as a totem, an examination of the mysticism and symbolism of feet should be examined. The feet are our support system; they are at the foundation of our structure. They enable us to move and to be upright. What are the feet of the peacock saying about you and your life? An examination and use of foot reflexology is beneficial to study for anyone with a peacock as a totem.

The feathers have been used for ritual and for decorative purposes. The colors and patterns of its feathers reveal why such mysticism has arisen in connection with the peacock. The blue-green iridescence creates a sense of awe. The bluish-green tint has often been associated with royalty. The "eyes" within the feathering have often been associated with greater vision and wisdom.

This idea of watchfulness is found in Greek Mythology. Argus, a watchman for the goddess Hera, had a hundred eyes. When he fell asleep during his duty and was killed, Hera placed his eyes in the peacock—her favorite bird.

Of all birds, the peacock most resembles the traditional descriptions of the phoenix. The phoenix is the legendary bird of resurrection that is sacrificed in the fires of life and then rises from the flames out of its own ashes. The peacock, as a reflection of the phoenix, has touched many societies. In Chinese mythology the plumage is a blending of five colors that have a sweet harmony of sound.

In Egypt it was linked to the worship of the sun god, Amon-Ra. Even in Christianity it was a symbol of the death and resurrection of Jesus. In Egypt, the peacock was associated with the all seeing eye of Horus. To the Hindus, it was associated with Hindra, the god of thunder who became a peacock to escape the demon Ravana, thus being endowed with 100 eyes in the feathers.

The peacock was often considered sacred in that it destroyed poisonous snakes. In Egypt it held a position second only to the ibis in this category. Because of its many eyes, it has been associated with wisdom and vision—heightened watchfulness. it has also been associated with immortality. Partly this is due to its similar appearance to depictions of the phoenix. This idea also arises from an old belief that its flesh would not putrefy.

An examination of these and other myths associated with this bird may reveal possible past-life connections for those with this totem. It will shed insight into the role it will play in your life. The lore associated with the peacock is closely tied to its characteristics and behaviors, and it will help you see how other societies were able to draw connections and make correspondences.

PELICAN

KEYNOTE: *Renewed Buoyancy and Unselfishness*
CYCLE OF POWER: *Year-round*

There are two species of pelican in the United States—the white and the brown. Both have the recognizable pouch and long bill. Contrary to what many believe, and as is often depicted in cartoons, they use this to scoop fish and not store them. Some reflection on that may reveal some insight into your own personal activities. Are you trying to store what shouldn't be stored? Are you not using or digesting what you have?

Both types of pelicans embody the keynote, along with other aspects that were once considered very magical and powerful. An old story tells of how the pelican wounded its own breast and fed its young on the blood. This explains the image of self-sacrifice often associated with it, and has come to be a very Christian correspondence.

The brown pelican often nests in bushes (mangrove thickets). By avoiding nesting competition with their neighbors, pelicans make room for more of their kind. Again this reflects a kind of unselfishness. This is further reinforced by the fact that they will often employ teamwork in fishing. This is especially true of the white pelican. The groups descend and drive the fish into the shallow areas.

Despite their size, they are very light and buoyant. They can float like a schooner. The brown pelican is often observed flying solo and then suddenly plummeting into the water. It then pops up to the surface. It has this ability because of a system of air sacs under the skin that make it unsinkable.

Symbolically, this hints at being able to be buoyant and to rest on top in spite of the heaviness of life circumstances. The pelican teaches that no matter how difficult life becomes, no matter how much you plunge—you can pop to the surface. The pelican holds the knowledge of how to rise above life's trials. This same idea is hinted at in regard to an old belief that pelicans once lived on the desert, in which they fed upon serpents.

Pelicans, in spite of their lightness, sometimes have a difficult time taking off from the water. Still they do manage, and again we can see the correspondence to freeing oneself from that which would weigh you down. The water is a symbol of emotions, and emotions often weigh us down. The pelican teaches how not to be overcome by them.

PENGUIN

KEYNOTE: *Lucid Dreaming and Astral Projection*
CYCLE OF POWER: *Year-round*

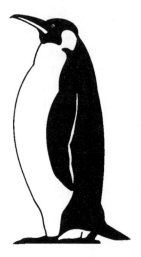

The penguin is a bird that doesn't fly. Its wings, though, do serve a purpose when it is in the water. The penguin is an excellent swimmer, and its movement in the water is as fluid and smooth as the flight of other birds. The wings serve as fins, helping the penguin to propel itself and steer in the water.

The penguin can literally jump out of the water, landing on its feet. It can leap five to six feet. This act, and its association with water, is very symbolic. The water is the astral plane of life, the dream dimension. The ability to maneuver so freely reflects an awakening of dream consciousness. For anyone who has a penguin show up as a totem, you can expect to experience lucid dreams. When you become aware in the course of the dream that you are dreaming, you can change the dream. As you change the dream state, you also change those same energies that are playing upon you in your waking life as well.

The leap from the water to land on its feet reflects the ability to leave the body. The penguin teaches how to consciously go out of the body. Out of body experiences (OBE's) are still one of the most fascinating areas of mysticism. This captures the imagination. The penguin is the expert at slipping in and out of the body—in full consciousness.

The behaviors and activities of penguins can reflect other energies operating in your life as well. The males of the emperor penguin family participate in the care and protection of the eggs. Emperor penguins do not build nests. When the egg is laid, the father puts it on its feet to prevent the egg from freezing to the ice. The father does not leave it alone for two months, until it hatches. The feathers of the father penguin cover it. He barely moves and doesn't eat until it hatches. At that point the mother penguin takes over the rearing.

This is also very symbolic. Remember that water is associated with the feminine, birth-giving energies. The emperor penguin reflects a greater assertion and expression of that within your life. For those who have a male emperor penguin as a totem, there will very likely be a two-month period in which you nurture, protect and help hatch your creative energies. The fact that the male has such a strong position in a traditionally feminine role, reflects greater awakening in dreams, altered states and creation.

PHEASANT

KEYNOTE: *Family Fertility and Sexuality*

CYCLE OF POWER: *Year-round*

Anyone with a pheasant as a totem would do well to also study the grouse and the chicken. Though of the same family, there are differences. The pheasant needs grasslands and grain fields, hedges and brush to survive in the wild. These environments should be studied by those with this totem.

Originally pheasants came from Greece, near the area of the Phasis River, from which we get the name pheasant. There they ran wild in the kingdom of Colchis. Today, some pheasants are wild as in the grouse or the quail which are distantly related. Others—most to be exact—are domesticated. Because of this, the pheasant is most often linked to the energies of family fertility and sexuality.

Most pheasants have splendid tail plumes. Tail plumes have long been associated with sexuality and the greater expression of it. The colors and kinds of feathers can provide even greater insight, as the feathering and types of pheasants varies greatly. A ringnecked pheasant, for example, multiplies in domestication successfully. The ringed markings on its neck reflect that fertility and growth within its family—a spiraling outward. Another example could be the badger feathers found on pheasants. These feathers have the appearance of striped, tapered markings similar to the badger. Anyone with a pheasant totem that has badger feathers would do well to study the characteristics of the badger itself.

The colors reflect much, and most pheasants have a variety of colors and feathers which should be examined. They all can reflect different aspects of the energies the pheasant symbolize for you. Pheasants are good teachers in how to set romantic moods through the warmth of colors.

PIGEON

KEYNOTE: *Return to the Love and Security of Home*

CYCLE OF POWER: *Year-round*

The pigeon is an unusual bird. Although most people think of it as a pest in the city environment, it has very unique characteristics. It is also tied to very gentle and loving archetypal energies.

Today the word "dove" and "pigeon" are used interchangeably. Although there is a difference, the two species are related. It would be wise for anyone with a pigeon as a totem to study the characteristics of the dove as well.

The pigeon has a long history associated with the home and with fertility. The real name of Christopher Columbus was "Colombo" which is the Italian word for "pigeon." Columbus helped discover a new home. The pigeon also has an extraordinary homing sense. It knows how to find its way back home, no matter how far it has gone.

It is because of this that they often are symbols for a time or a need to return to the security of home. Pigeons can teach us how to find our way back when we are lost. They help us to remember and find the love of home and homelife that we have either given up or lost. They are the only bird that can drink by sucking up water into their beaks. This reflects that ability to draw on the energies of home, no matter how distant.

They are reminders to us to remember that which has positively affected us from our early home life. Have we forgotten who we are? Are we falling into old patterns we vowed to remember and change? Have we forgotten our basic foundations, the heritage we have had passed on to us through home and family? This includes the morals, the behaviors, the attitudes, etc. Draw upon them and use them.

Because they breed rapidly and publicly, pigeons came to be sacred symbols for fertility gods and goddesses. They reflect the fertility of home and family that can occur when they are around. Pigeons will huddle together during a storm. If there are storms in your life, huddle with your family—biological or otherwise. There will be safety and security in that activity. Remember that pigeons remind us of the possibilities, real and ideal, associated with home and family.

QUAIL

KEYNOTE: *Group Nourishment and Protection*

CYCLE OF POWER: *Spring and Autumn*

The quail is a member of the chicken-shaped bird family known as the galliformes. This also includes, chickens, pheasants, grouse and such. In fact, quails have much the same habits as chickens. These should be examined as well, if a quail has flown into your life.

Because they are considered good eating, they have come to be associated with nourishment in many areas. Their frenzied mating antics though have also earned them a reputation for sexuality and fertility. In ancient Greece, they were considered a symbol of the return of spring.

The bob-white is a member of the quail family which speaks its name. This distinctive call has been associated with the mysticism of names. It is a bird which can help you to learn your soul name, the name that stays with you lifetime after lifetime. It has knowledge of the power of names and the naming process. Hearing the sound of the quail during the first week before or after the birth of a child can reflect you have chosen the most beneficial name for that child.

Quails live in groups called bevies. In cold weather, they will often nestle together to stay warm. They will often sit in a tight circle on the ground, tails together in the center, their heads facing the outer rim of the ring. They appear like the spokes in a wheel. This posture enables them to fly in all directions to confuse the predator when they are threatened.

The quail has a wonderful ability to easily spot danger. It takes off with a loud explosion. This startles the predator, distracting it and enabling them to escape. Quail can teach you to be mindful of dangers and how to explode to safety when threatened. It teaches how not to hesitate during times of crises.

RAVEN

KEYNOTE: *Magic, Shapeshifting, and Creation*

CYCLE OF POWER: *Winter Solstice*

The raven is one of those birds that has a tremendous amount of lore and mythology surrounding it, and it is often contradictory. It is a bird of birth and death, and it is a bird of mysticism and magic.

In the near East, the raven was considered unclean—because it is a scavenger. It is one of the foods listed as forbidden in the Bible. The raven is one of the birds that Noah sent out after the floods, but it did not return to the ark. On the other hand, also in Biblical lore is the tale of how a raven fed the prophet Elijah when hiding from King Ahab.

In Scandinavian lore, the raven played a significant role. The Norse god Odin had a pair of ravens who were his messengers. Their names were Hugin (thought) and Munin (memory). Odin was known to shapeshift as a raven himself. This reflects the idea of raven being a messenger of the great spiritual realm.

The raven has a long history of being an omen. During the Middle Ages the croak of the raven was believed to foretell a death or the outcome of a battle. It was even taught to the common folk in Christian communities that wicked priests became ravens when they died. Even today, some old timers tell how you can expect hot weather when a raven is seen facing a clouded sun.

The raven is a member of the corvids family, to which belong crows and magpies and other such birds. In truth, the only really significant difference between the crow and the raven is in size, the raven being much larger. It would be beneficial to study the information on the crow for anyone who has a raven as a totem. Much of the same information that applies to one, also applies to the other. It is simply a matter of degree. Rather than repeat that information here, I would like to give you some information not generally associated with the crow itself.

The raven has a wealth of myth and lore surrounding it. In many ways it is comparable to the coyote tales of the plains Indians, the Bushmen tales of the mantis and other societies in which an animal plays both a significant and yet confusing role. The coyote was both trickster and wise being—fool and wise one. This was true of the mantis in the tales of the Kalahari Bushmen.

In the Pacific Northwest, the raven has this same aura about him. In the Pacific Northwest, raven brought forth life and order. Raven stole the sunlight from one who would keep the world in darkness. Nothing could exist without raven. Raven is honored in art and on totem poles, reflecting the tales and mysticism that have developed around it.

With raven, human and animal spirits intermingle and become as one. This is reflected in its deep, rich shiny black. In blackness, everything mingles until drawn forth, out into the light. Because of this, raven can help you shapeshift your life or your being. Raven has the knowledge of how to become other animals and how to speak their languages.

Ravens are great at vocalizations, and they can be taught to speak. They incorporate and mimic the calls of other species. In the Northwest are tales of the Kwakiutl Indians who offered the afterbirth of male newborns to Raven so that when they grew up, they would understand their cries. Raven can teach you to understand the language of animals.

Ravens are playful, and they are excellent tool users. They will use stones and anything else that is available to help them crack nuts and such. They are birds not intimidated by others, and they are very fast and wary. Because of this, they are not easy prey for other animals or birds. This implies the ability to teach you how to stir the magic of life without fear. They are also known for their amorous behavior, reflecting the strong creative life force to which they have access.

This creative life force can be used to work the magic of spiritual laws upon the physical plane. It can be used to go into the void and stir the energies to manifest that which you most need. All this and more is what raven teaches. If raven has come into your life, expect magic. Somewhere in your life, magic is at play. Raven activates the energy of magic, linking it with your will and intention.

Raven speaks of the opportunity to become the magician and/or enchantress of your life. Each of us has a magician within, and it is Raven which can show us how to bring that part of us out of the dark into the light. Raven speaks of messages from the spirit realm that can shapeshift your life dramatically. Raven teaches how to take that which is unformed and give it the form you desire.

The winter solstice and winter season is the time of greatest power for those with the raven as a totem. The solstice is the shortest day of the year. The sun shines the least on this day, thus it is the darkest. From that day forth, the light shines a little more each day. This is symbolic of the influence of raven. It teaches how to go into the dark and bring forth the light. With each trip in, we develop the ability to bring more light out. This is creation.

ROAD RUNNER

KEYNOTE: *Mental Speed and Agility*

CYCLE OF POWER: *Spring and Summer*

The road runner is a streaked bird, approximately two feet long. It has a crest upon its head, and as with any bird with such, it reflects an activation of the mental faculties. It lives in cactus and mesquite areas, and these should be studied by anyone who has this bird as its totem.

The road runner eats grasshoppers in large quantities. Again for those with this totem, the qualities and characteristics of this prey should be studied. It will provide further insight into the role the road runner will play in your life. (Refer to part four of this text.)

The road runner is actually a ground-dwelling cuckoo. It has adapted to life on the ground. It has almost lost the power of flight, but on rare occasions they do fly. Its greatest ability is that of running. It can run as fast as 18 miles per hour.

The road runner teaches mental agility and speed. Those with this totem will learn to think quickly and on their feet. The road runner will help you learn to shift your thought processes with speed and agility. Mentally, you will find it necessary and easier to stop, shift, and then run in another direction if necessary.

The tail of the road runner works like an air brake. It facilitates stops and shifts in the mental process. It also implies an activation of the kundalini in a manner that will enable you to manifest your thoughts. Instead of planning and never completing, there will occur increased opportunity to plan and set those plans in motion.

Individuals with the road runner as a totem are always thinking. It is sometimes hard to follow their train of thought, but if they can be slowed down, they can show you connections and stimulate ideas you had not thought possible. Their minds are always at work.

ROBIN

KEYNOTE: *Spread of New Growth*
CYCLE OF POWER: *Spring*

Most commonly known as robin redbreast, this wonderful bird is a traditional herald of spring. Although robins often migrate, they do not always need to do so. Migration occurs due to lack of food and not to avoid colder weather as many believe. If the food supplies are beneficial, the robin will make its home year-round.

In spring, its song is often recognizable to all. In fact, few birds outdo the robin in overall distribution throughout North America. When a robin comes into your life, you can expect new growth to occur in a variety of areas of your life—not in just a single area.

There exists much myth and lore around the robin. The most common legend is that it obtained its red breast when it pulled a thorn from the bloodied crown on Christ's head while on the cross. In the more superstitious tradition, the stealing of a robin's egg was a means to court misfortune. Some believe that you should make a wish when you see the first robin of spring, before it flies off, or you will have no luck for the next year.

In spite of this lore, a study of the robin can reveal much of its true worth as a totem. Robins react to red. In males, it signals other males "to get out of my territory." The red is, of course, connected to the kundalini. In the robin, it is more of a rust, as if it has been diluted with other colors. This, along with the fact that it covers the entire breast area, reflects its activation in a manner that will stimulate new growth in all areas of your life.

The song of the robin is a cheery, rolling trill. Part of its purpose is to help the robin establish its territory. Two males in the same area will puff up and sing with all their force. Fights between robins over territory are usually in song. Physical confrontations are more symbolic without injury.

This is very significant for anyone with this bird as its totem. It reflects a need to sing your own song forth if you wish new growth. Any confrontations or hindrances are more show than actual threats, so go forward.

The robin lays a distinctive powder-blue egg. This is a color that is often used to activate the throat center in humans. This is a center associated with will force and creativity. The robin egg reflects the innate ability of those with this totem to assert the will force to create new growth in his/her life. When the robin comes to you it is to help you in this process. It may reflect you have been doing so inappropriately or ineffectually. Either way, the robin will show you how to do it successfully.

Both parents share in the feeding of the young—on the average of once every twelve minutes.[19] This is necessary, as the young are born entirely without feathers. Still, the robin has energy to raise more than one brood a year. Again this reflects the activation of the creative life force, reflected within the red coloring. It is the heart of the robin that gives it this ability.

SPARROW

KEYNOTE: *Awakening and Triumph of Common Nobility*
CYCLE OF POWER: *Year-round*

The sparrow has not always been considered the pest it is today. It is a perky, assertive bird that can hold its own against many forms of predation. The sparrow lives in all habitats. In the United States there were no natural checks upon it, and thus it multiplied at a fantastic rate.

The sparrow has its share of lore, as with many birds. One story tells of how it was the one bird present throughout the crucifixion of Christ, making it a symbol of triumph after longsuffering. It was a symbol of household divinities in Britain; and during the Middle Ages, it was a symbol for the peasants and lower classes throughout Europe. Peasants, at this time, were often helpless under the power of overlords. Because of this, they loved to hear tales of how the insignificant sparrow triumphed over such powerful enemies as wolves, bears, and eagles—the traditional symbols of nobility and those who mistreated the peasants.

Its ability to multiply and assert itself in spite of predation reflects the idea that nobility of the common person is inherently strong. For those who have a sparrow as a totem, look about you. Are you allowing others to take your dignity? Have you forgotten your own self-worth? Have you begun to think that you would always be under the heel of some tyrant—human or social? The sparrow will show you how to survive. It will awaken within you a new sense of dignity and self-worth, helping you to triumph in spite of outer circumstances.

The song sparrow is very symbolic of this. It has three spots in the form of an inverted triangle on its throat and breast. There is a dark spot on each side of its throat and a heavy spot in the middle of the breast. This reflects a drawing down of energy to awaken the heart and the throat centers. It is the assertion of will to bring out the inherent dignity so it can sing forth in your life. This is what the sparrow can teach.

---

19 Clement, Roland. *The Living World of Audubon* (New York: Grosset & Dunlap, Publishers, 1974), p. 224.

STARLING

KEYNOTE: Group Behavior and Etiquette
CYCLE OF POWER: Spring

The starling is a very sociable bird. When not nesting they gather together to form immense flocks. They almost always travel together, and they feed in flocks. Because of this, starlings reveal lessons associated with group behavior and etiquette. They can teach you how to be more effective within groups, as well as show you how your behavior is inappropriate for group situations. Anything dealing with community or group behavior falls under the teachings of the starling—good or bad. An example of inappropriate group behavior is reflected in the mobbing that starlings often do to other birds. Robins, bluebirds, wrens, and even the kestrel have occasionally been mobbed and beaten up by starlings. Only the screech owl is too tough for such starling behaviors.

If starlings have shown up in your life, ask yourself some important questions. Are you feeling as if life is ganging up on you? Are you applying undo pressure on others? How has your etiquette been lately in group situations? It may even be a warning to watch out for possible misbehavior. If you have been feeling mobbed, you may want to study and meditate upon the screech owl to help you deter this in your life.

In spring the bill of the starling is yellow. This reflects a stronger energy in regard to vocal expression. You may want to watch what you say, as people will have a tendency to take it incorrectly or blow it up out of proportion. It is usually an indication that you may want to watch your sensitivity to other people's words as well.

The starling has the ability to imitate dozens of birds. This reflects the lessons of community. For large numbers to live at peace in a community, there must be an ability to communicate in various languages. This is part of what the starling reflects. It is a symbol of being able to communicate more clearly (the yellow bill) with others in the flock.

STORK

KEYNOTE: *Birth and Unspoken Communication*
CYCLE OF POWER: *Year-round*

The stork is one of the most ancient and powerful symbols of new birth. It was a symbol in China with significances similar to that of the crane. It was also a bird believed to be sacred to the Roman goddess Juno—the goddess of home, children, and family fidelity. The stork has also been associated with the early lore around Christianity. One such story that I heard as a child tells how the stork circled around the cross, offering sympathy and strength to Jesus.

The stork has even been considered a close relative of humanity. In some fairy tales and legends, the stork is a bird that is capable of assuming human form at times. It has been said that when wounded it will weep human tears.

The stork is a wader; it has long legs that enable it to wade in shore areas and shallow waters. Such areas were often considered entrance ways to the Faerie Realm. It also reflects a connection to emotions and the creation symbology of water. Storks can help us to understand our emotions and how to enjoy the process of giving birth.

The stork is known for its dedication to its young. They are caring and very protective parents. This helps explain the connection between the stork and the Roman goddess Juno. Storks usually return to the same nests year after year, raising young from the same home nest.

This in itself can provide some insight into the stork's role within your own life. Do you need to get back home—back to the basics? Are you showing enough care for the child within you? Have you lost touch with your family roots? Are you taking the time to nurture and care for those projects and activities you give birth to within your life?

It has always been considered good luck to see a stork or have one as a totem. They are symbols of a new birth in your life. They reflect that on some level you are going to find life renewed and opportunities to awaken a new sense of joy and promise. In traditional folklore, a stork flying over the house reflected that birth was on its way.

The stork has no real voice for communication. They do have intricate postures, gestures, and dances that they perform for various purposes. They will rattle their bills, strut, and flap every posture having significance. This links the stork to the ancient mysteries of sacred dance.

Dance is a means by which we can awaken primal forces and energies. It is a means of linking other dimensions with the physical. The stork holds the ancient knowledge of sacred dance, especially fertility dances. Stork as a totem can teach you how to awaken your own fertility in any area of your life through movement and activity—rather than through words. It can show you how to use rattles and drums to empower and assist the awakening of your own fertility and creativity.

The stork can show you where you need to focus your movements for greatest success, and it can show you where your rhythms are off and hindering your development. It can show you how to invoke greater energy through proper dance. The stork will teach you how energies are created by dance, but rather invoked and challenged through it. It will show you how to transcend present conditions through sacred dance and create an opportunity for new birth.

SWALLOW

KEYNOTE: *Protection and Warmth for the Home and Proper Perspective*
CYCLE OF POWER: *Summer*

The swallow is often considered a favored bird that heralds the arrival of summer. Swallows have a tendency to follow warm weather, and thus they were considered one of the surest signs of summer. On the other hand, I have heard it said that one swallow does not make a summer.

The swallow has its own legends and tales unique to it. One Indian legend tells how the swallow stole fire from the sun and brought it to the earth, carrying it on its tail feathers. It is because of this action that its tail feathers are now forked and spinelike. Because of this and because the swallow comes with warm weather, it is associated with the sun and fire.

The southeastern Indians hung hollow gourds for purple martins, a member of the swallow family. An examination of martins will provide some further insight into the specific symbolism of this species.

In the Middle Ages, a variety of beliefs were attributed to the swallow. Many believed that swallows knew of a magical stone or a magical herb (Celandine) that could restore eyesight. A study of celandine (lesser) may provide some further insight. In a Scandinavian legend, the swallow hovered over the cross and cried "cheer up" to Jesus.

A swallow nesting on a house would reflect protection and preservation from disaster, especially fire and storm. A swallow flying high was an indication the weather would be good. Flying closer to the ground indicated rain. A study of the swallow's true characteristics and behaviors will help define its role and abilities as a totem.

The swallow is a small, insect-eating bird. Its bill is small, but the mouth opens amazingly wide. This hints at communications being more than what they appear. Are people saying things that actually have other meanings? Are we saying more than we realize? Do we need to listen more closely to what is being said and not be put off by who is saying it or how it comes out? It may even indicate that there is hidden wisdom in your own words or in the words of others.

The swallow feeds on many harmful insects. Swallows that nest near your home will help control pesky insects, reflecting a subtle protection of the home and the home environment. If a swallow shows up in your life, what does that say about the pesky insects within your life? Do you need to be more controlling of things in your life? Are there a lot of little irritations that are accumulating? Are you becoming too much of a "pesky insect" to others? Are you becoming too engrossed in the petty mundane activities of life and not moving on? Are others doing so? The swallow brings an energy that can help us with any aspect of this.

The swallow is a graceful flyer, and it actually spends little time on the ground. This is important for those with this totem to remember. Do not allow yourself to become too deeply enmeshed in the mundane. The swallow will often show up when you are allowing yourself to rehash old issues and problems and not move on. Its an indication you need some perspective.

The swallow has legs and feet that are small and weak. This reinforces the idea mentioned in the above paragraph. If a swallow has shown up, it may be telling you that you are weakest when trying to handle things from strictly a mundane perspective. Rise above it. Move beyond, so that you can gain a better perspective. You are weakest in solving problems when you do not distance yourself from them. A distance will help you to see clearly how to strengthen and protect yourself and others.

Objectivity is the key. By keeping your objectivity you will be able to easily protect the home and add greater warmth to your life and to the lives of those you touch. The swallow can help you to clean your environment of pests and create an energy of loving warmth in the home.

SWANS

KEYNOTE: *Awakening the True Beauty and Power of the Self*

CYCLE OF POWER: *Winter*

The swan is one of the most powerful and ancient of totems. This is reflected even in its name. It is one of the oldest names in the English language, and it has come down un-changed since Anglo-Saxon times.

The swan is a stately aquatic bird with a long graceful neck and beautiful white plumage. It is the largest of all waterfowl. It feeds on soft water plants, and its bill is so sensitive that it serves as a feeler underwater. For those with this totem, the emotions will become more sensitive, and you will find yourself becoming more sensitive to the emotions of others as well.

The swan is usually pure white (except for the bills and feet). This makes it a solar symbol. There is a black swan (Australian) and it is more of a nocturnal symbol. It is also considered a symbol of something rare and/or nonexistent.

The neck of the swan is long and graceful. It is one of the swan's most distinguishing features. The neck is a bridge area between the head (higher realms) and the body (lower worlds). In the swan totem, as you begin to realize your own true beauty, you unfold the ability to bridge to new realms and new powers. This ability to awaken to the inner beauty and bridge it to the outer world is part of what swan medicine can teach. It can show how to see the inner beauty within yourself or in others, regardless of outer appearances. When we are capable of this, we become a magnet to others. This is reflected in the familiar story by Hans Christian Anderssen, "The Ugly Duckling."

The swan is a cold-loving bird. They do not like the heat, and can stand the cold very well, as long as there is food. Those with this totem will find it easier to stand colder climates than warmer. Because of this, the swan also has ties to the direction of North, and its symbolism should be examined as well.

The kind of swan and its characteristics will have significance unique to themselves and to you. The largest of all swans is the trumpeter. It is named for its loud, far-carrying call. The whistling swan is our most common. The sound it makes is actually more of a whoop than a whistle. The mute swan, best known in America, is named for the belief that it loses its voice as it reaches maturity. It is not truly voiceless, but it does epitomize the idea of strength through silence.

Swans are powerful birds. They can break a man's arms with the beat of their wings, and they have strong bites as well. They are also devoted parents and they mate for life, and some live as long as 80 years. They reflect the power and longevity that is possible as we awaken to the beauty and power within ourselves.

The swan is the totem of the child, the poet, the mystic, and the dreamer. Swans fill mythology and folklore, usually as traditional symbols of beauty and grace. Swans were sacred to Aphrodite, the goddess of love. They were depicted pulling the chariot of Apollo. Zeus took the shape of a swan to make love to Ledo, a mortal—reflecting the ability of a swan to link different worlds and dimensions.

The swan fills folklore and fairy tales. Many speak of young maidens who turn into swans by putting on the magic garment of a swan's skin. If the skin were found, the beautiful maiden had to remain human and marry whoever found the skin, or do their bidding. The swan thus has come to be a link to the Faerie realm of life. Many of these tales involving swans ended tragically, hinting at the primal life-changing power of beauty when released freely. It hints of the control necessary to effectively work with such energy.

From Greece comes the mystery of the swan song. This belief taught that the swan sang its most beautiful song just before it died. The swan song has come to be synonymous with poetic fancy. The swan can teach the mysteries of song and poetry, for these touch the child and the beauty within.

SWIFT

KEYNOTE: *Speed and Agility in the Great Quest—*
The Magic Elixir of Saliva

CYCLE OF POWER: *Evening*

The swift is a small bird with wings that are swept back and stiff. Its flying is quick, and as its name implies, very swift. Its tail is short and barely shows, reflecting a need not to drag one's feet in any endeavor. If swifts have flown into your life, you should be asking yourself some questions. Are you not acting on opportunities when they present themselves? Are you or others around you hesitating too much? Are you trying to do things too quickly and losing control in the process?

The swift is a bird that can teach us how to respond to people and situations in life with speed and agility. It teaches us how to take advantage of any opportunity that arrives. The swift is most active in the evening, but it can be found feeding at almost any time of the day. This reflects its ability to assess and respond to opportunities with speed. The swift teaches us that hesitation can truly create loss of opportunity.

The swift makes a cup-shaped nest, glued with its own saliva. There is a tremendous mysticism around saliva and its uses for healing, and its connection to the primal fluids of life within you. The use of it as a gluing substance reflects the ability to draw on life energies and fluids for various purposes.

In tantrism and taoism there is a tremendous mysticism centered around saliva. The saliva of a sexually aroused woman is credited with great power, including healing and the charging of magical talismans. Saliva can be used as a "witness" for absent healing. A witness is anything which will psychically represent the person. It is a link to the person and their energy.

Saliva was considered a nectar in some eastern practices, nectar that could serve many functions. Physiologically, it cools the body and nurtures the system. The saliva of a woman is considered especially powerful—enough to heal and prolong life when taken while in an aroused state.

Kissing is often explored in tantric and Hindu love practices. Different kisses serve different functions. Anyone with the swift as a totem would do well to explore these as they involve the passing of saliva for specific purposes.

Kissing as a form of psychic protection is very ancient as well. The placing of a kiss (and the saliva) confers psychic energy and activates psychic centers. The saliva seals and protects areas of the body most susceptible to disharmony, and it helps to promote a wider distribution of love energy during sexual activity. This is reflected in the energies of the swift, as it seals its nest with saliva.

The cup-shaped nest has significance for anyone with a swift totem. The cup is a symbol for the Holy Grail, the quest of which leads us to find our spiritual essence and how best to manifest it in this lifetime.

All cups are associated with the feminine energies. A cup holds and contains elixirs (saliva). It can be used to pour them out like the horn of plenty. The nest is a reminder to act upon your feminine energies swiftly and powerfully. Learn to draw forth your waters and bring to life the magic within. In this the swift will assist you.

SWISHER

KEYNOTE: *Awakening to the Faerie Realm—*
Accomplishment For the Sake of Accomplishment

CYCLE OF POWER: *Dusk—Summer*

This bird is often referred to as a night-hawk, but it is no hawk at all. It is a cousin to the whip-poor-will.[20] It is a bird with a variegated plumage of white, black, and buff, reflecting that intersection of night and day that we call dusk.

Dusk is the time at which the swisher is most active. It is a time long associated with fairies, elves, and the awakening of spirits. The swisher is a bird of the "Tween Time," and it is often seen as a transport or vehicle for those of the Faerie Realm.

The swisher is part of a group of birds that used to be called goatsuckers

The Swisher

The swisher is a member of a family of birds that used to be called goatsuckers. They have a short bill and a wide mouth, and they feed on insects captured in the air.

(Photo courtesy of Brukner Nature Center, Troy, Ohio.)

because of an age old belief that they sucked the milk of goats. This probably originated with the folk ideas of mischievous elves and fairies who helped themselves to milk from goats and cows on farms near their homes.

Many misbehaviors and misfortunes were attributed to elves and fairies when there was no rational explanation. The souring of milk, the disappearance of objects, and even the stealing of milk was attributed to them. Since swishers and other "goatsuckers" of European origin were active at dusk and night (the time of elf and fairy activity), they were considered the vehicles for those of the Faerie Realm.

The swisher has a short bill and a wide mouth. It hunts at dusk and it feeds on insects that are captured and eaten in flight. They are most conspicuous and active at dusk and at night. This reflects much about those who have a swisher as a totem. They will often find themselves so active that they seem to live on the

---

20 The whip-poor-will is the only bird known to hibernate. In the fall it creeps into crevices and holes in canyons, and literally turns itself off. It is also a close relative to the owl. It was often believed that if a whip-poor-will landed upon your roof, someone would die. Many Europeans believed that the whip-poor-will would try and snatch the soul as it left the body.

run. It will be important for those who have a swisher come into their lives to pay attention to the 'Tween Times—dawn, dusk, midnight, noon, all times that are neither one nor the other. These will be times of greatest inspiration and power. You will find yourself more effective in all of your activities.

Unlike other nightjars[21] or goatsuckers, the swisher is more often seen than heard. Many people see them at night, but often don't realize what they are seeing. Many see this again as a direct correspondence to fairies and elves, with them being around and not being noticed.

If a swisher has come into your life you may wish to examine aspects of your life activities. Are you feeling neglected? Are you neglecting or not honoring important others in your life? Are you trying to get attention when you should be focusing on just accomplishing your tasks? Are you or others around you forcing attention? Are you feeling caught in the middle and as if you are not accomplishing things? The swisher will teach you to do your life tasks,and to do them well just for the sake of doing them, rather than for extraneous attention. It will teach you that there is no need to blow your own horn. When you do your job well, others will do that for you.

The swisher builds no nest of its own. It lays its two eggs upon the bare ground. This in itself is highly significant. It needs no glamour. It sees the earth as its nest, and it brings forth creative life. The two eggs also have symbolic significance for those who wish to explore the numerological correspondence.

TURKEY

> **KEYNOTE:** *Shared Blessings and Harvest*
> **CYCLE OF POWER:** *Autumn*

The turkey is sometimes called the earth eagle. It has a long history of association with spirituality and the honoring of the Earth Mother. It is a symbol of all the blessings that the Earth contains, along with the ability to use them to their greatest advantage. The turkey can live to be twelve years old. Twelve is a significant number in that the earth revolves around the sun in twelve months, reflecting a tie between the turkey and the honoring life cycle of the Earth. Those who have a turkey as a totem can usually expect a year of harvest.

---

21 The swisher is part of a family of birds called nightjars. They were called this because their voices would "jar" the night. Birds with weird calls in the night were often thought to have supernatural powers or to be links to supernatural realms.

Turkeys are native birds to this continent, and they were even raised by the Aztecs and Mayans. Almost every part of the turkey had usefulness. They were used as food. Their feathers were used for decorations, and even their bones were used to make whistles.

Turkeys have an intricate mythology among Native Americans. Turkey helped create the world, showing humans how to raise corn and fighting off evil spirits like the owl. Some stories teach how Indian sorcerers would turn themselves into turkeys and prowl around other villages.

The turkey is part of the chicken family, and the characteristics of it should be studied as well by anyone with a turkey as a totem. Some believe that the name for this bird came from the Hebrew name for peacock, "tukki."

The turkey is one of the most adaptable birds. Although once threatened, it is now surviving strongly again in the wild. It greatest threat is the loss of habitat. Although they can adapt to most environments, their preference is for forested lands.

The diet of the turkey is varied, but they can eat up to a pound of acorns a day. Nuts and acorns have often been associated with hidden wisdom and new seeds of growth. Animals and birds which feed on them often reflected that new nourishment, in the form of wisdom and/or growth, is likely to occur. The turkey has also been known to steal the food cache of squirrels.

The male turkey has a bright red, fleshy wattle, and a peculiar inflatable growth on the forehead. When limp it dangles along its beak like a loose antennae. It can swell, such as at those times when one male challenges another. This growth is very symbolic. It is linked to the ancient idea of the third eye, the inner vision often associated with the pituitary gland in more traditional metaphysics. The brow center or third eye is the center for higher vision, and is often considered the seat of the feminine energies within each of us. This reflects its tie to the Mother Earth and all of its feminine energies and possibilities.

The male will often keep several hens. The female must actually lie down in front of her chosen to get his attention. The hens will sometimes use a common nest for their eggs. This again hints at the concept of shared blessings, as does the way in which they protect themselves.

Many believe that the turkey cannot fly, but this is not so. The turkey is capable of quick take-offs and can fly up to 50 miles per hour for short distances. They also run well upon their stout legs. They also will perch in trees at night for safety, roosting together; and they will change their roosting nightly. They find a strength in numbers and thus reflect the energy of sharing.

VULTURE

KEYNOTE: *Purification—Death and Rebirth—New Vision*
CYCLE OF POWER: *Year-round—Summer and Winter*

In the earliest of times, the sun lived very close to the earth—so close in fact that life upon the earth was becoming unbearable. The animal world got together and decided to do something about it. They wanted to move the sun further

The Turkey Vulture
This unique bird derives its name from the Latin *vultur*, and although it does not kill its own prey, it is considered a raptor and a predator. It has a magnificent wingspan and an ability to soar effortlessly for great lengths of time. It is one of the most misunderstood birds, and yet it was one of the most powerful and mystical in many societies.

(Photo courtesy of Brukner Nature Center, Troy, Ohio.)

away. The fox was the first to volunteer, and he grabbed the sun in his mouth and began to run to the heavens. After a short while, the sun became too hot, burning the fox's mouth, and he stopped. To this day, the inside of the fox's mouth is black.

Then the opossum volunteered. He wrapped his tail around the sun and began running toward the heavens. Before long though, the sun became too hot, burning his tail, and he had to stop. To this day the opossum has no hair upon its tail.

It was then that vulture stepped forward. Vulture was the most beautiful and powerful of birds. Upon its head was a beautiful mantle of rich feathering that all other birds envied. Knowing that the earth would burn up unless someone moved the sun, the vulture placed its head against it and began to fly to the heavens. With powerful strokes of its wings, it pushed and pushed the sun further and further up into the heavens. Though it could feel its crown feathers burning, the vulture continued until the sun was set at a safe distance in the sky away from the earth. Unfortunately, vulture lost its magnificent head of feathers for eternity.

The vulture is probably the most misunderstood and misaligned bird. People see them as gross and associate them only with death, but myths and tales abound that reflect the exact opposite. Even a brief examination of the variety of myths about it and a cursory look at its behaviors will reveal a truly wonderful creature.

In the Greek tradition, the vulture was considered to be a descendent of the griffin, a mythical creature usually depicted with a combination of animal characteristics. It was a symbol of heaven and earth, spirit and matter, good and evil, guardian and avenger. It was considered the avenger of the nature spirits. To the ancient Assyrians, the angel of death would come in the form of a griffin. It embodied the union between the falcon and its solar aspects and the feline aspects of the night—a reflection of never-ending vigilance. The vulture is thus a link to the griffin as a guardian to the mysteries of life and death and the road of salvation. For more information on the griffin, you may wish to consult the author's earlier work, *Enchantment of the Faerie Realm*.

In Egypt the goddess of truth, Maat, is usually depicted carrying a vulture feather. In parts of Egypt the vulture was also a mother symbol, probably because it devours corpses, enabling other life to sustain itself. Often animals and birds represented a form of the divine power which would dispose of what could otherwise be dangerous to life and health. Life and death were both often mother symbols.

To the Pueblo Indians, it was a symbol of purification. Its medicine would restore harmony that had been broken. Its feathers were used in rituals for grounding after shapeshifting ceremonies, facilitating the return to the self. Turkey vulture assisted with such transitions. It was used to dispel evil, to break contact with the dead (as in channeling, shapeshifting or other forms of mediumship), to discharm objects and even to recover slain warriors.[22]

In folk beliefs, when turkey vulture comes back after the winter, there will be no more frost. Also the wearing of a feather of a black buzzard was thought to prevent rheumatism. They have also been associated wrongly with greed and heartlessness.

The vulture is a member of the raptor family, but unlike most raptors (hawks, owls, etc.), its weak feet and short talons make it unsuited for tearing and grasping. It relies on others to do the killing. Although their role as scavengers is often

---

22 Tyler, Hamilton A. *Pueblo Birds and Myths* (Flagstaff: Northland Publishing, 1991), pp. 225–229.

considered disgusting, it serves an extremely valuable and necessary function. It limits infections and bacteria from corpses that could otherwise spread to other animals who do not have the resistance. They serve to keep the environment clean and in balance. They prevent the spread of disease.

There are several varieties of vulture. Each has its own unique characteristics. All walk, stand and perch firmly and with dignity, a kind of unspoken confidence in themselves, regardless of their appearance.

The condor has the largest wingspan, and it is the world's largest flying bird. The wingspan of the Andean condor can reach 12 feet; the California condor can reach nine feet. The king vulture of Mexico—Argentina will fly alone or in pairs, usually high and far away from others.

Most people in this country are familiar with two types—the black vulture and the more common turkey vulture. Often called buzzards, they are simply vultures. The black vulture is named for its color. Its scientific name, *coragyps atratus*, means "vulture dressed in black." It usually is a solid black with a white spot at the end of each wing. The black vulture has a shorter tail and cannot soar as well as the turkey vulture. It spends more time on perches. It often nests in hollow logs.

The turkey vulture has a long tail and bi-colored wings. It is a creature of grace when in flight. Its scientific name, *cathartes aura*, means "golden purifier." They will congregate on communal roosts at night, and at dawn, in the early morning sun, they will outstretch their wings to dry the dew, giving the appearance of honoring the rising sun.

Although homely in appearance when just standing, in flight these raptors are magnificent specimens. They soar with a grace and an ease that is thrilling. For those with this totem, it speaks of a coming time when you will be noticed more for what you do than for how you appear.

The vultures have a wonderful ability to see and use the thermals rising from the earth, giving them lift. Their ability to use the thermals is often likened to auric vision, the ability to see the subtle energy emanations from the body. We have all experienced thermals in our lives. When we have driven down a road on a hot summer day and see the heat rising off the surface, this is a thermal. To the human ground observer, these currents are only visible for a few feet above the concrete. The vulture can see them as they rise into the sky. When on the ground, the vultures cannot see or feel the thermals, but in the air they are sensitive to every aspect of the currents. If turkey vulture has come into your life, you will probably soon start to see auras and colors around people and things. If not, the vulture can help teach you.

The vulture is a patient hunter. It can soar for hours without flapping its wings. They are tremendous symbols of flight without power. They ride the thermals and windborne updrafts. They use air currents to interfere with the pull of gravity and allow themselves to fly. In essence, they do not need to expend much energy to oppose gravity. This is seen in the fact that their wings rarely move, reflecting that the power for flight does not come from them. They simply use what is available.

One of the mystical secrets believed to be held by the vulture is the ability to levitate. Levitation is the law of spirituality. Gravity is the impulse toward the material and mundane (physical). The vulture denies the material. Its ability to float, rise and soar has been seen as a symbol of movement away from the mundane. It is a symbol of the disintegration of physical holds. It is a symbol of distributing one's energy so that gravity does not weigh and hold one down—be it the actual gravity of the earth or the gravity of mundane situations and experiences.

They can also fold their wings well above the horizontal level which is unique among raptors and most birds. It helps them in their soaring. When they do flap their huge wings, they provide a powerful thrust forward, and thus do not need to be used that frequently. This ability to use energy powerfully and efficiently is part of what vulture teaches.

Vultures are also noted for their keen eyesight. Some scientists believe they pass subtle messages visually from one bird to another, especially when a carcass is found. They can spot kills over many miles. Their eyes see eight times more sharply than human eyes.

One of its most powerful senses is the sense of smell. The turkey vulture has a highly developed sense of smell. They can find food simply by smelling it if necessary. The black vulture's sense of smell is not quite as developed. The sense of smell has long been associated with higher forms of discrimination in metaphysical traditions. Turkey vulture can assist you in developing your own sense of smell that you can use effectively in all areas of your life. It will help you to decide whether or not something doesn't quite smell right in your life. The sense of smell is also associated with aromatherapy, and for those with turkey vulture as a totem, this may be the most effective holistic health technique to develop or use on yourself.

The turkey vulture has a unique digestive system. When we examine the kinds of food it eats, it is no wonder. It has a resistance to botulism thousands of times higher than humans. The digestive tract contains chemicals that kill the virulent bacteria that is on the foods they eat.

It is not unusual for those with a vulture totem to have changes in their own digestive system occur. Foods that used to be enjoyed and have no side effects may become less compatible. On the other hand foods always thought of as incompatible may become compatible. Foods that you eat are going to have a more noticeable effect upon your energy system. Pay attention to how you feel physically, emotionally, mentally, and spiritually after eating various foods. You will soon discover which you may need to avoid and which you may need to increase.

When a turkey vulture comes in as a totem, there may also be changes in your eliminative processes. The turkey vulture is one of just a few animals that will eliminate over its own legs and feet. It will squirt excrement on itself. This is due partly to cleansing the feet and legs of bacteria that may have accumulated on them while the vulture was feeding on the carcass. The same antibacterial chemical in the digestive tract is found within the excrement, serving as a bactericide for the legs and feet.

This does not mean that those with a vulture totem are going to have problems with incontinence. Those with a vulture totem should make sure their own eliminative system is working properly and regularly. If your energy is down or you feel yourself coming down with a cold or such, check your bowel movements. They may need to be stimulated.

Another reason that the vulture does this is to cool off the legs and feet. This is something that is also healthy and beneficial for those with vulture totems, especially if they are having trouble handling the heat. Soak the feet in cool water, and you will find some wonderful and quick results.

The vulture actually keeps itself quite clean, and in the wild will bathe frequently. The featherless head enables the vulture to remain relatively clean as it dips its head into the entrails and carcasses. Had it feathers, bacteria would accumulate in them, thus the lack of feathers prevents infection. The sun's rays also serve as a disinfectant for the head. Each morning it will face the sun with wings outstretched to warm its feathers and to cleanse itself of bacteria that may still remain. In this fashion the wings actually serve as mini solar collectors.

The vulture has no real voice. It will force air out its bill and hiss. To some this reflects the lesson of acting rather than talking. To some it shows that vulture medicine has to do with performing rather than talking about performing.

Vultures usually lay their eggs on the bare ground. The young are extremely sensitive to interference. There is a long period of incubation in breeding and rearing a single chick, and thus the parent does not go far in search of food. The young do not leave the nest or fly until three months. For this reason there is the belief that it may take as much as three months before an individual begins to truly move past the death stage to rebirth, as is symbolized by the vulture.

In alchemy, the vulture was a symbol of sublimation, particularly because of its resemblance to the eagle. The vulture was considered a sign of confirmation of a new relationship between the volatile aspects of life and the fixed, the psychic energies and the cosmic forces. It was a promise that the suffering of the immediate was temporary and necessary for a higher purpose was at work, even if not understood at the time. It reflects that no matter how difficult the life conditions, rescue is as imminent in your life as was the rescue of Prometheus by Hercules.

WAXWING

> **KEYNOTE:** *Gentleness and Courtesy*
>
> **CYCLE OF POWER:** *Spring—Summer*

The waxwing is a beautiful and gentle bird of summer. It is a member of the cardinal family, and thus the cardinal should be studied as well. It is usually of a light chocolate color, with traces of pink or mauve and with a bright yellow band. It has a black chin and usually a black line running through the eyes, giving it the appearance of a mask. At the end of the wings is a patch of red that looks a bit like sealing wax.

A study of colors will provide some insight into the energies often associated with this bird. The mask-like appearance gives it an association with the art of mask making and ritual garb. Maskmaking is an ancient art, employed all over the world for ceremony, celebration, and magical practices. The waxwing has knowledge of how to use masks for fun and for healing, especially when combined with color healing.

Masks are tools for transformation, but most people fear change and transition. They believe it to be traumatic. The waxwing can show how change and transformation can occur as gently and easily as you desire. The waxwing shows how to use masks, head gear, and paint to create a doorway in the mind, a threshold that you can cross to new dimensions.

Like its relative the cardinal, the waxwing has a crest upon its head. This reflects an innate wisdom that it can awaken. It also has ties to ceremonial headgear and the use of it to shift consciousness.

The waxwing is actually a very gentle and polite bird. Waxwings are often known to pass food to each other. If a waxwing has come into your life, look at the gentleness you are experiencing or missing within your life. Are others extending to you the courtesy you deserve? Are you extending to them the courtesy they deserve? Do you need to start seeing yourself and others from a new perspective? Are you possibly not being gentle enough to yourself? The waxwing will show you how to awaken gentleness as a true virtue within your life.

WOODPECKER

KEYNOTE: *The Power of Rhythm and Discrimination*
CYCLE OF POWER: *Summer*

The woodpecker is one of those birds whose history is filled with myth and lore, much of it in connection with its most notable characteristics—the drumming. It is a relative of the flicker which was described earlier, and they share many of the same qualities and characteristics.

In the European folk tradition, the woodpecker was often considered a weather prophet, its drumming indicating forthcoming changes. It was even believed by some to be a thunderbird. In Babylonia, it was considered the ax of Ishtar and was associated with fertility. In the Greek tradition it occupied the throne of Zeus, considered sacred to this god of thunder. It was also considered the oracle of Mars, again because drumming was often used to accompany battles. The Romans also had a legend of the woodpecker. The powerful enchantress Circe fell in love with the woodland god Picus. When he rejected her love, she turned him into a woodpecker.

In the Native American tradition it is a bird connected to the heartbeat of the Earth itself. This drumming has many mystical connections, from new life rhythms to applications of shapeshifting. Many shamans learn to ride drumbeats into other dimensions.

There are, of course, different kinds of woodpeckers, each with their own unique qualities. Most are black and white, and some have red upon the head. The black and white reflects the need to see issues and aspects of life clearly. It reflects that things are fairly clear if we look closely.

The downy woodpecker is the smallest. It is also the most common and most friendly member of the woodpecker family. The pileated, found most often in forests, is the expert woodchopper. Often as big as a crow, it is the largest of the woodpeckers. It has the conspicuous red crest. The red-headed woodpecker is also very common. While most woodpeckers, particularly males, have some red on the head, the red-headed woodpecker has a red mantle of feathers that covers its head and neck.

The red found in the head area of any woodpecker reflects a stimulation of the mental activities and the head chakra centers. It reflects a stimulation and wakening of new mental faculties. This is even further symbolized by the pecking that is the trademark of this bird.

Woodpeckers peck holes in trees and wood to get at grubs and other insects. This digging in, especially with the head, reflects increasing analysis. Their bills are strong and sharply pointed, and their skulls are heavier, facilitating the hammering. Their sharp bill and its long barbed tongue can be likened to the art of discrimination.

If a woodpecker has drummed out a song for you, then you should ask yourself some specific questions. Are you looking at aspects of your life rationally? Are others around you not discriminating in their activities? Are you? Are you or others in your life just jumping into situations with little or no analysis?

Sometimes the woodpecker will show up just to stimulate new rhythms. Rhythm is a powerful means of affecting the physical energies. Sometimes it is easy to get so wrapped up in our daily mental and spiritual activities that we neglect the physical. This can be when the woodpecker shows up. It may also reflect a need to drum some new changes and rhythms into your life.

The woodpecker has strong hooked claws for firm holds upon a tree. Its tail feathers help to prop it upright. It also has a peculiar up and down flight. It will fly, coast down, fly and then coast down. It flies in a manner and rhythm unique to itself. All of this serves to emphasize the fact that it will become increasingly important for you to follow your own unique rhythms and flight. Do what works for you in the manner best for you. When woodpecker comes into your life, it indicates that the foundation is there. It is now safe to follow your own rhythms.

WREN

KEYNOTE: *Resourcefulness and Boldness*

CYCLE OF POWER: *Spring*

There are more than a dozen species of wren. It is a small, stocky bird that has often been cherished as much as the robin. It is usually brownish in color, and it will often cock its tail feathers up in the air. It seldom shows itself in the open.

Its feathers were considered fetishes against drowning, and it has usually been considered unlucky to kill one. In pagan traditions, wrens were considered sacred to the earth gods and goddesses. It has been thought a bird that stole fire from the sun and brought it to earth, giving it its short, cocked tail feathers. In medieval Europe it was considered the pet bird of the Virgin Mary, especially among the lower classes. This is probably due to the fact that most often the ruling classes were depicted in story and legend as eagles, hawks, bears—the greater birds and animals of prey.

The wren is a most resourceful and adaptable bird. It will build its nest in any convenient home. Usually their homes are built close to the ground or even upon the ground, especially in marshy areas. The male wrens do most of the building, and they will build several "dummy" nests as well as a true nest. Partly this is for protection, although some believe it is also to entice the female. Only after the dummy nests are built does the female settle in and have her brood. The male will sleep apart from the female and the young.

The wren is a bold and resourceful bird. One Native American tale speaks of a time when the wren tricked the boasting eagle into carrying it far into the heavens, until the eagle could go no higher. At that point the wren hopped off eagle's back and flew beyond the clouds, laughing at how much higher it was flying than the eagle ever would.

The wren has the vocal power of a bird much larger. It will sing from daylight to dark, as if overflowing with confidence. It is also a bit of a spitfire, and it will not hesitate to confront any threatening bird or animal.

If wrens have come into your life, it is time to ask yourself some important questions. Are you using the resources available to you? Are others? Are you not displaying enough confidence? Are you so wrapped up in daily worries that you are forgetting to sing? Are you not staying grounded? Are you not seeing the forest because of the trees? Are you not attacking your life with enough gusto? Wren holds the medicine for using what is available, and it can teach you the most effective means to build within your own environment.

PART THREE

UNDERSTANDING ANIMAL MEDICINE

In the beginning of all things, wisdom and knowledge were with the animals; for Tuawa, the One Above, did not speak directly to man. He sent Animals to tell man that he showed himself through the beasts, and that from them, and from the stars and the sun and the moon, man should learn . . . for all things speak of Tuawa.

—Chief Letakos-Lesa of the Pawnees Tribe
to Natalie Curtis, circa 1904[1]

---

1   Curtis, Natalie. *The Indians' Book: An Offering by the American Indians of Indian Lore, Musical and Narrative, to Form a Record of the Songs and Legends of Their Race* (New York, Harper Brothers, 1907), p. 96.

CHAPTER ELEVEN

HONORING ANIMAL TOTEMS

It is interesting to note that many societies, including the Native Americans, had no word to classify animals. They were simply considered a people, just as humans were people. To the Lakota they were brothers, sisters, fathers, and mothers. They were extended kin. The word "animal" was hardly used before the 1600s and then mostly by scholars. Animals were simply called "beasts" or "creatures" or some such designation.[1]

The word "animal" is derived from the Latin word "anima," meaning soul or breath of life. The wild in "wild animal" comes from the Anglo-Saxon "wilde," referring to living free within Nature and not under human control. Implied within this is the idea of the breath of the divine within the animal expression of Nature.

In old scriptures and writing, animals were often associated with divine forces, specifically with gods and goddesses. Every Eastern Indian god and goddess has an animal for a vehicle. The divine being is literally carried about on the animal. For example, the elephant-headed Ganesha is mounted upon a large rat, or Shiva rides the bull Nandi. The animal also is a messenger of the god or goddess, and the animal expresses the god's and goddess's nature and its relationship to Nature. The people recognized that the divine being was present within the animal, thus every bull was Shiva, as well as being sacred to Shiva.

The Hindu Temples were often constructed in concentric circles, and animals appeared in different forms on different levels of the circles. In the heart of the

---

1   Limburg, Peter. *What's in the Name of Wild Animals* (New York: Coward, McCann and Geoghegan, Inc., 1977).

temple (the sanctum sanctorum, the Holy of Holies), there is just one image of the divine who transcends all of those other physical forms.[2]

Several bestiaries of medieval times tried to attribute to animals certain specific cosmic qualities and phenomena thought to be constant. Two of these were *Physiologus* by Alexandria and the *De Animalibus* attributed to Albertus Magnus. Animals were used as symbolism of the lower aspects that humans must achieve victory over. Animals were often classified according to the four elements: aquatic and amphibian creatures = the water element, reptiles = the earth element, birds = the air element, and mammals (warm-blooded creatures) = the fire element.

Even with the old bestiaries and scriptures, the symbolism of animals often varied according to context—in spite of the constants the writers and teachers tried to assign them. The perception and meaning of the animal could be interpreted along natural, human, divine or even fantastic lines of thought. And usually it involved all.

This is what you must constantly keep in mind as you develop your own animal-speak. There is no simple interpretation. Each animal will speak to you individually, specifically and metaphorically. Begin with a solid knowledge base of the animal and then move into the more mystical and metaphorical associations. None is necessarily any more beneficial than the other, but the former will establish a foundation, upon which the latter will add the color to your relationship with the animal and the entire natural world. Keep in mind that each animal must be examined for its own characteristics and behaviors and related specifically to your own individual life. Any correspondence you can make is going to have some seeds of truth.

As you begin to honor and work with them, the task becomes easier and your interpretations and correspondences will become increasingly more exact. It will enable you to be at peace with the animals and help you to see the mingling of the divine and natural worlds. And your wonder at life will grow in proportion.

The animal totems you discover through the exercises in this book serve as an excellent bridge to the spirit realm. Animals will give you greater power and strength in working with those more elusive and ethereal realm while helping to keep you grounded.

As you discover your totems, you will find they come to you in dreams and in meditations frequently. You will encounter the animal in many ways, and these are confirmations to you. You will come across pictures, postcards and curios in which your animal is depicted. You may find yourself discovering television programs exploring its habitats and behaviors with greater frequency. Books, myths, and other depictions of it will cross your path. You do not have to indulge in all of these, but by acknowledging them and taking advantage of them, you honor the spirit and energy working in your life through that animal totem.

---

2   Snead, Stella. *Animals in Four Worlds* (Chicago: University of Chicago Press, 1989), p. 7.

There are five very specific things you can do to more firmly establish your relationship with your totem and with nature. They will help you to honor that relationship:

1. Learn as much about your spirit totem as possible. Read about it. Learn its basic qualities, habits, and behaviors. Research myths and tales associated with the animal. All of these will help you to define and understand how its energies are more likely to manifest within your own life.

   It is not unusual for people to discover animal totems that are frightening to them. There may be fears associated with them, or the animal may even be thought of as gross and unglamorous. When this happen, I recommend going to the children's section of any library and checking out a children's book on the animal. Most children's books try to present the animals in an interesting and intriguing way—especially those animals that children (and adults) are more likely to shrink from. A children's book on the animal will help you to become more comfortable with the animal, while usually presenting you with its most fascinating characteristics. Children's books are usually less threatening.

2. Find pictures and artwork of your animal totem. Make a collage of various depictions of it, all encircling a picture of yourself. Hang the pictures up where you can see them throughout the day. it serves as a constant reminder of the relationship you are establishing with your spirit animal.

3. Draw and sketch pictures of the animal. Don't worry about the quality of your artistic abilities. Don't compare your drawings to anyone else's. No one else has to even see your sketches. Remember that the relationship you establish is personal to you. You will find as you practice with the animal, your depictions will be surprisingly accurate.

   If you are a doodler while on the phone, doodle sketches of your animal. It helps you to build a relationship and no one ever critiques doodles. All artistic endeavors stimulate the right hemisphere of the brain which helps us in our intuitive perceptions of the entire spirit realm.

4. Buy figurines of your totem. They do not have to be large or expensive. Many bookmarks sold at bookstores have animal depictions on them. Buy these for yourself and for others.

   Small tokens and images (such as found on bookmarks) of your animal make wonderful gifts for friends and family. As you give the gifts, you are honoring the universality of the animal's spirit and its ability to help everyone. You do not have to tell everyone why you are doing so, nor do you have to explain its esoteric significance. Simply let them know it a favorite animal of yours, and that you thought it would make a nice gift.

5. Give anonymous donations to wildlife funds or specific organizations associated with your totem animal. Anonymity simply helps ensure that the honoring is for the sake of honoring rather than for recognition.

Volunteer time and energy at parks and nature centers. Most are always looking for reliable assistance. You may not work with animals directly, but your efforts help to promote the well-being of that natural environment. The tasks you do may not be glamorous, but every aspect has its importance.

At Brukner Nature Center in Troy, Ohio, I serve as a volunteer in several capacities. In one capacity, every Thursday morning I clean cages and feed the animals. The task can be time consuming and requires that you handle poop and other waste products which is not very glamorous—especially in the spring when the center is overflowing with babies and orphans who mess over everything. It also requires at times that you handle animals who can have a very nasty attitude. On the other hand it does allow contact with a variety of animals, and it frees the staff persons for more important duties in regard to rehabilitation, education and such. There is a trade off.

Remember that as you promote and protect any aspect of nature, you promote the relationship and life of your specific totem. Every aspect of nature is linked to every other aspect of nature in some way. We just do not always recognize the connection. As you work to promote and protect some aspect, the spirit behind it then works to promote and protect your life, for nature is not separate from us either.

Do not boast of what your totem is or does for you or others. Disbelief on the part of others, whether expressed or not, can hinder and restrict your connection to your animal. There is strength in silence. Speaking of your relationship can dissipate or weaken its energies before it gets a chance to work some real magic for you.

There is nothing wrong with simply letting others know you are fascinated by or like certain animals. If anyone asks, simply tell them you admire its energy and qualities. An animal totem is personal. Yes, individuals may have the same generic kind of animal, but the manner in which it works with you will be different from others. It is neither better nor worse, just different.

Learn to honor your relationships and allow them to unfold with respect. Learn the limitations, and allow your totem to learn yours. As you grow and unfold the relationship, do not be surprised as it changes. Be creative in the relationship and in your own way of honoring it. Give thanks to whatever divine source you worship for assisting your through this spirit animal.

CALLING YOUR SPIRIT ANIMALS

Once you learn your spirit animals, it is important to establish a positive working relationship with them. This will enable you to know exactly what they can and can not do for you. it will help you to call upon them and the archetypal energies operating through them for your particular purposes.

Begin by meditating upon the animal. Do simple visualizations, imagining it standing before you or drawing close to you. Let it speak to you telepathically. As it stands before you, tet it speak to you about itself. Let it tell you how it can help you in different areas of your life. Don't worry that it may all be in your mind. The more focus you give to it, the stronger the invitation and connection to its essence.

Practice visualizing it merging into you. Perform meditations where you see yourself as this animal. The exercises in the next chapter will help with this. If there are situations at work or at home where you know you need this animal's energy, take five minutes before entering into the situation to see your totem alive within you. Feel its energies strong and vital. Know they will help you in handling the situation with great success. See the situation turning out successful as a result.

As you begin to know your animal spirit and are able to recognize its energies around you and within you, you can begin to experiment with calling it to you. Music, chanting, and drumming can all be used to help call your spirit animals forward. Drumming and chanting are powerful tools that can assist in shifting consciousness and opening doors to the spirit realm. Although we do not have the time and space to cover all of the aspects of drumming and its applications to working with animals, it will be examined in greater detail in the next chapter.

Make up songs and chants to your totem. They do not have to be complicated. Two to three lines that are simple, melodic, and repetitive can serve as a wonderful tool. If there is a simple song or chant that you are already familiar with, alter its words so that it honors your totem. In your meditations, you can easily ask your totem to teach you the prayersongs that will call it forth more quickly.

One of the most powerful chants that I use for all of my spirit animals comes from adapting an old Renaissance performance piece. I use its three-line chorus as a call to my animal totems. It is also protective and energizing, and it celebrates the animal.

The piece is called "Riu Chiu," and it is a 16th-century, anonymous Spanish work. It is one of the most frequently performed Renaissance pieces at Christmas, but, as with many such pieces there are both religious versions and secular versions.

The three-line chorus has twelve syllables per line and three lines. Three is a creative number, and it is inherent within the twelve. Twelve also has its own great mystical significance, with ties to the twelve signs of the zodiac, the twelve months of the year, etc. These numbers give the chant a creative rhythm. For those who study numerology, the significance will not be missed. (You may wish to refer to my earlier work, *Sacred Sounds*, for some of the significance of rhythm and for more specific techniques in writing magical and mystical chants and prayers.)

The translation of the lines also has ties to the mysteries of predator and prey as discussed earlier in this book. The adaptation of the third line reinforces the idea that the divine manifests through specific animals and expressions of Nature.

"RIU CHIU" (original)

Riu Riu Chiu, La guardo ribera.
(Riu, Riu Chiu. Who guards by the river.)

Dios guardo el lobo de nuestra cordera.
(God guards/keeps the wolf from our ewe.)

Dios guardo el lobo de nuestra cordera.
(God guards/keeps the wolf from our ewe.)

"RIU CHIU" (my adaptation)

Riu, Riu Chiu. La guardo ribera.
(Riu, Riu Chiu. Who guards by the river.)

Dios guardo el lobo de nuestra cordera.
(God guards/keeps the wolf from our ewe.)

_____ guardo el lobo de nuestra cordera.
(_____ guards/keeps the wolf from our ewe.)

In my adaptation, I do not use the word "dios" in the third line. Instead I substitute the name of the animal I am calling. Since this is a Spanish piece, I use the Spanish name for the animal. In this way I emphasize the idea that God or the Divine manifests through an animal, and it is the energy of the animal which keeps the wolf away from the ewe. It is the animal who activates the energies for the balance of magic in predator and prey.

SAMPLE ADAPTATION

Riu, Riu Chiu. La guardo ribera.
(Riu, Riu Chiu. Who guards by the river.)

Dios guardo el lobo de nuestra cordera.
(God guards/keeps the wolf from our ewe.)

Halcon guardo el lobo de nuestra cordera.
(The hawk guards/keeps the wolf from our ewe.)

The animal is the form in which the divine manifests, and this is reflected within the third line. If I am working with several animals, I will repeat this, each time substituting a different animal. I will usually repeat this song three times for each animal, keeping that magical rhythm of three. Experiment with it. Find what works for you. This is a powerful piece, and I have found it effective in calling to me those animals that I do not normally work with.

At the end of this section is the melody for this piece. If you have access to a piano or a musical instrument, it will help you in learning to sing it. I recommend going to your local library, a college music library, or even a music store which has access to Renaissance pieces, and getting a recording of it. Hearing someone sing it will help you learn the melody much more easily. Most libraries, if they do not have it, can help you find it.

The effort you put into it finding it and learning it will be well rewarded, as it is a powerfully effective piece. Drums and rattles can be used with it as well, enhancing the effects.

A simple Spanish-English dictionary will help you with the Spanish names for animals that can be substituted. Some names may not fit easily into the rhythm, so you may have to be creative. For example, the Spanish word for owl is "lechuza" which does not fit smoothly into where "Dios" was. I simply blend it together, dropping the last syllable, so that instead of three syllables, "lechuza" seems to have two—"lechuz." Your intention will carry through.

The following are some samples:

Deer	— venado, ciervo (masc.)	Kangaroo	— canguro
Hawk	— halcon	Owl	— lechuza
Eagle	— aguilla	Rabbit	— conejo
Fox	— zorro	Turtle	— tortuga
Horse	— caballo	Vulture	— gallinazo
Elephant	— elefante	Whale	— ballena

Below is the music for this call to the animals. Work with it. Experiment. Your efforts will bring swift reward. As you learn it, you will be able to use it to call animals, send them with messages and help you to shapeshift. It has a magic to it that will work.

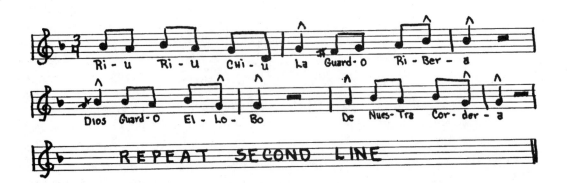

CHAPTER TWELVE

ANIMAL RITES

Animal rites and animal rights are frequent subjects for discussion among metaphysical and other "new age" groups. It would naturally be assumed that the two go hand in hand, but in some circles this just is not so. It is amazing how often I hear stories of animal rites that involve sacrifice.

There is the popularity of voudoun in parts of the country where chickens are frequently slaughtered in ritual. With the return and popularity of shamanism, many assume that animal sacrifice is a natural part of attuning to nature and that it is okay—as long as the animal is honored. At the time of the harmonic convergence I heard many horror stories of shamanic groups making sacrifices of chickens and such to Mother Earth.

Hunting seems to have become more popular of late and even encouraged among some groups. One woman who was consulting me told me how happy she was that she could send her husband out hunting so that she could have skins to make her ritual garments and thus become more at one with the animal.

Nothing is more dangerous than a little knowledge. All such activities I find appalling. It displays ignorance and a great disrespect toward Nature. Some may argue that the animals die in Nature anyway, and so no real harm is done. This is true, death is part of Nature. The death, though, occurs as part of the natural cycle of predation or sickness, not through artificially induced elements. No matter how it is rationalized, hunting is not a sport. A sport involves a contest between individuals equipped with the same tools. I have no qualms about reporting abuse activities to the proper authorities.

Many shamanic purists believe that this is the only way to truly attune to Mother Earth, but no matter how they rationalize it, these individuals are operating under some grave misconceptions. In more primitive times these kinds of rites were a part of life. An animal killed was killed for survival. It was an act as much for self-preservation as for religion. Every part of that animal served a function and was used, often because there was nothing else available, or that the people did not have the right knowledge. These societies also had extremely poor hygiene, a short lifespan, and an extremely difficult existence. Do we want to return to those aspects as well?

In some ancient societies the letting of blood was a means of releasing a form of psychic energy found in the blood that could amplify the energy of the priest, the priestess, the shaman, the magician, or the medicine person. It was the only way they knew. Today, humans have evolved beyond the need for such activities. The human psychic energy is too strong and vital, and such activities simply contaminate the human energy field—no matter what kind of cleansing and purification activities are combined with it. They pollute thoughts, emotions, and even the physical health.

Those who proclaim its necessity are misguided. They are either individuals who refuse to take the time to develop their abilities in a more natural manner or they still believe that magic and mysticism is something supernatural and beyond themselves. Eventually in such cases, the law of reciprocity will kick in, but at what expense?

Remember that mimicry is impotent. Many mystical and magical formulas have come down to us through the ages, and many groups hold strictly to them, never altering the rites and prayers. And then they often make excuses for why the energy invoked and expressed was less than what it was designed to be.

For true magic and spirituality to occur we must take what we have learned and then add our own creative intuition and imagination to it. This alone gives it power. This is what makes it truly magical. Being responsible and living a mystical life requires that you take what you can find from whatever source you can find—extract it, reshape it, and then synthesize it into a system of creative and productive growth that works for you individually. It is using what you learn in the manner that is best for you and all life around you.

We can never again experience those good old days of the ancient shamans. Nor should we want to. If we believe that we must kill an animal or sacrifice it to become at one with it, there will soon be nothing left but pictures. Which would you rather see: a wolf in the wild or a picture of a wolf in the wild? What we can do is take what the ancient shamans taught and adapt it to our present lives and circumstances. We can search out beneficial ways of gaining the attunement.

I know a number of individuals who have found a wonderful compromise. In our society of high traffic and the impingement of roads upon natural lands, most people are familiar with road-kill animals. An increasing number of individuals are carrying gloves and plastic bags in their cars. When they come across a road kill, they stop and gather it up, and later they perform their own ritual to honor it, maybe even saving some feathers or pelts. Some just stop and move the animal off the road so that other animals which scavenge upon it will not be hit by traffic as well. This is a tremendous honoring of the life of the animal and of nature. It says to the spirit of the animal, "Your life was beneficial."

I carry gloves, a blanket, and bags in my car. With all the traveling that I do, I often come across hurt or dead animals. It is sad to see the numbers and kinds of animals that are hit. I have seen hawks, crows, opossums, raccoon, groundhogs, bob cats, coyotes, and many others. I have even been unfortunate enough to hit and kill small animals that freeze in my headlights. It is a horrifying feeling. I have not always been in a position to stop, but when possible I do—if only to move it off the road. I say my own prayer to release its spirit, I express sorrow for its sudden and unfortunate death, and I wish it well, promising to try and aid its kind in the future.

In the spring it is not unusual to see opossums that have been hurt or killed. When possible, I try to stop and check it. If it is a female, there is a good possibility it is carrying young in its pouch. Though the mother may be dead, the young may live.

Once, while returning from Colorado, I was driving through Missouri. It was after several days of heavy rains. The ground had become so soaked that hundreds of turtles from the woods along a stretch of highway had come out and onto the road. They were found in both lanes of the highway covering an area of about five miles. It was difficult to avoid hitting them. I checked my rear view mirror to see how other drivers were doing.

Some drivers did not even bother trying to miss the turtles, but I was amazed by the driver of a semi-truck. He slowed to minimum speed and went out of his way, maneuvering his truck around the turtles, not harming a single one. It was amazing seeing him handle that big rig and being able to avoid every turtle. Considering the number of turtles, it was an impressive piece of driving. As I left the turtles behind, I sent them a prayer of protection and a special prayer to the truck driver as well.

Such activities are rites which honor the natural world. Rites to honor and connect with the natural world can be as simple as a prayer or as intricate as a shapeshifting ceremony. The ones which follow are designed to be both simple and effective. Do not be afraid to adapt them or to create your own. They will stimulate ideas for working with your spirit animals more creatively.

PREPARING FOR ANIMAL RITES

Mention the word ritual to a dozen people and you will receive a dozen different reactions. The responses always vary and are often confusing. Much has been written about ritual in the past, but unfortunately, it is often absurd and ludicrous derivations of true ritual techniques. Most opinions that people hold toward rites of any kind come from the fabric of the imagination—as stimulated through television and movies. Most of it is hype, revealing little understanding of the true potential for aligning ourselves with the variety of energies existing in the universe.

A good deal of information on ceremonies and rites, and those who partake in them, is conceived and performed for the dabbler or the psychic thrill seeker. Many invent ritual practices to cover their own misbehaviors or to cloak their own ignorance.

It was once believed that rituals only concerned themselves with angels and demons, but we must realize that we all use ritual every day of our life. How may of us follow a set routine every morning? Do we get up, shower, drink our coffee, read the paper and then go to work? That is a ritual. We have personal rites, military rites, religious rites, social rites—rites associated with every aspect of human expression.

What we will explore through the rest of this chapter are rites that will help you to honor and attune to the natural world and the animals within it more effectively. We will show you how to create routines that will enable you to look at nature and the life within it in a manner that will reveal the higher forces at play within your life. The rites will help awaken a greater love for all manifestations of life within the world.

Ceremonial rites stimulate inspiration. Their primary purpose is to awaken within the participants a greater realization of connectedness to all energies of the universe. They help us to recognize that we are a microcosm. Everything we do affects everything else in the universe, and everything else in the universe is reflected within our own lives. To fulfill that purpose, you do not need intricate tools, instruments, robes, and temples. It simply involves a creative application of your mental faculties along specific lines. Nothing more than an open mind, an expanding awareness, and persistence is necessary to see results.

A ritual or ceremonial rite is anything done with strong purpose, intention, and emphasis. It provides a means for experiencing the inner worlds more fully. It rewards you with greater self-expression, self-discovery, and self-exploration. Keep in mind though that most of the rituals of the past will no longer work effectively with the energy of the present. Today an effective ceremonial rite involves the emergence and the harmonizing of ancient sacred traditions with modern creative impulses. We build upon the old, but we add our own creative intuition to them.

There are many ritual traditions to choose from. Most have had their own animal rites and ceremonies. The Qabala, Egyptian, Orphic, Celtic, American Indian, Macumba, and African and other shamanic societies had their own unique methods of rituals. It is always a good idea to study the ritual techniques of a tradition thoroughly before creating and adapting it for your own purposes. Be familiar with what the symbols and energies of the rites were designed to do. Otherwise you may find yourself uncomfortably surprised by what you invoke.

A successful rite—whether it is to connect with Nature/animals or any other purpose—will focus and improve your memory. It will enable you to experience certain energies without being overwhelmed by them. it will expand your consciousness, stimulate creativity, and increase your overall confidence levels. Usu-

222

ally within three to seven days you will get a tangible confirmation that it has fulfilled its purpose or is in the process of doing so.

There are several preliminary considerations necessary before beginning any work with your spirit totem:

1. LEARN AS MUCH ABOUT YOUR ANIMAL AS POSSIBLE. I know I have said this frequently throughout this book, but it is essential. Read about it. Study it. Make a list of its most outstanding and unusual characteristics. Every aspect of its behavior will have some significance to you or to your life. It may have shown up either to help you awaken and develop some of those same characteristics or to control those that need it in your life.

2. KNOW THE PURPOSE OF YOUR RITUAL OR MEDITATION. This should be done before you create any meditation or ceremonial rite to align with your spirit animal. Know why you personally want to involve yourself with it. Determine the most appropriate time(s) and place(s) to perform it. Remember that specific tools are not necessary to have an effective rite. Tools and wardrobe help the mind to stay focused on the purpose, but they are not essentials.

3. KEEP YOUR ANIMAL RITES AND MEDITATIONS SIMPLE. They do not have to be of any great length to be effective. The most effective rites are those which do not employ intricate tools and/or costume. What makes you feel the most comfortable?

4. MAKE PREPARATIONS BEFOREHAND. Prepare the place of meditation and ritual. Make sure that both the place and you, yourself, are neat and clean. Use a smudge or incense that is purifying. Ensure that the phone is off the hook and that you will not be disturbed. Perform a progressive relaxation before beginning the actual rite or exercise.

5. USE MUSIC AND DRUMMING TO ENHANCE THE CONNECTION. The right music can be a powerful enhancement to any ritual or meditation, but it must be music suitable to your purpose. Just employing music for the sake of music will detract. Experiment with different types to find what works best for you.

   You may wish to make up your own song to honor the animal spirit. I touched upon this earlier in this book. You may also find that one of the benefits of performing animal rites is that it establishes such a dynamic link between you and your animal that it will teach you the animal's song.

   One of the most effective tools to empower animal rites is the drum. It is a basic tool of shamans. A true shaman does not inherit gods, goddesses, or other divine entities through a family, a tradition, or religion. A shaman is one who opens himself/herself so that the expression of the divine in whatever form is most suitable is experienced directly.

Rhythm is the pulse of life and it affects all physical conditions and states of being. To the Native Americans, the drum beat is the heartbeat of the Mother Earth. In Voudoun, the drum is used in specific ways to block out the rational mind during the rituals. It serves to activate the sexual energies or even induce trance.

Rhythmic patterns have always been a part of ritual and healing. Pure, specific rhythms were associated with definite ideas, experiences, and physiological responses. There are drum and rhythm patterns to stimulate or calm the emotions, and there are those which aid in the exploration of inner consciousness.

In many shamanic practices, the drumbeat is used to induce an altered state of consciousness. The drum beat is concentrated upon and followed by the participant as if riding it on a mythical journey into levels of the mind that could not otherwise be as easily accessed. The drum connects or bridges the individual to magical states of consciousness.

Some are so skilled at drumming that they can duplicate the rhythms of various animals. There is snake drumming, wolf drumming, hawk drumming—a drumming for every animal. As the rhythm is created it plays upon the metabolism of the individual causing entrainment—the individual's own heart and metabolic rhythm is brought into synchronization with the drum beat. This is used to facilitate a shapeshifting, an aligning with the archetypal forces represented by the animal.

This text does not have the capability to explore all of the intricacies in the use of ritual drumming. (There are several sources in the bibliography which can help you explore this subject more fully.) Get a drum or a rattle, or make one. Even the clapping of two sticks together is a means of creating a rhythm. Practice sitting and slowly tapping out a repetitive, slow rhythm. Pay attention to the changes in your body. Incorporate those rhythms when performing the exercises in this chapter. Remember that you are simply using rhythm to alter your own physiological and spiritual rhythms for specific purposes.

6. USE MOVEMENT TO HELP ESTABLISH THE LINK WITH YOUR ANIMAL. As we have mentioned, movement and dance were often incorporated to help align the individual with the energies and essence of the animal. The animal's movements, postures, and gestures were imitated. This is especially effective when performed for five minutes or so at the beginning. It is a means of drawing the animal to you, and into you as well. As you mimic its movements, visualize yourself becoming the animal, or see it drawing closer to you as it would to one of its own kind. Then imagine it melting into you, coming alive within.

Have fun with the movements. Watch nature programs on your animal so you can observe how it moves. Visit zoos or nature centers that house animals and observe them so that you can imitate their movements. Then be creative with it. Make your own dance of celebration to your animal totem. You do not have to confine yourself to only its movements. You may wish to explore my earlier book *The Magical Dance* to help you with this.

7. KEEP PROPS AND TOOLS SIMPLE. It takes very little to connect in with the powers of nature. Sometimes though props such as feathers or portraits or costumes can be used to help you focus and concentrate the mind. You may wish to explore mask making and make one for your animal spirit. You will find it very empowering, even if you do not find it artistic. It is simply a means of expressing honor and reverence to it. Just the making of such, whether you use them or not, is a powerful attunement meditation itself.

Some people make robes that have the animal spirit painted on. Some use face and body paint and paint themselves in the image of the animal or its markings before the meditations and rites to help focus and concentrate the energies and the attention. Again, you do not have to become that complicated to connect with your totems. It can be fun to do at times, and if you feel drawn to do so, go ahead. It is especially effective when combined with the dance and song. This is also a powerful enhancement to the sample shapeshifting technique described later in this chapter.

Special Reminders

1. The animals (and their energies) with whom you work are all found within you. You are the microcosm. All energies within the universe live within you.

2. The animals and the energies associated with them will express themselves through you and in your life. By meditating and using animal rites to align with them, you become the focused point of manifestation. Be assured that if you meditate and create rites to connect with the animals, you will experience their energies somewhere in your life. Initially, you may need to be a little more observant to recognize those points of manifestation. As you develop the connection with your spirit animal, you will develop ways to control how and where its energies manifest.

3. There will be some trial and error in developing the relationship with the animal and its energies. As with any relationship, there will be boundaries. Just recognizing your power animal does not mean it will be effective to use in every avenue of your life.

4. There will be an urge to share your new-found connection and joy once you start achieving noticeable results. This is natural. It is also usually your first test in developing a working relationship with the animal. Discretion and discrimination are essential. Be very careful with whom you share your experiences. Others can create barriers and color what should otherwise be a personally joyful experience.

5. Preparation is always the key. Familiarize yourself completely with the animal, its symbols, qualities, and energies. Learn its myths and its lore, and keep an open mind. If you find that the energy is uncomfortable or too intense, break the connection. Remember that you are establishing a relationship, and in any relationship everyone involved has to learn the boundaries of the others.

6. As you connect to one aspect of Nature, you automatically open to others. As you connect with one animal, others will show up within your life, making themselves known. It reminds us that all things, all animals and all humans are connected. It is one of the truly wonderful benefits of learning animal-speak.

Exercise #1: Creating an Animal Speak Dictionary

To some this may seem more of a task than a rite, but it is a powerful way of beginning to attune to animals. For ages, people have tried to mimic animal sounds. Ornithologists have often catalogued and attempted to describe the calls of birds:

Crow — "Caw, Caw, Caw"
Chickadee — "Chick-a-dee-dee-dee"
Duck — "Quack, Quack"
Barred Owl — "Who cooks for You—who cooks for You all"
Mourning dove — "Whooooooo-who-who-who"

Anyone who has ever had a pet knows that pets are constantly speaking to us. Their movements, postures, and vocalizations send a variety of messages to us. They rub against our legs, bark and purr, show their teeth when threatened, crouch when scared, and lick to show affection. We, in turn, communicate with the animals, teaching them. We may rattle a food bowl to call them. We talk softly when showing affection and sternly when upset.

To understand animals, you have to be able to interpret their language. The language of every animal is different from every other animal. There are certain messages that are common to them all, often those having to do with survival. Threatening postures and sounds are the most common, and all animals use them to some degree. We have to keep this in mind when learning to speak the language of animals.

We must also keep in mind that animals communicate with other animals and with people. Sometimes the communications are different, and sometimes we have to interpret the language a little more symbolically. Many creation myths speak of the time when humans and animals spoke the same language, but that time has passed. We have forgotten, so we must relearn it. Paying attention to the number of crows, the number of times a crow caws, and what it does immediately before and after such occurrences all are filled with meaning to the Native Americans.

If you wish to learn the language of animals, you must develop a new vocabulary. This is where the development of the dictionary comes in. This can be done with both domestic and wild animals. For most people, beginning with the domestic is usually simpler.

1. Choose one animal at a time to work with, and give yourself a specific time to focus on it. This may be as simple as a week or two week period. Some may wish to devote an entire month to observing one animal. Find what works for you.

2. Keep a notebook or journal on the animal. Read about it. Watch nature programs devoted to it. Most importantly, take time to observe its activities yourself. Now, of course, this will be very nearly impossible with certain kinds of wild animals. Most people do not have access or opportunity to observe animals in the wild, but even in city environments there are some opportunities with commoner animals. Begin with those you see most often: birds, squirrels, pets, etc.

3. Make notes of sounds, movements, and behaviors that you observe. When you observe them, also make notations about what you think they mean. Some will be obvious, but others won't. You should be able to come up with at least two possible interpretations. One possibility is to try and explain what the movement or sound may mean to other animals (especially those of its own species). The other possibility is an interpretation along the lines of what it may mean to you. Jot down all possibilities, no matter how far fetched they may seem.

4. Pay particularly close attention to sounds and activities that occur when you are around or approach the animal. Are these different than when you observe from a distance? Try mimicking the animal's sounds and movements. How does the animal respond? Keep notes on anything that occurs.

5. Then pay attention to what goes on in your own life shortly after the observation or communication. Look back at the end of the day. Does anything the animal did reflect the kind of experiences you had in the course of the day? Can you draw any parallels? Observe this over a 24-hour period. Don't worry about stretching the correspondences. It will help you to recognize the subtle nuances in the communication.

When you encounter the same sounds and behaviors, do you have similar kinds of experiences as those you recorded the first time? Remember that through this process you begin to develop parameters that help you to understand the specific communication from the animals you encounter. Eventually you will be able to say to yourself, "Now the last couple times the squirrel acted this way, this is what happened . . . So it is a good likelihood that this is going to occur again."

As you create your dictionary, you are developing a greater ability to understand animals in the world around you. Your dictionary will enable you to translate the meanings of sounds and motions of the common animals around you.

The more you work with it, the easier it becomes. In just a year, you can lay a solid foundation in the language of a number of animals. You will have developed a beginner's vocabulary. You will also find that it will be easier for you to understand and interpret some animals than others. Sometimes these animals serve as a catalyst, helping you to realize that the ability to learn animal-speak is inherent. Everyone has the ability.

Exercise #2: Flights of Fancy

Animals stimulate the imagination. They touch and stir deeper aspects of ourselves that we sometimes forget we have. One of the most wonderful rites to perform on a regular basis to enhance and maintain attunement is to create a fanciful meditation involving your animal. It is especially beneficial as a prelude to the dance exercise that is described in the next exercise. It can also be an excellent preparation for more powerful shapeshifting techniques such as that which is described later in this chapter.

This kind of rite frees the emotions and helps us to move past our usual mental blocks. It helps us begin to loosen the more primal fabric of our energy, that part of the subconscious which responds to and understands Nature. It is relaxing and it also relieves stress. It stimulates creativity and invites a more intimate relationship with Nature in all of its forms.

1. Choose an animal. It can be any animal. In fact, it is beneficial to do this exercise with any animal that appeals to you at the moment. It does not have to be your own personal totem.

2. Do some preliminary reading about the animal, its habitats and behaviors. You don't have to be thoroughly acquainted with every aspect, but you should be familiar enough with it to be able to visualize it clearly in your mind.

3. Choose a time in which you will not be disturbed. Make sure the phone is off the hook. If possible, perform the visualization outdoors.

4. Close your eyes and take a few deep breaths. Begin a slow progressive relaxation. Focus on each part of the body, beginning with the feet and moving up to the head. Send warm, soothing, and relaxing feelings to each part in turn.

5. Now imagine that you are the animal. If it is a bird, see yourself with your ankles long and your nose and mouth joined together to form a beak. Your eyes are on the side of your head and your body is covered with feathers. If an animal, see yourself covered in fur.

The fields, the woods, the mountains and forests is your home. As you imagine yourself in this form, A great urge to be outside comes over you. Your senses are sharp. Fragrances that would normally have gone unnoticed are strong. Your eyes are sharp and your ears detect the slightest sound. It is as if all of your senses are amplified.

Now see yourself in your natural environment. You may be running or flying, but the movement makes you feel strong and alive. Never have you felt so vital. As each muscle stretches and works, you grow stronger and more vibrant. Then envision yourself slowing until you are standing or perching at rest. Your senses are sharp and vital. You are feeling more alive than you have felt in ages.

Now breathe deeply and slowly. As you begin to relax and your breathing steadies, you feel your body changing back once more. The feathers become the clothes you are wearing. Instead of being in a forest or field or atop a mountain, you are in your seat where you first started. Though the image fades, the energy, strength, and balance remains within.

A variation of this exercise can be used effectively as well. Instead of visualizing yourself changing, it is beneficial to see the animal approach you. As it does, it invites you to ride upon its back. Simply imagine yourself the size necessary to be able to ride upon the animal, as it carries you through its environment, showing you what it feels and experiences every day of its life. Imagine what it would be like to ride or fly with the animal you have chosen.

Allow your imagination to run free. Do not try to hold it tight. Do not worry if what you imagine is not truly an aspect or quality of the bird. This rite is designed to loosen the imaginative faculty so that you can access those levels of the mind that will facilitate understanding and speaking the language of animals.

Exercise #3: The Rite of Gifting

Gifting is a simple way of expressing gratitude for opportunities to share with nature. In essence, it is an act of balance. If you take something, you give something in return. What you give can be in the form of an actual gift or simply your time. It is a means of honoring that which you are working to understand. This is most important for when you do your studies and actual encounters with Nature and her animals—be it a wooded area, a park or your own backyard. For anyone learning animal-speak, regular visits to natural environments will become essential.

The Native Americans will offer tobacco to the earth or the animals, leaving it in the environment. Tobacco is sacred to them and it has great significance. When you acknowledge the encounter with a gift, it sends a message to all of Nature that you are receptive and respectful. It facilitates further encounters.

Gifting is a means of awakening a greater sense of gratitude in life and for life. It is most important to do in some form when you are out in nature and are specifically observing and studying some animal or aspect of nature. For example, if there is a chosen area for your observations, search for a special gift to leave in that area when you are ready to leave. This can be any number of things: an acorn, a crystal or colorful stone, a special leaf, a flower that is special to you, dried herbs, or any natural object. It should always be a natural object so that it can become a part of nature and not clutter or destroy the intrinsic beauty of the spot. I will leave a flower, often a rosebud, or a small crystal point.

This rite of gifting completes the circle. Nature gives to you and you receive, and thus you give back to Nature and it receives. This is a powerful rite. It requires no fancy prayers, activities, or formalized ceremonies. It is simply a circular rite of gifting.

In situations where animals are being observed in artificial environments—zoos, nature centers, etc.—you cannot always leave a tangible gift within that environment. Such environments are controlled for the safety and well-being of the animals and the visitors. In cases such as these, a monetary gift to the center is beneficial. It helps promote the well-being of the environment. If it is a case in which you observe the animal frequently, you may wish to donate some time as a volunteer. In this way, you are giving back, and the circle is completed.

It is not right to assume that you can visit and observe without permission, especially in natural environments. It is always a good idea to at least mentally ask the environment and animals within it for permission to observe before taking a position to do so. It helps to build greater mutual respect. You are less likely to take Nature or the experience for granted. It makes the experience more meaningful.

Hints to Make the Gifting More Effective:

1. Always return to the same spot in Nature so that you can build a relationship with that part of the environment. You don't have to limit yourself solely to that spot though.

2. At the end of your visit, leave the gift with a mental "thank you" for the experience and for what you were able to observe. You may even wish to ask mentally for permission to return again at that time.

3. Keep the gifts simple and natural so that they do not intrude upon the intrinsic quality of the natural environment.

4. It is a good idea to carry a plastic trash bag with you whenever you go out into a natural environment. Pick up trash, litter and any other form of clutter you may come across. It shows respect, and Nature will gift you in return.

5. Visit the sites at different times of the year and for different lengths. Make note of the animal activity, plant life and such within the area. At the end of each visit, always leave a gift upon departure.

6. Part of the circle of gifting is receiving. Practice sitting quietly and observing. Make notes, but do not discuss. Listen, smell, and watch what Nature gives to you. You may even wish to visualize yourself as part of that environment, connected to and growing out from the earth. The more you feel connected to the earth, the easier the cycle of receiving from it grows.

7. All movement should be slow. Remember that Nature is very wary of human life, so trust is sometimes difficult to develop. Slow movements that do not startle or frighten are a gift that you can give to the animals. It will help them feel more comfortable. After all, you would not like for someone to come into your home and disturb your life. It is a gift of respect—simple but effective.

8. As you learn to naturalize yourself, feel a part of Nature, then the animal life, the insects, and the birds will accept you as part of the surroundings. When they do that, they will gift you with more activity and they will draw closer.

Exercise #4: Dance Rites

There are many ways of using dance to honor and connect with animals and other aspects of Nature. This book cannot cover them all, but perhaps it will stimulate ideas that you can take and develop for yourself. Many people in societies all over the world have dances that honor animals. Costumes, elaborate or simple, are used to help awaken in the individual the experience of the animal's energies.

Dancing to the animals is a way of honoring them and activating their energies dramatically within your life. One of the most common forms of sacred dance was the imitation of Nature and life within it. Individuals would perform the dance of an animal to align themselves with its power and to awaken it within their life. It is a powerful tool to use in conjunction with the shapeshifting exercise described later in this chapter. Through dance we can shift our energy to that of a pattern similar to our animal totem.

To understand how this works, you must understand the human body. It is a complex, bio-chemical, electro-magnetic energy system. Every time a muscle is used there is an electrical stimulus. The study of the electrical impulses associated with muscular movement is part of the study of kinesiology. When we move or dance in imitation of animals, we help adjust our own body's electrical frequency to one similar to that of the animal. We create resonance.

For this to be most effective, you must perform a close study of the animal. Learn about the way it moves and the way it stands. How does it hold its head? How does it place its feet when it walks? Practice pantomiming those same postures and movements. These movements will be at the heart of the dance. They do not have to be long or extended. Several minutes is all that is necessary to invite the animal's energy into your life, if done appropriately.

The following sample dance is effective to use with any animal. Its movements will lead you into the imitation of the animal and its energies, and symbolically draw them out into your life. It is done with simple circular movements, combined with the basic postures and movements of your animal totem.

1. Begin by researching your totem, focusing on three or four basic movements or postures that it assumes, and which most reflect the energies of it.

2. Practice mimicking and pantomiming its movements.

3. Choose a room or clear the center of a room so that you will have adequate space to move. Prepare it with incense or some pictures or symbols associated with your totem.

4. Choose music or have a drum that you can carry and play. You may even wish to have someone perform the drumming for you. Initially keep the drum beat slow and steady. A two-beat rhythm is easy to perform and imitates the steady rhythm of the heart. The first beat is played a little harder than the second.

5. Begin the dance by marking off a sacred space. This is done in a circular movement (see diagram on page 233). This creates a sacred space in the mind, a place between worlds—a point in which the subtle and tangible can intersect and touch. A circle movement is a dynamic way to initiate any dance ritual. Circle the dance area at least once in a clockwise direction. (I recommend three circles as three is the number of birth and creation).

   A simple toe-heel step is easy to perform. If you use a simple two-beat drum rhythm, on the first (harder) beat, place the toes of one foot down, and on the second (softer) beat bring the heel of the foot down.

6. Keep your focus on the center of the circle. All dance is a series of movements around a central point. The movement in the circle and your focus on its center adds energy to your purpose. Focus on knowing that you are awakening and inviting the energy of the spirit animal into the circle.

7. Now slowly begin to spiral in toward the center. You may even wish to visualize that you are walking or dancing in the animal's natural environment. Imagine and know that as you draw closer to the center, you draw closer to the archetypal energies represented by the totem.

8. Once in the center of the circle, pause and close your eyes. Imagine the animal around you. Feel its energies and essence. Now begin imitating its movements and postures. See yourself as the animal. Imagine and feel its energies coming alive within you as you.

9. After several minutes of this, or when you feel its energies vibrant within you, pause again in the center. Know that the animal is within you and can now be called out of you when needed. Then slowly begin the dance again, spiraling out toward the perimeter of the circle. This time, you move in a counter-clockwise direction. As you spiral outward, visualize yourself bringing

Diagram for the Dance Rites

Create your sacred space by dancing a circle in a clockwise direction. It opens you to experiencing the energies more fully.

Now slowly spiral in toward the center—the point where the forces of the animal can be met.

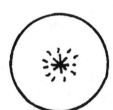

Next perform your movements, imitating the animal. See yourself as the animal and its energies alive within you.

Then in a counterclockwise direction, slowly spiral out to the perimeter of the circle, coming back into yourself but with the energy of the animal.

Slowly dance the circle in a counterclockwise direction to dissipate its energy. Use the same number of revolutions as in #1.

the essence of the animal out with you. Imagine and visualize how its energies will help you in the days ahead. See it being beneficial in as many specific situations as you can.

10. When you reach the outer edge of the circle, begin dancing the perimeter—moving in that counterclockwise direction. This closes off and dissipates the sacred space. Use as many revolutions as you used in the beginning to create the circle. Know that you have brought out some of the energies of the animal totem with you. Remember the responsibility and honor it.

Exercise #5: Learning the Art of Shapeshifting

In the early evolution of humanity, before we were so solidly locked within the physical form, we could probably mold our shapes. When the body was less dense, we may have indeed been able to metamorphose into another shape. Today we must use the faculty of the imagination.

Shapeshifting is natural to all of humanity. It involves more than just transforming oneself into a beast. Every day, on some level, we shift our energies to meet the daily trials, responsibilities, and obligations of life. We learn early on in our lives when to smile, when to be serious, how to appear apologetic, or how to express a wide variety of personas according to need.

Shapeshifting is not just transforming into a beast, as often described in ancient myths and tales. Most of the tales of shapeshifting were either symbolic or reflected a time in human evolution when we were not so grounded in the physical. Shapeshifting is a matter of controlling and shifting your own energies to fit the needs of the moment—being able to draw upon those qualities and energies necessary.

Anyone who can discipline himself or herself to achieve a goal is a shapeshifter. If you can adapt to change, pleasant or otherwise, you are a shapeshifter. If you can turn a foul mood into a pleasant one, then you are a shapeshifter. If you can adjust your behaviors to relate to a wide variety of people and life conditions, then you are a shapeshifter.

It is this kind of shapeshifting that we all can develop to a high degree. We can learn to adjust our energies to that which is similar to a particular animal totems and manifest it beneficially within our life. When we can do this, then we begin to realize that there truly is a magic to the world.

Today, most magic takes place within the mind at a different level of perception. It doesn't make it any less real or useful in our outer lives. When we can accept that, then we are on the way to becoming a true magician. With practice you can strengthen the imaginative faculty and learn to consciously control and shapeshift it along any lines you desire. And when we change the imaginings, we change the world. We can learn to shapeshift the imagination so that for all intents and purposes, we become the shape.

Examples of positions to aid in shapeshifting.

This is what this exercise will help teach you. It is only a beginning, and it won't make you a master shapeshifter. It will help you to stretch and strengthen your imaginative faculty, assisting you in attuning to and manifesting the energies and qualities you desire from your spirit animal.

To be a good shapeshifter, you must master the art of observation. You cannot shapeshift to a bird's body—even in the mind—if you do not know how a bird's body works. Begin by observing two or three basic forms or postures of your animal. Visit zoos. Observe the animal's behaviors and make notes. Mimic its movements and its sounds. Begin the process by thinking yourself into the part. Think about what it would be like to be the animal.

You may want to assist yourself in making the transformations through incorporation of dance and/or costume of the animal. The following outline includes aspects of the previous dance rite, but takes it a step further. You may wish to review it, to enhance the effects.

1. You *must* have privacy for this exercise. No phones, no interruptions.

2. Begin the exercise by dancing off your sacred space, as outlined in the previous exercise. Then begin to spiral in toward the center. You may wish to have a chair or a cushion that you will want to sit upon.

3. When you reach the center, pause. Feel and imagine the unformed energy of the animal spirit around you. Now begin the movements and postures associated with your totem. As you take the stance and make the steps within the inner circle, mimicking the animal, feel its energy becoming stronger within you and around you.

4. Now take a seated position, and within your mind, build the image of your animal. See the image forming and growing over the area of your solar plexus. See it form solidly within your mind's eye in front of you, at the level of the solar plexus.

5. When you can imagine it fully in front of you, begin to visualize it being absorbed into your body through the solar plexus region. Take its full essence into you through that center.

6. Now start with the feet or the hands. Feel them begin to change. Imagine and feel claws, paws, or talons forming. Where there was skin, imagine fur or feathers forming. Allow the change to come slowly and to move up the body. The last part of the body to change should be the head. This will help you to maintain control.

7. As you imagine yourself transforming, also visualize a door forming for you, a door that has engraved upon it the image of the animal you are becoming. This is a door to the inner world. It is easier to maintain the form on the inner levels than in the outer, so visualize the door opening and you going through it as the animal.

8. Initially you will be imagining all that you wish to experience as the animal. Eventually though, the experience will become alive. It will take on the quality of a very vivid dream. You won't just be observing yourself doing this, you will be experiencing it.

9. On the other side of the door, you may wish to explore the environment of the animal. You may use the animal form to travel on the inner levels to outer destinations—visiting people, the past, the future. You are the animal.

10. After a time, imagine yourself coming back through the door, and it closing solidly behind you. Then slowly the body begins to change once more, starting with the head. The fur/feathers become skin once more. Do not rush the transformation. When you have changed back, allow the image of the animal to withdraw from the body, again through the solar plexus. Imagine it fully and completely outside of you once more. Then allow its image to slowly dissipate until it is simply an unformed energy surrounding you in the center of your circle.

11. Slowly open your eyes and stand. Perform several of the animal moves as a way of honoring and thanking the spirit of the animal, and then begin the slow counterclockwise spiral out to the perimeter of the circle. Visualize the energy dissipating as you do.

12. Dissipate the sacred space, visualizing yourself fully grounded and balanced as you dance the outer circle in a counterclockwise direction. Use the same number of revolutions as you did to create the sacred space.

There are some important precautions and considerations in performing this exercise or any like it. If you find that your mind is scattered or changed too much in the next day or so, stop the activity. If you see, or others around you see, changes in your personality, stop the exercises immediately. This kind of exercise should not be used too often.

Frequently there are those who have never meditated or worked to control their energies, and who desire to jump in and learn to "shapeshift." This can create problems. If you find yourself rushing home to do a shapeshifting exercise or neglecting other important aspects of your life, then stop immediately. It is creating imbalance.

Be flexible in the above steps. Adapt and experiment with them. Dance and shapeshifting are both creative processes. For them to become truly magical, you must apply your own creative imagination and intuition.

As you will find, the effects of any dance ritual are seldom subtle. Expect sometimes dramatic physical responses and releases. You may even want to consider only taking on the aspects of the totem under the guise of someone knowledgeable of deep altered states. If not, go very slow.

Even though the shapeshifter may not change physically to outside observers, internally he or she may have undergone an profound transformation and believe it to have occurred physically. This should not be treated casually or dismissed. Time and care must be used in assimilating and balancing the energies invoked through shapeshifting.

For the beginner, it is best to work with simple movements and postures. *Always use the door.* This way, if you should temporarily lose yourself in the transformation, you will have already trained the mind to use the door to trigger the reversal.

Some may wish to try ecstatic dancing to facilitate the transformation. If you are unsure of your ability to control and handle the transformation, do not use it. No dancer or shapeshifter should ever go until "they drop." This is extremely unhealthy and very damaging to the entire energy system of the individual.

Many shamanic techniques use drums to induce the altered state and facilitate the shapeshifting. If you are working with others, the drum can be used to draw the individual back into reality. One drum technique involves using a slow, heartbeat rhythm, and then building in intensity to release the consciousness and facilitate the transition. Reversing this and moving from the frenzied rhythm to the regular heart rhythm will draw the consciousness back to normal. This is especially effective because the individual does not then move from the deep altered state to normal consciousness too abruptly.

Taking the hands of the individual and performing joint deep breathing assists in grounding the individual back into reality. Massaging the feet to open and activate the chakras that connect us back to the earth and its reality is also beneficial. Assuming a seated or prone position will assist in this, especially when accompanied by removing any fetishes or costumes that were used to aid the transformation.

It is also beneficial to stroke the spine downward from the crown of the head. This stabilizes the chakras, and it draws the consciousness back into present reality. Remember that always the goal is to connect with the energies and to develop conscious control and awareness of them at all times.

CHAPTER THIRTEEN

DICTIONARY OF ANIMAL TOTEMS

It is important, when you begin to examine your animal totems, to relate to them from an entirely different perspective. You will actually begin to develop a kind of empathy toward them. You will no longer simply observe Nature objectively. You will become involved once more with all aspects of it. You are drawn in.

Books may describe the qualities and characteristics of the animal, but only by working with it and applying it to your own self and your own life can you develop a relationship with it. You cannot help but be connected with environmental and social ethics involving Nature and animals. You will develop both passion and compassion for all aspects of Nature. You will feel what Nature feels. The numbness that modern society has helped to foster in regard to Nature fades. "Empathy is the tangible sense of our interconnectedness. When we feel what another person feels and when we understand that Earth is a living organism whose parts also have an awareness, even though different from our own, we want to help because we share that emotional experience."[1]

Just as with the birds, begin the process by asking yourself basic questions concerning your animal:

- What is its color?

- What is its size?

- What is its shape?

---

1   From *Keepers of the Animals: Native American Stories and Wildlife Activities for Children* by Michael J. Caduto and Joseph Bruchac, Fulcrum Publishing, Inc., 350 Indiana Street, #350, Golden, CO 80401 (303) 277-1624.

- How does it behave?

- Where is it from and what direction is that to you?

- When is it most often seen?

- What kind of home does it make?

- What kind of sounds does it make?

- What is its favorite food or prey?

- What feeds or preys on it?

- How does it adapt to seasonal changes?

- When does it usually mate?

- What are its survival adaptations?

Some may find it easier to begin by examining the most significant feature of the animal. Does it have sharp claws or great strength? Are there sharp teeth or skillful intelligence? Focus first on its most outstanding feature and then move to other aspects. That which most strikes you first about the animal will be most important.

For example, horns and antlers may be the first thing you notice about an animal. They have long been a symbol of strength and power. Horns are permanent growths, while antlers are shed each year and new ones then grow again. Both reflect an antennae-kind of connection to that which is above the head. In some animals, it bestows beauty and indicates maturity. A singular horn was often used to symbolize the masculine or solar aspects, while doubles reflected the feminine and lunar energies of life.

There is no possible way all animals could be covered in the following dictionary. It focuses primarily on mammals from the North American continent, but there are mammals from other continents included. Even if you have lived your entire life in this country, it is possible to have a totem from another country. This may reflect past-life connections. It may also help reflect that we are connected to the entire Earth and not just our continent. The world is smaller today in that we have the influence of all societies. We speak of the United States as being a melting pot—this holds true for spirit totems as well.

You may wish to also study about mammals in general. It may provide some insight. Mammals are our closest relations among animals. What distinguishes mammals from other animals is that mammals breathe air and they give birth to live young. They are not hatched. Mammals are the only animals that produce milk and suckle their young. Only mammals grow hair or fur. They are also warm-blooded.

There are roughly 4300 species of mammals in the world and over 400 on this continent alone.[2] There are twelve orders of mammals, ranging in size from the tiny shrew to the great whale. They are found both in the wild and in cities. Each group has its own characteristics, and a study of them will help you to understand more about this animal's influence in your own life.

Study the animal's living environment. If it is an animal found within urban areas, what does it need to survive and live close to people? If it is found in the wild, what does it need to survive there? Remember that every species has value. One is no more magical or powerful from a spiritual perspective than another. They all serve a vital role. Every animal has its own magic, no less essential to our lives and the life of the Earth.

This dictionary will give you a starting point. Do not limit the study of your totems to it and it alone. It is sketchy. You may even find that the interpretations of animals and their behaviors from a mystical point of view may differ from your own. This is fine. Each must relate to the animals in his or her own unique way. Establish your own relationships. Only then will the essence and magic of the animals come to life for you.

ANTELOPE (Pronghorn)

KEYNOTE: *Speed and Adaptability of the Mind*
CYCLE OF POWER: *Spring and Autumn*

The pronghorn is the only antelope native to North America, but it is not a true antelope in that it does not shed its antlers, as is common among all antelopes. As with all horned and antlered animals, it reflects a connection to the brow and crown chakra and all aspects of mental ability. In the case of the pronghorn, it reflects a mental agility and quick wittedness that will enable it to survive in the most difficult of environments.

The antelope is usually specialized for living within different environments— deserts, grasslands, thickets or even swamps. They have a thick hide, sometimes an inch thick, which helps protect them from the environment. The thick tubular hairs have large air cells which serve as an insulation during winter. This insulating factor is partly what enables them to survive.

For anyone with an antelope totem, there may either be a need to insulate oneself or a need to come out of hiding. The pronghorn can show how best to

---

2   Ibid, pp. 161–162.

work with your insulation and help you develop a new sense of timing in relation to it. It is not unusual for someone who is very emotional or empathic to have the antelope show up at times as a totem.

All antelopes have great speed. They can run at speeds up to 60 miles per hour. Even baby fawns can run around 25 miles per hour in the first day or so. Those with an antelope totem have always had extremely quick wits. The ability to communicate those thoughts is part of what the pronghorn can teach.

Pronghorns have a dynamic ability to communicate with others, and they have a great curiosity. Children with pronghorn totems are often those who drive parents nuts with continual questions. Their minds and imaginations are always active.

A pronghorn will signal danger to others by raising the white patch on its rump. Most pronghorns depend mostly on their sense of sight. They have large eyes and a wide angle of vision. They have eight times the vision of humans, so the moment the white patch flashes, they do see it—even from a great distance.

This ability to see at a distance can be developed into a heightened psychic ability for prediction. This is further reflected with the branched set of horns, giving the antelope totem the ability to awaken your own higher psychic antennae. Clairvoyance is part of what it can teach. Most individuals with a pronghorn totem are intrinsically psychic. They came in with the lights on, although they don't always realize it. They can usually sense imminent danger, and as long as they pay attention to it, they will seem to lead charmed lives—always just avoiding the catastrophes that seem to befall those around them.

Pronghorns also have a strong sense of smell. At the first sign of danger, a strong musk scent is also released. This totem can teach people how to know when people and situations don't quite "smell" right. In traditional spiritualism there is a form of mediumship known as clairaugustus or clear-smelling. Some mediums and psychic pick up fragrances of spirits or around individuals and interpret them. This is an ability that this totem can help awaken. It is not unusual for those with this totem to encounter strange fragrances throughout the day from unidentifiable sources. Usually when this begins to awaken, it begins with the aroma of musk. Musk is a fragrance that can be meditated with to help facilitate connecting with this totem.

Pronghorn males often have harems. The females usually have twins, and they give birth to them in different spots. It is not unusual for those with this totem to find that their energies are divided, come spring. Two avenues of activity usually open up. They each will be distinct and different, even though there may be connections or they may have opened up at the same time from the same source. It is always a good idea to look for new opportunities about to surface in your life when the pronghorn shows up.

For the protection of the fawns, the mother stays away from them after giving birth, except to nurse. The fawns are born with practically no scent, so as long as the mother does not leave hers, they will be safer. This implies several things. First, the opportunities that are about to open will not need a great deal of attention. Second, it indicates an ability for the new opportunities to grow quickly with just a little nurturing.

The pronghorn feeds on shrubs and sagebrush. It can actually go for months or even a lifetime without drinking water. It has the ability to get water from the plants that it eats. This reflects that the pronghorn can teach you how to replenish yourself in whatever environment you live. It can teach you how to use your adaptive ability to find life in areas not normally considered liveable. It can help you extract the life essence out of the most parched life experiences and develop a new mental perspective and attitude toward them, so that you can move quickly into new areas of your life.

ARMADILLO

KEYNOTE: *Personal Protection, Discrimination, and Empathy*

CYCLE OF POWER: *Year-round*

Armadillo is Spanish for "little armored one." It is a burrowing animal whose armor is the shield it carries on its back. The armor is comprised of overlapping bony plates, covered with horns. The undersides are ordinary hide and are its most vulnerable area. The armadillo and those with it as a totem are most vulnerable when they expose their undersides, or inner workings. Armadillo teaches how to protect yourself and when to let your defenses down.

The armadillo is actually a member of the sloth family. It has no canine teeth or incisors, but it does have 80 or more molars that never stop growing. It lives in burrows that are really multichambered dens. These dens can be as much as five feet below ground. Its claws are excellent for digging, reflecting an ability to dig through the surface of things to see what is beneath. The armadillo teaches discrimination.

All animals with armor of any kind have connections to the European knights of medieval lore. The armadillo can be a past-life link specifically to the 16th-century Spanish conquistadors, probably best known for the conquering of Mexico and Peru. Chivalry, strength, and protection were often the ideal qualities to be developed by the European knights. This is reflected in the fact that the armadillo's best offense is a strong defense.

The early armor was often heavy and made it awkward to move in, in spite of the protection. The armadillo teaches how to carry your protection with you and how to use it only when it is necessary. They have an ability to protect without causing undue harm to others. The armadillo can reflect past-life connections to the knights, or the need to develop the same qualities and characteristics that the knights possessed.

The armadillo links those with it as a totem to other animals—including those which prey upon it, and these should be examined as well. The armadillo is often preyed upon by big cats and coyotes. They will often flip them over to expose the underside. The armadillo also will sometimes bask in the sun during cold periods. They tend to fall asleep at such times, on their backs with their undersides exposed. They are thus more vulnerable. Along health lines, the armadillo teaches those with this totem to be extra cautious in dress and covering during times of cold, or there will be a greater susceptibility to illness. Again there is the issue of protecting against exposure to certain climates.

The spotted skunk and the burrowing owl benefit from the armadillo. Both will make their homes in abandoned armadillo dens. It is not unusual to find that an individual with an armadillo totem will have friends who have skunk and owl totems also. There is a positive relationship. The Aztecs called the armadillo "rabbit turtle." The qualities of both are somewhat embodied by the armadillo—especially in its appearance. An armadillo as a totem can also reflect a past-life connection to the ancient Aztecs.

The primary diet of armadillos is invertebrate insects. In one summer it can consume 200 pounds of insects. Ants and earthworms are a large part of its diet, and the qualities of them should be studied as well.

When threatened, the armadillo will roll itself up into a ball, covering all its vulnerable areas. If an armadillo has strolled into your life, you should be asking yourself some questions. Are you not protecting yourself as you should? Are others around you needing protection? Are you being too sensitive and protecting yourself from attacks that are not there? Are you imagining attacks or being too sensitive to the energies of others?

The armadillo has a tremendously powerful sense of smell. It can smell insects six inches underground. This strong sense of smell has ties to higher forms of discrimination and psychological stimulations. Anyone with the armadillo as a totem would do well to work with aromatherapy and the development of their own sense of smell. Do things just not smell right? Do people or situations smell fishy? Learning to trust what you smell is part of what the armadillo can teach.

The sense of smell also has ties to the sexual energies. It is a strong stimulant to the sex drive. The armadillos only pair for mating, and then they go on their way. The usual gestation period is around eight to nine months, just as with humans. Unlike humans though, if distressed, the armadillo can delay giving birth for up to two and a half years.

This reflects much about the energy that comes with an armadillo totem. It usually signals that the opportunity for a new birth is coming within the next 8-9 months. It will be important, though, not to roll ourselves up and hide from the opportunity for fear we may be vulnerable. On the other hand, if we are too worried and stressed to act upon the opportunity, its movement can be delayed for up to two years or more. Armadillo can show you how to adjust your rhythms so that what you wish to create will occur at the safest time.

The armadillo can move fast if it needs to. It is also a good swimmer. It will swallow air and inflate its intestines until they are able to float. Other times they will hold their breath and walk on the bottom of streams and other natural water sources. They can hold their breath for up to six minutes.

This and their ability to dig reflects an the ability of the armadillo to teach you how to move from one dimension to another. It can teach you how to move through all elements. This can be linked to specific forms of mediumship, in which the individual is able to move consciously into new dimensions and stay protected all the while. It hints of an ability to explore and walk the threads of life and death, and work with the spirits of the dead.

It also hints of the ability to explore the emotional sides not often exposed, even though individuals with this totem may be reluctant to do so. If in the position, they can explore many emotional and mundane aspects of themselves. THey often try to keep these more sensitive aspects of themselves protected and hidden. It will be important for those with this totem to learn when to expose these more subtle sides and when to cover them up. This is part of what armadillo teaches.

Oftentimes individuals who are extremely empathic will have an armadillo as a totem. An empathic individual's body will become a barometer for whatever is experienced. If around someone with an ache or pain, empathics will experience it within their own body as if it is their own ache or pain. This can lead to an actual manifestation of the problem. Empathic individuals are very susceptible to outside influences—physical, emotional, mental, and spiritual. This heightened sensitivity needs to be controlled and balanced. Armadillo can teach you how to do this or show you how to help others in this position.

ASS

KEYNOTE: *Wisdom and Humility*
CYCLE OF POWER: *Year-round*

Although most people associate the ass with negative qualities, it has not always had this association. As with many animals, it has had mixed significance throughout the ages. It has been associated with the planet Saturn in astrology, probably because Saturn is the strict teacher. It makes sure we learn our lessons. Thus we have threads of the ass's association with stubbornness.

In Chaldea, the goddess of death was pictured on an ass. Thus it was also a symbol of death, and, of course, the life after. Its image has been found in Palatine in mock crucifix in which Jesus was depicted with the head of an ass. It was also found in medieval emblems and art as a symbol of patience and humility.

In Christian gnosticism, it is aligned with the mysteries associated with the triumphal entry into Jerusalem—or that point in New Testament scripture we now associate with Palm Sunday. In the scripture Jesus is depicted riding upon a white ass as palm leaves are waved in celebration.

This kind of processional is symbolic of the path of the candidate who is victorious in transfiguring his/her life. It represents the outer recognition that comes to those who express the higher, inner potentials. The white ass is symbolic of the awakened soul wisdom and the palms are the symbols of the victorious attainment.

If an ass is a totem for you, you should be asking yourself some basic questions. Are you expressing your own wisdom or following the wisdom of others? Are you displaying the appropriate humility for what you have accomplished? Are others around you doing so? Are you recognizing and acknowledging what you have accomplished so far on your life path? Are others around you not recognizing or acknowledging their own accomplishments appropriately?

The ass is the promise of awakening wisdom and the approach of new opportunities of even greater work. Don't be stubborn and refuse to move with the flow. Don't hold on only to what you have done to this point. Remember that it is not the goal but the path to that goal. Do not become content and complacent, for the ass promises even higher wisdom and greater opportunities.

BADGER

KEYNOTE: *Bold Self-Expression and Reliance—Keeper of Stories*
CYCLE OF POWER: *Late Spring*

The badger is the giant of the weasel family. Those with this totem should study the weasel as well. The badger is gray, black, and buff, with a white stripe from the nose to the back of its head. This in itself is very symbolic of how open it is, the keeper of much light and knowledge of other animals and the Earth.

The badger may look fat, but it is muscular and powerful. Its outer skin is loose, so it is difficult for bites from other animals to injure it. Its own jaws are exceedingly strong. The jaws are the symbols of powerful expression. This ties the badger to the mysteries of the "word"—particularly the magic of storytelling.

"I would ask you to remember only this one thing," said Badger. "The stories people tell have a way of taking care of them. If stories come to you, care for them. And learn to give them away where they are needed. Sometimes a person needs a story more than food to stay alive. That is why we put these stories in each other's memory. This is how people care for themselves."[3]

The badger is a remarkable digger. Fast and quick , it can dig beneath surfaces easily. It can outdig a gopher or a mole, moving rapidly through the Earth. This ties them to all earth spirits and gnomes of lore. It also hints at the ability to see beneath the surface of all things and people. It lives in an underground complex of burrows that are called "earths." It has several living chambers, along with latrine and storage chambers. These earths hint at the stories beneath the outer, the inner places, and homes of the outer world.

The badger is active both day and night. It is a carnivorous animal, living primarily on rodents such as rabbits, gophers, mice, squirrels, and other underground dwellers. It eats many cropconsuming rodents. It will often store the animals or parts of them in its earths. Because of this it can be thought of as the keeper of the stories of other animals.

It is basically an unsociable animal. It does not "relate" well with others— even its own kind. This might be why stories are its symbolic means of communication. It is often easier for those with badger medicine to relate through stories than to have to do it directly.

The young badgers, usually two to three, are born in May or June. The family always separates in the fall, when the young and the father move to find their own homes. Sometimes the father will help with the raising of the young, but as a whole the badgers are loners and solitary. They are comfortable within themselves and are very self-reliant. They can teach this or help those with this totem to teach it to others.

The dachshund (badger dog) was bred specifically to hunt and dig after the badgers and to chase them out of the burrows. Dachshund owners probably have some badger medicine or can easily connect to it.

Because it is such a powerful digger, the badger has knowledge of things beneath the earth. This includes minerals, roots, and other plants and herbs. This makes the badger also a dynamic healer. Sometimes the badger healer is overly aggressive, but the technique is usually effective. Badger can teach the long forgotten knowledge of roots and their mystical and healing powers.

The badger is bold and ferocious, and it never surrenders. If a badger has come into your life, you should do some examination. Are you or those around you not digging deep enough? It may indicate a need to get beneath the surface. It may reflect a time of greater connection to the earth and its animal spirits. It may be telling you to draw upon the stories that intrigued you and held you fast during childhood. They may be symbolic of things going on or about to go on in your current life. Whenever badger shows up, there will be opportunities to develop self-expression and reliance. It speaks of a time to begin to tell a new story about yourself and your life.

---

3 Excerpts from *Crow and Weasel* by Barry Lopez. Text copyright © 1990 by Barry Holstun Lopez. Reprinted by permission of North Point Press, a division of Farrar, Straus, and Giroux, Inc.

BAT

KEYNOTE: *Transition and Initiation*
CYCLE OF POWER: *Nighttime*

The bat is one of the most misunderstood mammals. Modern depictions in movies and television have given it a sinister reputation, but it plays an important role in Nature and as a symbol in the totem traditions. Although more modern lore places the bat in cohorts with the devil, with its dragon-like wings, in more ancient times it was a powerful symbol.

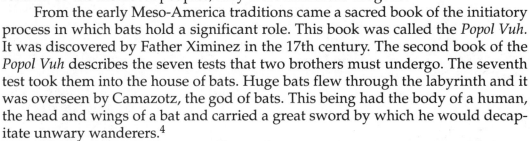

In Babylonia bats represented the souls of the dead. In China they were symbols for happiness and long life. To the ancient Mayans, they are symbols of initiation and rebirth. To the medieval peoples, they were miniature dragons.

From the early Meso-America traditions came a sacred book of the initiatory process in which bats hold a significant role. This book was called the *Popol Vuh*. It was discovered by Father Ximinez in the 17th century. The second book of the *Popol Vuh* describes the seven tests that two brothers must undergo. The seventh test took them into the house of bats. Huge bats flew through the labyrinth and it was overseen by Camazotz, the god of bats. This being had the body of a human, the head and wings of a bat and carried a great sword by which he would decapitate unwary wanderers.[4]

This powerfully symbolic story and imagery reflects the process of transition—part human and part bat (animal). It implies a loss of one's faculties if unwary about the changes. It also holds the promise of rebirth and coming out of the darkness.

The authors, Jamie Sams and David Carson, refer to the bat as reflecting the traditional shaman's death—the breaking down of the former self through intense tests.[5] It is a facing of your greatest fears—that it is time to die to some aspect of your life that is no longer suitable for you.

Most people fear transitions, holding onto a "better the devil you know than the one you don't" kind of attitude. If a bat has flown into your life, then it is time to face your fears and prepare for change. You are being challenged to let go of the old and create the new.

For many, change is always distressing. When the bat comes into your life, you may see some part of your life begin to go from bad to worse. That which worked before may no longer. This is not negative though! And it will only be upsetting to the degree we are emotionally attached to the old way of life or to the degree we focus on the past rather than the infinite possibilities of the future.

---

4   Hall, Manly P. *The Secret Teachings of the Ages* (Los Angeles: The Philosophic Research Society, Inc., 1977), pp. CXCIV–CXCVI.
5   Sams, Jamie and Carson, David. *Medicine Cards* (Santa Fe: Bear and Company, 1988), pp. 205–207.

Changes and transformations are blessings. They are not triggered from without but from within; and the world is our mirror. As we change, even within our consciousness, everything reflected within the world also begins to change. To understand and enjoy the blessing of change, begin by taking or renewing responsibility for your life. This means opening to the power within which will override all fears.

Look beyond the immediate and limited circumstances. There can be no death without there also being rebirth. Everything reflects the divine. Remember that fear and death is a choosing to block or go against the Divine energies that are yours by right of inheritance. Rebirth and life are found by choosing to follow the flow within. The choice is always ours. Remember that each time you trust your own inner promptings, you chase the fears within the dark corners of your mind away. What you choose to do today will have repercussions for years down the road. Do you want those repercussions to be positive or negative?

Though small in stature, the bat is a powerful symbol. Its medicine is strong and can even be traumatic. It is a nocturnal animal, and the night was often considered the home of fears. Home fires and lights are often used to chase back the night and the fears rather than facing them and transmuting them. Are you avoiding facing something that is inevitable?

Sometimes bats are a symbol of facing our fears. They have very sharp, needle-like teeth. They can also be carriers of rabies. Rabies is an infectious disease of the blood, created by a virus. It was often associated with madness. Fears that are allowed to spread, uninhibited, will eventually permeate our system and can create a kind of madness within our lives. Bats can reflect a need to face our fears. The imaginings that result from fears that are incubating are often much worse than the actual facing of the fears, themselves. What are you most fearing right now?

From a naturalistic view, bats are not sinister. They play a very valuable role in nature. They feed on insects and are essential to the pollination of many plants. Their waste product, guano, is also used as a valuable fertilizer. This hints that every aspect of facing our fears will have value to us, no matter how messy it may seem to be. It holds the promise of empowerment.

The bat is also the only flying mammal. Its tremendously elongated finger bones support the wings which are made of a tough leathery skin. Its flight seems fluttery and jerky, but it is flight nonetheless. All flight implies a rising above. You may wish to study the general symbolism of flight as described in part two of this book.

Because humans are mammals as well, the bat is an even more important symbol for us. It becomes a symbol of promise amidst the sometimes chaotic energies of change. It reflects the ability to move to new heights with the transitions. Yes, our own flights may seem fluttery and jerky, but we will be able to fly.

We will not only be able to fly as a result of the changes, but we will be able to see the world from an entirely new perspective. Bats sleep with their heads down. This posture has always reminded me of the Hanged Man card in the tarot deck. This card reflects the piercing of new barriers and the opening to higher wisdom. It symbolizes a new truth being awakened. It also implies great strength and stamina to handle the ordeals that may beset you as you open to new consciousness. Its message contains the promise of new horizons and unexpected views about to manifest. Meditation upon this card would be most beneficial for those with a bat as a totem.

The bat is actually a sociable animal. It lives in flocks, and thus its appearance usually reflects either a need for more sociability or increased opportunity with greater numbers of people.

The bat has a medicine which awakens great auditory perception. The idea of "blind as a bat" is wrong. Bats are not blind, and their eyes are large and developed. They can easily navigate by sight in lighted situations.

On the other hand, they are expert at maneuvering through the dark. They have a form of sonar in their nose that gives them perfect navigation. Their ability at echo-location enables them to perform amazing flying feats even within the flock. They rarely, if ever, collide. This sonar and echo-location can be linked metaphysically to the gift of clairaudience or clear-hearing. It awakens the ability to hear spirit.

Those with a bat as a totem will also find that they have an increasing ability to discern the hidden messages and implications of other people's words. Listen as much to what is not being said. Trust your instincts. The nose is the organ of discrimination, and with its sonar located in its nose, the bat reflects the ability to discriminate and discern the truth in other people's words.

The bat is powerful medicine. It can be trying, but it always indicates initiation—A new beginning that brings promise and power after the changes.

BEAR

KEYNOTE: *Awakening the Power of the Unconscious*

CYCLE OF POWER: *Spring and Summer*

The bear is a powerful symbol and image in both myth and lore. Stories abound of individuals turned into bears, bears into humans, and bears as gods. It has stirred imagination so much that even a constellation was named for it— Ursus Major, The Great Bear. Seven stars of this constellation are probably the most easily recognized in the northern hemisphere. These seven stars form The Big Dipper, and they have links to the seven great rays of light of the Divine.

The bear has lunar symbology as well, giving it ties to the subconscious and even unconscious mind. It was an animal associated with the goddess Diana, a goddess of the moon. It is also a symbol for alchemy, the nigredo of prime matter. It relates to all initial stages and primal instincts.

Like birds, the bear is often considered among Native American peoples as kin to humans because, like birds, it can stand and walk upon two legs. For many, the bear and the wolf are the last true symbols of the primal, natural world, and many ecologists believe that how humans respond and protect their lands and their future will be the most honest depiction of how serious humanity is about preservation of our environment and the natural resources within it.

The bear is the largest of the carnivores, but it will eat almost anything. It is omnivorous, eating both plants, fruits, and meat. It actually eats less meat than many smaller carnivores, such as the fox.

Contrary to popular belief, bears do not truly hibernate. They do live to a great degree on their stored-up fat. The body temperature will drop a little (around 13 degrees) and the breathing rate can be cut in half. The depth of their sleep depends greatly upon the amount of fat stored. This reflects the bear's ability to teach those with it as a totem how to go within to find the resources necessary for survival. The bear can teach you to draw upon all of your inner stores of energy and essence even those which have never been tapped or accessed. Meditating and working with bear will help you to go within your soul's den your inner sanctum—to find your answers.

During the winter sleep the black bear's kidneys shut down completely, and scientists are studying this activity, hoping it will provide clues to more successful kidney transplants. Physicians would love to find a way to duplicate this in humans so that diseased kidneys would have time to heal. This is part of what bear medicine is about.

The kidneys serve a vital function in the body, excreting urine, and also filtering the blood plasma. Metaphysically, the kidneys are symbols of discernment and discrimination. If bear has shown up in your life, ask yourself some important questions. Is your judgment off? How about those around you? Are you not recognizing what is beneficial in your life? Are you not seeing the core of good deep within all situations? Are you being too critical of yourself or others? Are you wearing rose-colored glasses? Bear medicine can teach you to go deep within so that you can make your choices and decisions from a position of power.

All bears are astonishingly swift. The black bear and grizzly can reach running speeds of 35-40 mph for short distances. All bears, including the polar bear, can climb. Only the size of the tree will discourage the climbing. Bears are often associated with trees. Nature programs love to photograph bear cubs high up in trees or adults scratching themselves against them. There are even "bear trees," trees marked with claws as signposts along the well-worn and traveled path of a particular bear.

The tree is a powerful and ancient symbol, just like the bear. It is a natural antenna, linking the Heavens and the Earth. Different trees do have different meanings, as was discussed briefly in an earlier part of this text, but in general, it represents knowledge. It is a symbol of fertility, of things that grow.

As bear teaches you to go in and awaken the potentials inherent, the tree serves as a reminder that we must bring what we awaken out into the world and apply it—make our marks with it. Anyone with a bear totem should keep the cub in themselves alive and occasionally climb trees—if only to get a clear perspective.

For those with a bear as a totem, it is important not to hide away and try to hibernate all year-round. You must come out of the den. This is even reflected in the birthing process of bears. Female bears give birth during their heavy sleep, semi-hibernation stages. Usually two cubs are born, sometimes three. They are born helpless and semi-conscious. The cubs nurse in the safety and warmth of the den throughout the winter.

As spring approaches, the mother and her cubs will emerge. The cubs will have become strong enough to follow their mother. This is tremendously significant for those working with a bear totem. It often reflects a need to go deep within yourself, to have periods in your life when you can be more reclusive. During these times, you will be able to go within yourself and even give birth to two or three ideas or projects. They can be nursed through the winter, and then as spring approaches, emerge with your babies to help them grow.

Those who have a bear as a totem will find this cycle of semi-hibernation and reclusiveness during the winter very natural. They will also find that with the spring will come opportunities to act more assertively in regard to that which has been nursed through the winter months. Bear people should be patient though, as the cubs will usually stay with the mother for up to two years. This can reflect that those project you nursed may not come to full fruition until the second year of the cycle.

Although distantly related to the dog, the bear is a closer relative to the raccoon. There are a variety of bears. The most common bear is the black bear. This is a kind of misnomer, as not all black bears are black. They can be brown, cinnamon, and various combinations. They are very playful, both as adults and as young cubs. This is a reminder for those with this bear as a totem.

The largest bear is the Alaska brown bear. A relative of the grizzly, the brown bear is relatively solitary. The grizzly has long been known for its strength and ferocity. Although it can be quite fierce, it is not naturally aggressive.

By far the most outstanding hunter of the bear family is the polar bear. This white bear has no fear. It is the most carnivorous and aggressive of all the bears. It is at the top of the food chain and has no enemy other than humans. It feeds to a great degree on seals, and those with this totem should study the qualities of the seal as well.

All bears have a great fondness for honey. Honey is the natural sweetness of life. It is usually found in the hives, located in trees, again reflecting a connection between bears and trees. It is a reminder for those with this totem to go within to awaken the power, but only by bringing it out into the open and applying it will the honey of life be tasted.

BEAVER

KEYNOTE: *The Building of Dreams*

CYCLE OF POWER: *Dusk and Night*

The beaver is the largest of the rodent family. It disappeared from Europe and Asia, and is found now only in this hemisphere. It is adapted for life in the water. It has webbed feet, and its tail serves as a rudder. It is an excellent swimmer, and it can stay submerged for up to 15 minutes at a time. It has extra-large lungs, and it can take in more oxygen and tolerate more carbon dioxide than humans. Because of this, beaver can also teach lessons about breath and its control for the greatest health and effectiveness.

Water has long been associated with emotions and with dreams. One of the most common dreams the average person has is to have a home and a family. This dream is embodied by the beaver. It lives in a close-knit family, and beavers will mate for as long as both are alive. If beaver has appeared in your life, it can reflect the opportunity to build upon your dreams.

Beavers are also master home builders. They perform magnificent feats of engineering in the felling of trees and the building of dams. Their homes can have intricate canals, and they keep their dams in constant repair. This magnificent skill at building may even link those with this totem to the ancient and mystical Masons. A study of the Masonic tradition may open many doors.

A beaver lives less than twelve years in the wild. Its most noticeable characteristics are its large incisor teeth and its tail. One of the reasons that the beaver is always chewing is that its teeth continue growing until it dies. Without the chewing, the teeth would become too large, and it would be unable to eat. If a beaver loses a tooth, it will usually die. For those with the beaver as a totem, proper dental hygiene and care will be essential.

Tree bark is the beaver's favorite diet, and poplar and aspen are its favorite trees. A study of the qualities of these trees may provide you with even more insight. The actual tree felling is accomplished through teamwork. One beaver rests and keeps watch, while another chews. The trees are often stored in the dam to provide food throughout the winter.

Although some see the beaver as a pest, it actually serves wonderful benefits. Its felling of trees enables brush to grow, thus providing food for deer and moose. Its dams even help make farmlands for humans. A beaver pond will fill with silt. When the beaver leaves it, eventually the dam in that pond will break. The water drains off, leaving a flat pocket of rich soil.

If beaver has come into your life, ask yourself some important questions. Have you been neglecting your most basic dreams? Are your dreams in need of

253

some repair work? Are you or others around you becoming too lost in their dreams—always dreaming and never acting upon them? Is your home in need of repair?

Remember that the beaver reminds us that we have to act on our dreams to make them a reality. When it shows up, it is a time for action. Beaver can show you how to construct wonderful dreams.

BISON (BUFFALO)

KEYNOTE: *Manifesting Abundance Through Right Action and Right Prayer*

CYCLE OF POWER: *Year-round*

The American buffalo is actually a bison. Buffalo is a name that applies to the animals of Asia and Africa. To the plains Indians it was a symbol of sacred life and abundance.

Once a beautiful woman dressed in white buffalo fur appeared. She brought to the Lakota the sacred pipe which showed how all things were connected. She taught the men and the women many mysteries of the earth, and she taught them how to pray and follow the proper path upon the earth. She showed them how to pray for and bring forth abundance. As she left, she rolled upon the earth and became a white buffalo calf and then disappeared over the horizon. No sooner had she disappeared and great herds of buffalo were seen all around the Indian camps.

The bison or American buffalo is a symbol of abundance and the manifestation. Part of what White Buffalo Woman taught to the Lakota is that they did not have to struggle to survive if the right action was joined with the right prayer. By uniting the mundane and the divine appropriately, all that would be needed would be available. This same idea is embodied even within Biblical scripture: "The Lord helps those who help themselves."

The bison is a large animal and can weigh up to a ton and a half. It has a massive head, humped shoulders, and an almost exaggerated appearance because of its shaggy fur. Humps are often symbolic of stored forces—reservoirs that can be tapped. In the case of the bison, it reflects the abundance that is available if we know how to tap it. The fact that the hump occurs at the shoulder level, implies that we must incorporate our own efforts. Shoulders are symbols of the ability to embrace and hold life. Upon shoulders are carried either our burdens or our rewards. The humped area on the shoulders implies the need for our own efforts.

The massive head also implies the need to combine our efforts with the Divine. The head is the upper region. It is a symbol of the heavens and the divine, the higher faculties. In the case of the bison, both aspects are amplified. Both the mundane and the spiritual is necessary for manifesting what we are seeking.

The bison is very unpredictable and can be dangerous. This can serve as warning about not keeping yourself well grounded as you begin to work toward greater abundance in some area of your life. It is a four-footed animal, and thus implies groundedness.

The bison also usually follows the easiest path. When we join the right action with the right prayers, the path is not difficult. We do not have to bull our way through. The path opens and flows easily. The bison will use its head to bowl and push with on occasion, but it is usually during the winter. Its massive head is used to clear patches of snow so that it can feed upon the grasses beneath.

If a bison has shown up for you, it may indicate opportunities to manifest or move toward manifesting abundance in some area of your life. This has hidden within it several cautionary notes, though. This is not a time to push or force. Follow the easiest path.

The appearance of the buffalo also implies that the law of synchronicity is operating within your life at the moment. Things will happen in the time, manner and means that is best for us if we allow it. This doesn't mean we should sit back and do nothing, but rather that we should do what we have to do and then let the events take their natural course.

It's nice to get from point A to point B, and there are ways of forcing it. If you force it though, you may end up at the destination at a time when there is nothing to be gained. If you allow the natural flow to take you, you still end up at your destination, at an advantageous time, and you usually get some nice side trips along the way. Bison teaches us how to work with that natural rhythm.

If bison has shown up in your life, look for opportunities for abundance and increase. Also ask yourself some important questions. Are you honoring that which you seek? Are you remembering that the divine is essential to all things in the physical? Are you giving honor to yourself and to the efforts of others within your life? Do you show gratitude for what you already have? The quickest way to stop the flow of abundance is by failing to honor that which has already come to you.

BOBCAT

KEYNOTE: *Silence and Secrets*

CYCLE OF POWER: *Late Winter and Spring*

The bobcat is sometimes called the wild cat. It has a short, bobbed tail from which it gets its name. It also has tufts of hair on its ears and sideburns. It is often confused with a lynx which is usually grayer and always larger. In fact, the bobcat is sometimes called the red lynx.

The bobcat is a solitary animal, and those with it as a totem often find themselves in the same situation. Coming to terms with that—learning to be

alone without being lonely, is part of what the bobcat teaches. The females often have a small territory, but males can be quite nomadic, overlapping the territories of five to six females. Mating is usually in late winter, and then the males and females go their separate ways.

Because it is solitary, those who have the bobcat as a totem will find that their friends often share secrets. It is important for anyone with a bobcat or lynx as a totem not to break confidences. This will always have strong repercussions and will usually be found out quickly.

The tail is very symbolic. Tails have a long connection symbolically with the sexual energies and the kundalini. The tail or the tail end is the seat of the life force. The tip of the bobcat's tail is black, and its underneath side is white. This reflects the ability to turn on and off the creative forces as is needed. This is part of the medicine of the bobcat.

It also ties the bobcat to some forms of sexual magic and mysticism. Using the cloak of darkness and secrecy, the bobcat can teach how to project and utilize the life force in silent but powerful ways. The bobcat's magic is always most powerful when others do not know of it. Speaking of it dissipates its power. For those with this totem, learning when to speak, how much, and to whom will be essential. Bobcat people must be cautious about what they share with others. Things will have a tendency to be distorted or blown out of proportion. What may be white to the bobcat person can be mistakenly perceived as black, and vice versa.

The bobcat's keen eyesight, sensitive whiskers, and tufted ears make it a superb nighttime hunter. Those with a bobcat as a totem will be most effective at night. These characteristics have ties to most of the predominant psychic arts. Bobcat's eyes will enable them to see what others may try and hide or cloak. Their sensitive whiskers give them the ability for a form of psychometry, holding an object against the face will enable the individual to pick up impressions. The tufted ears also have connections to clairaudience and to hearing what is not being said.

An individual with a bobcat totem may find others uncomfortable around them. They will know that you can see what they are not showing and hear what they are not saying. This ability can make someone a dynamic counselor or a dynamic manipulator. If a bobcat has shown up in your life, look for that which is hidden. Not all is as it appears to be. Trust your own senses. If it doesn't feel right, trust it—even if there is no logical reason to think otherwise.

The bobcat can see very well in the dark, and its hearing is acute. Oftentimes, bobcat people choose to be solitary because they hear, see, and feel so much hidden garbage about people around them that they begin to believe all humans are like this. Bobcat people should never become completely reclusive. Meditation on the Hermit card in the tarot deck will help you to know when to be alone and when to be social. It will help you to attune to the energies of this animal.

The bobcat is found all over the United States, but it is endangered. It makes its home under rocky ledges and in piles of rocks, and the symbolic significance of this should be studied as well. (Refer to chapter five.) Although not very fast, it can leap six to eight feet. Its primary food is rabbits and woodchucks, and the significance of these should be studied as well to fully understand the power of the bobcat.

The young are born in the spring, and up to four bobkittens can comprise a litter. The mother starts training early. By about seven months the young have learned to hunt alone and around nine months they have left the family to search out territory of their own.

For those to whom bobcat comes, expect some new learning formal or informal. In either case, within 7-10 months you will have what you need. Bobcat people usually learn quickly and thoroughly. If you are a parent who has a bobcat totem, begin the training of your children early. Trust your own instincts on how best to do this. The children will become strong and independent.

If bobcat has come into your life ask yourself these important questions. Are you being too solitary? Do you need to look for new learning opportunities? Are you or those around you being indiscreet? Are you not trusting your inner senses? Are you allowing others' outside appearances to sway you? Whenever bobcat is around, it will teach you that there is true power and strength through silence.

BULL

KEYNOTE: *Fertility*
CYCLE OF POWER: *Year-round*

The bull, and its female counterpart the cow, have long been symbols of fertility. While the cow is predominantly a symbol of motherhood and nourishment through non-injury (it's an animal able to furnish food without being slaughtered), the bull is an animal which brought nourishment through slaughtering and so came to be known as an animal symbolizing fertility through sacrifice.

While the cow usually embodied lunar aspects, and goddesses sometimes wore horns of the cow, the bull was a symbol of the sun. To the Assyrians, the bull was born of the sun. The Hindu divine being Indra is often depicted riding on a bull, while Brahma is depicted upon a cow.

Bull worship was a part of Egypt and Greece. The Egyptian god Osiris is often depicted with the head of a bull. In Roman and Greek mythology are several powerful legends of the bull. Probably the most familiar is the tale of the Minotaur. A study of the myth and lore of the bull may provide insight into past lives for those with this totem.

The bull is, of course, associated with the astrological sign of Taurus, an earth sign. It is a sign that has to do with possessions. It is a sign that has links to making the mundane and earthy more fertile. The sign of Taurus should be studied for further insight.

The bull is masculine and implies a fertilizing of the Earth, a feminine planet in traditional astrology. In the bull then we have the union of the male and female. The bull is sometimes depicted as lunar (female) and sometimes as solar (male). The horns of the bull resemble the lunar crescent, giving it the link with the feminine. Anytime the male and female come together there is opportunity for fertility.

If a bull has shown up as your totem, you should ask yourself some important questions. Are you being as productive as you can? Do you need to sow some new seeds? Are you being stubborn and rigid? Do you or those around you need to become more sensitive? Are you rushing when you should be allowing things to become fertile in their own time? Are you or those around you insecure?

The bull can help you to understand and work with the mundane aspects of fertility and the relationships necessary for it. it will teach stability without stubbornness. The bull can help you to assert your feminine energies with the greatest success.

CAT

KEYNOTE: *Mystery, Magic, and Independence*
CYCLE OF POWER: *Nighttime*

Although a domesticated animal, it would be unjust not to at least touch upon the energies and essence of the cat as a totem. Many of the larger cats are examined in this dictionary separately, but cats in general—wild or domestic—have certain qualities in common.

In myth and lore, the cat predominates. In ancient Egypt they held a position of special privilege. The goddess Bast was often depicted either as a cat or with a cat's head. In Scandinavian lore, the cat was associated with the goddess of fertility, Freyja. In the Hindu tradition Shasthi, the goddess of childbirth, is depicted riding upon a cat. Cats appear frequently in the tales of the Brothers Grimm and many other folk stories from around the world.

To cats have been attributed a wide variety of traits—often contradictory. Curiosity, nine lives, independence, cleverness, unpredictability, and healing are but a few. A witch's pet cat was usually regarded as her familiar—a spirit in the form of a cat. It was often believed that witches could take the form of cats.

Cats are at home after dark, and yet most humans want them to be traditional pets during the day. When they do not respond in this manner, they are accredited with independence and unsociability. Because the dark is the home of fears and those things humans do not want to see and can't see, the cat has come to be associated with magic and mystery. The truth is that cats have more rods in the retinas of their eyes, which enhances light perception. It enables them to see effectively in the dark. The traditional prey of a cat is the mouse, but it is by no means limited to it. Cats still effectively hunt birds and rabbits.

The traditional enemy of the cat is the dog, but this is not its only enemy. For anyone with a cat totem, the study of the qualities of the mouse and the dog will be beneficial for helping you to understand the magic and the balance of energies with the cat.

Examine the colors, the character, the behaviors of your own cat. Everything about it will be significant. Many books exist on the lore and the character of cats. Whether domesticated or wild, anytime a cat becomes predominant, look for magic and mystery to come alive.

COUGAR

KEYNOTE: *Coming into Your Own Power*
CYCLE OF POWER: *Year-round*

Throughout its history the cougar has been known by many names: puma, mountain lion, cougar, catamount, mountain screamer, sneak cat, panther, and more. Cougar, panther, and puma are the most common. Cougar is its South American name and the name puma comes from the Quechua language spoken by the Incas. The Florida panther is part of the same family, but it should not be confused with the panther of the leopard/jaguar family as is described later. In your studies of the cougar, is there a name which draws you more? This may provide some insight into past life connections with this totem.[6]

The early colonists mistook the cougar for a female lion. "Dutch traders in New Amsterdam (now New York City) asked the Indians why they only brought in skins of the female. The Indians relishing a joke on the ignorant white traders told them that all of the males lived in a distant range of mountains and were so fierce that no one dared hunt them. Thus the name mountain lion came to be."[7]

The cougar is the second largest cat in the western hemisphere. It is also one of the fastest and most powerful of animals, but it tires quickly. It is powerful enough to kill with its bite or its claws. It can leap over forty feet.

It is a stealthy hunter, and many of the qualities of the panther described later hold true for the cougar. If cougar has shown up in your life, it is time to learn about power. Test your own. Most young cougars learn how to use their power through trial and error. It strengthens them and hones their skills. When cougar shows up as totem, much of the trial has been worked through. Now it is time to assert.

---

6   Limburg, Peter. *What's in the Name of Wild Animals* (New York: Bobbs-Merrill Comp., 1975), p. 140.
7   Ibid, p. 140.

People may not like your asserting. They may try and keep you in the category they have always kept you. You can choose to remain so, or you can stretch your muscles and show your capabilities. Those with cougar medicine fall easily under attack, especially by those who have grown comfortable with the status quo and do not wish to truly see you grow. Remember that there will always be some who will not wish to see you come into your own power or will ever acknowledge that you have. If cougar has shown up, there is a choice to be made, and it should be made quickly and strongly. A cougar leaps at its opportunities.

The deer is the cougar's favorite prey. Anyone with a cougar totem should also study the deer. One of the qualities embodied by the deer is gentleness. For those with the cougar totem, remember that power can be asserted gently. There is strength and power in gentleness. It is also a reminder that there are times to be gentle and there are times to assert your power forcefully. This is part of what the cougar teaches.

The cougar also has connections to the porcupine, and its qualities should be studied as well. The cougar is one of the few animals capable of killing a porcupine without harm to itself. In fact, about one third of its food can be made up of porcupine. The cougar has developed the ability to flip the porcupine upon its back, exposing its vulnerable underside.

The cougar teaches decisiveness in the use of personal power. When it attacks, it does not hesitate. When threatened, it goes for the most vulnerable place. The cougar can teach you how to bring out your power and fill your heart with it in a manner that will enable you to take charge of your life. You will find you can use it to defend yourself or to attack—with equal effectiveness. Cougar teaches you how to take charge of your life and your circumstances most effectively.

COYOTE

KEYNOTE: *Wisdom and Folly*
CYCLE OF POWER: *Year-round*

The coyote is an amazingly adaptive animal, and the Native American lore about this animal is rich and plentiful. It is the creator and the jokester. Much magic has been associated with the coyote, but the magic does not always work. Even in its not working, it serves a purpose. There is always hidden wisdom where the coyote is concerned.

In many ways the coyote is to the plains Indians what the raven is to the people of the Northwest—creator, teacher, and keeper of magic. Both are playful and love to have fun. Both are skillful, but often look for ways to do things that will not involve the use of their own skill. They often look for short cuts. Both remind us not to become too serious, and both remind us that anything is possible.

Oftentimes in many of the tales, the coyote makes things more complicated than they need to be. If coyote has shown up as a totem, you may wish to ask yourself some questions. Are you or those around you being too serious? Have you forgotten that play time is essential to health? Are you complicating what is really simple in some area of your life? Is someone playing tricks on you?

The coyote teaches the balance of wisdom and folly and how they both go hand in hand. The image of the wise fool has been used in the lore of many societies. This is the individual who seems to be a simpleton and yet the words and actions have a much greater wisdom than is initially recognized. Are you not seeing the wisdom of your life and its events? The coyote will help you.

In the tarot deck is The Fool card. This card is good for anyone with a coyote totem to meditate upon. Its energies are tied to simplicity and trust. It is the card for developing poise in the chaos of life. It stimulates and renews innocence, and it reawakens a childlike wisdom in response to the world. It is the card that reminds us that true teachers of wisdom have a wonderful sense of humor. Through the coyote, we learn to become again as little children with a reawakening of the intellect, creativity, the artistic mind and all of the intuitive faculties.

Although often seen as a pest to be eliminated by many groups, it has managed to extend its range. It is found in every part of the country. It has been able to do so because it has used its keen intelligence and adaptive ability. The coyote used to be most active hunting at dawn and dusk. Today it is most active at night. This is done to avoid other hunters.

The coyote will often use cooperative hunting techniques. They have a well-organized system of running down smaller prey. The chase occurs in relays. While one coyote rests, another gives chase. This kind of cooperation hints at the energies that coyote can bring to your life—an ability to stimulate cooperation to accomplish important tasks in the most efficient manner. Sometimes the coyote has even teamed up with badgers and they have hunted together, reflecting the coyote's ability to adapt to the situation.

The howl is one of the coyote's most significant qualities. It is generally accepted to be primarily a social gesture. It can express loneliness, warn of danger, or call for assistance. It touches the soul of whoever hears, reminding us of our primal connections.

A coyote's den can be located anywhere. They usually prefer the side of a hill near a water source. The coyote will often return to the same den for each litter, but they rarely use the den year-round. It is a place they work out of. This same kind of pattern is common among those who have a coyote as a totem. They are most effective when they work from a place, but do not limit themselves strictly to it. It hints of the need for mental stimulation, and those with this totem require a lot of it.

Coyote's have a very close-knit family unit. They will sometimes mate for life. The father is very conscientious and participates in the care and raising of the young. Both parents train the young in hunting techniques. The male cares for the mate while she is pregnant, helping to protect and feed her. If something does happen to the mother, then the male takes over the care of the young.

The coyote is one of the most fascinating animals, and it is not easily locked into any particular category. It is filled with paradox, but at the heart of its energy is the balance of wisdom and folly that makes for a fulfilling life.

DEER

KEYNOTE: *Gentleness and Innocence—Gentle Luring to New Adventure*
CYCLE OF POWER: *Autumn and Spring*

Deer have always captured the imagination of humanity. It is one of the most successful families of mammals, native to every continent except Australia. They have been able to adapt to every sort of habitat. The white-tailed deer, the mule deer and the caribou are three that are prominent on this continent. The moose and wapiti (elk) are also part of the deer family, but they are treated separately in this work.

Each type of deer has its own special qualities and characteristics, while sharing some of the qualities of all deer in general. Caribou, for example, make long migrations twice a year, reflecting a need for those who have it as a totem to use that same pattern in their life. They begin rutting in fall and early winter, and these then are the power times. The mule deer is also a wanderer. It never follows the same path twice. This is part of its natural defense, making it less predictable to predators. Most of the information in this section will focus on deer in general, and the white-tailed specifically.

The name "deer" has several variations on its origin. These may provide clues to past lives for those with this totem. The Anglo Saxon word "deor" was a general word for animals and was often used just in the general sense. In the German language, it has its root in "tier," simply meaning wild animal also. It can also be traced to the Sanskrit "mriga," also meaning wild animal.

To many the deer is considered the most important animal ever hunted. The hunt of the deer is what transfers our civilization to the wilderness. There are many stories and myths of deer luring hunters or even kings deep into the woods until they are lost and begin to encounter new adventures. One such example is found in the tales of King Arthur and the Knights of the Round Table. Sir Gawain follows a white hart to many adventurous encounters.[8] A reading of Sir Thomas

---

8 Knowles, Sir James. *King Arthur and His Knights* (New York: Longmeadow Press, 1986), pp. 103–119.

Malory's *Le Morte D'Arthur* will also provide more examples.

The deer is also a central religious image for Buddhism. Buddha is often pictured with a deer, and legend tells how he first preached in a deer park. This image itself reasserts the meaning of the deer as representing innocence and a return to the wilderness.

The white-tailed deer is the most common in the United States. One of its most outstanding features is the set of antlers that the male develops. In other members of the deer family, i.e., reindeer and caribou, both the male and females grow them. The antlers are solid bone, and they are shed every year. Antlers grow behind the eyes and are very protective.

Each year until the age of five, the antlers grow bigger and with more points. If you encounter a deer in the wild, try to make count of the number of points. This will tell you some of the significance the deer will have for you. Remember that numerology can help define the essence.

Antlers are symbols of antennae, connections to higher forms of attunement. Deer with antlers thus can be a signal to pay attention to your inner thoughts and perceptions, as they are probably more accurate than you think.

The antlers are shed every year, and each year they grow back larger and with more points, for five years. If a deer has entered your life, look for new perceptions and degrees of perceptions to grow and expand for as much as the next five years. It can indicate that there will be opportunities to stimulate gentle new growth increasingly over the next few years.

The antlers grow behind the eyes, again hinting at the symbolism of heightened perception. When the antlers are shed, they are eaten by deer and rodents who gnaw on them to assimilate the calcium.

One to two young are born. Fawns are born a color that protects and hides them. In the first few days, they hardly move, and the mother nurses them often. This is very significant for those with this totem. Many societies taught the importance of staying with the newborn for a prescribed period of time. No visitors, no family members other than the father were allowed contact with the newborn. Even today in the Muslim religion, a mother who breastfeeds for a prescribed time makes that child her own, whether it is her biological child or not. This kind of attention and separateness enables the child to link with the family more strongly and protects the newborn from subtle outside influences.

It has always bothered me to see new mothers with week-old babies walking around busy malls and stores. I understand the desire to get out, but it reveals a lack of understanding of the subtle energy influences of the human body. Our auras or energy fields are electro-magnetic and exchanges of energy do occur with other people and places. The kind of energy a child is exposed to in a mall can have strong effects. No one has ever done any significant studies on this, and it is an area that truly needs to be explored. Until that child's energy is strong and firmly grounded, it should be protected from extraneous influences.

The deer leads us back to the primal wisdom of those old teachings. It reminds us to establish a strong healthy connection with the child before we expose it to many people and other strange energies. It is a reminder that there is a tradition that is natural and suitable for family units and for the health of the young. It is for the child's best interest.

After the first few days, the fawn can usually stand and follow its mother about. Doe fawns may stay with the mother for as much as a year. The buck or male will usually leave after a few months. The father takes no part in the rearing of the young; it is all the rule of the mother. Again this can be a reminder for us to move gently back to the traditional family unit and roles. It may indicate, if the deer has shown up in your life, that you have gotten too far away from the role that would be most beneficial for you at this time.

A deer's senses are very acute. Its vision is designed for clarity at a distance. It is especially effective at detecting contrasts and edges in dim light. Its hearing is equally acute. Anyone who has deer as a totem will find increasing ability to detect subtle movements and appearances. They will begin to hear what may not be said directly.

When deer show up in your life it is time to be gentle with yourself and others. A new innocence and freshness is about to be awakened or born. There is going to be a gentle, enticing lure of new adventures. Ask yourself important questions. Are you trying to force things? Are others? Are you being too critical and uncaring of yourself? When deer show up there is an opportunity to express gentle love that will open new doors to adventure for you.

DOGS

KEYNOTE: *Faithfulness and protection*

CYCLE OF POWER: *Year-round*

Dogs are domesticated canines. Their descendants are coyotes and wolves, and thus they should be studied as well. Dogs are companions to humans, providing faithful protection. Every dog and every breed has its own unique qualities. Many breeds were designed for specific purposes and functions. Studying the history of your breed will help you define the kind of energy specific to this totem.

Different dogs will mean different things. Herding dogs were for protection and to assist in the labors of herding domesticated farm animals. Some dogs were raised specifically for sporting activities—hunting and retrieving. Thus they may have qualities unique to them—a love of water, a need to run, etc. Some dogs are mixed, embodying qualities from a variety of breeds, reminding us that we each are unique.

Examine the qualities of your breed and the individual dog. It will reveal much about the energy associated with it. Examine the individual personality. How does it behave most of the time? What does this say about you? Earlier in the book, I gave an example of how my four dogs are unique, and how I use their behavior as messages for my self. If my dog Cheyenne, who is usually standoffish and a loner, becomes very friendly and pesters me to play, it usually indicates I need to take some time off and socialize and play a little. Our animals can tell us so much.

Most Native American tribes had dogs for protection and warnings, but dogs have held symbolic importance in other societies as well. In India the dog is a symbol of all caste systems, reflecting the small becoming great. In early Christianity it was a symbol of guardianship (as in the sheepdog), and it was even an allegory for the priest. In Greece it was a companion to and guardian of the place of the dead. It has also been a symbol of motherhood because dogs are very caring and nurturing parents.

It takes a lot to break a dog's spirit. It's ability to love, even when abused, is tremendous. It's spirit and willingness to love and to be a companion is great.

Study your dog. This will tell you more than what can be elaborated on here. If dog has come into your life as a totem, ask yourself some questions? What is this saying about your need for or lack of companionship? Are you being faithful? Are others around you? Are you showing unconditional love, or receiving it? Do you need to be more protective of your territory? Do you need to play a little more? Are you being faithful to yourself? Does your spirit need bolstering? How about those around you? Examine your territories. Dog knows its home ground, and if it has shown up, its energies and lessons will touch you personally.

The dog is a powerful totem, reflecting faithfulness and companionship. Many times it is easier for individuals to begin working with totems that are domesticated rather than the wild. (Pictured above are the author's own four dogs: Cheyenne, Akasha, Avalon, and Kodi.)

DOLPHIN (Porpoises)

KEYNOTE: *The Power of Breath and Sound*
CYCLE OF POWER: *Year-round*

The dolphin is a mammal of the sea. Many people think of dolphins and whales as being fish, but they aren't. They nurse and contain most of the qualities that separate mammals from other animal species. The largest member of the dolphin family is the killer whale which also embodies the quality of patience.

The fact that dolphins make their home in the sea is very significant. Many myths speak of how life began in the primordial waters of life. Water is the symbol of creation, passion, and even sexuality. It is the element of all life. It is a symbol of new dimensions and forces.

Dolphins can open new creation and dimensions to a great degree. Water is essential to life, but so is breath. Many techniques for breathing exist that teach how proper use of breath can be used to induce altered states and align oneself with new dimensions and life. Learning techniques of breathing can help you to become more passionate and sexual, and to heal the body, mind, and spirit. For example, tension and stress can be released by simply imitating the spouting breath that dolphin uses upon surfacing. People with lung and breathing problems can benefit greatly by aligning themselves with dolphin medicine.

Dolphin has a rhythm to its breathing and to its swimming. Learning to breathe like a dolphin can be beneficial. Breath control is the key to the power of the dolphin. When you can align yourself with dolphin through breathing you can have dolphin take you to all the places and times that existed before the great seas covered most of the world. Dolphin can lead you to underground caverns and the primordial beginnings of yourself.

Dolphin also has a sonar ability. It uses a series of clicks and responds to the feedback of those clicks as the sound reverberates. Sound, breath, and water are all considered the sources of all life. Sound is the creative life force. Sound came forth out of the womb of silence and created all things. Learning to create inner sounds so that you can create outer manifestations is part of what dolphin can teach.

Sound requires breath, and water is the unformed creative element that we can shape into any manifestation, if we know how to combine breath and sound. The sacredness of sound and breath has been taught in many societies. In the Babylonian cosmology, the gods formed by the goddess Tiamut in the waters of life did not come into being until she called them forth.

Dolphin can show you how to enter into the waters of life and then with breath and sound call forth from the waters what you most need or desire. There are breathing techniques and sounding techniques essential to manifestation. If we don't use them properly, we find that our prayers are unanswered and our affirmations manifest in an obtuse manner. Dolphin can show us how to do it properly. (You may also wish to refer to my earlier work *Sacred Sounds* for further information on this.)

The dolphin was a symbol of salvation to the early Christians. To the Greeks it was a sacred messenger of the gods, a dynamic blessed symbol of the sea. Because of this it was rarely killed. The dolphin often displays an altruistic behavior. It has a large brain and a great intelligence. Even today, rather than be wary of humans who would kill them, they enjoy the company and their curiosity draws them close.

If dolphin has shown up as a totem, ask yourself some important questions. What are your words and thoughts creating for you? If unsure, when dolphin arises, you will soon discover. Are you getting outside and enjoying fresh air? Are you holding in tensions? Are others? When dolphin shows up it is time to breathe some new life into yourself. Get out, play, explore and most of all breathe.

ELEPHANT

KEYNOTE: *Ancient Power, Strength, and Royalty*

CYCLE OF POWER: *Year-round*

The elephant is the largest living land mammal. Although not native to this continent, I have included it because I have encountered a number of people to whom it has become a significant totem. It has an ancient ancestry in the mammoths. There are two types still in existence, the Indian and the African. The African is larger and the shape of the ears differ.

The elephant has a tremendous amount of myth and lore surrounding it. Of all elephants, the white elephant is considered the most sacred. This is similar to the sacredness often reflected in Native American traditions associated with the white buffalo. It is said that mothers of great teachers and masters will dream of white elephants. One story of Buddha's mother tells how she dreamt a white elephant had entered her womb.

In India and southeast Asia elephants are venerated, and the symbolism of the elephant is multiple. It is a symbol of royalty and fertility. The Hindu god of wisdom and success, Ganesha, is usually depicted with an elephant's head. The god Indra held several roles in which an elephant played a part. As the king of gods, the elephant was the royal mount. As the god of warriors, the elephant was

Indra's super weapon. As the god of rain, Indra used the gray elephant to bring forth the monsoons.

The elephant is both strange and terrifying to those unfamiliar with it. Much of what the average person believes about elephants is fallacy. Mice do not scare them. They respond to the sound, not to the movement of a mouse. Although they do have good memories, the idea that an elephant never forgets is misunderstood. It actually refers to never forgetting someone who has caused injury. They have been known to seek revenge if the opportunity presented itself. There also are no elephant graveyards, special places where elephants go to die. These tales are very mystical and symbolic. Elephants do show interest in the dead and the dying, even going so far as to display sorrow.

The elephant has a most auspicious symbolism. They embody strength and power, especially power of the libido. Male elephants are more likely to rage out of control when in rut. Because of this the elephant is seen as a symbol of great sexual power.

Because of their size, color, and shape, elephants and clouds have been linked together. They were seen as symbols of clouds, and many believed that elephants created the clouds. Those with an elephant totem should study the symbolism and significance of clouds. In general, they are symbols of the mist that separates the formed worlds from the unformed. They have been associated with Neptune, prophecy, fertility, and even family. Because they are always in a state of metamorphosis, they can reflect the same for those with the elephant totem.

On several occasions in the past, I have participated during the summer in psychic events that were held outdoors. On these occasions for a change of pace, I did "cloud readings," using the cloud formations to stimulate the psychic energies. I would hold the individual's hands, and look up into the sky and then talk about what I saw in the cloud formations and how it reflected in the individual's life. It is fun and can be a nice change of pace. On every occasion I have done this, one of the first things I would see is a cloud formation shaped like an elephant. It would be years before I understood the connection.

One of the most outstanding features of the elephant is its trunk. Because the elephant has relatively poor eyesight, it relies heavily upon its sense of smell. It breathes smells in through the trunk and discerns from the smells. The sense of smell is a long time symbol for higher forms of discrimination. Those with an elephant totem should pay attention to what smells good and what smells bad. Are you not discriminating as you should? Are others? Does something smell funny? Are you not responding, even though things don't smell right?

For those with an elephant totem, working with incense and fragrant oils can be a powerful and effective tool. Aromatherapy should be studied and used. Oils and fragrances will enable you to shift your consciousness most effectively.

The sense of smell is also strongly connected to sexual drive. It is one of the most powerful stimulants. Smells may become an aphrodisiac for those with this totem. It can be a powerful means of seducing or being seduced. This further enhances the symbol of the elephant as a sexual symbol.

The trunk is very versatile, and it is used for drinking, showering, and defense. Elephants even greet by touching trunks. The trunk has two fingerlike extensions. This specialized nose and upper lip combination makes it work almost like a hand. WIth it they can feed upon twigs, leaves, and grasses that it would not otherwise have been able to reach. Again it reflects that through the increased sensitivity of smell that the elephant stimulates, you can open to energies and worlds otherwise unaccessible.

The tusks are another important part of the elephant. Unfortunately, poachers kill an outrageous number of African elephants, simply to cut off the tusks of ivory. For anyone with an elephant totem, the significance of ivory from a spiritual and metaphysical aspect should be examined. The tusks are used as weapons and as tools for digging edible roots. This gives the elephant links to things beneath and above the earth—a knowledge of plants and roots.

The elephant society is divided by age and gender. Cows and calves live in all female herds, led by a wise old cow. This reflects the ancient tradition of three forms of the feminine energies in life—the child, the mother, and the old wise woman. These three forms have been found in most societies in which mystery teachings of life and the universe exist.

Bulls occasionally join the female herds. This is usually just for mating. The rest of the time they usually live in bachelor herds which are run by an older tougher bull. Again this has been duplicated in many societies around the world. Both men and women had their societies and their sacred teachings about elephants.

Elephants show great affection and loyalty to each other. Older calves will help younger siblings. Grown elephants will help sick or wounded comrades. In the elephant are the ideals of true societies.

Those who have the elephant as totem will usually find themselves in a position where the opportunity to reestablish powerful family and societal ideals will occur. Mutual care of the young, respect for the elderly and the sick, being strong in your own self—these are the foundations of a great person or a great society. If the elephant has come to you, you will have the opportunity to work toward establishing this within your own life or the lives of others. If elephant has come to you, prepare to draw upon the most ancient of wisdom and power. You will have an opportunity to either help yourself or others reclaim your most primordial royalty.

ELK (Wapiti)

KEYNOTE: *Strength and Nobility*

CYCLE OF POWER: *Autumn*

The elk is one of the most regal animals of North America. It is powerful and strong. At one time it was found all across North America, but by the late 1800s it was wiped out in the eastern United States. Today it is protected, and the western mountains provide range and refuge for it.

The Shawnee Indians named this animal wapiti, which is probably a more appropriate name. White settlers gave it the name of elk, calling it after a European relative which actually more resembled the moose.

The elk is an animal of great strength, power and stamina. It can run at a fast trotting pace for extended periods of time. One of its primary defenses is to outrun its predators. Elk can sustain a strong pace for great lengths of time.

If an elk has come into your life it can mean that you are about to hit your stride. Elk may also have shown up to teach you how to pace yourself more effectively. Have you been overdoing? Have others around you? Have you given up or thought about giving up too soon? Are you not pursuing things enough? Are you trying for the quick and easy when the long and steady will be most effective for you right now? An elk takes four to five years to reach maturity. If you have started new projects or tasks recently, you may need to give them four to five years to see them reach the peak of success.

An elk is in its power time during the fall. This is its rutting season. Except during the season of rut, elks stay with their own gender—males with males, females with females. Sometimes elk will show up as a totem to remind us that we need to have the company of the opposite sex occasionally for balance. Have you been neglecting your need to relate to others of the opposite sex? Are you keeping company of just one gender—to the neglect of the other? Have you been spending too much time with the opposite sex and not enough with your own?

The neck of the male swells during the rutting season and its bugle call sounds throughout the area. It is a way of declaring territory and affirming the relationship with the cows of the species. The neck is a bridge area, a point of crossing over. We all need the company of the opposite gender. It does not have to be a sexual relationship but simply spending time with them helps in balancing and bridging our own energies to higher levels.

Few elk are ever loners or solitary. They congregate and live in herds, staying mostly with their own gender. If elk has shown up, it may reflect a need for companionship or group support in some fashion.

Herds of elk usually have watchouts. These elk will sound alarms through long whistles (bugling) and through raising and revealing a large rump patch. There is always a group interaction occurring. Sometimes elk will show up to teach us how to live cooperatively in herds or groups. Are you trying to do everything by yourself? Are others? Do you feel as if you have the strength and energy to handle all tasks alone?

Elk even make use of babysitters. One or two will take charge of the young, while the others wander for food. If threatened, they will defend the young with sharp hoofs. It is the young that are most vulnerable, and elk and moose are both extremely protective. Parents with elk totems can be very protective and fierce in defense of any possible threat, imagined or real. The most common predators are the mountain lion and grizzly, although coyotes will often group hunt. As long as it is a healthy adult, the elk can usually outrun its predators. This is not so with the young and the sick, but this is how the herd stays strong. A study of the elk's predators will provide further insight into the kind of energies likely to be manifesting within your life.

Elk eat mostly grasses and vegetation. They do not migrate much. Their fur is thick and heavy and they can withstand the severe cold. If the weather is extremely bad, with very heavy snows, they may spend the winter in the foothills where vegetation is more accessible.

Anyone working with elk medicine would do well to hold to a predominantly vegetarian diet. The energy levels will be stronger, the stress levels will be lessened and the stamina will increase. If you find yourself becoming sluggish, call upon elk medicine. Adjust your diet, and in just two to three days you will notice a considerable difference in your overall energy levels.

FOX

KEYNOTE: *Feminine magic of camouflage, shapeshifting and invisibility*
CYCLE OF POWER: *Nocturnal, Dawn, and Dusk*

The fox is a totem that has touched almost every society on the planet. It is a totem that speaks of the need to develop or the awakening of camouflage, invisibility, and shapeshifting. It is one of the most uniquely skilled and ingenious animals of nature. It can teach these skills to those whose life it enters.

There are 21 species of fox and they can be found in most parts of the world and in varied climates. It is found along seashores and in the mountains, in the deserts and in the Arctic. It lives in North and South America, Europe, Asia, and even Australia. The fact that there are 21 different kinds of foxes found throughout the world has great metaphysical significance.

Card 21 in the tarot deck is The World. It is a card that reflects a new world opening up, that the process of creation is beginning. It reflects that the world is growing and shapeshifting itself into new patterns that will be beneficial. For those with a fox as a totem, meditating upon this card can be of benefit to understanding how fox energy will be helping with creation. It can reveal what is growing and shapeshifting (or needing it) within your own world.

The fox has a long history of magic and cunning associated with it. Because it is a creature of the night, it is often imbued with supernatural power. It is often most visible at the times of dawn and dusk, the "Between Times" when the magical world and the world in which we live intersect. It lives at the edges of forests and open land—the border areas. Because it is an animal of the "Between Times and Places," it can be a guide to enter the Faerie Realm. Its appearance at such times can often signal that the Faerie Realm is about to open for the individual.

In the Orient, it was believed that foxes were capable of assuming human form. In ancient Chinese lore, the fox acquires the faculty to become human at the age of 50, and on its hundredth birthday, it becomes either a wizard or a beautiful maiden who will ultimately destroy any man unlucky enough to fall in love with her. "There are several American Indian tribes that tell tales of hunters who accidentally discovered their wives were foxes."[9] This is very symbolic of the idea of magic being born within the feminine energies, and that unless a male can recognize the magic of the feminine—in himself or others—and learn to use it to shapeshift his own life, it will ultimately lead to destruction.

The Cherokees invoke fox medicine to prevent frostbite, and Hopi shamans always wear fox skins in their healing rites. The Choctaw saw fox as the protector of the family unity. Apaches credited fox with the killing of the evil bear, and for sticking its tail fur into the flame and stealing fire for humans. In other societies, fox was also held in great esteem. In Persia it was sacred, for it helped the deceased get to heaven. In Egypt, fox fur was thought to bring favor with the gods. The Indians of Peru had a fox god. The fox was often believed to reward those who did it service.

An examination of fox behaviors and characteristics will reveal much about the role and the energy it represents for you individually. Almost all foxes have sharp snouts, large ears, long, bushy tails, and long, thin legs. The large ears help the fox to keep cool in the summer, as they dissipate heat through them. For someone with a fox totem that has difficulty with summer heat, combing the hair behind the ears will almost always bring relief.

The most common fox in North America is the red fox, but not all red foxes have reddish fur. The fur of the red fox has variations, just as human hair does. Some may have the reddish coat, others may be more brown, and still others may have a black and silver fur. In general the red fox is associated with sexual energy, the kundalini, and the freeing of the creative life force. A study of colors and their symbology may help you further define the role of your fox in your life.

---

9   Lavine, Sigmund A. *The Wonder of Foxes* (New York: Dodd, Mead and Company, 1986), p. 13.

The red fox is a powerful totem. This animal has long been associated with the magical arts of invisibility and shapeshifting. Its natural ability for camouflage stirs wonder in all those who encounter it.

(Photo courtesy of Brukner Nature Center, Troy, Ohio.)

Except for the Arctic fox, the fur does not change color with the seasons. The Arctic fox also has more rounded ears, providing more insulation against the cold.

The coat of the fox serves as camouflage, and most fox coats have variations of color within them. This facilitates their ability to stay camouflaged and remain relatively unseen. Practicing and using camouflage is something everyone with a fox totem should learn to do. Working to blend in with the surroundings, to come and go unnoticed, moving silently about without revealing your intentions is all part of what fox teaches.

Much of this is reflected in learning to control the aura, the energy field around your body. You can adjust its frequency and intensity so that you harmonize more with others. You can focus on changing its appearance so that you blend in. Practice by standing against a wall and see yourself (and your aura) becoming the color of the wall, just as if you were fading into it.

The next time you go to a party, take a seat in a chair or on a couch and see yourself as a fox that blends in perfectly to its surroundings. Remember that a fox is most often seen when it is out in the open, so visualize yourself as taking on the color and pattern of the chair. Then sit quietly and watch how many people, accidentally bump into you or even begin to sit on you because they did not "notice or see" you there. You will be amazed.

Practice seeing yourself as a fox when you enter or leave a party or gathering. See yourself as blending into the gathering, melting into it. Do not be surprised as the night goes on when people make such comments as, "When did you arrive?" "How long have you been here?" "I didn't see you come in," or "When did you leave?" The more you work with fox, the easier this becomes.

The historical character of Merlin had to have used fox medicine and energy to accomplish much of what he did, but he practiced it. "Even during his lifetime Merlin was largely ahistorical and unrevealed . . . He was largely unknown to the greater public, except as `Merlin.' When he was summoned by kings or needed desperately to recruit other allies, he came silently, disguised as a poor shepherd, as a woodcutter or as a peasant. Even the sovereigns failed to recognize his in his various disguises. He practiced concealment habitually and for a long period of time."[10]

For those with fox totems, it will be important to learn this art of camouflage, and its related arts of invisibility and shapeshifting. The fox uses its ability at quiet camouflage to its benefit. With practice you can develop this same kind of ability and apply it so that you may see and hear things you otherwise could not.

Another aspect of fox fur has significance as well for anyone with a fox totem. Hair is often associated with psychic energy serving as antennae. The fox has two kinds of fur. It has a short, dense, wooly undercoat, and it has long, stiffer guard hairs that overlie the undercoat. This serves as a protector and it is usually darkest on the back.

Hair and fur are ancient symbols for energy and fertility, and layers of fur reflect levels of energy and levels of fertility. With the fox it is the undercoat which is the primal energy source from which an individual draws his/her abilities. The outer layer protects and defines how that energy is being used by the individual. As the outer hair changes so does the expression of the inner creative force. Hair should become very important to an individual with a fox totem. If a change is needed on certain levels, learning to change the hair to reflect the change desired helps to activate fox energy so that shapeshifting can begin.

The brush or tail has always been considered the most sacred part of the fox, although this is not necessarily true. It does hold great significance for one with a fox totem. When it runs, the fox tail is always in a horizontal position out from

---

10 From *Merlin* by Norma Lorre Goodrich. Copyright © 1987 by Norma Lorre Goodrich. Used with permission of the publisher, Franklin Watts, Inc., New York.

the body. This acts as a rudder. This horizontal position is the feminine form. Thus the fox tail is a symbol of directly guiding the feminine creative forces. It is especially beneficial to the fox when making abrupt and sharp turns. If the focus stays on the creative energies, any sharp turn in the individual's life will be accomplished with ease.

The tail also serves as insulation from the cold for the nose and feet, as the fox wraps itself up in its tail. Individuals with fox totems have an ability to insulate themselves from anything that may seem to be cold, especially in relationships. They can become warm and cozy in themselves.

The overall thickness of the fur makes the fox look much larger than it really is. This is especially significant for those with fox totems. These individuals have the ability to make themselves appear larger than they actually are. Because of this, an individual schooled in working with this aspect of fox medicine can use it to his or her advantage, for personal protection or for making greater impressions in various areas of his/her life.

In the winter, a thick tuft of hair grows on the toe pads on the bottom of the feet. This helps keep the feet warm and gives better traction, something that those with fox totem should be careful to do.

Although a fox dislikes getting wet, it is an excellent swimmer. This is also very significant, for it says something about the innate character of those with a fox totem. They have learned to draw upon and express the feminine energies, the creative force, in the outer world. For them, there is no desire to go back into the waters of life (feminine), but they will do so if it is necessary.

The legs of the fox are adapted for running. There is a tremendous stamina to them, an ability they can bring to others. Their favorite gait is a trot, and it is believed that they can trot indefinitely without exhaustion or the appearance of such. Few animals of a similar size can outrun a fox. Learning to establish a trotting pace is essential to those with a fox totem for their overall health and success. The fox also runs in such a way that the tracks look like a single line of footprints. During the trot the feet are placed almost directly one in front of the other. This reflects a straight-forward expression of the feminine energy.

Fox walks and runs on its toes, something very catlike. This is also significant for the fox is part of the canine family (dog), but it embodies a feline characteristic. The feline is the feminine energy given greater expression and movement. This quality reflects a need to assert the feminine, creative energies.

The fox also has the ability to run up trees if it is necessary. This reflects an ability to move into new dimensions and call upon new resources instinctively. The gray fox particularly has the ability to climb a tree much like a cat would, by using the claws of its back feet to push it up.

The senses of the fox reveal much about the potential within those who have it as a totem. Its hearing is very acute. They are like mini-antennae. They can pick up the squeal of a mouse over a hundred and fifty yards[11] away. Those with fox

---

11 McDearmon, Kay. *Foxes* (New York: Dodd, Mead and Company, 1981), p. 26.

totems have an excellent ability to hear what is not being said, as well as any whispering that may be going on. This ability is also tied to clairaudience, the ability to hear spirit.

The fox also has excellent eyesight. In fact they have elliptical eyes, just like a cat. They are color blind, but they have a great ability to see varying shades of lightness and darkness. This gives an individual the ability to size people up very accurately. They also have a great ability to see moving objects, especially at the edges or borders of areas. Because of this, it is not unusual for those with fox totems to develop the ability to see spirit; actually see those beings of the "Between Places," the fairies and the elves. This will happen if fox has come to you.

By far its keenest sense is the sense of smell. It hunts as much or more by smell as by the other senses. The fox is fascinated by unusual odors, and those with fox totems respond strongly to smells, detecting subtle differences in odors. Smell is one of its forms of social communication—deciding who to socialize with. It would be beneficial for anyone with fox medicine to study aromatherapy.

Sexually, the sense of smell is one of their strongest stimulants, and it has a key impact upon the degree and intensity of arousal for those with fox medicine. There is strong connection between fragrance and sexuality, and for those with fox medicine, this is critical. The sexual energy is our most creative energy; it is part of the kundalini energy force within the body. This force is critical in all activities. If controlled and channeled, it can be used for a variety of purposes—one of the most dynamic being for the art of shapeshifting. A fox entering one's life as totem may reflect the awakening of the kundalini. Such an individual to whom fox comes often has a great capacity for sexual expression with an ability to practice it in rich and varied ways—often with little inhibition. This aspect may often be camouflaged until the right moment.

The sense of smell is also associated with higher forms of discrimination and discernment. One working with fox medicine should sniff out each situation. This will let them know who to avoid and who to connect with. Does this person smell right? Does something smell funny about this situation?

Most foxes have only one partner. They are very monogamous. They also live alone about five months of the year. They are often solitary and comfortable with that state most of the time. The red fox vixens (females) search for a den usually only when they are pregnant. If possible they return to that same den year after year, adding to it and making it larger and more comfortable.

This same quality and love of the home is found in those with fox totems. Although foxes are territorial and travel within that territory, they do return to their home, their den. Those with fox medicine may find themselves as territorial in activities, but also inclined to return to their home and improve it.

A litter of fox cubs usually numbers from one to six. They are blind and deaf when they are born, but they move from that extreme to one of great sight and great hearing as they get older. If the cub survives its first year it will usually live several more, establishing its own territory. This reflects that those with fox medicine may have their greatest tests in childhood, but also their greatest instinctual education in the art of survival.

The fox is a survivor and a great hunter. In spite of encroachment on its territory and the history of being hunted it has been exposed to, it still manages to survive. Its instincts are great. Some have said it has survived because of its cowardice, but this "cowardice" is nothing more than the fox having learned to avoid potential danger. It will go out of its way to do so.

The fox is actually the farmer's friend, although many farmers accuse them of stealing and killing chickens and such. Usually the fox that does this is old and unable to hunt more difficult prey. The fox actually consumes vast numbers of beetles, crickets, grasshoppers, and especially mice and other rodents. Mice, in fact, are its favorite food, and those with fox totems should also study the characteristics of mouse.

The fox has a small appetite, but it may eat small amounts frequently throughout the day, caching away extra food in its den. This can reflect a beneficial eating habit for those with a fox totem.

Foxes are dainty, graceful, and lightfooted in hunting. They actually hunt more like a cat, often leaping upon their prey and holding it with their front paws. The fox is crafty and patient, and it will lie in camouflage intensely studying its prey until just the right moment to attack.

Probably the fox's cleverest hunting technique is "charming." In this technique, the fox is seen near a prey, performing various antics. It will leap and jump and roll and chase itself, so that it charms the prey's attention. While performing, the fox draws closer and closer without its prey realizing, as it is caught up in its seemingly non-threatening antics. Then at the right moment, the fox leaps and captures its prey. This is a camouflage technique, one associated with behavior. It is one that those with fox totems can use to capture any prize. As you develop attunement to the fox and learn its magic, any prize can fall to you.

GIRAFFE

KEYNOTE: *Farsightedness*

CYCLE OF POWER: *Year-round*

The giraffe is the tallest of all mammals. Although not a native of this continent, it is worth discussing, as many people all over the world experience the giraffe as a totem. This tallness enables them to see great distances. This has ties to foreseeing events that are to come.

The most outstanding features of the giraffe are, of course, the long thin legs and the slender and long necks. The neck is their most outstanding feature. As I have mentioned in regard to several other animals, the neck has great symbolism. It is the point of connection between the head and the trunk, the upper and the lower. It is the bridge. All bridges help us to cross over into new realms and new perceptions. The long neck, in combination with the giraffe's exceptionally keen eyesight, makes it a powerful totem for farsightedness and for seeing what lies on the horizon for you.

The neck is very strong. Male giraffes twist their necks around each other to test strength. The force of a head blow, directed by the neck muscles in defense, is great. It hints at using what is most natural for the greatest power.

The throat and neck are also associated with expression and communication. The giraffe makes no noise other than an occasional snort. It can moo and bleat, but most of its communication occurs through body language. If the giraffe is your totem, are you saying things you shouldn't? Are you not saying things that you should? Are you allowing others to speak inappropriately or allowing their words to affect yourself?

If a giraffe has come into your life, ask yourself some important questions. Are you seeing what is ahead of you? Are you afraid to look ahead? Are you seeing other people's perspective? Do you allow other's refusal to see your own perspective affect your life? Are you seeing the consequences of your thoughts, words and deeds? The giraffe can help you in answering these questions.

The long thin legs of the giraffe are symbolic as well. Legs enable us to move. They are symbols of balance and represent an ability to progress. With the giraffe, you have your legs and feet on the ground and your head in the sky.

Are you resisting moving into new areas you see for yourself? Are you resisting change? Are you afraid of the future? The giraffe can show you the future and how best to move toward it. When running, the legs and the neck of the giraffe work together, reminding us that it is not enough to see the future, but you must move toward it as well. The giraffe can teach how to do this most gracefully.

The giraffe is a browser, eating twigs, leaves, and buds. Its tongue is used to strip the leaves from trees. Its long legs do make it difficult for it to get water, so it has developed the ability to go several days without. The giraffe is most vulnerable when it spreads its legs out and lowers its head so that it can drink. This is a reminder to those with a giraffe totem. You will be most vulnerable if you move your sights from the horizons for any great length of time. If you become too static and complacent, you will find life becoming increasingly difficult.

The giraffe has a dainty head which reflects a lot of its social character. Giraffes like each other's company. The strongest ties among giraffes are between the mother and her baby. Giraffe people usually have strong family relationships and friendships as well.

On the head of the giraffe are horns that are unlike any other animals. These blunt, long stubs are never shed, and they are covered with skin. As has been mentioned, horns and antlers are symbols of antennae for higher mental faculties and perceptions. With the giraffe, there are actually three horns. The third actually looks more like a lump under the skin, but it is located just above the eyes. This placement is very significant as this is the area of the body associated with the third or inner eye—the seat of higher intuition. This only serves to reinforce the farsighted perception that the giraffe and its energies can awaken within you.

GOAT (Mountain)

KEYNOTE: *Surefootedness and Seeking New Heights*

CYCLE OF POWER: *Late Fall and Early Winter*

Everything about the mountain goat enables it to survive in the higher altitudes of mountain regions. Its thick wool insulates, its greater skeletal flexibility aids it in climbing, and even its feet are adaptive to their environment. Anyone with a mountain goat as a totem would do well to study the significance of its living environment—the high mountainous regions.

The mountain goat is noted for its dynamic climbing ability. The toes act like pliers, aiding their grip as they move up steep ledges. The soft pads on the bottom act as suction cups, giving them greater surefootedness. They can stand on their hind legs and pull themselves up with the front. Even the kids can stand almost immediately upon birth and begin climbing shortly after.

Their highly flexible skeletal system is very significant. Comprised of bones and cartilage, it is the support system for the framework of the body and assists in its movement. If a mountain goat has shown up as a totem, ask yourself some important questions. Are you getting the support you need as you move up into new areas? Are you giving the proper support to others as they move? Are you being too inflexible in exploring new possibilities? Are you feeling a lack of support or a need for support? Is something wrong with the basic structure of your life?

The mountain goat can, of course, descend much quicker than it can climb. The flexibility of its spine and its surefootedness enables it to maneuver precarious paths and ledges that would kill other animals. It has been known to make leaps of thirty feet or more to small ledges, barely large enough to stand upon. This reveals much about the flexibility of its skeletal system, but also the ability of its knee joints to absorb shocks. The mountain goat holds the knowledge of how to stretch and reach for new heights and goals. It can teach how to have trust in your own ability to land on your feet.

The mountain goat has links astrologically to the sign of Capricorn. You may want to look toward this time of year as being a significant one for culminating new moves or initiating them. The goat may have shown up to get you prepared. Anyone with a mountain goat as a totem should study the qualities and characteristics associated with the sign of Capricorn.

Because of its connection to Capricorn types of energy, ask yourself important questions. Are you being too serious? Not serious enough? Are you not preparing diligently enough for the new moves in your life? It can reflect a time of studiousness and industry, but it can also help when ambition and opportunistic behaviors get out of hand.

The horns of the mountain goat give it the ability to perceive what lies ahead in the future, and, with its natural climbing ability, it can reveal how you personally can best achieve the future. Mountain goats will fight with their horns. When threatened, they circle and try to stab with their sharp points. They have been known to even kill grizzly bears.

The thick coat of the goat enables it to withstand severe winter conditions. This reveals much about this animal's abilities as a totem. It can help you to keep focused and move step by precarious step to new heights, all the while protecting you from any severe life conditions. It is not unusual to have a mountain goat show up as a temporary totem when conditions become difficult and we fear slipping back. Its energies help us to regain balance, perspective, and continue the climb.

The goat may also link you to past lives associated with Greece. It is a symbol that shows up prominently in Greek mythology. It has ties to the nature god Pan, and to Amalthea and the Horn of Plenty. A study of the lore around them will provide insight into the role the goat will play within your own life.

If the mountain goat has climbed into your life, this is a time to begin new climbs and new endeavors. You will not need to rush into them. With proper foresight, you will see what is ahead and will be able move forward with greater surety.

GROUNDHOG (Woodchuck)

KEYNOTE: *Mystery of Death without Dying—Trance—Dreams*
CYCLE OF POWER: *Winter*

The groundhog or woodchuck is a burrowing rodent, actually a member of the squirrel family. It has chisel-like teeth, and it lives at the edges and open areas of woods and forests. It is known for its digging and tunneling ability.

Symbolically this reflects the ability to get deep within an area of interest. It is not unusual to have a groundhog appear at a time when a new area of study is about to open up. Since a groundhog does not fully mature for about two years, its appearance as a totem can reflect an endeavor that may take two years to come to full fruition. This may reflect two years of intensive study, digging, and building.

The groundhog makes elaborate dens with multiple exits and storage rooms. It spends half its time underground. The bedroom area is always located above the lowest end of the tunnel. This is so it won't be flooded. They clean up after themselves, burying their own excrement. Within their burrows they have separate toilet chambers.

Groundhogs are generally non-territorial, but they will not allow others in their tunnel. Groundhogs can tell if a burrow is occupied, as fresh dirt will be piled outside of its entrance. For anyone with a groundhog totem, it is important to give definite signals to the boundaries you wish to have respected in your life.

Groundhogs go into a true hibernation and spend about four to six months in that condition. They prepare for this by fattening themselves. They gorge through summer and late fall. They will curl up in a frost free chamber of their burrow, and their life processes will slow. Their temperature will drop from its normal 96 degrees to about 40 degrees, barely above freezing. The respiration slows to one breath per minute and the heartbeat plunges from 110 beats per minute to about four or five. They achieve a state of unconsciousness and will usually awaken in late winter or early spring.

Hibernation has always had great significance to it. It symbolized death without dying. Some societies used methods to induce these states as a symbolic ritual of death and rebirth. Thus hibernation reflected a time of initiation. Winter is the season of power, for that is when the groundhog reveals and uses its most effective medicine—hibernation.

It is also a symbol of opening fully to the dreamtime, the heavy winter sleep, allowing the individual to use the dreamtime more powerfully. Those with a groundhog totem will find that there will be increasing ability to develop lucid dreaming—especially during the winter. Any time groundhog shows up, the clarity and power of altered states will be amplified. Dreams will become more significant.

Many shamans, yogis, and mystics would teach methods of slowing down the metabolism of the body. This was often used to create trance conditions. This could facilitate healing or be directed toward out of body contacts. It can also be used to develop shamanistic trance. In this form of trance, the individual learns to shut down the body and then leave the body (leaving it protected), and then goes off into other dimensions to learn and to bring back knowledge.

When groundhog shows up as a totem, there will be opportunity to explore deeper altered states of consciousness. Lessons associated with death and dying and revelations about its process will begin to surface. Groundhog holds the knowledge of metabolic control. Its medicine is that of going into the great unconscious to touch the mystery of death without dying.

HORSE

KEYNOTE: *Travel, Power and Freedom*

CYCLE OF POWER: *Year-round*

The horse is rich in lore and mythology. An entire book could be written on the significance of the horse alone, for no one single animal has contributed more to the spread of civilization than the horse.

It has been associated with both burial rites and birth—with individuals riding into and out of the world upon it. The Norse god Odin rode upon an eight-legged steed. In the Hindu tradition, the chariot of Surya, the sun god, is pulled by stallions, as is the chariot of Apollo in Greek Mythology.

In Chinese astrology the horse is associated with appeal and persuasiveness. Horses are symbols of freedom—oftentimes without the proper restraints. Horse people in Chinese astrology are friendly and adventurous, and they can be very emotional.

Before the horse's domestication the distances between peoples and societies was great, and there was little interaction. It served humanity in travel, in war, in agriculture, and in most other major areas of life. Today the horse is limited mostly to recreation and agriculture, but its energy is expansive. Because of it, the world has been brought closer together.

The horse enabled people to explore and find freedom from the constraints of their own communities. This enabled them to travel and thus discover the multiplicity of life and all of its powers. Horses have great appeal to most people. We are fascinated by them, and riding one raises us above the mundane, and renews our sense of power. Riding horses has been likened to flying by more than one poet through the ages. They signify the wind and even the foam of the sea.

Horses were given powers of divination. More than one legend speaks of the clairvoyance of horses and their ability to recognize those involved in magic. They are symbols that can express the magical side of humans.

The symbolism of the horse is complex. It can represent movement and travel, or maybe it showed up to help you with movement. It has been a symbol of desires—especially sexual. The stallion was often used as a symbol of sexuality. The taming of a stallion would then be the taming of sexuality and dangerous emotions.

As with many domesticated animals, there are a wide variety of horses—each with its own unique abilities. Riding, plowing, pulling—the horse still serves a variety of functions. To understand your own particular horse totem, try to determine which kind it is. Horses, like dogs, are bred today for specific purposes and determining that can help you define the purpose of it within your own life.

Take your totem and examine it in regard to yourself. What is its color? Its kind? How does it appear to you? Does it run? Is it always perceived standing? Do you see yourself riding it or watching it?

If a horse has shown up in your life, it may be time to examine aspects of travel and freedom within your life. Are you feeling constricted? Do you need to move on or allow others to move on? Is it time to assert your freedom and your power in new areas? Are you doing your part to assist civilization within your own environment? Are others? Are you honoring what this civilization has given you?

Horse brings with it new journeys. It will teach you how to ride into new directions to awaken and discover your own freedom and power.

LEOPARD

(See the separate entry for the "Snow Leopard." Information on the leopard has also been included in the category of "Panther." Although technically they are not the same, panther was a name often given to both the leopard and the jaguar.

The qualities of both are very similar. Study the panther information and then research the leopard to find its unique significance to you.)

LION

KEYNOTE: *Assertion of the Feminine and the Power of the Female Sun*
CYCLE OF POWER: *Year-round*

The lion is the second largest member of the cat family. The traits of cats should be studied in general, for the lion embodies many of them. It makes its home on the savannas of Africa, and those with this totem would do well to study the significance of the savannas. The lion's main prey is the antelope and this should be studied as well.

The lion has been symbolic of a variety of energies through the years. It is a symbol of the sun and of gold. It was a symbol for the sun-god Mithra. The Egyptians believed that the lion presided over the annual floods of the Nile. Early Christians believed it to be the earthly opponent of the eagle. The medieval alchemists associated it with the fixed element of sulphur, and a young lion was often the symbol of the rising sun and all that is implied by it.

The lion is unusual among members of the cat family in that it will live in groups called prides. If a lion has shown up as a totem, you can expect lessons and issues dealing with community and groups to surface. There may be a need to examine your own role in the group.

Within the pride, the females are the best hunters. Although most lions are clumsy hunters by themselves, they have developed an excellent cooperative hunting technique. The females, though, do most of the hunting and the rearing of the cubs. The lion cubs lead a relatively care-free existence. Their parents are patient and affectionate with the cubs, and most individuals with lions as totems will find those same qualities developing within themselves.

The males are most noticeable by their large mane. They do very little work. They can be passionate and excessively jealous of the lionesses. They protect the pride against predators. When hunting they use their roar to scare prey toward the waiting lioness. If a male lion has shown up as your totem, you may need to examine your usefulness within some group or community in your life. Do you need to do more than you are? Do you need to be more protective? Do you need to cooperate more?

The lion does not fight for the sake of fighting. It avoids confrontations, and will leave the scene of danger if possible. This is a tactic to keep in mind if the lion is your totem. Lions also hunt primarily by stealth, and the most common method of killing it is by strangulation. This technique is something for those with this totem to practice developing when pursuing new endeavors and objectives in any area of life. Be stealthy for the greatest success.

The idea of the young lion being associated with the rising sun is most significant. Since the females of the pride do most of the work, it actually reflects the idea of the rising of the feminine energies. The sun has not always been a masculine symbol. It does give birth to new days, and it nurtures and warms life. Thus it is not stretching the correlation to see the lion as the assertion of feminine energies to bring forth birth and new power.

When a lion has shown up, there will be opportunity to awaken to a new sun. Trust your feminine energies—creativity, intuition and imagination. These will add new sunshine to your life. Don't be afraid to roar if you feel threatened or intruded upon.

LYNX

> **KEYNOTE:** *Secrets and Vision of the Hidden and Unseen*
> **CYCLE OF POWER:** *Winter*

Much of the information concerning the bobcat also applies to the lynx. Both animals are similar, and the bobcat was sometimes referred to as the red lynx. Both have short, stubby tails, tufted ears, and a ruff about the face. The lynx is chunky and muscular. It has long legs and big furry paws that serve as snowshoes during the winter. The lynx is also found further north and its territory is not nearly as widespread as that of the bobcat. For anyone with the lynx as totem, also study the significance of the northern direction.

Its facial ruff gives the lynx an aristocratic appearance. Still abundant in Alaska and Canada, they are starting to make a comeback in other northern parts of the country. The lynx has no trouble maneuvering in the snow. Its feet are wider than those of its relative, the bobcat.

Lynx kittens are usually born with blue eyes. After about two months, the blue eyes turn to the yellow like their mother's. The blue hints of the expansiveness of the sky or heavens open to the lynx from birth. The transition to the yellow reminds us that the lynx can draw knowledge from the heavens.

The mother teaches the young to hunt. Summer and fall is spent in passing on the skills. These skills will be needed as winter approaches, for by late winter the family breaks up and the lynx go their own way—seeking out their own life and knowledge.

The main prey of the lynx is the snowshoe hare. On its wide feet it is able to pursue the hares, even when the snow is piled deep. It will feed on smaller rodents, but the snowshoe hare is its main diet, and the qualities of it should be studied as well. "So closely is the fate of the lynx tied to that of the hare . . . that when the hare population plummets during a regular eleven-year cycle, so does that of the lynx."[12]

---

12 Weidensaul, Scott. *American Wildlife* (New York: Gallery Books, 1989), p. 4.

This eleven-year cycle is very symbolic. From a metaphysical standpoint, eleven is a master number. It is associated with inspiration, revelation, mysticism, and occult teachings. The fact that the lynx is a gray color also adds to this significance. The gray is the symbol of clouds that hide the ancient wisdom, that separate the seen from the unseen. The lynx is the animal whose powers enable it to cross back and forth and draw out knowledge and secrets from behind the clouds.

The lynx has connections to mythology and occult groups in history. These links (no pun intended) can provide clues to possible past lives. In the Scandinavian and Norse traditions, the lynx was sacred to Freyja, and her chariot was sometimes depicted being drawn by lynx. The Greeks believed the lynx could see through solid objects. In fact, it is named for Lynceus, a mythological character who could also do this.

In 1603 Italian scholars formed the Academy of Lynxes, dedicated to the search for truth and the fight against superstition. Galileo was a member, and its symbol was that of a lynx tearing Cerberus with its claws. Cerberus guarded the entrance to the underworld. The implication was that knowledge would conquer darkness and suffering.[13]

The lynx has acquired the reputation for supernatural eyesight. It has been attributed with the ability to see error, falsehood, secrets and all that is hidden. If a lynx has shown up in your life, look for that which is hidden. Trust your instincts in believing others. The things you imagine are probably more accurate than you think. No matter how strange and how irrational the imagining, it probably has a core of truth.

Lynx has the ability to teach you how to know the inner workings of others. Jamie Sams and David Carson refer to it as a special type of clairvoyance in which you see that which people hide—from others and themselves. This may be fears, activities and even abilities.[14]

Individuals with lynx as a totem need to be very careful about breaking confidences. Things said have a greater potential of being made public or distorted, so words must be chosen and used cautiously. Strength through silence should be the motto. The breaking of confidences usually brings quick and strong repercussions.

If lynx has shown up in your life, you will find that other people increasingly share their secrets, taking you into their confidence. You will "accidentally" discover things about people, and some of it you may not wish to know. You don't have to do anything with the knowledge. Hold onto it. Use it for your own benefit, but be careful of sharing it inappropriately.

It is not unusual to find that some people will become very uncomfortable around you. On some level they will recognize that you can see within them. When they avoid you, trust what you imagine to be the reason.

To help you awaken the lynx ability to see hidden knowledge, Sit back and watch. As you observe how people behave and what they say, you will also get

---

13 Limburg, p. 115.
14 Sams and Carson, p. 109.

images of things behind them. Visualize yourself inside the other person. In many ways the lynx medicine is like X-ray vision. You are able to see the inner workings. Learn to go into the silence and trust what images and knowledge come to you from it.

MOOSE

KEYNOTE: *Primal Feminine Energies and the Magic of Life and Death*
CYCLE OF POWER: *Late Fall and Early Winter* (**November**)—
The Time of Approaching Shadows

The moose is one of the most ancient and most unique of the power totems. To the Algonquin Indians, it was known as "mong-soa" or "twig eater." To the Athapaskan Indians of Alaska it is Dineega. To the latter there was a tremendous relationship between Raven and Moose. The Athapaskan hunters would protect and talk constantly on their hunts to Raven who they knew helped shape the world. They would pray to Raven to assist in the hunt for Moose. Thus when a moose appeared, it was a special, sacred gift. For anyone who aligns with Moose—no matter how it may occur—a unique and sacred energy is opened.

The moose is an animal of contradictions. It is strange and yet majestic. It seems awkward, but there is a tremendous gracefulness to it. While it makes us smile, it also causes us to catch our breath. Those with Moose as a totem will find these same contradictory feelings stirred in others about them.

Except during mating season, it is a predominantly solitary animal with a unique ability to make use of its territory—whether it be lake, pond, grassy, plains, or spruce forests. Those with this as a power animal have that same ability.

The moose has an uncanny ability to camouflage itself, in spite of its great size and power. And it uses this ability to its advantage. Those who would align with the moose can also develop this ability. Part of this involves the ancient magic of invisibility, but it also involves an aspect of shapeshifting.

This unique "shapeshifting camouflage" is reflected in the life of the historical Merlin. When he was summoned by kings or needed desperately to recruit other allies, he came silently, disguised as a poor shepherd, as a woodcutter or a peasant. Even sovereigns failed to recognize him in his various disguises. He practiced this concealment habitually.

Despite the size of the moose, it does have a unique ability to move silently and speedily. Its appearance of ungainliness is misleading and deceptive. It is this deception which enables it to survive so well. One reason for their ability to do this is that they have excellent depth perception. They can accurately judge the negotiability of an area. The moose has a speed and grace at negotiating territory that others could not. It can move through great depths of snow and through marshes that would trip up many others. This same ability can be strengthened, awakened, and even taught to those who align with the medicine power of the moose.

The moose is often associated with the feminine energies, the maternal forces of the world, and those who align with the moose will find these forces awakened. Part of this revolves around the association with water. Water is the primal symbol of the feminine forces of the universe. It is the symbol of creativity and dynamic forms of intuition and illumination.

The Penobscot Indians of Maine relate tales of how the moose once was the whale, the greatest mammal of the waters. The MicMacs of Nova Scotia tell how when the moose is too persistently hunted, it returns to the sea.

The association with the water and sea is important to understand for anyone who aligns with the moose power. The sea is the point from which all life comes and to which all life returns. It is the great womb of the universe. The moose is often seen in marshy areas and standing in lakes.

They also have a unique ability to plunge to the bottom of lakes, and can remain there feeding for up to a full minute before surfacing in a burst with fresh greens dangling from their mouths. For those who want to work with the full mystery of moose power, this should be carefully studied and meditated upon. It reflects the ability of the individual to learn to go back into the depths and draw new life and nourishment from it. The moose can teach the ability to move from the outer world to the inner. It can teach how to cross from life to death and back to stronger life. It teaches how to use the thin thread that separates life and death to one's advantage. It is not unusual to find individuals with strong mMoose medicine working in soul retrieval.

This aspect of working with life and death and the energies and life forms on both levels is reflected through a sacred tradition of the Athapaskan Indians. To these people "potlatch" is a memorial ceremony to help dispatch the spirit of the dead. The belief is that when people die, they do not leave right away. They stay nearby and so food is burned for them to eat. At first it is once a day, then every other day, then once a week and so on for a year—at which time a memorial potlatch is served. This potlatch involves a sharing of special food, particularly moose head soup, sacred because it is not always available. This service then sends the spirit on.

This reflects much about the inherent mediumship and ability to work with spirits of the dead by those who align with moose medicine and energy. Moose people can learn to go into the icy waters of the void (death) and come back out.

Another reason for its association with the primal mother/feminine energies of the universe is because the female moose is extremely protective of its young. Very few creatures will ever challenge a female moose with its calf. There is a great maternal energy that has a primal strength to it.

Moose also have a highly developed sense of smell and a highly developed sense of hearing. The sense of smell has its spiritual or metaphysical counterparts in emotional idealism and spiritual discernment. The hearing lends to the human the abilities of clairaudience and spiritual comprehension. When Moose aligns with an individual (which is usually how it happens, rather than an individual aligning with a moose), the individual should pay more attention to that inner voice and that sense of smell. Do things not smell or sound right—even if you can't define why? Trust those feelings, for they will define themselves shortly.

Moose calves are also born with their eyes open, which is very significant. Most of those who are open and resonate with Moose medicine came into this world with their inner eyes already open. It is not unusual to find such individuals getting discouraged when they work to "click on those inner lights," as so many others describe their own awakening psychic and intuitive capabilities. These individuals must understand that they came in with their inner lights already on, so there will be no clicking. Learning to trust what they so often think is simply the imagination, etc. is part of the task of maturing into full Moose power.

If a moose calf lives through its first month, it will most likely survive to become an adult. This reflects much about the lives of those who moose aligns with. It is not uncommon to find those with moose medicine having had their most difficult (and sometimes traumatic) lessons in life during their childhood. The survival through this reflects that innate ability to draw from the creative force of the feminine waters of life to strengthen and sustain them. The two most powerful parts of the moose are the paws, which will cut like a knife, and the antlers which are both decorative and defensive. The head and the feet—these two areas are parts of the body most sensitive in those of moose medicine. Foot reflexology and head, neck, and upper back massages are important to release stress. I would imagine, although no research has been done on this, that cranial sacral work would facilitate healing and release most beneficially for those of moose medicine.

Along health lines, the moose is herbivorous, and this says much about the dietary needs of those who would truly align with its power. This does not mean that one should become a vegetarian, but rather that it should be a strong part of the diet. It also reflects that the body will respond most strongly to herbal alternatives rather than traditional chemical medicines.

You cannot discuss the power of the moose without also discussing its antlers. Their antlers are the largest of all antlered animals. Antlers are ancient symbols of antennae—of crownings that activate the upper chakras of the head.

Only the male of the species grows antlers, unless there is a hormone imbalance in the female. Maybe this reflects the idea that the male must attune even more strongly (through these antennae) to the intuitive promptings. The rubbing of the antlers to remove the velvet covering has a lot of significance as well. It reflects the need to massage the head area to release the past for the antlers are shed each year.

The moose is a symbol of the sexual energies as well. This sexual energy is a physical reflection of the primal creative energies. That energy has its cycle within the body and within the rhythms of the year.

Autumn is the power time of the moose, and late October and November especially is the month for honoring the moose. The hunting season is over. The mating is being completed, and a new cycle is about to begin. For those of moose medicine the autumn is a powerful time. The smell of dry leaves, the sound of their crunch as they are walked upon, touches a primal core, stirring life forces anew within the individual. In many ways it is aligned with Samhain, All Hallow's Eve, All Saint's day, Harvesting Rituals and all the traditional energies associated with this season.

The Moose has always been a powerful omen. When it appears in dreams, it reflects a long, good life. It was known to give strength, and more than one Indian tribe believed that you could travel three times as fast and three times as long after a meal of moose. (The mystical significance of three should not be bypassed here. It is the creation, the new child born from the womb of the mother.) The hoof was known as a cure for epilepsy. Moose was known to banish headaches and dizziness, and Moose medicine was also considered the antidote for snakebite.

The moose has no enemy that it fears other than a grizzly bear, but even then it can outrun and outswim it. Its maneuverability and intuition, along with its highly developed senses sustain it.

Almost all northern Indian tribes have legends and tales of the moose—reflecting its universality and its great mysticism. The Menomini of Wisconsin even had a moose phatry or clan at one time. The Dog-Rib Indians south of the Arctic Circle (near Great Bear lake and Great Slave Lake) speak of Hottah, a two-year-old moose who was the cleverest of all northern animals, and who helped create the Rocky Mountains.

When moose comes into your life, the primal contact with the great feminine force and void of life is being awakened. It is an invitation to learn to explore new depths of awareness and sensitivity within yourself and within your environs.

MOUSE

KEYNOTE: *Attention to Detail*

CYCLE OF POWER: *Five- to Six-Week Cycles*

There are many kinds of mice. Most have certain qualities in common. These will be examined in this section, along with a specific look at the common deer mouse (also called the wood mouse or whitefooted mouse).

The deer mouse has big eyes and ears. and has white gloves on its feet. Most mice are nocturnal, but this is especially true of the deer mouse. It sees well in darkness, but in sunlight it will act somewhat blind. This is not true of other mice.

The deer mouse will nest in abandoned squirrel and bird nests, hollow logs, cracks, and crevices. Its nest will often be globe-shaped, and the entrance will have a plug or door which can be closed for warmth. The male and female work together to remodel the nest. Most mice change their nests often.

The deer mouse is fastidious about keeping its fur cleaned and groomed. This is not so with the more drab house mouse. The deer mouse is good about its appearance, but it is a sloppy housekeeper. This reflects that, for those with a mouse totem, there will be areas in which fastidiousness and attention to detail is highly concentrated, while in other areas there may be neglect. This paradox is often a source of confusion and sometimes irritation to those who live and work with mouse people.

Most mice store food, as well as search out food all year round. The deer mouse eats seeds, berries, and bark and is less destructive than the meadow mouse in regard to farmers crops and grains.

All predators feed on mice. To compensate for this, mice will have three or four litters a year. They survive because of their numbers. The deer mouse mother, as with most mice, will care for the young about five weeks. Then the young are on their own. Because of this, if a mouse has come into your life, its energies will be most strongly felt for about five to six weeks.

When mouse shows up as a totem, it is either time to pay attention to details, or an indication that you cannot see the forest for the trees. You may be getting so locked into details that you forget the big picture.

Ask yourself some important questions. Are you taking care of the trivial but necessary things in life? Are you getting so lost in the big dreams that you are neglecting other aspects of your life? Are you becoming so focused on one or two activities that you are neglecting to see other opportunities? Are you missing what is right in front of you? Is there something obvious that you are missing or need to focus on? Are you trying to do too many things at once and thereby scattering your energies?

Mouse medicine can show you how to focus and pay attention to detail. It can show you how to attain the big things by working on the little things. Whenever mouse shows up there are lessons associated with attention.

OPOSSUM

> **KEYNOTE:** *The Use of Appearances*
> **CYCLE OF POWER:** *Spring*

A number of years ago when my workshops were just beginning to grow in popularity, an individual in the metaphysical field was spreading rumors about me among certain groups, to undermine my work. Apparently he felt threatened by the increasing attention I was receiving. After a workshop one evening, several people spoke to me about what was being spread around. I remember fuming all the way home. I couldn't believe that this person would make up stories—after all we had done some traveling together. I knew that I was going to have to confront this person.

When I got home and raised my garage door, my headlights flashed on a pair of eyes in the back of the garage. An opossum had taken up temporary shelter. I got a broom and tried unsuccessfully to sweep it out. Finally, I left the garage door open, hoping it would leave on its own and went into the house, temporarily distracted from my fuming.

About an hour later I went outside to check the garage, and the opossum had disappeared. I drove the car into the garage, and pulled on the garage door. It only moved about five inches and then locked. I pulled again and still it locked. Since it was dark, I couldn't tell if the runners on which it sat were jammed or what was going on. Finally, I grabbed the handle with two hands and yanked as hard as I could. The door freed and came down. As it did, the opossum tumbled off the top of the garage door and fell on top of my head. I must have jumped six feet. I don't know who was scared worse—me or the opossum. Apparently it had climbed on top of the garage door and was lodged in a way that hindered closing the door.

It left rather abruptly, after bouncing off my head and hitting the ground. It appeared just as dazed and unhurt as I was. I tried to get my heart started. I began laughing as I walked back into the house. My anger from earlier that evening was dissipated. It was then I decided to not respond. I would just appear to play dead or ignorant to the rumors. Within several weeks, the rumors had ceased and numerous phone calls reaffirmed that I had responded appropriately. No one was believing the rumors, and my invitations to teach and lecture increased even more.

Opossum teaches us how to use appearances. Sometimes it is necessary to "play dead." Sometimes it is necessary to put up a particular front to succeed most easily and effectively. This is what the medicine of opossum can teach. It also can show you when others are putting up false fronts and deceptions. Opossum has an archetypal energy that helps us to use appearances to our greatest benefit and that helps us to recognize when others are creating false impressions. Opossum can help us learn to divert attention or to get attention any way we need.

Sometimes it is necessary to behave or act in a strategic manner. We may need to appear fearful or fearless in spite of how we truly feel. We may need to show submission or aggression. We may need to be apathetic or extremely caring. Opossum is the supreme actor, and those in the acting field or that need to learn something of it can do no better than to work with the opossum.

The opossum is a nocturnal animal. It is the only marsupial on the North American continent. Marsupials are animals that raise their young in a pouch on the abdomen. When the young are born, they are blind, but they are still able to climb up into the pouch immediately after birth. There they stay for about one month.

During the spring, I often stop and check opossums hit and on the road. There may be young in the pouch if it is a female opossum. The young can live for a while in the pouch even after the mother has died, but only for a short while.

In the pouch are located the nipples. Most opossums have 13 nipples. In a litter, there can be many more than thirteen young, but only thirteen will be able to survive. This number is very symbolic. Although many associate it with bad luck,

The Opossum

The opossum is a wonderful animal with the unique ability to divert attention by displaying the right appearance. It can teach us how to adjust our behaviors and appearances for the greatest benefit.

(Photo courtesy of Brukner Nature Center, Troy, Ohio.)

it is also a symbol for the one great sun around which the twelve signs of the zodiac revolve. It is a symbol of the sun within.

The pouch, especially in regards to the opossum's defense of "playing dead," links it to the ability to help us draw from our own bag of tricks that which will most benefit us. It can show you which appearance to draw from the pouch to use for the greatest success. The milk of the mother is rich in calcium, as young opossums need high concentrations of it. Those with this totem should examine their own calcium levels.

The playing dead that the possum is famous for is a self-induced state of shock. The pulse becomes minimal. The heartbeat slows. A musk scent of death is released, and for all appearances it will seem dead. The opossum can enter and leave this state abruptly—pretty much at will. This act serves to confuse many predators. The surprise distracts them, and the opossum is able to make its escape. It is this kind of flexibility and ease of appearance that the opossum can teach to those with it as a totem.

When opossum shows up as a totem, ask yourself some important questions. Are you acting or about to act in an inappropriate manner? Do you need to strengthen your own appearance? Are others putting up false appearances in front of you? Do you need to divert attention away from some activity? Are others trying to divert your attention? Is it time to go into your bag of tricks and pull out some new strategy? Learning to pretend and act in ways and with realism is the magic that opossum teaches.

OTTER

KEYNOTE: Joy, Playfulness, and Sharing
CYCLE OF POWER: Spring and Summer

The otter amuses and fascinates must humans. Their playful expressions and activities capture our imaginations. Whether a sea otter or the river otter, there is a natural, joyful curiosity about them.

Once on a canoe trip in northern Ontario, Canada, a river otter popped up about ten feet from the front of the canoe. It raised itself up out of the water and peered over its nose as if curious as to who would be up so early and coming into its playground. It would dive and disappear and then reappear off to one side or the other, as if trying to size up the situation from every angle. When its curiosity was satisfied, it dived and disappeared, going about its own activities.

Otters awaken curiosity. They remind us that everything is interesting if we look at it from the right angle. They are playful and seem to have fun at whatever they are doing.

Otters always have their homes close to the water. During the summer, they are rarely on land, especially river otters. They usually have a large home territory around and in the water, and they usually mark their homes with a scent.

Their connection to the water links them to the primal feminine energies of life—especially the pleasurable aspects of the feminine—creation, imagination, joy and love of the young. Otters remind us to keep the inner child alive or to give birth to it. They remind us that life can be fun if we approach it with the right attitude. Otters are seldom seen alone. They are either with others or playing with some object.

The adult otter has practically no natural enemies. They protect their young very well. They are agile and fast in the water, with the ability to outswim fish. If there is a threat, they usually swim away fast, but they can be ferocious fighters.

The mother otter usually chases the father out of the den when the young are born, again reflecting the otter's tie to primordial feminine and mothering energies and patterns. When the young are out and about, the father is allowed to rejoin. Usually two to four young are born, but they must be taught to swim. This task is handled by the mother. Sometimes otters show up to help awaken the primal mothering energies and responsibilities. It can indicate a need to set up your boundaries within the home and define your feminine role.

Otters are extremely agile and acrobatic in the water. They love to slide on their bellies and dive in and out of the water. When under water, the nostrils and ears close. Remember that water is an ancient symbol for the feminine and creative forces of life. An otter's activities and playfulness reminds us all—male and female—that we all need the feminine qualities in some form for the greatest joy in our life.

If otter has surfaced in your life, it may be time to find some play time. Involve yourself in some creative activity. You do not have to be god at it; just have fun with it. Or are you being too playful? Are you not staying focused? Are you afraid to have fun? Are you getting too serious? Are you worrying? Do you need to awaken your inner child? Treat yourself to something special. Honor otter and it will teach you not only how to have fun, but it will reawaken a new sense of wonder at life and all things within it.

PANTHER

KEYNOTE: *Reclaiming One's True Power*

CYCLE OF POWER: *Dark of the Moon—New Moon—Winter*

The panther is a very powerful and ancient totem. The name panther is more generally associated with a particular species of leopard or jaguar, although in the Florida area, the cougar is also referred to as panther. For the purposes of this work, we will explore it as part of the leopard and/or jaguar family and not of the cougar.

As with most of the large cats, the panther is a symbol of ferocity and valor. Like the tiger and the lion, it embodies aggressiveness and power, but without the solar significance. In the case of the black panther, there is definitely a lunar significance.

As with any totem, a study of the individual characteristics can provide much insight into the energies being awakened within those who align with this animal. Panthers of the leopard family are found in Africa, Asia Minor, China, and India. Those we associate with the jaguar family are found in the southwest United States (rarely anymore), throughout Mexico, Central America, and parts of South America. Meditation upon this totem, when it reveals itself to you, will help you determine whether it is part of the leopard or the jaguar family. Regardless, there are still traits that both embody and reflect.

The panther, in general, is smaller but more fierce than lions or tigers. They have over 500 voluntary muscles that they can use at will. This reflects a lot about an individual who has such animals as a totem. It reflects an ability to do a variety of tasks as he or she wills. It is simply a matter of deciding and putting to use those particular "muscles"—be they physical, mental, psychic, or spiritual.

As a whole panthers are loners (solitary) although they do associate with others, they are most comfortable by themselves or within their own marked territories. They are drawn to those individuals who are likewise often solitary.

The panther is an enchanting combination of beauty and utility. They have a wonderful gracefulness, with an ability to move with ease or freeze entirely. They are quiet when they are stalking, hunting, or pursuing. Those who have a panther as a totem will find their greatest power in silence as goals are pursued. Revealing too much or speaking too much about pursuits can counteract some of the effectiveness.

Panthers are excellent sprinters, but they are not great long distance runners. From a health perspective, those with a panther totem must learn to pace their work, allowing time to rest and to play. They must not push too far or too hard on any one task. If they do, they are more susceptible to imbalances. In times of trouble—in any environment—those with panther totems are often the first and the fastest to respond, and especially in the work environment they respond effectively to deadlines and to pressures.

After mating, the panthers only stay together for a short time. The female handles the rearing of the young, disliking intrusions from the outside. This is often similar to women who have panthers as totem guides. They do not like others—even their mates—interfering with how they feel the young should be raised. The female panther almost always raises the cubs alone, and women with panther totems often find themselves doing likewise—whether out of divorce or simply through asserting dominance in that area of the couple's life.

All cats have binocular vision. Each eye can work singly, providing greater depth of vision, magnifying images, and facilitating judgment of distances. Thus anyone who aligns with the panther will begin to develop greater depth of vision—of their life, of events, or other people. This is more than just psychic sight. It is an inner knowing.

Often people enter the metaphysical field, taking up exercises and meditation to have their inner lights "clicked on." Individuals with panthers as totems are usually individuals who came into the world with the lights already on. Thus they should not be discouraged when they do not experience what others describe when their lights turned on. They should trust their thoughts and their inner visions (imaginings) for there is probably a strong foundation in reality.

To those with whom the panther links comes the ability to develop clairaudience, to hear the communications of other dimensions and other life forms. The panther has very strong hearing. It can move its ears to locate the direction of sounds.

The panther also has extremely sensitive hairs on the body, especially the face. Those with a panther totem will find their own sensitivity to touch increasing, from the time the panther enters your life. The skin is our largest sensory organ, and we experience much more of the world through it than we realize. Those with panther totems should pay attention to how they feel when someone touches them or when they touch someone else.

The facial hairs of the panther are especially sensitive, and those with this totem can develop a special form of psychometry. Rather than holding and "reading" an object's vibrations through the hands, placing it against one's cheek or forehead will bring strong impressions.

This skin sensitivity—the touch faculty—will heighten responses in the overall body. Things—such as foods—that are generally revolting will be more so to individuals with these totems. Touches that are sensual and erogenous will intensify as well when the panther enters one's life. The arrival of the panther initiates a time of awakened sensuality and passion, two powerful tools of the feminine powers.

It is in the hours of darkness that panthers find its greatest element of power. This is even more true of those who have as a totem a black panther. The season in which their power is greatest is the winter. The lunar cycle most powerful is the dark of the moon through the new moon.

It has been noted mythically that a panther of the leopard variety have a distinctive sweet breath by which it lures animals to it for food. Leopard varieties kill by biting the back of the neck. They do not attack from the front, they pounce from behind. Those with a panther totem who are angered will not confront another individual head on—and are better off not doing so. They must stalk patiently, waiting until close enough to strike strong and hard. They don't play when they hunt. These individuals will go for the throat, so to speak.

The jaguar variety of the panther will also stalk, but they are more powerful. Because of their position and power they will simply bite through the temporal bones of the skull. They have also been known to shear the heads off of animals with a single swipe of their claws. Because of their sensitivity, individuals with the jaguar panther as a totem will instinctively know how best to attack if placed in such a position—and they can do so lethally whether in defense or in response to anger. Because of this natural ability, individuals with this totem must learn to temper their responses, or they may unintentionally wound others more deeply than they mean to.

Of all the panthers, probably the black panther has the greatest mysticism associated with it. It is the symbol of the feminine, the dark mother, the dark of the moon. It is the symbol for the life and power of the night. It is a symbol of the feminine energies manifest upon the earth. It is often a symbol of darkness, death, and rebirth from out of it. There still exists in humanity a primitive fear of the dark and of death. The black panther helps us to understand the dark and death and the inherent powers of them; and thus by acknowledging them, eliminate our fears and learn to use the powers.

In China there were five mythic cats, sometimes painted like tigers or leopards. The black reigns in the north with winter as its season of power, and water its most effective element. This is the element of the feminine. This is the totem of greater assertion of the feminine in all her aspects: child, virgin, seductress, mother, warrioress, seeress, old wise woman.

When the black panther enters your life as a totem, it awakens the inner passions. This can manifest in unbridled expressions of baser powers and instincts. It can also reflect an awakening of the kundalini, signaling a time of not just coming into one's own power. More so, the keynote of the black panther is *Reclaiming One's True Power.*

In mythology and scripture, the panther has been found in all parts of the world as a dynamic totem. It has been a symbol of the "Argos of a Thousand Eyes," who guarded the heifer IO who was loved by Zeus. After his death, the eyes were transferred to the feathers of the peacock. The panther always brings a guardian energy to those to whom it comes.

The panther has also been attributed to Jesus. In the *Abodazara* (early Jewish commentaries on the scriptures), it is listed as a surname for the family of Joseph. It tells how a man was healed "in the name of Jesus ben Panther." Because of this the panther is often signals a time of rebirth after a period of suffering and death on some level. This implies that an old issue may finally begin to be resolved, or even that old longstanding wounds will finally begin to heal, and with the healing will come a reclaiming of power that was lost at the time of wounding.

The panther was also a symbol associated with Bacchus/Dionysus. One story tells how Bacchus was nursed by panthers, and he is sometimes depicted riding a chariot drawn by them.

The myths and stories of Dionysus are very symbolic. He is, to many, a symbol of unleashing desires, and thus the awakening of the kundalini forces. He—and thus the panther—symbolize a time of moving from mere poles of existence to new life without poles or barriers. The panther in a Dionysic manner awakens the unconscious urges and abilities that have been closed down. It signals a time of imminent awakening.

The panther is a symbol of awakening to the heroic quest. All of the Greek heroes were born from the union of a god and a mortal mother—the linking of the great fire and the great femininity. The heroes thus had the seeds of the divine force, that would eventually provide impetus to reach beyond the normal bounds and restrictions—to negotiate new stages in progression and purification. The heroic tales tell us that no matter the depth of degradation—whether self-inflicted or inflicted from outside forces—there is always the promise of light and love to lead us back. When the panther enters your life, the path leading back is about to begin.

Dionysus had to overcome many years of wandering, plundering, madness, destruction, and suffering before he could take his place within the heavens. His is the lesson of overcoming negative tendencies and sufferings inflicted upon ourselves by ourselves, or by others to attain to our divinity. His story is that "we are gods and goddesses in the making."

Usually, in the lives of those with a panther totem, there either already exists or will soon arrive upon the scene an individual who will serve as teacher and nurturer and guide upon the heroic path. For Dionysus there was the centaur Silenus and the satyrs. They symbolize the alternate realities that do exist around us and the increasing ability to view them at will as we become the initiates of the heroic path.

These alternate realities will open to those with panther totems. These alternate realities, the beings within them and the energy of the panther all have ties to powerful sexual energies. It may reflect a time of resolving old sexual issues, or it may simply reflect learning to embrace these energies as a true power without being judgmental. We must recognize and learn the transforming nature of the sexual energies and how to direct them consciously.

Dionysus was a god of life and rebirth, passion and resurrection. He was twice born. The panther reflects a coming time of opportunities to become twice born ourselves. This often means we may have to face offending malignancies of our life—a process similar to what has come to be known as "Meeting the Dwellers on the Threshold"—those aspects of ourself or our life that we have painted over, glossed over, shoved to the back of the closet or pretended didn't exist. Sometimes this means we must suffer the loss of what we think we love the most.

The panther holds the promise of rebirth and guardianship throughout. It is the extra protection we need in those times. It is the symbol of power reclaimed from whatever darkness within our life has hidden it. The panther is the promise that whatever is lost will be replaced by that which is greater, stronger, and more beneficial.

In the myth of Dionysus, the hero bears the magical thyrsus, a wand entwined with vines, upon which rests a pine cone. It gives the individual the ability to create delusion and illusion. There awakens within the individual upon this path and with this panther totem an ability to cause people to see and think as you desire them too. This ability is earned and strengthened through self-discipline. Like the black panther, you can blend into your surroundings with ease and to whatever degree you desire.

To the Indians of North and South America, the jaguar especially in the form of the black panther—was endowed with great magic and power. The jaguar panther climbs, runs, and swims—even better than the tiger. Because it could function so well in so many areas, it became a symbol of immeasurable power to the Latin American natives. It was a symbol of mastery over all dimensions.

To the Tucano Indians of the Amazon, the roar of the jaguar was the roar of thunder. Thus the black panther was the god of darkness and could cause eclipses by swallowing the sun. This reflects the tremendous power inherent within the feminine forces. To those with the panther as a totem, this power will increasingly be experienced.

The Arawak Indians say that everything has jaguar. Nothing exists without it. It is the tie to all life and all manifestations of life (thus ties to the eternal feminine within all life). To them, becoming the man-jaguar was the ultimate shapeshifting ritual. The Olmecs created monuments to the jaguar, and the Aztecs and Mayans spoke and taught about the power in becoming half-human and half-jaguar. One who can become a jaguar is shorn of all cultural restrictions. The alter ego is free to act out desires, fears, aspirations.

The Indian shamans would perform rituals to borrow jaguar power. One who could do such could do great good or great ill. Stories abound of revenge, abductions, and great cures of disease through use of jaguar power among the Latin-American Indians.

Even in Egyptian rituals, a panther tail was worn about the waist or knotted about the neck to help protect and strengthen. It was used in a process called "passage through the skin"—their own version of shapeshifting to engender themselves with the panther's power.

Nietzsche once said that "that which does not kill us makes us stronger." It is this same idea that is awakened in the lives of those who open to the power of the panther totem. Those things of childhood and beyond that created suffering and which caused a loss of innate power and creativity are about to be reawakened, confronted and transmuted.

The panther marks a new turn in the heroic path of those to whom it comes. It truly reflects more than just coming into one's own power. Rather it reflects a reclaiming of that which was lost and an intimate connection with the great archetypal force behind it. It gives an ability to go beyond what has been imagined, with opportunity to do so with discipline and control. It is the spirit of imminent rebirth.

PORCUPINE

KEYNOTE: *Renewed Sense of Wonder*
CYCLE OF POWER: *Autumn*

Porcupines are fascinating mammals that are often misunderstood. The porcupine is a member of the rodent family. It is sometimes called a hedgehog, but this is a mistake—the true hedgehog is an entirely different animal.

Porcupines are rather good-natured, and they shuffle along at their own pace. Though they look clumsy and slow on the ground, they are excellent climbers and can climb 50 to 60 feet. The legs are short but strong, and they have a unique ability to use them to test the strength of the limbs they may climb upon.

Porcupines live in arboreal areas, mostly in pine forests. They eat the barks of various trees and evergreens, and they enjoy blossoms, young leaves, and water lilies. They also have a great craving for salt and will eat anything that has the faint flavor of salt. Individuals with this totem may need to watch their salt intake. There may be a tendency to crave and overindulge in salt.

I encountered my first porcupine in the wild in northern Ontario, Canada. I had to portage my canoe, and as I came to the next stage of river, a porcupine was at its edge, about three feet out, feeding on water lilies. It looked up more curious and amused, and then simply resumed its feeding, more fascinated by the lilies than it was by me.

This reflects much about the personality and character of the porcupine. It has a good nature, and it seems to enjoy just about anything that it does. It has a strong sense of curiosity, and seems amazed and filled with wonder at most things it encounters. It is this same quality that the porcupine can awaken in those with it as a totem. Although it has poor eyesight, it remains extremely curious, and not overly cautious in response to its visual limitation.

The most noticeable characteristic about the porcupine is its quills. This is also the most misunderstood. The quills—around 30,000—cover all parts of the body except the face and the underside of the belly and tail. The quills are controlled by a layer of muscle and they can be made to lie flat or straight up. When molested, disturbed, or threatened, they stand up. The quills are filled with air, making the porcupine buoyant in water. This reflects the ability of the porcupine to swim and move in emotional areas (symbolized by the water).

The porcupine does not shoot its quills. When threatened the quills stand up. To protect its face, it will lower it between the front legs so that quills guard it. The quills are loosely attached and easily discarded. It will lash with its tail, usually aiming at the predator's head. If it hits, the quills are left.

There is no venom on the quills, but they do have barbs on the end. As the quill penetrates the skin of an opponent, the barb expands. Each movement of the predator then causes the quill to work deeper in. It is impossible for other animals to remove them.

The porcupine's greatest predator is the fisher, a member of the weasel family. For many years, naturalists believed that the fisher flipped the porcupine on its back to kill it, but they now know that it grabs the porcupine by the nose, biting its face repeatedly until it dies. The fisher is so good at preying on the porcupine that it is becoming more and more scarce in the wild. Anyone with a porcupine totem should also study the weasel family, and especially the fisher member.

Cougars are also successful at preying on porcupines. They have learned the knack of flipping it onto its back, exposing its vulnerable belly. The cougar should also be studied by those who have the porcupine totem.

Porcupines usually live in hollow logs, caves, and holes. In the winter, they will spend a lot of time in trees. It is easier for them to climb than it is to shuffle around through the snow.

Porcupines are usually born one at a time, although occasionally there are twins. They mate in the autumn, and the young are born about seven months later. Only the mother raises the young. Porcupines can live to be anywhere between 9-15 years.

As the young get older, they are often seen standing upon their hind legs and rocking to and fro, waving their paws. This is a rhythmic exercise. When observed, it looks very much like a dance, and porcupines can help us come into a new rhythm in the dance of life—one that will awaken wonder. Dance is also an avenue of pure enjoyment that anyone with a porcupine totem could find great pleasure and relaxation in.

Porcupines are also susceptible to snuffles. This is a flu-like disease that affects animals. It is usually the result of a lack of nutrients. Anyone with the porcupine totem should be careful to have a diet rich in nutrients and vitamins. Especially eating green vegetables will be beneficial to the health, as the porcupine is an herbivore. If you feel your energy weakening or are coming down with cold and flu-like symptoms, check your diet.

Porcupine people have a knack for sticking it to people sharply and intensely if aggravated. They have a knack for saying or doing that which will cause the most hurt for the longest time—like a quill barb working deeper into the skin. They do not always use it, but when they do the point is well taken.

When porcupine shows up, take a look at your life. Are you allowing other people's opinions to prevent you from exploring activities that could otherwise be fun and enjoyable? Do you have recreational time in your life? Are you overly sensitive to the barbs of others? Are your barbs inappropriate or taking the joy from others? Are you still allowing the barbs from long ago to aggravate you and sting you? Sometimes it is necessary to remove the old barbs, no matter how painful, so they do not fester and poison the system.

Porcupines can show you how to resist the barbs of others. They can teach you how to enjoy life and maintain a sense of wonder about it, in spite of negative conditions. They can show you how to shuffle along, without too much seriousness, and still achieve. They can teach you how to protect the inner child from all of life's barbs, and can show you the strength in your vulnerability.

PRAIRIE DOG

KEYNOTE: *Community*

CYCLE OF POWER: *Spring and Summer*

No other animal, except for perhaps the wolf, epitomizes the idea of community more than the prairie dog. A prairie dog community is always filled with activity. A prairie dog is a member of the squirrel family, and there are two main kinds. The blacktailed live predominantly on the plains and are the most common. The second has white-tipped tails. They live in the mountains and are not as sociable.

Prairie dogs live in a town, a network of underground tunnels. The burrows or homes are comprised of individual tunnels and rooms. The entire town is divided into coteries or individual communities in which the members depend on each other. Each section of the town is inhabited by members of separate "clans."

In the digging of the tunnels, the dirt is kicked out behind them. This gives a raised mound area at the entrance above the ground. They then cut down the plants around the entrance, enabling the prairie dogs to watch out for predators more easily. The watchman prairie dog will send out alarms in the form of high-pitched yips.

The primary predator used to be the black-footed ferret, which now only exists in captivity. Efforts to restore it to the plains have had very limited success. Today its primary predators are owls and snakes, and these should be studied by anyone with a prairie dog totem.

Prairie dogs eat grasses and plants. They rarely drink water, getting moisture from plants instead. In the winter they live predominantly off their accumulated fat.

Individuals with prairie dog totems may need to make sure they have lots of vegetables in the diet. Water intake may not be as important to them as long as a great quantity of fresh vegetables are eaten regularly. Individuals with these totems may also experience a sensitivity towards the sun, and sunglasses would be very beneficial. Prairie dogs have orange-colored lenses in their eyes to filter out some of the sun's glare. This helps them as they are often seen sunbathing.

Prairie dogs are very sociable animals. They greet each other by kissing and hugging. With mouths open, they touch their teeth together. They love to show affection. If a prairie dog has shown up as a totem, examine your own sociability. Are you or those around you being sociable? Unsociable? Are you trying to be reclusive when you shouldn't? Do you need to demonstrate more affection than what you have in the past?

Examine your sense of community—be it your family, work or social community. Are you participating fully? Are others? Do you need to learn to live with others, each sharing in the responsibilities? Prairie dog usually indicates that there are going to be changes in your perceptions about community life and your part in it. These lessons may extend over a five- to seven-year period, as this is the usual life span of the prairie dog.

Because prairie dogs are diggers, when they show up as a totem, you may want to examine how much digging you should do in different aspects of your life. Do you need to get more deeply involved in the lives of others around you? Are you too deeply involved?

Although many people feel the prairie dog is a pest and should be eliminated, it actually serves a valuable purpose in Nature. The digging aerates the soil, causing plants to grow more easily. Their burrows allow more moisture to get beneath the surface of the land. When prairie dog shows up it is usually time to become more actively involved in the community. Changes are necessary. Involve yourself, and don't allow others' accusations to dissuade you from your participation.

RABBIT (HARE)

KEYNOTE: *Fertility and New Life*
CYCLE OF POWER: *Year-round*

The rabbit is an animal whose essence and energy is a paradox. It is found in both myth and folklore, and, depending upon the society, it was perceived in a variety of ways. In Greek mythology, it was associated with the goddess Hecate. In Egyptian hieroglyphics it is associated with the concept of being. The ancient Hebrews considered it unclean because it was lascivious (Deuteronomy xiv, 7). "Among the Algonquin Indians, the Great Hare is the animal-demiurge."[15]

In China, it is one of the twelve astrological signs. It was considered a most fortunate sign, giving those born under it the ability to possess the powers of the moon. Hare individuals are considered sensitive and artistic. The hare is imbued with ambition, finesses, and virtue, along with living on the moon.

The rabbit is known for its ability to procreate, its fleetness, its ability to make great leaps and hops. It moves primarily by hops and leaps, and individuals with this totem find that their endeavors do so as well. All of these characteristics are significant for those with the this totem.

The rabbit is found mostly in thickets and tall grasses. It is active both day and night, but is most visible at dawn and dusk. These are times long associated with the Faerie Realm of life, and because of this, the rabbit is often seen as an animal that can lead one unknowingly into the Faerie Realm. The most common example of this is found in Lewis Carroll's story of *Alice's Adventures in Wonderland,* in which Alice follows a white rabbit down a hole into a wondrous world of adventure.

Rabbits and mice are the two most common prey animals. Because of this Nature compensates them with a tremendous fertility. Rabbits can have between two and five litters of young per year, usually with three to six young per litter. It is because of this that the rabbit has long been a symbol for sexuality and fertility.

The mother only feeds the young in the morning and in the evening. She spends the rest of the day away from the nest, feeding herself. This is a protective gesture for the young, so as not to draw attention to them. Unfortunately many people come across baby rabbits while the mother is away, and they assume they are abandoned. People then proceed to move the young.

Within one month, 28 days, the young are able to be out on their own. They can stay in the nest, but they can survive on their own. If a new litter arrives, the mother will kick the old litter out. This 28-day period again reinforces the lunar

---

15 Cirlot, J. E. *A Dictionary of Symbols* (New York: The Philosophical Library, 1971), p. 139.

connection with the rabbit. Usually if a rabbit totem shows up, you will begin to see a cycle of 28 days beginning to manifest in your life.

The two most common rabbits are the cottontail and the jackrabbit. The ears of the cottontail are shorter than the jackrabbit, and its coat stays the same all year round. The fur of the jackrabbit will lighten or even turn white in the winter. Both animals can leap and hop. Those with rabbit totems will see movement occur in their life in varying degrees of leaps and hops. It won't be a steady step-by-step movement. The leaps and hops do not usually take more than the cycle of one moon (28 days) to occur.

Although some associate fear with the rabbit, it has wonderful abilities for defense. Those with this totem would do well to apply them to their own life. Rabbits often create forms to use for hiding and resting. To create a form, the rabbit scratches a shallow bowl into the earth or grass that is open in front and in back to enable it to escape if necessary. Rabbit people should plan for possibilities. If a rabbit has shown up, it may indicate a need to do some more planning or check those you have already set in motion. You do not want to box yourself into a corner. Rabbits have a knack for avoiding being seen. They can freeze, holding perfectly still. They know that movement can be detected from great distances by many predators. If you are involved in competition—in work or in play—it will be important not to foreshadow your moves.

Rabbits are also clever at doubling back, making quick and rapid turns. If they need to flee they can be extremely fast. Learning to shift from freezing to great speed is something all with this totem should learn. It will aid your success and enable you to take advantage of opportunities that may only present themselves for brief moments.

Rabbits are vegetarians. Those with this totem may need to examine the kinds of foods being consumed. For the greatest health and healing, a vegetarian diet, even if only temporary, will strengthen and heal.

Rabbit can show you how to recognize the signs around you. It can help you to attune to the lunar cycle and recognize the tides of movement within your life. This in turn will enable you to become even more fertile in your life.

RACCOON

KEYNOTE: *Dexterity and Disguise*

CYCLE OF POWER: *Spring and Summer—Nocturnal*

Raccoons are fascinating animals. They are distantly related to the bear, and thus it should be studied as well by anyone with this totem. The raccoon is one of the most adaptable animals, and in spite of encroachment on its natural habitat, it is even able to live within the city.

The name raccoon is believed by some to come from the Algonquin Indian

---

16 Limburg, p. 147.

word "arckunem," meaning "hand scratcher."[16] The paws are very dexterous. Raccoons can be expert at opening lids, latches, doorknobs, and such. Because of this they often have the reputation for thievery—of being able to get into things they are not supposed to. It would not be surprising to find that individuals who are thieves and burglars have raccoon medicine, even though it is not being used positively.

Raccoons are fascinated by water. They like to slosh their hands and their food in it. This has given rise to the belief they never eat anything without washing it first. Actually, water increases the sensitivity of the raccoon's hands, and they can feel their food better.

The raccoon will eat almost anything available. It will capture small prey, but it usually eats mostly vegetables and fruit. This is something that those with this totem should also keep in mind.

Raccoons are extremely curious, which is partly why they often get into things they shouldn't. They love to explore. Their nocturnal excursions can be likened to mini-adventures. They can be very curious about new realms and will examine anything that fascinates them.

One of the most striking features of the raccoon is the mask that it wears. Although some associate this with thievery, it actually gives the raccoon a very powerful mystical symbolism. The use of masks to achieve altered states and for other healing and ritual purposes has been a part of every society. Mask making is an ancient art employed all over the world for ceremony, celebration, and in magical practices.

Concealed behind a mask, people could become something or someone else. We can become whatever we want by wearing masks. Masks are invested with mystery. They are tools for transformation. The hidden aspect, the secrecy, helps promote the transformation. It helps us to change what we are to what we want to be, giving us magic.

Just as there is with the raccoon, with masks there is ambiguity and equivocation. When we wear a mask we are no longer who we thought. We make ourselves one with some other force. We create a doorway in the mind and in the physical world a threshold that we can cross to new dimensions and new beingness.

This is the magic of raccoon. It is an expert at disguise and secrecy. It knows how to wear masks for a variety of purposes. It can teach you how to mask and disguise and transform yourself. Each must develop the relationship with the raccoon in their own unique way, but raccoon medicine can teach you how to become dexterous in the masks you wear. It can show you how to wear a healing mask or show you the face you shall become. The raccoon holds the knowledge of how to change our faces.

Whenever I take trips to teach classes and workshops, I look for any animals that may appear to determine the kind of energies associated with the upcoming session. The first time I taught a class on mask making, I saw no animals other than those I normally see on trips. I was kind of surprised because usually with new classes, some new animal shows up.

The class went well, and as I pulled away in my car, the headlights flashed off the eyes of an animal. I slowed, thinking a cat or dog was stepping out onto the road. As I drove closer, I saw a raccoon sitting on the edge of the street, its masked eyes fixed solidly upon me. I drove slowly forward, and stopped alongside it. It didn't move. It simply stared at me. Goosebumps appeared as I nodded to it and thanked it for helping with the class. It never occurred to me before that the raccoon would show up to add its energy to the mask making class. Every time since then, I always encounter raccoons either going to or coming from the class on mask making. I have honored the raccoon for its help.

Raccoon holds the knowledge of transformation through masks and disguise. This knowledge can be applied to religious and ritual practices or within normal everyday life. Do you need to present a different face to people for greater success? Are you hiding your true self? Are others hiding their true self? Raccoon can help you find the answers.

Raccoons do not hibernate, but they do go into a heavy sleep during the winter, living off their body fat. This has connections to learning to use masks to put to sleep one aspect of yourself so that another can be awakened. This is also part of what raccoon medicine can teach. It will help you develop dexterity in using masks to achieve new altered states and dimensions.

Raccoons are very courageous and they can be quite ferocious. Litters of raccoons are brought in to Brukner Nature Center every spring and early summer. Working and handling them has taught me a great respect for their ferocity—even when young. When they get older, they can become very surly. In the wild, raccoons are deceptive and agile. They are experts at self-defense.

Raccoons enjoy hollow logs, especially for their dens. They will have one to two litters per year, usually with two to seven young. At about twenty weeks a raccoon can live on its own, but they are very sociable, and where you find one raccoon, you will usually find another. They also live longer than most animals in the wild—around ten years.

If a raccoon has shown up, you may see its influence for an extended time. If you are trying to make changes or endeavoring to hide changes you are making from others until you are in a better position, plan on using about a 20-week cycle. You will find it more effective. For longer and greater life transformations and such, when raccoon shows up you may want to make longer plans.

RAMS (Bighorn Sheep)

KEYNOTE: *Seeking New Beginnings*

CYCLE OF POWER: *Late Fall and Early Winter*

The ram has long been a symbol in many societies. For many it was a symbol of sacrifice. It was killed in ritualistic traditions for a variety of purposes. This is found often in biblical lore. Moses initiated Passover with the sacrifice of a lamb. It also symbolized the quest for great rewards, as is seen in the Greek heroic tale of Jason and the Quest for the Golden Fleece. It is also a symbol of great force and power. Battering rams were used in many societies to knock down doors and gates of enemies.

If the ram has shown up in your life, prepare to seek out new beginnings in some area of your life. The ram is the symbol for the astrological sign of Aries, the first month of the astrological year. It falls in the spring, a time of new beginnings. The ram tells us to assert ourself in new areas.

In Chinese astrology the goat and the sheep (ram) are often interchanged, representing one of the twelve months of the year. It is a sign associated with sensitivity and perseverance. They are somewhat stoic, never coming out and speaking their minds directly, and they can also have a tendency toward impracticality in the Chinese tradition.

In real life, rams embody many of the characteristics associated with them in mythology and lore. Their power and strength is often depicted in nature films where they are seen butting heads in duels of strength.

Rams and ewes of the bighorn sheep family live above the timberline. They eat tender grasses and the flowers of certain herbs. Throughout the spring and summer they build up layers of fat and a thick coat which enables them to survive the winters.

The horns are a predominant feature of the ram. In individuals with this totem, they stimulate great mental activity. There is a curiosity and an active imagination that must be constantly fueled and that gets stronger with each passing year, just as the horns of the ram grow larger with each passing year.

The horns of the ram are weapons, a form of defense and a status symbol. They grow throughout the life of the animal, eventually forming a full curl or spiral. The spiral is a symbol of great creativity, and because it is associated with the head in the case of the ram, it has even more significance. For those with this totem, there will occur a new stimulation of mental faculties, imagination, and inspiration—along with the energy to act upon it.

Young rams often play a form of king of the mountain, testing strength and new positions. This is most evident in the autumn, when the pecking order becomes more focused. There begin challenges for the right to mate with the ewes. The rams spin, lunge through the air and heads crash, horns knocking together. This continues until one admits defeat. For those with this totem, autumn may bring a time for you to assert your strength and move to new challenges.

A ram can live to about 14 years of age, but the life expectancy decreases with the size of the horns. The larger the horns the more frequent the duels. The rings on the horn actually mark the age of the ram.

Bighorn sheep, like mountain goats, have toes that pinch. The hooves are covered with an elastic material that helps absorb the shocks and aid the grip. The joints of the sheep act as miniature shock absorbers when they make their great leaps down. The bighorn sheep only need a two-inch space to get a foothold.

This is very important for those with this totem. It is a reminder that the openings for new beginnings may be small, but if acted upon, they can be secured. Those with this totem must learn to trust in their ability to land safely on their feet as they make new moves and new beginnings.

If the ram has come into your life, do some examination—but don't take too long with it. It is usually an indication of a time to make some new beginnings, to initiate new endeavors—rather than just think about it. Are you taking advantage of opportunities that are presenting themselves? Are you staying balanced as you make new leaps and climbs? Are you initiating things appropriately? Are you acting on your ideas or just talking about them? When the ram shows up, it will teach you to bring forth the powers of the mind and imagination and use them to seek out new heights and new adventures.

RAT

KEYNOTE: *Success, Restlessness and Shrewdness*
CYCLE OF POWER: *Year-round*

The sight of a rat usually distresses most people. Rats often carry contagious diseases, and though rats don't have a very elegant reputation, they are tremendously adaptable.

In Chinese astrology, the first year is assigned to the rat. A legend tells how at one time Buddha summoned all of the animals to him. Of all the animals, only twelve showed up, and the first was the rat. To honor each of the animals, Buddha named a year after each one, giving the first year to the rat. People born in the Chinese year of the rat are said to be success-oriented, sometimes restless and nervous, but always very shrewd.

Although the city rat can be a pest, its cousin the wood rat, or country rat, is a most exceptional animal. It is intelligent and often displays an ability to reason. Studies have shown that wild rats are brighter than laboratory rats.

The rat has succeeded in proliferating in spite of the efforts of humanity. This drive for success may be what the rat has come to speak of with you. Are you driving too hard? Are you not pushing hard enough? Do you need to be more aggressive in pursuing your goals?.

Rats are highly social and often cooperate in survival efforts. They store food, reflecting an interesting economy. They are the most adaptable of animals with an ability to survive in most environments.

Two rats were introduced into this country—the black rat from the orient and the Norway or brown rat. Of the two, the Norway is often considered the most harmful because it can easily destroy great quantities of stored foods. If possible, identify the rat. Begin by asking yourself: Is this a country rat or a city rat? And then go from there.

If a rat has shown up as a totem, you may find yourself getting more restless. It may indicate a time to be more shrewd in all of your dealings. Are you not handling the pests in your life properly? Do you need to become more adaptable? It may even reflect a time to more aggressively pursue endeavors for success. The behavior of the rat when you see it will help you to determine the kind of energy it specifically brings to you.

RHINOCEROS

KEYNOTE: Ancient Wisdom

CYCLE OF POWER: Year-round

There are five species of rhino in existence today, two in Africa and three in Asia. The African rhinoceros can be distinguished from the Indian by its two horns. The exact species of your totem will provide more specific insight— including possible past-life connections to those areas of the world where it is found. The rhino is a survivor of the age of giant mammals. It takes its name from the two words, "rhino" and "keras," meaning nose and horn, respectively.

All rhinos are basically solitary, and because they are descendants of ancient times they bring with them an energy of comfort in one's own solitude. They teach how to be comfortable within yourself. They are the embodiment of the mystery school axiom: "Know thyself!"

The most significant aspect of the rhino is, of course, its horn. Unlike most animals, the horn is located on the nose and not on top of the head. Although all horns give higher sensitivity from a symbolic perspective, in the case of the rhino it lends to those with this totem greater sensitivity to that area of the body of the olfactory senses. The sense of smell has long been a symbol of the energy of higher discrimination, spiritual idealism, and the application of higher wisdom. When we look at the sensory development of the rhino, this is further exemplified. Although it has relatively poor eyesight, its senses of smell and hearing are keen.

If the rhino has shown up as a totem, you need to examine your own innate sense of discrimination. Are you not trusting your own inner wisdom—what you know to work and be best? Are you distrusting or discounting the foundation of your own learning? Are you forgetting that ultimately no one knows better for you than you? Are you only looking at appearances and refusing to see beyond the surface?

The African white rhino is endangered. It has become a symbol of African ecology. It suffers from loss of habitat and from poaching by those who pay a great deal of money for the rhino's horns, because of the ignorant superstition regarding its magic abilities. The horn is a symbol and has no medicinal value. The horn is not even comprised of the bony material that makes up normal horns and antlers. It is rather flimsy and is made of skinlike material.

The white rhino is found in the African savannas. It likes tall grasses. Despite its size, it can be surprisingly agile if need be. It can be a rather peaceable animal. The rhino only bears one young at a time, and the gestation period is about 17 to 18 months in the case of the white rhino. For those with this totem, look for new access to ancient wisdom and the assimilation of it into your own life to occur in about this same time-frame.

Those with this totem would do well to also study the oxpecker bird. This bird is a companion to the rhino. In fact it is sometimes called the rhino bird. It will land on the back and eliminate stinging flies and ticks.

The rhino will help you to see the wisdom of your life. It has a solidity that will help you to put life into its proper perspective. The ancient side of the rhino will help you to draw upon your own innate wisdom and find application to the present time.

SEA LIONS and SEALS

KEYNOTE: *Active Imagination, Creativity and Lucid Dreaming*
CYCLE OF POWER: *Year-round*

Seals and sea lions amuse and fascinate most people. Although similar in appearance, they are not the same. They do share many of the same characteristics, but they should not be confused. Both are part of the order of mammals known as pinnipedia, which is usually translated as "fin-feet," but it literally means "feather feet." The name seal comes from the Anglo-Saxon "seolb" meaning to drag, named after the manner in which they move upon the land.

Although both seals and sea lions will spend time on land, the seal is more at home in the water. Sea lions are not completely the water animals that seals are.

They also are much more mobile upon land than the seals. This is due to the fact that a sea lion has much more flexible hind flippers than does the seal. Its neck is also more flexible than the seal's. Most of the time what the general public refers to as performing "seals" are really sea lions.

There are more varieties of seals than there are sea lions. The elephant seal is the largest of all. It got its name for its size and the droopy snout of the males. During the mating season, males will have ferocious battles, and although sometimes a great deal of blood is shed, rarely is anything injured more than their pride. In the late 1800s the elephant seal was reduced to a mere 100 before laws to protect it were instituted. Today, it has rebounded. The harbor seal is the widest ranging of all seals. Like the sea lion and other members of the seal family, it will give birth out of the water. The specific kind of seal or sea lion should be studied to determine its specific role within your own life.

The most distinguishing characteristic between the seal and the sea lion is that seals have no external ears, simply small openings. The sea lion does have external ears. Because both are small, they stand out even more in their symbolic significance. Ears are the center for hearing and balance, and this significance should be applied to your own life.

If a seal or sea lion has shown up as a totem, it is time to do some questioning. Are you getting out of balance? Has the imaginative faculty opened so much that you are not staying grounded? Are you listening to things and people that you shouldn't? Are you not listening to that which you should? Are you listening to the inner voice (especially in the case of a seal totem)? Are you following the words of others rather than your own?

Both the seal and sea lion are associated with water. They spend great amounts of time in and around it. Water is the creative element. It is a symbol of the feminine, the emotional, the imaginative, and the dreamtime. When these animals show up, you can expect your dreams to become even more vivid and significant. Pay attention. Much of what you are dreaming and imagining may have a strong basis in reality—no matter how far-fetched.

Keep a notebook with you, as the imaginative faculty is about to be awakened and stimulated. Seals and sea lions can teach you how to develop and focus the imagination. They can teach you to draw upon their energies to impact upon the "real" world in which you operate every day. Seals and sea lions can also keep us grounded so that we don't get lost or caught up too strongly within the imagination.

Remember both come out of the water for rest and mating. They always bear their young on land. This is very significant, as it reflects the ability to bring the creative force out from the inner and set in motion in the outer. For seal and sea lion people, it will be important to pay attention to the creative imagination and inspiration that is strong within them. These individuals are highly imaginative and very creative, needing activities that channel and direct those energies.

This kind of creativity, stimulated by these totems, is similar to the kind of creative life force often associated with beings of the Faerie realm in legend and lore. The Selkies of the Shetland Islands and Iceland were water spirits who took the form of gray seals. According to legend, at night they would come on shore and shed their seal skins, walking and dancing in the moonlight as men and women. The women selkies were very beautiful and desirous, while the male selkies were handsome and amorous. Human women who wished to have children would cry seven tears into the water to draw out a selkie lover from its depths.

There are no limits to the creative energies stimulated by this totem. They enliven dreams and awaken the imagination so they can be applied to the outer. The archetypal force of the seals and sea lions helps those with them as totems to learn to balance the inner imagination with the outer realities—making both aspects more colorful and beneficial.

SKUNK

> **KEYNOTE:** *Sensuality, Respect, and Self-Esteem*
> **CYCLE OF POWER:** *Year-round*

At Brukner Nature Center where I volunteer in the animal program and as a trail guide lecturer, there is a tradition in giving the animal talks. Before the skunk is brought out to be shown, the audience is made to raise their hands and repeat after the speaker: "I promise . . . not to . . . hold my nose . . . or go `Ooooh!' . . . when the next animal is brought out." Of course, everyone usually knows by then that it is the skunk they are about to see.

The skunk is one of the most widely recognized mammals, but it is also one of the most misunderstood. It is a very powerful totem with mystical and magical associations. Just look at how people respond to it. They show great respect for it and what it can do. This is part of what skunk teaches. It teaches how to give respect, expect respect, and demand respect.

The Skunk

The skunk is most noted for its spray which has such a recognizable fragrance. Although the spray does not kill, it awakens a healthy respect in those who encounter it.

(Photo courtesy of Brukner Nature Center, Troy, Ohio.)

312

It helps you to recognize your own qualities and to assert them.

The skunk does not get out of the way of any animal. It moves along at its own speed, with its own mind. It is self-assured and confident in itself. If skunk has shown up, it can be to help you with this particular aspect. It can teach you how to be more self-assured and how to assert yourself.

The natural enemy of the skunk is the great horned owl. Skunk is its favorite food. This owl should be studied as it is also part of the contrary or balancing medicine of the skunk. Its essence can help you in seeing how best to apply your skunk medicine.

Skunks are fearless, but they are also very peaceful. They move slowly and calmly, and they only spray as a last resort. Because they are peaceable by nature, they always give warnings before spraying. This warning involves three stages. First, it will stamp its feet and turn its back to you. Second it will raise its tail up, as the gland which sprays is located underneath it. When the third step arrives, it is usually too late. After raising the tail, the skunk will look back over its shoulder. This is to line up the correct angle for spraying. Once the skunk has seen you over its shoulder, it is too late.

The skunk can spray 12-15 feet with tremendous accuracy. It can repeat the spraying five to six times before it must build up again naturally. The spray is an irritating chemical. It won't kill, but it can sting the eyes and numb the senses. Sometimes a skunk can show up as a totem to teach us how to get more attention without being arrogant and irritating. Sometimes it shows up to help us deal with those people in our life who are outrageously irritating. Tomato juice is still the one thing which helps to eliminate skunk odor. Those with this totem may find they have a sensitivity to tomato, or a need for more within their life. The qualities and characteristics of the tomato should be studied as it is part of the contrary or balancing medicine associated with the skunk.

The skunk smell is one that almost everyone can recognize. This has links to how skunk awakens in others a greater recognition of you and your own abilities. The sense of smell also has ties to sensuality and sexuality. Research is currently being conducted that reveals the various connections between fragrance and sexual response. This includes work with pheromones and studies that reveal a surprising similarity between the cells of and response of the olfactory nerves, and those within the genitalia.[17]

Fragrance has long been used as an aphrodisiac. Those with skunk medicine will find that the use of fragrances will elicit dynamic responses in those they associate with. People will respond to the fragrances you employ. A study of aromatherapy would be very beneficial for those with this totem. When skunk shows up, you can usually expect to experience stronger sexual responses to others and in their response to you. A greater ability to attract people will begin to unfold.

---

17 According to the *Random House Dictionary of the English Language* (New York: Random House, 1970), p. 1081, a pheromone is "any of a class of hormonal substances secreted . . . stimulating a physiological or behavioral response . . . "

It is interesting how people respond to some fragrances. They complain that certain smells drive them nuts. How often have you heard people say, "I wish I knew what that smell was. It reminds me of something and it's driving me crazy."

Skunks usually have one litter of young per year, with about ten babies. Skunks can spray from the moment their eyes open. This again reflects the intense energy levels that individuals with this totem are often born with. In the early years, they may find extreme cycles of either repelling or being pushed away by others, or drawing lots—many friends or no friends, never alone or always alone. At 20 weeks they are capable of being out on their own. A skunk can have a lifespan in the wild of up to ten years. This reflects the kinds of cycles likely to manifest for those with this totem.

Skunks are known carriers of rabies. Mothers that have rabies will pass it on to the young, although the young may not show any symptoms of it for up to six weeks after being born.

Individuals with skunks as totems must learn to balance the ability to draw and repel people. There is a natural cycle. The skunk is a solitary animal for the most part. Skunks can remind us that there are times best for drawing people and there are times best to avoid people. Finding the correct balance is what can ensure prosperity.

There are two main types of skunk—spotted and striped. The striped is the most common and most easily recognized. It actually has a double stripe that runs from its head to its tail. This stripe, whether single or double, is an indication of the active flow of the kundalini or life force. (The kundalini has ties to the sexual energies nd to the life force that is active in every aspect of our life processes.) In individuals with this totem, the kundalini is usually already active. Skunk shows up at a time to amplify and to teach the control and use of this life force more effectively.

In eastern metaphysics, students are taught of three channels of energy that flow through the body along the spine—the ida, the pingala, and the sushumna—the moon, sun, and the balance of the two. This reflects the ability of those with skunk medicine to be able to turn on and off the creative force and direct it along several lines.

Skunks are usually quite silent, so it is good for those with this totem *not* to blow their own horns. It will backfire and only serve to push others away. Sit back and let others do the noticing for you.

Skunks are very adaptable and this is what those with this totem must also learn. Skunk can teach you when its best to be noticed and how to go about it most effectively. They are carnivorous, but they will eat almost anything, particularly insects, berries, and fruit. Skunk does its hunting at night.

When skunk shows up as a totem you are going to have opportunities to bring out new respect and self-esteem. It indicates lessons and times associated with increased sensuality physically, sexually, psychically, and spiritually. Examine your self-image. Remember that people are going to notice you. How they notice and remember can be controlled by you. This is what skunk can help teach.

SNOW LEOPARD

> **KEYNOTE:** *Overcoming Our Demons and Haunts, and Renewal of Vision and Vitality*
>
> **CYCLE OF POWER:** *DAWN—Early Morning, and Dusk—Early Evening*

Leopards and jaguars are the two spotted members of the big cat family. Often they are linked and called the same thing—given the generic name of "panther." A study of the section on "Panthers" will reveal even further insight.

Of all the big cats, leopards are the best at stalking prey. They can remain silent and inconspicuous until they are within only a few feet of their prey. Then they reveal themselves only for a few seconds at the instant of attack.

Leopards have a strong hunting instinct and intuition, which usually shows up in cubs at an early age. Those with any leopard totem usually have strong intuitive faculties and heightened sensibilities. Leopard cubs learn quickly what is within their ability to capture and how best to approach it. Trusting that inner instinct is part of the life lesson for those with this totem. This can be difficult in developing trust, especially in Western society where we are often taught to ignore the intuitive and only follow the logical.

The leopard negotiates its environment in silence. Imitating the walk of the leopard can be a means of helping those with this totem attune to it. The leopard walks with each paw turned inward. The outer edge of the paw will touch the ground first, and thus objects which could cause noise can be avoided before the leopard's full weight comes down on them.

The leopard hunts best at night, and it will often store its prey in a tree. One of the traditional trademarks of the leopard is the tail dangling down. The long graceful tail is often a symbol of sexuality and innate potential.

The snow leopard is found in the high mountains of Asia. This may reflect possible past-life connections to those areas in which it is commonly found. Its green eyes and grayish white coat dappled with rosettes make it one of the most beautiful members of the leopard family. For those with this totem, meditation on its green eyes, the northern direction, and its mountainous and rocky homes may provide insight into its specific role in your life.

Of all leopards, snow leopards are considered the least aggressive. Although many big cats are known to occasionally take human prey, the snow leopard does not do this, even though they are quite capable of taking down prey much larger than themselves. Their environment forces them to be extremely agile and excellent leapers. This hints at its ability to teach those with this totem how to make great leaps over new obstacles in their life.

The snow leopard has been surrounded by mystery and lore. In Central Asia arose a belief that snow leopards do not eat the flesh of their victims, but only suck their blood. Although this probably originated because of the puncture marks created when the leopard suffocates its prey, it has great symbolism. The blood of anything is its life force. In most societies there existed the belief that what one ate, one became. An animal that only took the blood and not the flesh may indicate great discrimination so that only the powers and life force of the prey is assumed and not its weaknesses (symbolized by the flesh). For those with this totem, it can reflect opportunity to learn how to find the lost life force and drink from it once more, without becoming enmeshed in the old patterns.

There is also an old story of Milarepa, Tibet's poet-saint, who was stranded for six months in the Great Cave of Conquering Demons. When his followers went to find him, they found he had been transformed into a snow leopard. The snow leopard is a totem that can reflect a renewed energy, ability, and opportunity to conquer one's own great demons. Those with this totem would do well to research and meditate upon the life of Milarepa.

The snow leopard lives in the high mountains. Mountains have always been places separate from humans. They were the abodes of gods. They are places of good vista. The animals of mountain gods and goddesses were often sacred to the divine in some way. When a snow leopard reveals itself, it hints of divine protection and a reawakening of one's own spark of divinity.

The snow leopard is solitary and secretive, so for it to be seen is a rare and precious experience—even if only in a vision. The snow leopard has an uncanny ability to blend into the rocky vastness of its environment. Although they have a stocky appearance, due to their thick coat, they are actually slightly smaller than regular leopards, but they are equally good predators. The qualities of the bharal (blue sheep) should also be studied by those with this totem as it is one of its most common prey.

If a snow leopard has revealed itself, look for a time to clear out the haunts and demons within the mind. The strength and vitality to do so will be there—vibrant and plentiful. Great leaps in overcoming them will occur.

It can reflect a period of 22–24 months in which the old demons are chased away and new vistas open up. (At the age of about 22 months, the young are able to be out on their own.) The snow leopard holds the promise of new life, new perception, and a renewed perspective on life.

SQUIRREL

KEYNOTE: *Activity and Preparedness*

CYCLE OF POWER: *Year-round*

Everyone is familiar with the squirrel. It is a member of the rodent family, and is often seen scurrying about, as if always busy or bursting with nervous energy. Squirrels can be quite sociable, but they don't like strange squirrels. They are often observed scrounging about for food and digging holes in the earth and storing nuts and other food sources for later times. Their keen sense of smell will enable them to find their stored caches even if they do forget where they buried their nuts.

There are two main types of squirrels, the gray and the red. There is also a black squirrel which is a more aggressive strain of the gray. The gray is found most often within the city, while the red is found more commonly in forests and woods.

There is also the flying squirrel, which does not really fly. Its skin stretches and enables it to glide from tree to ground or tree to tree. Unlike the gray and the red, it is nocturnal. It strongly dislikes being disturbed

The Gray Squirrel

Squirrels seem to always be active and busy, scurrying about. Much of their time is spent gathering and storing foods they will need for the winter, as they do not hibernate. They will eat heavily and put on weight and thicken their fur in preparation though. They are symbols of preparedness and activity.

(Photo courtesy of Brukner Nature Center, Troy, Ohio.)

during the day. Owls are usually the flying squirrel's chief predators.

Red squirrels are the sentinels of the forest. They chatter and scold when strangers appear. It seems as if they are literally reporting the news to all who can hear. The red squirrel is more aggressive and is usually a much better fighter than the larger gray. The marten is the red squirrel's most dangerous enemy, and it should be studied as well. Red squirrels usually have two litters per year, with two to seven young. Within twelve weeks of birth they are usually capable of being on their own. This twelve-week cycle would be good to examine in regard to your own life, if red squirrel has come to you.

The gray squirrel is the most common and the most enthusiastic. Like all squirrels, it does not hibernate. It builds its nests in the hollows of trees or in tree-tops. The nests are usually ball-shaped, and the entrance is on the side. Even though it is bigger than the red, if confronted the gray will usually run and avoid any fight. Its predominant predators are foxes and raptors such as the owl and hawk. Gray squirrels, like the red, usually have two litters per year, and they also are usually able to be on their own in about twelve weeks.

All squirrels can be quite sociable. They wrestle for play, and they are extremely observant and imitative. This imitation of other squirrels is how they learn. Individuals with squirrel totems learn best by doing rather than by studying.

Squirrels are also quite communicative. Their chatter can often be heard in the trees when disturbed or playing. Their bushy tail adds to their expressiveness, along with providing warmth, shade, and balance. The squirrel will often express emotion through flicks of its tail.

Every squirrel is unique, and its medicine will be activated differently for everyone. If squirrel has scampered into your life, examine your own activity and preparedness. Are you too active? Not active enough? Are you not planning at all for the future, distant or near? Are you becoming too erratic—running to and fro and not accomplishing anything? Do you need to learn how to save and ration on any level—including money, time, energy, etc.? Are you afraid you will never have enough? Are you getting too hung up on collecting and accumulating? Are you gathering and not giving?

Squirrels can teach us balance within the circle of gathering and giving out. If we are doing too much of one or the other, squirrel may appear to help us. Squirrels are the masters at preparing, but they also are reminders that in our quest for our goals, we should always make time to socialize and play. Work and play go hand-in-hand, or the work will create problems and become more difficult and less fruitful.

TIGER

> **KEYNOTE:** *Passion, Power, Devotion and Sensuality*
>
> **CYCLE OF POWER:** *Nocturnal—Full Moon and New Moon*

Tigers are magnificent and stir a feeling of awe in all who see them. There are a number of varieties of tigers—bengal, Siberian, etc.—and each should be examined for its own characteristics. The information on cats and panthers should also be studied as there is often an overlap.

All tigers are known for their ferocity and their power. They are also excellent swimmers, unlike other large cats. This gives them ties to all the energies and mystical qualities so often associated with the element of water. All tigers also display great motherly devotion with their offspring. The mother raises the young and teaches them to hunt. Most tigers are solitary, and they come together usually only to mate. They also have immense territories.

The Siberian tiger is considered by many to be the most magnificent, and most experts agree that this species of tiger originated in the northern part of East Asia. It would later migrate and evolve to live in warmer areas. The Siberian tiger is an untiring traveler. It can cover great distances in a single day. Tigers prey upon all types of animals, but wild boar is a frequent victim.

The Bengal tiger lives in southern Asia. Its main prey is deer. It will usually live in several lairs, one of which is used to bring up the young cubs. At eight weeks old the cubs join their mother in hunting. At six months, they have learned to kill, but they are not capable of feeding themselves until they are around sixteen months old.

Most tigers hunt slowly and silently, a tactic beneficial to learn for those with this totem—regardless what is being sought. They can be selfish with their kills, and they have the power to drag a several-hundred-pound carcass over a quarter mile, just to hide it.

Tigers are nocturnal hunters. Individuals with this totem will find their most effective work accomplished at night. The traditional black and gold/orange patterning links the tiger to the mysticism surrounding the new and full moons.

The sleek and powerful muscles and the soft thick coat of the tiger stimulates thoughts of sensuality. All cats stretch languorously and rub up against other cats and objects. For those with this totem, there will be awakened a new sensuality—a sensitivity to touch.

There has always been a great deal of mysticism and mythology centered on the tiger. A study of these associations will help you to identify its role within your own life and possibly even past-life links to other parts of the world.

In Korea, the tiger is the king of beasts. In the Hindu tradition, the tiger was sacred to the goddess Kali, the goddess of creation and dissolution, of sexuality and death. In Greece, it was associated with the mythic character Dionysus, the twice-born.

China is filled with myth and legend of the tiger. In Chinese astrology, one of the twelve signs is the sign of the tiger. Those born in the year of the tiger are assigned the traits of being both colorful and unpredictable. They are adventurous, powerful, and passionate.

In China, the tiger is both a symbol of darkness and the new moon, as well as brightness and the full moon. There are five mythic tigers in Chinese lore. The red tiger is a symbol of the south, summer, and fire. The black tiger is a symbol of the north, winter, and water. The blue tiger is a symbol of the east, spring, and vegetation. The white tiger is a symbol of the west, autumn, and all metals. The yellow tiger is supreme among all five. It is the ruler of the Earth and all energies upon it.

If a tiger has entered your life, you can expect new adventures. It will awaken new passion and power within life. Expect it to begin within 6-8 weeks and last for at least a year and a half. Examine what is going on in your life. Do you need more passion for life? Are you expressing your life passion inappropriately? Has your energy been down? If tiger has shown up, there will begin to manifest new adventures and renewed devotion and passion for life.

WEASEL

KEYNOTE: *Sly and Secret Circumvention and/or Pursuit*

CYCLE OF POWER: *Nocturnal*

The weasel is a member of the mustelid group of mammals. This family includes, skunks, badgers, fishers, minks, otters, martens, and wolverines. They are all recognizable by their long bodies, short legs, and ears that are generally rounded and especially small. All produce a strong musk scent and usually have underground homes. They are also all carnivores.

There are three branches of mustelids. Some dig for their food and are not strictly carnivores, although meat entails a large part of their diet. This branch includes skunks and badgers. A second branch are those who are expert at swimming and catching prey in the water, such as the otter. The third group are almost strictly land carnivores, and it is this group in which weasels belong.

Weasels are almost entirely meat eaters. They kill mice, rodents, and other pests, and in the wild they stick strictly with natural foods. For those with this totem, this behavior may need to be examined in regard to their own best health interests.

Weasels require tremendous amounts of food. A weasel will eat from one-third to one-half of its weight in food every day. They eat small amounts all day long because they expend a lot of energy. This is a dietary practice that those with this totem will find most effective for their own health and well being. The weasel will also do all the killing necessary for it to eat through the day before it ever eats a bite. It will take the food to its own den and enclosure.

The weasel is a great chaser. It has an excellent sense of smell, so once it has its prey's scent, it can trace it. The long, slim body enables it to follow mice into burrows. It has a wonderful ability to squeeze through narrow spaces. Weasel medicine can help you get out of tight fixes and to squeeze through and into areas of life that others would not be able to enter.

The weasel is graceful, solitary and very silent. Though weasel people may often be loners, they uncover a lot about people in their lives. Their ability for silence enables them to go unseen and unheard, even in the company of others. Because of this things are said and done in front of weasel people without others realizing. Weasel can show you how to use your powers of silent observation to sniff out what is hidden or secretive without anyone being the wiser.

In the Native American tradition, the weasel has the medicine for seeking out secrets. Trust your own senses in regard to other people, and you will come out all right, even if it means going alone. This is part of what weasel teaches.

Ferocity is probably greatest among the weasel family of all mammals. Mothers will even attack humans if they feel their young are threatened.

Weasels usually bite their prey at the neck and hang on until the spinal cord is cut or the animal bleeds to death. Individuals with this totem have a knack for going for the throat of those who threaten or try to best them. Once aroused, they will hang on until the damage is done. Remember that weasels are carnivorous, and weasel people, if angered, do not hesitate to attack in some way. This can be verbal assaults that cut deep and sure and inflict lasting wounds. Weasels are naturally silent when hunting, but they have a wide range of vocalizations. The worse thing an individual could do would be to assume that a weasel person was weak simply because he/she was silent.

When weasel shows up as a totem, examine your life. Do you need to develop your observation skills? Are you being too vocal in your pursuits? Telling others about your goals will undermine your own pursuit of them. Are you not digging hard enough? Is there a narrow space that you may have to squeeze through? Are you or others around you being fully honest? If not, weasel will help you to see it. Are you missing the obvious? Are you not trusting your own feelings and senses—regardless of others?

Weasel medicine awakens your innate ability for silent and secret observation. It will show you the best techniques for circumventing trouble. It can teach you how to pursue your goals on any level with the greatest success.

WHALE

KEYNOTE: *Creation, Power of Song, Awakening Inner Depths*
CYCLE OF POWER: *Year-round*

The whale is the world's largest mammal. Whales form part of a large group of warm blooded mammals adapted to life in the sea. Many myths speak of how all life upon the planet, especially human, sprang from the seas. Because of this and other reasons we will discuss, the whale is an ancient symbol for creation—be it of the body or our world.

The people of the Arctic are often considered the most careful observers of Nature, for only this would enable them to survive the most unforgiving of climates. The Inuit (Inupriaq) had a special relationship with the bowhead whale, and one of their legends tell how it was the most magnificent creation that the Great Spirit had made.

There are ninety or so different species of cetaceans or whales—including dolphins and porpoises. There are sperm whales, killer whales, pilot whales, narwhals, humpback whales, and the largest mammals on the planet, blue whales. All whales have blowholes by which they exhale. Imitating the spouting breath of whales can aid in freeing your own creative energies. All whales have blubber which serves to insulate and store energy for the whales. The whale can help teach you how to insulate yourself and use your own creative energies more conservatively. All whales also conserve oxygen under water by decreasing the blood flow to areas of the body where it is non-essential. Whales have an ancient knowledge of how to use the creative force of breath for a variety of purposes.

Most whales are divided into one of two groups, toothed and baleen. Toothed whales have sharp teeth by which they catch and eat fish and other marine animals. This group includes sperm whales, pilot whales, dolphins, and such. Most eat fish, squid, and other marine animals. They usually are found in herds or pods. Toothed whales have demonstrated great reasoning capabilities and even creative thinking at times. They can stimulate this in those with them as a totem.

Baleen whales do not have teeth. Their mouths are lines with bony plates made of hardened keratin. They strain sea water through these plates, feeding on the plankton or sea life within it. The baleen whales are the largest.

The humpback member of the baleen family is most noted for its wonderful song. The beautiful sounds are sung by the males, and each breeding season brings with it corresponding song changes. This reflects the ability of the whale to teach us how to create through sound and song, adjusting it to the time and place and individual. By drawing upon your own creative instincts, you can sing forth your own song.

Whales also have a form of sonar or echo-location. This sensitivity to sound again links the whale to the primal creative sounds of life. Sound is the creative force of life. Directing it and responding to its feedback is part of what the whale teaches. This can be used to tap hidden levels of your own mind or even to accelerate the manifestation of goals.

Whales at one time were also symbols of containment, concealment, and even resurrection. The Biblical story of Jonah and the whale is the prime example. For three days, Jonah lived within the belly of the whale before he came forth. He was given a second birth. He was resurrected. When we learn to go deep within our selves, the creativity that we awaken can resurrect our lives—if we bring it out and apply it.

Whales will occasionally breach—coming completely out of the water. Whale people are very creative, but they have to come out of those creative waters. They must stay in contact with the real world. Are you becoming lost in your own creative imagination? Are you not taking it and using it in your outer life? Are you keeping everything inside and afraid to let it out? If so, it is time to breach. Show the magnificence and power of your own creativity. Do not hold back.

If whales are showing up in your life, you should examine your use—or lack of use—of your own creativity. Are you not simply mimicking what others have done or are you building upon it in new and dynamic ways? Are you applying your own creative intuition to old processes and life formulas? This and this alone is what imbues them with power and magic.

Remember that the whale was a gift of the Great Spirit to the Inuit people. It was what enabled them to survive. It was the most beautiful of all beasts but it had practical uses as well. Creativity for the sake of creativity is not what whale teaches. It awakens great depths of creative inspiration, but so it can add color and light to your outer life to make it more wondrous.

WOLF

KEYNOTE: *Guardianship, Ritual, Loyalty, and Spirit*
CYCLE OF POWER: *Year Round—Full Moons—Twilight*

Wolves are probably the most misunderstood of the wild mammals. Tales of terror and their cold-bloodedness abound. Although many stories tell otherwise, there has never been any confirmed attack and killing of a human by a healthy wolf. In spite of the negative press, wolves are almost the exact opposite of how they are portrayed. They are friendly, social, and highly intelligent. Their sense of family is strong and loyal, and they live by carefully defined rules and rituals.

Wolves are the epitome of the wild spirit. Their positive characteristics are so numerous it is no wonder that Native Americans and others practically deified them. Many believe that the true test of America's sincerity about protecting the environment will revolve around whether or not the wolf remains protected and is allowed to be reintroduced into areas of the country where it has heretofore been eliminated. The wolf is the true spirit of the free and unspoiled wilderness.

There are several kinds of wolves in North America. The red wolf is the smallest and it may even be extinct in the wild, although there are efforts to reintroduce it. Its territory was in the southern United States. The Mexican wolf is a subspecies of the more common gray wolf. It is found in the southwest United States and Mexico. It was hunted almost to extinction, and is now part of a recovery and captive breeding plan. The Arctic wolf is probably the purest breed. Living in an isolated area around the Arctic circle has enabled its survival.

The gray or timber wolf is the most common. Only in Alaska, Canada, and the region around the Great Lakes area is it found today. It was hunted to extinction in all other areas of the country. The gray wolf is not always gray. It may be black, gray, brown, white, or various combinations.

Probably the biggest misconception of wolves is about their size. They are not nearly as large as most people imagine. Their thick fur gives an appearance of greater size, but they are usually no taller than a good-sized German Shepherd.

Wolves are very ritualistic—in as many ways as humans. They live by carefully defined rules. There are specific territories that are sacred. Their social behavior is based upon a hierarchical structure. Each has its place and function within the hierarchy. There is an "alpha" male and an "alpha" female.

Wolves do not fight unnecessarily. In fact, they will often go out of their way to avoid it. Though they are extremely strong and powerful, disagreements rarely end in serious fights. Often a glance, a posture, a growl is all that is necessary to determine dominance. They don't have to demonstrate it, but they are capable if it comes down to it. This is part of what wolf medicine teaches. The wolf teaches you to know who you are and to develop strength, confidence and surety in that so that you do not have to demonstrate and prove yourself to all.

Wolves have a complex communication system—using body language. The movement of the head, an erect tail, direct eye contact—all have great meaning. The postures are often subtle, but each wolf learns from the time they are pups how to read and respond. The facial expressions of the wolf are varied and useful in conveying the mood to other members of the pack. It is a most important visual center of communication. It also uses its tail position to effectively communicate as well. Usually those with wolf totems are very expressive with hands, posture, face or in some other manner. If you have difficulty conveying your moods and ideas to others, meditate and study the wolf. It will teach you how to empower your verbal communications with appropriate body language.

Wolves also have a complex system of vocal communications. They howl, whimper, whine, growl, and even bark. Even the howls for which they are famous have a variety of meanings. The howls may serve as a signal to call others of the pack or to locate the other members. They may be a social expression. They are used to greet one another and to define certain territories. They even howl just for the joy of it.

Every member of the pack knows its position in relationship to everyone else within that pack. The ritualistic behaviors that establish the wolf ranks are part of its magic. Wolf packs are not entirely autocratic—under the supreme rule of the alpha member. Neither are they democratic. There are times when both occur, and it is this flexibility which adds to the success of the wolf government. Wolf can teach the lesson of proper governorship—a balance between authority and democracy. Wolf can teach you how to use ritual to establish order and harmony within your own life. Wolf helps us to understand that true freedom requires discipline.

The alpha male and female often mate for life. Breeding season is usually in late winter, with the female giving birth about two months later. All members of the pack show great care and affection toward the playful pups. They are extremely tolerant. If the mother or father is unable to care for them, then another member will adopt the young. Some wolves will even serve as babysitters. Adult wolves are friendly and amiable toward pups, and wolf medicine teaches respect and honor for family and for children.

Wolves become sexually mature at about the age of 22–24 months. For those who have a wolf come to them, look for its energies and influence in your life to take this same possible time pattern.

Wolves are, of course, predators. Their prey consists most often of the sick, the young, and the old. Deer is their most common prey animal. Wolves will not waste much time on a healthy adult moose that stands its ground. Wolves travel great distances in their hunting. They have a stamina and strength that enables them to travel far, and for extended periods. They have been clocked at 24 to 28 miles per hour. Although the wolf can't maintain that speed for any great length of time, it does seem able to trot indefinitely at about five miles per hour. In winter wolves will use frozen lakes and rivers as travel routes and can travel 15-25 kilometers in a single night.

Wolves usually consume all that they capture, gorging themselves. For those with wolf totems, this can indicate a need to make use of all that is available to you. Sometimes wolves show up as a totem to remind us not to waste, as much as to remind us to keep our spirits alive.

The wolf has an extreme intelligence. It goes out of its way to avoid trouble or danger. Some believe that wolves even use ravens as aerial spotters for possible food sources.[18] The raven has a connection to the moose in Eskimo lore, and since moose can be a prey of wolves, raven is linked to them as well. Ravens will often follow wolves. They will fly ahead, land in a tree and wait for the wolves to pass, and then fly on again. Wolf expert David Mech reported a playful behavioral relationship sometimes displayed between wolves and ravens.[19] Raven should also be studied by those with wolf totems.

Wolves have extremely keen senses, particularly that of smell. It is said to be one hundred times greater than that of humans. The sense of smell endows it with great discrimination, and the sense of smell has often been associated with spiritual idealism in metaphysical circles.

The wolf also has an excellent hearing sensitivity. Its hunting depends strongly upon its sense of smell and hearing. This would be a reminder to those with this totem to listen to their own inner thoughts and words. The intuition will be strong. This idea is even further emphasized by the thick coat of fur the wolf has. Fur and hair have long been symbols of psychic abilities. The wolf has both an inner coat and an outer, giving it the ability to reflect the archetypal forces associated with psychic insight.

The wolf has a capacity for making quick and firm emotional attachments. Learning to trust your own insights and to secure your attachments accordingly is part of what wolf medicine teaches. The wolf can help you to hear the inner and guard you from inappropriate actions. It will guard you as it teaches you—sometimes strongly, sometimes gently—but always with love. When wolf shows up, it is time to breathe new life into your life rituals. Find a new path, take a new journey, take control of your life. You are the governor of your life. You create it and direct it. Do so with harmony and discipline, and then you will know the true spirit of freedom.

---

18 Brower, Kenneth. "The Wolf Man of Riding Mountain," *Harrowsmith*, *ii:11* (September/October 1987), p. 75.
19 Mech, L. David. *The Wolf* (Minneapolis: University of Minnesota Press, 1970), p. 288.

PART FOUR

THE EXOTIC LANGUAGE OF INSECTS AND REPTILES

The children opened Elder Brother's bag and out of it flew the first butterflies. Their wings were bright as sunlight and held all of the colors of the flowers and the leaves, the cornmeal, the pollen and the green pine needles. They were red and gold and black and yellow, blue and green and white. They looked like flowers dancing in the wind. They flew about the heads of children and the children laughed. As those first butterflies flew, they sang and the children listened.[1]

---

1   From *Keepers of the Animals: Native American Animal Stories and Wildlife Activities for Children*, by Michael J. Caduto and Joseph Bruchar, Fulcrum Publishing, Inc., 350 Indiana St., #350, Golden, CO 80401, (303) 277-1623.

CHAPTER FOURTEEN

INSIGHT INTO THE WORLD
OF INSECTS

Seldom does anything cause as strong emotional response in humans as a close encounter with insects. Some respond with fear, while others respond in awe. Still others try and ignore the most plentiful group of animal life upon the planet. It is estimated that there are over 800,000 species of insects, with a multitude of varieties within those species.[1]

Insects are both ancient within the history of this planet, and also as symbols within the history of humanity. Humans have long attributed characteristics to certain kinds of insects. Although this is a form of anthropomorphism, it is important to understand that often the qualities associated with insects were attributed to them because of a characteristic they displayed. Again, as with any animal, we do not have to believe that they have a creative intelligence, but we can recognize that the behaviors, instincts, and patterns they do display can reflect and symbolize certain archetypal forces as yet not fully understood.

Many modern shamans issue precautions about working with insect totems, implying that the archetypal force or spirit behind it is too primitive and difficult an energy with which to effectively work. I believe each must determine this for himself or herself. In spite of these warnings, insects have been used as totems in many societies for a long time.

To the Kalihari Bushmen, the praying mantis is an animal bushmen. Their legends and lore are filled with the teachings of Mantis and its mystical qualities.

---

1 Farb, Peter *The Insects* (New York: Time-Life Books, 1968), p. 17.

The spider in the Native American tradition is both grandmother and creator, a symbol of the ability to weave new energies into being. To the medieval peoples, dragonflies were often miniature dragons and signs of doorways into the Faerie Realm. We must be careful about making generalizations. Remember that the key to learning animal—speak is to understand the behaviors and qualities of the animal. This will help you to determine its role in Nature and its symbolic role within your own life.

Examine insects in general, and then the specific ones you seem to continually encounter. Especially pay attention to those unusual ones that you come across. Recently upon a trip to Florida, I visited a nature center. I had gone with the expressed purposes of meditating upon certain changes and activities I was hoping to initiate while in Florida. All along the trail I had dragonflies and butterflies buzzing and flying around me. Every time I'd stop, they'd light upon my hand, head, or shoulders. Later I was to encounter the most beautiful spider I had seen in ages. It was called a Golden Orb Weaver, and its web was artistic, beautiful, and intricate. The significance of these insects was not lost on me. They held the promise of new adventures and new beginnings. It turned out to be one of the most successful in that area, and it opened new doors for the future.

Usually, anything small, creepy and crawly is classified as an insect, but this is not accurate. Ticks, spiders, centipedes, and such are members of another class of animals entirely. Insects have jointed legs and three body parts—the head, abdomen, and thorax. They also have three pairs of legs, and most have at some time, one or two pairs of wings attached to the thorax and a set of antennae attached to the head.

Spiders have eight legs and no antennae. Their eyes are simple and small, and the head and thorax are fused together. They are arthropods like insects, but of a different class. For the purposes of this book, I am including spiders along with the other insects within the dictionary.

Insects are opportunists, something from which we all can learn. They are the most diversified lifeform, and there are so many types that one-third to one-half are estimated not to even have names. Insects are enduring, and they seem to possess an uncanny wisdom, doing many of the same things humans do but with greater efficiency—including raising their own crops (fungus), herding insect "cattle," and living in highly structured and complex social organizations.

Insects succeed as a group because of six primary qualities. First, their ability to fly enables them to spread. Second, they are extremely adaptable to the environment and climactic conditions. Third, they have an external skeleton which provides a kind of armor for themselves. Fourth, their small size keeps their demands meager and more accessible. Fifth, reproduction enables the species to survive. They can delay fertilization until the food supply and living conditions for the young are most likely to be beneficial. And finally, they have the ability for metamorphosis. They can undergo multiple (usually four) changes to facilitate and carry on life.

All of these characteristics can be viewed symbolically as ideas which would assist humans to be more successful within their own lives. We, of course, can not fly, but we can make sure that we don't get stuck in what is too comfortable. It can reflect a need to continue to explore new avenues in life and not to become too content. We can't wear our skeleton on the outside, but we can develop our sensitivity to the energies around us and strengthen our own auric fields so that we are less likely to become victimized. We can keep our demands small, and not be so wasteful within our lives. Many people fail at life because they try to accomplish the great all at once, rather than building and doing a little at a time so that it becomes great over time. The delaying of fertilization until living conditions can support it has multiple applications—the most obvious having to do with all the problems of overpopulation in the world.

Lastly is the process of metamorphosis. Change is inevitable in life, and life only becomes more difficult and dangerous on many levels when we resist its natural flow. Change ensures growth. We have to shed the old before we can come into the new. Metamorphosis is the magic inherent within insects. It is the magic of life that they can teach.

Biologically and physiologically, humans recognize that there are changes—childhood, puberty, adulthood. Change should occur on other levels and is necessary at other times. Everything we create in life has to go through stages. These align with the four stages of insect metamorphosis. All insects and thus all ideas and creations begin as eggs. The eggs hatch into caterpillars which feed and spin cocoons. From a cocoon comes its final expression of life—usually with wings.

In the egg stage, there is the fertilization process. We give birth—to an idea, an activity, a new quality, or something. From the egg stage comes the larva. In insects, the egg becomes a caterpillar in this stage. The caterpillar feeds and works

to strengthen itself and achieve its foundation. Ideas and creativity need to be worked with, shaped, formed, developed, and honed. When this is accomplished, when the caterpillar has laid itself a new foundation, the stage of chrysalis begins.

A cocoon is woven around itself by the caterpillar, and a mummylike pupa forms within. In this stage there is a reorganization of the caterpillar's cells even though there is the appearance of lifelessness. Sometimes individuals need to back off, after laying a foundation, and then go deeply within so that creation will be able to come forth strong and in new light. There are points in the creative process where we must be passive and let things take a natural course. We do what we must, and then let it move on its own. This is reflected in the chrysalis stage.

From the chrysalis comes yet a new and final form—a winged insect. The fact that it has wings in its final stages is very significant, and all of the symbolism associated with wings apply to insects as well as birds. The adult only comes out of the cocoon in the warmth of spring—again reflecting the ability to go within and determine the best time to set the new creations in motion on a higher level. Wings are the emblem of the adult insect and thus the adult creation. Flight now becomes a way of life for however long the adult survives.

Within the stages of metamorphosis are the keys to creating and manifesting anything. Those with or without insect totems would do well to study and meditate on how insects molt old forms, shedding the old to come into new forms. Insects remind us that we are never the same. We are always changing, and that is the only constant. But that is also the force of creation. This may have been exactly what the Caterpillar had in mind as he spoke to Alice in *Alice's Adventures in Wonderland:*

> ". . . Being so many different sizes in a day is very confusing."
>
> "It isn't," said the Caterpillar.
>
> "Well, perhaps you haven't found it so yet," said Alice; "but when you have to turn into a chrysalis—you will some day you know—then after that into a butterfly, I should think you'll feel it a little queer, won't you?"
>
> "Not a bit," said the Caterpillar.
>
> "Well, perhaps your feelings may be different," said Alice; "all I know is, it would feel very queer to me."
>
> "You!" said the Caterpillar contemptuously. "Who are you?"[2]

Many insects live in groups or colonies—bees, wasps, and ants being the most common. These types of insects are called social insects, and there are different jobs and functions within their community. Insect totems can reflect lessons in sociability and working for and within the community.

Most insects breathe through openings within the body, located on the thorax or abdomen. Because of this insects can teach techniques on how to use cellular

---

2 Carroll, Lewis. *The Original Alice in Wonderland* (Newmarket, England: Brimax Books, 1988), p. 41.

breathing techniques to enhance overall health. This type of breathing process is part of many teachings in yoga, taoism, and other oriental traditions on the use of breath for power and health.

Each insect will have its own unique qualities and characteristics. These can reflect the energies active within your own life or needing to be developed by you. Only a study of the insect will provide the insight. Pay attention to its most unusual characteristics. For example, an ant can lift a stone 50 times its own weight. A bee can haul a burden 300 times its own weight.

This hints at the kind of energies and the symbolism attributed to insects through the ages. Such feats often have rational, as well as metaphysical, implications. The great displays of strength have to do with the fact that most insects have a different muscle development than humans. A human being has a little less than 800 individual muscles. A grasshopper has over 900; and the grasshopper, along with most other insects, has a great resistance to fatigue.[3]

Insects have many ways of protecting themselves and insuring successful survival. These should be studied and meditated upon as well. Similar applications can be used by those with insect totems. The most common is concealment and camouflage. Some employ an armor plating, some use cocoons, and some are armed with claws, stingers, chemicals, tusks, and such. What does your insect use? Are you using something similar? Should you be? Or are you using it inappropriately?

The worst enemy of insects are other insects. This is significant when we apply that same aspect to humanity. Humans are their own worst enemy. How often do we hear people say, "I did it to myself. I'm my own worst enemy." If things aren't working around you, and an insect is prominent in your life, take a look at yourself. Is there something you should be doing but you're not? Is there something you are not doing that you should?

Humans are in direct contact with their environment. We have nothing shielding the skin and senses. Insects are not in direct contact. Because of their exoskeleton, they must use other means to sense the environment.

The most dynamic sensory organ is the antennae or feelers. All antennae, antlers, horns, and head appendages have been symbols of higher consciousness, intuition, and heightened perception. The antennae of insects are constantly in motion, feeling the environment about them. This feeling aspect is what links insects with the psychic ability of psychometry in mystical traditions. Psychometry is the ability to hold an object and read its vibrations—attuning to those things and people that have occurred around the object.

The antennae of insects vary in size and shape. They are usually larger in those insects with poor eyesight. With their antennae, they can feel, smell, taste, and determine temperature. They can also use them to create sounds. The antennae have numerous tiny pegs upon them which serve as receptors.

---

3   Farb, p. 12.

The sense of touch in insects is highly developed. They have numerous touch hairs upon the legs, body, and antennae. Individuals with insect totems will find their own sensitivity to touch becoming greater. Are you too sensitive to your environment and the people within it? Are you not paying enough attention to what is around you? Are you out of touch? Are you getting too mental and ignoring the physical?

It is not unusual to find those with insect totems becoming more sensitive to touch. The skin is the outer covering of our body and our largest sensory organ. It protects while it senses. It is an ancient symbol for sensitivity and self—worth. It is also a symbol of birth and rebirth, as the cells of the skin are continually regenerating.

Insect totems may show up at times where issues of insensitivity surface. Are we being insensitive to others or they to us? Are we trying to deaden our senses to outside influences? What is bugging you? Who are you bugging?

The hearing of insects is very acute. They are even capable of detecting ultra-sound. Their hearing organs are found on the legs and the abdomen. These enable them to sense the vibrations emitted around them. Individuals with insect totems should develop their listening skills. Pay attention not only to what is being said, but also to what isn't. Pay attention to what is said through the body language of others. Trust your impressions.

Insects have no voice, but they do make noise through stridulating, the rubbing of one body part against another. The sounds serve a variety of communication functions. It helps them in finding mates and even to frighten enemies.

Insects pass messages to each other in a variety of ways. They use scent, touch, chirping, and even dances. Ants touch their feelers together. Grasshoppers rub their wings together to create communication noises. Bees will perform dances that communicate where food can be found and how plentiful it is.

The visual acuity of insects is limited. Their vision is only sharp to about three feet in most. They actually have compound eyes. This does not enable them to see more clearly and more focused than humans, but it does aid them at detecting the subtlest of movements. Insect mysticism then can teach you to pay attention to the subtlest of movements and communications within your own life.

Insects are the keepers of knowledge on subtle, non—verbal communication. They can teach us how to use these same subtleties within our own life. A good experiment is to spend a day not using any verbal—written or spoken—communication. Use gesture, posture, movement, utterances of sounds, and touch. See how well you can communicate in this manner. This is part of the wonder and the magic that has long been attributed to the forces associated with insects. This is its truest medicine, regardless of the kind of insect.

CHAPTER FIFTEEN

DICTIONARY OF INSECT TOTEMS

The following dictionary is by no means complete. It is even minuscule when compared to that of the birds and mammals given within this book. There are too many different kinds and variations of insects to cover them all. It also includes spiders which are not insects at all. They are being included in this category simply for the ease of description.

The examples given are those which have the greatest abundance of myth and lore surrounding them. The myths and their origins would make for beneficial study as well. This may provide further insight and even provide clues to possible past-life connections. Not all are described in as great detail as many of the other animals within this text, as the field of insects is too large and too intricate to explore within this book's confines. Also, many of the characteristics of insects overlap, and most of the information in the previous chapter can be applied to most insect totems.

As with all totems, study each one individually. Its behaviors, characteristics, and such will have significance. What activity is it involved in as you discover it? What time of year does it show up? What has been going on in your own life within the previous 72 hours that might be connected in some way to the energies of this insect?

Also, no *Cycle of Power* is given for them as it will vary according to the season, the lifespan (which can be relatively short in many insects), and the stage of metamorphosis. Most insects become most active in the spring and summer, with activity declining as autumn and winter approach, with winter usually bringing some form of dormancy. In spite of this, remember that even the creepy crawlies will speak to us if we will listen.

ANT

KEYNOTE: *Industriousness, Order, and Discipline*

The ant has long been a symbol of work and industry. Partly this is due to the Greek tales of the ant, such as is found in *Aesop's Fables.* Their wisdom and intellect in their endeavors is often acclaimed. There are many types of ants, some of which are solitary, but most of which are part of a larger community. Though drudgery is often associated with them,  this is far from true. When by themselves, they display simple and uncomplicated behavior patterns. Within the community, there is a repertory of activities and behaviors.

Ants are social. Much of their work centers on community activity. The primary activities are gathering, hunting and growing. Yes, some ants do farm, growing a kind of fungus. Ants also participate in food exchanges within the community, and they will often make slaves of other ants to perform labors.

There is discipline and order within most ant communities, and everyone knows his/her place. Predominantly, there are three castes: (1) the queens who found new colonies, (2) the winged males who fertilize the queens for life, and (3) the sterile females who serve as babysitters and laborers.

The queen ant has wings and the ability of flight until fertilized. Once she is fertilized, she pulls off her own wings, sacrificing her own flight for the birth of newborn. The queen usually dies after twelve years. Those with ant totems may find that the cycle of industriousness and building of goals may increase over a period of twelve years. The cycle of twelve—days, months, years, will be of significance. For those who are into numerology, this would be a beneficial number to study if the ant is your totem.

The worker ants are skilled architects. They build complex homes, galleries, and even vaulted ceilings. Their skill and undaunted efforts reflect much about what this totem can awaken. The ant is the teacher of how to build, how to become the architect of your own life. It can show you how to construct your dreams into a reality. It will show you that the greatest success occurs with persistence.

If the ant has shown up as a totem, examine your own industriousness. Are you disciplining yourself enough to accomplish the tasks at hand? Are you or those around you looking for the quick and easy way? Are you neglecting important activities? Are you laying a good foundation? Are you adding new structures to your life with each passing year in some fashion—education, jobs, hobbies, etc.? Are you being patient with your efforts? Are you being patient with yourself? With others? Are you making things greater and more difficult than they need be? Are you missing an opportunity to initiate new creations and endeavors? Ant can teach you how to harness your own power to design and recreate your life and its circumstances from the ground up. Ant can show you how best to work with others for the good of everyone. Ant teaches us that regardless of circumstances, if the effort is true, the rewards will follow—in the most beneficial time and manner. Ant is the promise of success through effort.

BEE

KEYNOTE: *Fertility and the Honey of Life*

Bees have been mythical symbols throughout the world. In Hinduism, depending upon how depicted, the bee could relate to Vishnu, Krishna or even Kama, the god of love. In Egypt it denoted royalty. In Greece, it was used in the symbology of the Eleusinian Mysteries, and the Celts associated it with hidden wisdom.[1] Probably the most significant and consistent symbolism is that of sexuality and fertility, due primarily to its stinger and its part in pollination.

Bees are also long-time symbols for accomplishing the impossible. For many years, scientists were unable to determine how bees were able to fly. Aerodynamically, the body was too large for the wings. It has only been in more recent times that science has determined that bees move their wings at such a high rate of speed that it makes flight possible. Still, it remains to many as a symbol of accomplishing quests that appeared to be impossible.

All bees are essentially "honey" bees. They gather and pollinate. Bees are often considered the busiest and most useful of insects. Without them no flowers and many fruits would never blossom. It occurs through the pollination. As the bees land upon one flower, collecting its nectar, pollen also attaches itself to the leg fibers. It is then transferred to other flowers, creating a fertilization process.

Pollination is just one productive process the bee participates in. It also furnishes food, i.e. honey, and it also preys on other insects, helping to keep the insect population in balance. Bees that build their homes in the ground help turn over the soil, often much better than the earthworm itself.

If a bee has shown up in your life, examine your own productivity. Are you doing all you can to make your life more fertile? Are you busy enough? Are you taking time to savor the honey of your endeavors or are you being a workaholic? Are you attempting to do too much? Are you keeping your desires in check so they can be more productive?

The legs of bees are one of their most sensitive organs. A bee actually tastes through its legs. It is able to determine if there is nectar in the flower it lands upon. Are you taking time to enjoy the labors and activities you involve yourself in? The bee helps remind us that activities are more productive and sweeter if we take time to enjoy them.

The stinger is often seen as a phallic symbol. Most bees only sting once. There is a barb attached to the stinger, which pulls the stinger off when used. The queen can sting more than once, but it only fights when another queen is born.

Most bees have organized communities. This is most evident in the bumble-bee family. There are the queen, the drones, and the workers. The first brood the

---

1 Cooper, J. C. *Symbolism—The Universal Language* (Northamptonshire, Aquarian Press, 1982), p. 71.

queen lays become workers, and they take over the building and maintenance of the nest. Bees, like ants, are excellent builders. The honeycombs are constructed in a six-sided shape, called a hexagon. This geometric shape has had long mystical significance associated with it. It is a symbol of the heart and the sweetness of life found within our own hearts. It is a symbol of the sun and all the energies associated with it.

The bee is the reminder to extract the honey of life and to make our lives fertile while the sun shines. The bee reminds us that no matter how great the dream there is the promise of fulfillment if we pursue it. The elixir of life is as sweet as honey, and the bee is a symbol that promises us that the opportunity to drink of it is ours if we but pursue our dreams.

BEETLE

KEYNOTE: *Resurrection*

The beetle is the most varied of all insects. There may be as many as 280,000 kinds of beetles. To put this into perspective, the number of vertebrate animals—including fish, reptiles, amphibians, birds and mammals—may be around 44,000.[2]

In Egypt, the scarab, or sacred beetle, had great significance. The beetle would take a piece of ox dung and shape it into a ball by rolling it from east to west. The eggs were laid within this and then buried. After about a month, the beetle would dig it up and push it into the water, and the young would emerge. Because of its east to west rolling, it came to be associated with the sun and its movement across the sky. The scarab thus came to be a symbol for solar deities and for new life.

As with many insects, the beetle goes through a tremendous metamorphosis from the grub stage to the winged. Because of this, it is associated with resurrection and change. In its winged stage, the front set of wings are thickened into hard covers which fold and protect the soft underside. This may indicate for those with this totem a need to be more protective, or possibly that you are too closed off.

If the beetle has shown up in your life examine the need for metamorphosis. Are you in the process? If so, what stage? Do you need a change? Are you needing new sunshine? Is it time to resurrect some aspect of your life? Is it time to leave the past behind? The beetle can show you how to do this with the greatest success.

---

2   Farb, p. 12.

BUTTERFLY

KEYNOTE: *Transmutation and the Dance of Joy*

Probably no animal or insect has come to represent the process of transformation and shapeshifting more than that of the butterfly. For those with this totem, the process of metamorphosis should be studied closely. With butterflies and moths there are always four distinct stages of change, as outlined in the previous chapter. (The cocoon is only spun by the moth, and not by a true butterfly, for the chrysalis stage).

When butterfly shows up, make note of the most important issues confronting you at the moment. This is probably why butterfly has shown up. What stage of change are you at in regard to them? To determine that, you may have to examine and determine what you wish the outcome to be, and how best to accomplish it.

The butterfly is a powerful symbol in myth and religion. In early Christianity, it was a symbol of the soul. In China, it was used as a symbol of conjugal bliss and joy. In the Hopi tradition, unmarried girls of the butterfly clan wore their hair in the shape of butterfly wings. In Indian lore are stories of how butterflies come when called by children of the Nez Perce tribe.

To the Native Americans, the butterfly is a symbol of change, joy, and color. The colors of the butterfly should be examined for its significance and to help you understand its role within your life. Prior to a workshop on fairies and elves recently in Florida, I was performing a meditation at a nearby nature center in preparation for the workshop. When I opened my eyes, I was surrounded by approximately a dozen black and yellow butterflies (Zebra Heliconius). There were even several on my lap.

This was very significant to me for several reasons. First, there has long been an association in folklore of a relationship between those of the Faerie Realm and butterflies. The black and yellow was even more significant. In traditional angelology, these are colors often associated with the archangel Auriel in her guise of overseeing the activities of the nature spirits. It was a wonderful indication of the energy that would accompany me to my workshop.

Butterflies appear to dance as they light upon flowers and such. They remind us not to take things quite so seriously within our lives. They awaken a sense of lightness and joy. They remind us that life is a dance, and dance, though powerful, is also a great pleasure. Butterflies can be reminders to get up and move, for if you can move you can dance. Dance brings the sweetness of life back. This is further exemplified by the fact that butterflies actually have taste receptacles on their front legs. They taste flowers by walking upon them.

Butterflies bring color and joy with them. When butterflies come into your life look at how much or how little joy is within your life. Lighten up. Look for change. Don't forget that all change is good. Butterfly medicine reminds us to make changes when the opportunities present themselves. Transformation is inevitable, but butterfly will help teach you that growth and change does not have to be traumatic. It will teach you that it can occur as gently, as sweetly, and as joyfully as we wish.

DRAGONFLY AND DAMSELFLY

KEYNOTE: *The Power of Light*

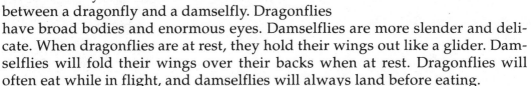

Dragonflies and damselflies are very ancient with estimates of having been around for over 180 million years. They have a beautiful, jewel-like coloring. The bright colors take time to develop, reflecting the idea that with maturity our own true colors come forth. This is part of dragonfly medicine.

For many it is difficult to tell the difference between a dragonfly and a damselfly. Dragonflies have broad bodies and enormous eyes. Damselflies are more slender and delicate. When dragonflies are at rest, they hold their wings out like a glider. Damselflies will fold their wings over their backs when at rest. Dragonflies will often eat while in flight, and damselflies will always land before eating.

Both are known for their fast flight and their dazzling aerial feats, as if imitating how light itself can be moved and directed. They twist, turn, change direction in an instant, hover, move up or down, and even fly backwards. Dragonflies are sometimes known as mosquito hawks. Both the damsels and the dragons are excellent hunters of flying insects. They can fly at speeds up to 30 miles an hour, and their eyes help spot flying insects. They can spot a movement forty feet away. They use their sharp, spiny legs and strong jaws to capture their prey.

Dragonflies and damselflies inhabit two realms—water and air. The significance of these should be examined. In their early life—as a nymph—they live within the water. As they mature and go through their metamorphosis, they move to the realm of air. It is not unusual to find individuals with dragonfly totems to be very emotional and passionate in the early years, but as they get older, they learn to balance it with greater mental clarity and control. Sometimes it can indicate that the emotions have gotten shut down because of emotional issues in the early life. Remember that the dragonfly and damselfly are always found around water. There must be expressions of the emotional and the mental together.

If a dragonfly has shown up in your life, you may need some fresh air in regard to something emotional. You may need to gain a new perspective or make a change. It may even indicate that you are neglecting your emotions. Are you being too rational about everything? Are you not keeping the color of emotions alive?

Dragonflies are very territorial. They will lay their eggs within their territory near the water. The egg eventually develops into the nymph stage of metamorphosis in this insect, and remains as a nymph for almost two years before it transforms into an adult dragonfly or damselfly. This can reflect a number of possibilities for those with this totem. It can indicate that an approximate two-year period of change is about to reach its culmination. It may reflect that you are coming into a two-year period of transformation. It may even reflect a need to institute changes that may culminate in the colorful transformations you desire within a two-year period. Only by examining your life and activities will you begin to understand its specific role.

Just as light can bend and shift and be adapted in a variety of ways, so can the archetypal forces associated with the dragonfly. It is one of the most adaptable of insects. It is why it has been able to survive for so long. Dragonflies have two pairs of wings, but if need be, they can fly with one. Their eyes are kept clean with special combs on their legs and by washing the eyes with water drops collected in the mouth.

Their main predators are frogs and birds. Particularly the frog should be studied by those with this totem. Examining its information found in the last chapter will help you with this.

Their realm is the realm of light, and they are only out during the day, as they are cold-blooded. Summer is their most powerful time, as they need the warmth and the light of the sun. For those with this totem, this will be important to consider. Spending time outside in the sun near fresh water sources will be beneficial for restoring and changing health conditions for the better for those with this totem.

Although some have color pigments in their skin, for most the colors are caused almost the same way rainbows form. Structures in their shell scatter and refract the light, making them look iridescent green and blue. As they age, they may pass through several color changes. This ability to reflect and refract light and color has caused it to be associated with many forms of magic and mysticism—including color magic, illusion (causing others only to see what you wish), and more. Dragonfly's magic is the power of light and all that has ever been associated with it.

Dragonflies and damselflies are often depicted in Japanese paintings, representing new light and joy. To some Native Americans, they represent the souls of the dead. Some stories speak of the time in which they used to be real dragons. Often we assume that dragons have to be gigantic beasts breathing fire, but the fantastic creatures of the Faerie Realm often come in many shapes and sizes. Dragonflies because they are mythical relatives of the ancient dragons are wonderful links to working with nature spirits. For more information on them, you may wish to refer to my earlier work *Enchantment of the Faerie Realm*.

The dragonfly and damselfly reflect and work with the sun and light. The light changes throughout the day. The dragonfly and damselfly undergo their own transformations. If they have shown up, look for change to occur. Are you resisting change when you shouldn't? Dragonflies remind us that we are light and can reflect the light in powerful ways if we choose to do so. "Let there be light" is the divine prompting to use the creative imagination as a force within your life. This is part of what dragonflies and damselflies teach us.

Life is never quite the way it appears, but it is always filled with light and color. Dragonfly can help you to see through your illusions and thus allow your own light to shine forth. Dragonfly brings the brightness of transformation and the wonder of colorful new vision.

GRASSHOPPER

KEYNOTE: *Uncanny Leaps Forward*

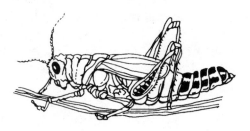

Although the ancient Hebrews saw the grasshopper as a symbol of the scourge, in other societies it held a position of honor and respect. In China grasshoppers and crickets were symbols of good cheer, good luck, abundance, and virtue. Some even believed that relatives would come back to life as a grasshopper or cricket, and they would construct small cages for those they would find. Even to the ancient Greeks the grasshopper was a symbol of nobility.

As its name implies, the grasshopper moves by leaping and hopping. This is also how it escapes. Grasshoppers have a tremendous jumping ability, and they can leap horizontally up to twenty times their own body length. For those with this totem, it is important to get off the haunches and move. Take a chance; take a leap forward.

The hind legs of the grasshopper differ from the rest of its legs and the legs of other insects. They are extremely long and large. The hind legs have delicately controlled muscles. Those with this totem will usually find that things don't move or flow the way they do with other people. Progress is not usually made step by step. Instead, others may seem to be progressing while you seem to be sitting still. Do not become discouraged. When grasshopper shows up, there is about to be a new leap forward—one that will probably carry you past the others around you in your life.

Grasshoppers have an instinct for finding the sunny sides of mounds and other places so they can be exposed to the sun. They have a knack for being in the warmth and light and knowing when to make their leaps. Trust your own instincts and rhythms if this is your totem. What works for others will not necessarily work for you. (Also remember that what works for you probably will not work for anyone else.)

Listen to your own inner voice to know when to make your moves in any area of your life. Grasshoppers possess a tympanic organ on the front legs. As they breathe, this organ is activated. By moving the legs in different directions they are able to locate a sound's source. This connection between sensing sounds and the legs is highly significant. *Trust your inner voice.*

Those with grasshopper totems have an uncanny ability to leap into success-ful ventures. This becomes even more true when they learn to listen to that inner voice and follow their own instincts. Sometimes grasshopper can show up if we are not listening or if we are afraid to make the leap off our mound. Many times such fears have to do with the fact that "no one else has done it this way." Grasshopper people have to learn to make new leaps. Life only becomes difficult when they refuse to move. At such times they may feel as if they are experiencing a scourge themselves. Remember a grasshopper always leaps up or forward. It doesn't leap backward.

PRAYING MANTIS

KEYNOTE: *Power of Stillness*

Mantis has shown up in mythology and lore. In China, a system of the mar-tial arts evolved around the activities of the praying mantis. Kung Fu is based upon the imitation of animals and aspects of nature. One form of it is the praying mantis form.

Most prominent though are the tales of the praying mantis found within African lore. To the Kalihari Bushmen of Africa, Mantis was a Bushmen. There are abundant tales that speak of Mantis and his adventures. In many ways, they are similar to the coyote tales of the plains Indians and the raven tales of the North-west Indians. Whenever Mantis got himself into trouble, he would go off and hide. He would then go to sleep and dream a solution to his problem.

This epitomizes the keynote for this insect—the power of stillness. Through learning to still the outer mind and go within, we can draw upon greater power—physical, emotional, mental, or spiritual. That stillness can be simple contempla-tion, a meditation, or even sleep and dreams. The ancient mystics spoke of seven levels of silence that can be used by us, the first being simple contemplation and the last being death. In between them are dimensions that can add tremendous power to our life. This is part of what the praying mantis teaches. It teaches how to still the outer, so that when it is time to act (in any form) it is done with surety, accuracy, and great power.

According to *The Random House Dictionary of the English Language,* mantis comes from a Greek word meaning "Prophet."[3] If we learn to go into the stillness, we can open ourselves to prophecy. One form of meditation sometimes taught in conjunction with traditional kung fu is called "chi kung." This meditation helps the individual to go within and direct the body's life force along specific avenues, strengthening and empowering it through the various organs and systems of the

---

3   Stein, Jess. *Random House Dictionary of the English Language* (New York: Random House, 1970), p. 873.

body. This has healing and strengthening applications. We can learn to use the stillness in varying degrees—whether for creativity or for healing—and this is part of what the praying mantis teaches.

It is this ability for stillness that makes the mantis a great hunter and enables it to survive. It will wait motionless, blending into its surroundings. Then at the most opportune time, it will suddenly grasp its prey in its long forelegs which fold over its victim like closing a jackknife upon it.

For those with this totem, some examination may be necessary. Are you letting others know your plans before they are even laid? Are you being indiscriminate in what you say and to whom? Are you being impatient? Are you needing help meditating and quieting the outer mind? Are you missing opportunities to grasp life's rewards because you act or speak too hastily? All of these things praying mantis can help with.

SPIDER

KEYNOTE: *Creativity and the Weaving of Fate*

The spider has shown up in myth and lore throughout the world. Usually its symbolism has been very similar wherever it is used. In India it was associated with Maya, the weaver of illusion. It has had connections to the Fates in greek mythology and the Norns in Scandinavian lore— women who would weave, measure, and cut the threads of life. To the Native Americans, spider is grandmother, the link to the past and the future.

Unlike insects, spiders have a two section body instead of three, often giving them a figure eight kind of appearance. This in conjunction with its eight legs (unlike an insect's six) links it to all the mysticism associated with the geometric form of the figure eight. On its side, this is the symbol of infinity. It is the wheel of life, flowing from one circle to

The Spider

The spider is the master weaver. To the Native Americans Grandmother Spider kept and taught the mysteries of the past and how they were affecting the future. Spider reminds us to awaken our own sensibilities to be more creative in life.

(Photo courtesy of Brukner Nature Center, Troy, Ohio.)

the next. The difficulty is learning to walk those circles or even hold your position within the middle between the two.

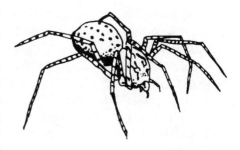

Spider teaches you to maintain a balance—between past and future, physical and spiritual, male and female. Spider teaches you that everything you now do is weaving what you will encounter in the future. In the tarot deck is a card—The Wheel of Fortune. This is a card that has to do with rhythms—the rise and fall, the flow and flux. It is linked to the energies of honor and fame, and the sensitivities necessary to place ourselves within the rhythm of Nature. Meditation upon this card would be beneficial for anyone with the spider as a totem.

The spider awakens creative sensibilities. It weaves a web of intricate and subtle fabric, as if to remind us that the past always subtly influences the present and future. Often the webs will take a spiral shape, the traditional form of creativity and development. The spider found within the web reminds us that we are the center of our own world. The ancient mystery schools had one precept inscribed above their portals: "Know Thyself and Thou Shalt Know the Universe!" Spider reminds us that the world is woven around us. We are the keepers and the writers of our own destiny, weaving it like a web by our thoughts, feelings, and actions.

The spider, because of its characteristics, has come to be associated by mystics and in mythology with three predominant expressions of magic. The first is the magic and energy of creation. It is a symbol of creative power, reflected in its ability to spin a silken web. It is also associated with assertiveness of that creative force, of keeping the feminine energies of creation alive and strong. As will be discussed further, this has ties to the characteristics of some spiders, i.e. the female black widow, which will kill and eat the male after mating has exhausted it.

The third predominant magic of the spider is associated with its spiral energy, the links with the past and the future. The spiral of the web, converging at a central point, is something to be meditated upon by those with this totem. Are you moving toward a central goal or are you scattered and going in multiple directions? Is everything staying focused? Are you becoming too involved and/or self-absorbed? Are you focusing on others' accomplishments and not on your own? Are you developing resentment because of it—for yourself or them?

Spider is the guardian of the ancient languages and alphabets. Every society has had myths about how the different languages and alphabets were formed. The Chinese alphabet is attributed to Ts'ang Chien, the god with the dragon face and four eyes. He formed it from the patterns of the stars, the marks on the back of the turtle and the footprints of birds in the sand. The Norse god Odin created the Runic alphabet after hanging upon the great tree of life for nine days and nights. After this time, the twigs fell off and spelled out certain formulas and words.

To many, there was an alphabet even more primordial. It was formed by the geometric patterns and angles found within spider's web. To many this was the first true alphabet. This is why spider is considered the teacher of language and the magic of writing. Those who weave magic with the written word probably have a spider totem.

The spider has long been associated with death and rebirth. Part of this may have to do with the fact that some female spiders will kill and eat the male after mating. This is often found in the insect world, the praying mantis being another such example. Because it is constantly building and weaving new webs, it has also been a lunar symbol, with ties to the waxing and waning of the moon. For those with this totem, this pattern is a reminder to maintain balance and polarity in all aspects of life. Spider teaches that through polarity and balance creativity is stimulated.

Books, movies, and television have had a tendency to promote a fear of spiders in the general public. Most spiders are poisonous. This is how they kill or stun their prey. They serve a vital function in controlling insect populations.

The black widow probably has received the worst reputation undeservedly. It is found all over the United States. It is jet black, but it has a red hour-glass shaped marking on the belly. It is a poisonous spider, but it is not fatal to humans as many assume. It is actually a very timid spider, and it is usually as much or more afraid of humans than they are of it.

Tarantulas are another common big spider that people are familiar with. The tarantella, a folk dance of Southern Italy, was named after the tarantula. They believed incorrectly that its bite caused convulsive movements in humans. The dance with its circular direction and quick foot movements was named for it.

The tarantula is one of the largest spiders, and it is hairy. Its mouth is underneath its body. Its bite is poisonous, as with most spiders, but it would not affect the average human any more than a bee sting. Tarantulas do spin a thread, but they do not weave a web. They dig a burrow or a hole in the sand and hide in the bottom of it. As soon as they feel something walking around the opening, they will jump up, grab it, and pull it back in. That is how they catch their food.

Most spiders are actually very, very delicate. If you were holding a tarantula and dropped it, it would break and die. Spiders are a combination of gentleness and strength, and they have learned to combine both for successful survival. This is an important lesson for those with this totem.

As delicate as they are, spiders are also very agile. They can maintain balance and walk the tiny silken threads with ease. To walk the threads of life and maintain balance has been one of the mysteries throughout the ages. Myth and lore often speak of individuals who have learned to walk the threads between life and death—waking and sleeping—between the physical and the spiritual. This is part of what spider medicine can teach, for spiders are the experts at walking threads.

Most people have little or no contact with the bigger spiders, but they will often see a wide variety around the house and home. Many of these serve vital functions, killing more harmful insects. Most of their movement occurs in the dark, and they move into inaccessible areas. This reflects much about how to express the creative energies. Don't be afraid to employ it in seemingly inaccessible corners. Weave your creative threads in the dark and then when the sun hits them, they will glisten with intricate beauty.

If spider has come into your life, ask yourself some important questions. Are you not weaving your dreams and imaginings into reality? Are you not using your creative opportunities? Are you feeling closed in or stuck as if in a web? Do you need to pay attention to your balance and where you are walking in life? Are others out of balance around you? Do you need to write? Are you inspired to write or draw and not following through? Remember that spider is the keeper of knowledge of the primordial alphabet. Spider can teach how to use the written language with power and creativity so that your words weave a web around those who would read them.

CHAPTER SIXTEEN

THE MAGIC OF THE REPTILE WORLD

Reptiles are one of the most ancient forms of life. They are also the most adaptable, which has enabled them to survive through millions of years of evolution. There are over 6000 species of reptiles found around the world and living in all environments, except the extremely cold. Four main groups have survived since the time of the dinosaurs:

- Snakes and lizards,
- Crocodiles and alligators,
- Tortoise and turtles, and
- The tuatara found in New Zealand.

Of these groups, the turtles and crocodiles survived the great extinction of the dinosaurs. They have remained relatively unchanged since that time. Because of it they are replete with myths and tales from all parts of the world.

Reptiles have basic characteristics that distinguish them from over forms of animal life. Reptiles are first and foremost coldblooded. Their body heat changes with the temperature of the air and environment around them. While mammals have an internal thermostat to maintain a steady body temperature, the reptile must seek out an environment that will help it survive. This is why snakes and lizards are often seen basking in the sun. They need that warmth to help them survive. They must use an outside source to raise and lower their internal temperatures.

To those with a reptile totem, this is very symbolic. It indicates a great sensitivity to the environments to which they are exposed. It is not unusual to find individuals with prominent reptile totems to have dramatic mood swings in accordance to what their environment is. These individuals often take on the tone and temperature of the environment. If in a group that is partying wildly, they can easily go along. If in a group that is studious, they will become so as well. If in a group that is cheerful and loving, they will display similar characteristics.

Parents of children with reptile totems should be careful to make sure the children keep the right company and participate in beneficial activities. Learning to handle peer pressure in a positive manner will be part of the lesson of anyone with a reptile totem. Reptiles teach us to be selective about what we expose ourselves to. Learning to control and work with the human aura and its interaction with other energy fields would be beneficial for those with this totem.

This is even further emphasized by the fact that reptiles have a skin that is covered with tough scales. This is a second characteristic that distinguishes reptiles from other animal life. These tough scales are protective and in the case of some reptiles, facilitate ease of movement. For those with reptile totems it can be a reminder to keep your tough side outward. This can be a difficult lesson for many people. We are often raised to be open and friendly to everyone. Unfortunately, there are people who take advantage of this.

Some reptile people will object to displaying a tough side. If these individuals will look closely at the scaly skin, it will usually appear smooth and even shiny in some cases, as with snakes. I try to remind these people that there can be strength and yet gentleness in them. Finding the balance can be difficult and can be part of the life lesson of those with a reptile totem. Being tough does not mean that you have to come off looking like the bad guy, and that is also what reptile totems can teach. You can be as strong and protective as necessary and still remain "shiny" in the eyes of those you are tough with.

Reptiles do breathe air, and most have at least one full lung. Most reptiles lay eggs. The symbolism of eggs in general was covered in the bird section of this book, and most of it applies here as well. The eggs of reptiles differ from birds, though, in that they almost always have a leathery shell. Many reptiles also lay their eggs, bury them and abandon them, which is partly why they have such a tough shell. Only a few reptiles will care for the eggs and the young, the crocodile being the strongest example. When the eggs hatch, most reptile young must survive on their own.

Young children with reptile totems often learn early in life how to take care of themselves. They must develop self-sufficiency and self-reliance to a great deal. Some children with reptile totems come into the world with the mind set and a strong sense of determination. Others must develop it for their own success. For most people with reptile totems, it is not unusual to find that the early years were often the most difficult, often having the most difficult lessons.

Some people will acquire reptile totems as they grow older or go through specific changes in their life. Such changes can be very dramatic—a kind of death/rebirth process, or they may be gentle assertions of new opportunities. When a reptile comes into your life, look for opportunities to assert yourself and develop self-reliance on some new level. The unfoldment of self-sufficiency will begin to occur.

The diet of reptiles varies. Reptiles eat everything from plants to large animals. It depends on the reptile itself. Garter snakes will eat earthworms, but black rat snakes will eat rats and mice. Some lizards feed only on plants and/or insects. On the other hand, turtles are omnivorous; they will eat both plants and animals. Individuals with a reptile totem in a powerful position in their life may find that certain diet restrictions may not work.

As with any totem, studying its most common food source or prey can provide insight. If it is an animal or insect, learn something about it. If it is a plant, study it as well. Remember, even plants have certain characteristics which can be related. One of the most ancient forms of divination was through the symbolic interpretations of trees and flowers.

For the purposes of this book, I will be including amphibians among the reptiles, but as you will see, they are not the same. Many people assume that such creatures as frogs, toads and salamanders are part of the reptile family, but they aren't. They may have similar adaptive characteristics, but they are as different from the reptiles as spiders are different from insects. Herpetology often includes the study of both reptiles and amphibians.

Amphibians lead a double life, which is significant and should be meditated upon by anyone with an amphibian totem. The word amphibian comes from two words—"amphi" = "double" and "bios" = "life." Amphibians divide their life between land and water, and it is usually the second half that is spent at least partially on land.

From a symbolic aspect, this can reflect much about what has always been taught in lore about the power of amphibians. They are often the keeper of dreams (water element). The ability to live in water and on land can then reflect that lucid dreaming is going to be stimulated. Many amphibians are thought to be the keepers of knowledge of astral projection. On a more psychological level, they can also reflect a need to learn to use the emotional energies (water) constructively (land).

The most commonly recognized amphibians are frogs, toads, and salamanders. Most people think that salamanders are more closely related to lizards and reptiles than to amphibians, but this is not so. In spite of its appearance, a true

salamander is more closely related to the frog. It must stay in moist areas, and it does have a slimy coat which lizards do not. A salamander could never survive in the heat and sun fire like a normal lizard.

So how do we distinguish an amphibian from a reptile? An amphibian is a vertebrate animal but it has no feathers, fur, or scales. It will usually have toes at some stage but no claws. Amphibians are cold-blooded like reptiles, needing the environment for a heat source. Their temperature fluctuates with their surroundings. Those with amphibian totems will find themselves being just as sensitive to the environment.

Amphibians, like some reptiles, will shed their skin as they outgrow the old one. The skin is usually eaten by amphibians though. This shedding of the skin is very symbolic of transformation, resurrection and rebirth. Any totem which does this usually indicates the same kind of rebirth energy about to manifest within your own life.

Amphibians do not drink water. Water is absorbed directly through the skin. Individuals with amphibian energy strong in their life will need to be around water. It is not unusual to find them spending great amounts of time in the bathtub or shower. Being around natural water sources will be essential for their overall health and well-being.

Amphibians usually go through metamorphosis of some kind. This is most obvious in frogs and the change from egg to tadpole (polliwog) and then to frog. Most people with amphibian totems can pinpoint specific periods in their life where major transitions have occurred or been triggered. They are very definable stages. If amphibian totems show up in your life, you may need to ask yourself in what stage of development or metamorphosis are you presently.

Like reptiles, amphibians lay eggs. Frogs and toads fertilize the eggs outside of the body and salamanders have internal fertilization. With most amphibians, preparation for reproduction begins the preceding autumn before the actual process in the spring. Because of this, these two times of the year can be the most powerful for individuals with amphibian totems. These can be the best times to initiate new ideas, projects and such.

A study of the foods your amphibian totem eats will also provide insight. Many amphibians eat insects, especially in the adult stage. As with any totem, study its unique characteristics and behavior patterns. This will hint at much of the energy pattern about to or already manifesting within your own life. With its double life, the amphibian will help you while asleep and awake.

CHAPTER SEVENTEEN

DICTIONARY OF REPTILE TOTEMS

The following dictionary is by no means extensive or complete. There are too many varieties to give complete elucidation to all. It would probably take several volumes of books to do them complete justice. The ones given are very common and ones in which a great deal of myth and lore still survives. The list also includes amphibians which are not reptiles at all.

As with all the animals, there is a lore about those in this section from different parts of the world. This may reflect possible past-life connections to those areas if you have the reptile or amphibian totem. A study of the myth and lore of the animals will also help you to understand how they have been looked at by people throughout the ages.

Study about reptiles and amphibians in general. Most share common characteristics, only some of which I have mentioned in the previous chapter. Then study each one individually. Each will have its own unique characteristics as well.

Then try and apply it to your life. What were you doing or thinking when you first encountered this totem? Does it show up frequently or is this something new? What has been going on in your life in the previous 72 hours that may have invited its essence and energy into your life? As with the insects, I have not included a *Cycle of Power* for these totems. Most reptiles and amphibians have their own unique schedules and rhythms, based upon their own growth patterns and speeds. Determining this for yourself will be a means of honoring them and attuning to them more effectively.

ALLIGATORS and CROCODILES

KEYNOTE: *Primal Energies of Birth, Motherhood, and Initiation*

Alligators and crocodiles have had mixed symbology and imagery throughout the ages. To the ancient Egyptians they have been associated with fury and ferocity—the same aspects often given within mythologies to the unbridled feminine/creative forces of the world. The viciousness and destructive power was often symbolized as a mother swallowing her young. Inherent within this was the idea that there could not be death without life or life without death.

All alligators and crocodiles inhabit the water and the land. Water was always associated with the Great Mother, the feminine principle of life and therefore birth. Water, though, can also swallow you up. Creation and destruction and the more creation. This is the primal essence reflected within these reptiles.

Birth and death in any form are initiations, events that mark the end of one period and the beginning of a new. This indicates the culmination of knowledge on one level and the seeking for newer knowledge on others. All of this is reflected within the essence of alligators and crocodiles.

They patrol the waters and the shorelines that separate land from water—birth from death, etc. In this sense they can be seen as the keepers and protectors of all knowledge. They are the primal mothers in whom all knowledge rests and waits to be born.

This becomes even more significant when we realize that crocodiles and alligators are excellent mothers, which is unusual among reptiles. Both lay between 20 and 60 eggs, and when the young develop enough within the eggs to begin squeaking from the inside, the mother answers and helps them to hatch. She then carries them gently in her mouth down to the water.

Aside from the mothering energies attributed to these reptiles, they have been depicted in other ways as well in mythology. In the Hindu tradition Varuna, the god of waters, rides on a crocodile's back. Also in Egypt, because of its association with mud, it was often used as a symbol for fertility and power—with mud being the mixture of water and earth that enables new life to grow.

In medieval Europe and earlier, because of their appearance (long body and tail), the alligator and crocodile were associated with the dragon. Sometimes it had the dragon's negative correspondence and sometimes the more positive. The dragon was often the guardian of treasures, often symbolic of hidden wisdom. Because alligators and crocodiles seem to hide within the water while guarding them, they were given the same role as the mythical dragons—the guardians of mystical treasures and wisdoms. To encounter an alligator or crocodile was to indicate an opportunity to begin to unfold and develop some new wisdom—wisdom that could swallow you up if not used carefully.

They are different animals, although close relatives. One of the primary differences is that the crocodile has a tooth that sticks upward from the lower jaw and the alligator does not. Alligators will build a nest of mud and leaves while the crocodile will dig a hole in the sand.

Crocodiles and alligators both have their eyes high on their head. This, of course, serves a practical purpose, enabling them to remain relatively hidden beneath the waters while still able to seek out prey. On a more symbolic level it hints at higher vision and clairvoyance.

Although often considered silent creatures, they do vocalize. They hiss loudly when threatened. During mating season, they are known to roar.

Alligators serve a wonderful function in the conservation of other water animals. They will dig "gator holes"—small ponds of fresh water. These potholes in the mud slowly fill with the last remaining water in an area, creating a miniature oasis that will enable it and other animal life to survive.

The alligator has a much more rapid growth rate than the crocodile. The average adult can grow to be around twelve feet. It can grow as much as a foot a year until it reaches its ultimate length. In cooler climates, the growth rate is less. Alligators rarely live past the age of 60. For those with this totem, you will see opportunity for initiation and the accumulation and use of new knowledge and wisdom occur more rapidly than with a crocodile totem, but it can also be more dangerous if not balanced. An alligator digests its food very slowly, reflecting a need to not go too fast too soon. Digest what you have experienced and learned before moving on to the knew.

The crocodile has its own unique characteristics as well. It is most famous for shedding its "crocodile tears" a phrase that hints at fake sympathy and sadness. A crocodile does shed tears, but it is not out of pain or sorrow. It is done to rid the eyes of salt. For those with the crocodile totem, care of the eyes will be important. If it has shown up as a totem, ask yourself some questions. Are you refusing to show emotions when you should? Are you showing emotions that are not true? Don't allow yourself to be blinded by emotions.

A crocodile will also keep its mouth open for extra cooling. Yoga teaches different breathing techniques in order to affect different systems in the body and the flow of energy. There are "cooling breaths." Studying and practicing these would be beneficial for anyone with this totem—especially when emotional situations around you begin to get hot.

If an alligator or crocodile has shown up, look for an opportunity to touch very primal energies. There is going to be an opportunity for strong birth and/or initiation that will open new knowledge and wisdom in some area of your life.

CHAMELEON

KEYNOTE: *Clairvoyance and Auric Sensitivity*

That which we call a chameleon in the United states is usually not a true chameleon. Growing up, I remember going to the circus and seeing them sold. In the United States what most people refer to as a chameleon is actually an anole.

The chameleon actually has a third eye, located on the back of the animal's head, and it blends perfectly with the body. It does not see in the sense of the other two eyes, but it is capable of distinguishing light and dark. For those with this totem, new awareness of their own psychic ability and intuition is being awakened. There will be greater ability to recognize when it is functioning and when it isn't.

A chameleon does not actually blend into its surroundings. It is already the natural color of its normal habitat. It does change color in degrees according to temperature, humidity, and even emotions. When frustrated or angry it turns brown. When happy and/or contented, it turns more of a light green. This reflects a sensitivity to the environment.

Those with this totem will find their own sensitivity to the environment and other people increasing. Our auric fields are partly a combination of electro-magnetic vibrations. We are constantly giving off (electrical) and absorbing (magnetic) energies, and most of the time we are not cognizant of it. Every time we come in contact with another person, there is an exchange of energy. We give them some and they give us some.

Those with this totem will begin to realize and recognize this exchange much more distinctly than in the past. Trust what you feel and sense. The changes and such will be important for your own health and well being. Learning to read and interpret the aura would be beneficial.

FROGS

KEYNOTE: *Transformation through Water and Sound*

The frog is our most recognizable amphibian. Though often confused with toads, there is a distinct difference. Frogs are associated with water, while toads are always found on dry land. Frogs have a smooth surface, and toads have a bumpy skin surface. Toads also have glands (paratoid) on the side of the head which make a thick mucous that is poisonous. Frogs do not.

Frogs have an ancient mythology about them. Being amphibians with links to the water and the land, they are often associated with the magic of both elements. This also links them to the lore of fairies and elves. Many shamanic societies—especially North and South American—link the frog with rain and control of the weather. Its voice is said to call forth the rains.

Because of its connection to water, it is also linked to lunar energies (the moon moves the tides of waters upon the planet) and those goddesses associated with the moon. The frog was an animal attributed to the Egyptian goddess Herit, who assisted Isis in her ritual for resurrecting Osiris.

Frogs have been known to be heralds of abundance and fertility, especially since in their polliwog stage they resemble the male spermatozoa. This is also due to the fact that after rains, a greater number of frogs come up to dry land and feed on insects and worms who have come out of the rain-soaked land. It is also associated with fertility, for rain makes things grow.

Even as adults, frogs remain semi-aquatic. They live in damp areas. They need water and all that is associated with it symbolically or otherwise. If frog has hopped into your life, you may need to get in touch with the water element. It may reflect that there are new rains coming or that you need to call some new rains forth. Maybe the old waters are becoming dirty and stagnant. Frog can teach you how to clean them up.

Emotions are often associated with water. Individuals with frog totems are very sensitive to the emotional states of others, and seem to know instinctively how to act and what to say. They know how to be sincerely sympathetic.

Frog holds the knowledge of weather and how to control it. Frog medicine can bring rains for every purpose—to cleanse, to heal, to help things grow, to flood, to stir. Its energies can be used to bring light showers or downpours for most any purpose.

The call of the frog is the call of the waters. The spring and summer are the times when frog's voice is strongest. These are its power times. Its call serves a variety of functions. It calls mates to it. It also serves as a release call for non-receptive females. It defines its territory and it warns of predators.

The frog is a totem of metamorphosis. It is a symbol of coming into one's own creative power. It changes from an egg, to a polliwog, to a frog. Even after if becomes a frog, it lives close to and spends much time in the water. It always has contact with the creative force out of which it came. Usually frog people have strong ties to their own mothers.

This connection to water should also serve as a reminder to those with this totem. Are you becoming too mundane? Are you becoming mired in the mud of your day-to-day life? Are you needing to dive into some fresh creative water? Are those around you? Are you feeling waterlogged, becoming bogged down, or drowning in emotions?

Frogs are tuned keenly to sound. Over each ear canal is a round membrane, a tympanic organ—which enables them to recognize and respond to certain sounds and their locations. Science has known for a long time that water is one of the best conductors of sound. This sensitivity to sound should be developed by frog people. Their taste in music will probably not run mainstream, but they can learn to use their voice to stir the emotions and to call for the rains or change the climatic conditions of their own lives.

357

LIZARDS

KEYNOTE: *Subtlety of Perception*

Lizard is an animal of great subtlety. Its movements are quick. It has four legs and can run with great speed. Some lizards can live in the house, and they help to control the insect populations. The gecko lizard is one of the few reptiles that has a voice, and this should be meditated upon by anyone that has it as a totem. The Komodo dragon of Indonesia is a monitor lizard, and it is the largest of all lizards. If at all possible, try to identify the kind of lizard and study it individually.

Most lizards have long tails which help them maintain balance and can also serve as a defense mechanism, as you will learn later. Most also have a crested back, ruffs, or spines. These serve as protection but they are also very symbolic. Some have ruffs about the neck. The neck is an area that bridges the higher and the lower, and lizards with them are those that can teach you how to bridge the subconscious with the conscious—dreaming with waking. They can stimulate lucid dreaming.

Those with spines and crests along the spine usually reflect that the sensitivities of the chakras are heightened or about to be. Are you being too sensitive or not sensitive enough? Are you being too picky or are you missing the obvious? It can also reflect that the kundalini or life force is active and flowing strongly, which will heighten all sensitivities—physical, emotional, mental, psychic, and spiritual.

The Lizard

The lizard is the expert at subtle perception. It can sense vibrations through the ground. Its eyes can detect the subtlest of movements, and it has extremely acute hearing. All of these are symbolic of specific forms of clairvoyance practiced in many societies.

(Photo courtesy of Brukner Nature Center, Troy, Ohio.

A lizard has an ability to recognize the subtlest insect movements, and it can remain still or relatively so to mislead its prey or protect itself. This indicates that your intuition and psychic perceptions are either already active or about to be activated more strongly. Pay attention.

There are a number of characteristics that distinguish a lizard from other reptiles. They too, have a dry skin, and like many, they also have claws. They are also sensitive to vibrations in the ground. They feel it with their feet, tail, and body. Their eyes are sharp with an ability to detect the slightest movement around them. They also have acute hearing.

All of these characteristics give it a symbolism associated with the psychic and the intuitive. The ability to perceive subtle movement—physical and ethereal, waking or sleeping—is what lizard medicine teaches. To some within the Native American tradition, the lizard is associated with dreamtime.[1] Dreams contain some of the subtlest perceptions of the mind of which we may not be conscious. They are translated to us through dreams to make us more conscious. These can be fears or foreshadowings, but almost always they are the things to which we do not pay attention.

Individuals with a lizard totem should listen to their own intuition over anyone else's. Lizard usually reflects heightened sensitivity. You feel what others may not. You will see things that others may miss. You will hear things that are not being said. No matter how strange it may seem, learning to follow those perceptions is what will enable you to succeed most frequently.

One of the most significant characteristics of some lizards and their claim to fame is the ability of the tail to come off. A predator may grab for it, its paw landing upon the tail, only to be surprised as the tail breaks off and the lizard scampers to freedom. The lizard then begins the process of growing another in its place.

This detachment is also part of what lizard can teach. They can help us to become more detached in life to survive. Sometimes it is necessary to separate ourselves or part of ourselves from others to be able to do the things we must desire to do. The lizard helps us to awaken that ability for objective detachment so that it can occur with the least amount of difficulty. Lizard can show up to help us break from the past. It may even indicate a need to explore new realms and follow your own impulses before you get swallowed up in what is not beneficial for you.

Like most reptiles, the lizard will often bask in the sun. It is cold-blooded, and it needs the warmth of the sun to stay warm. This basking is often a feigned sleep, and it serves a secondary purpose of fooling insects that may mistakenly come too close. This ability of feigning sleep while basking in the sun is sometimes related to controlling the sleep state—especially dreams. Lizard, as mentioned earlier, is the totem that can help us understand and use this state more effectively.

---

1   Sams, pp. 181–183.

SNAKE

KEYNOTE: *Rebirth, Resurrection, Initiation, and Wisdom*

Of all the reptiles—and maybe even all animals—the snake has been the subject of great controversy and paradox. Religious sources argue over whether it is the symbol of the higher or the lower. Sometimes seen as devil and sometimes as healer, it is an animal that truly has earned the mythical reputation.

In the Americas, the snake served as a prominent symbol in art and lore. To the Native Americans, the snake is a symbol of transformation and healing. Snake ceremonies involved learning to transmute the poisons within the body after being bitten multiple times. Survival of this would then enable the individual to transmute all poisons—physical or otherwise. It activated the energy of kill or cure, ultimately leading to dramatic healings.

In the Meso-American societies, the serpent or snake was depicted as feathered and flying. It was a symbol of their greatest god and hero, Quetzalcoatl. Quetzalcoatl's story is the myth of a dying god who would someday return. In many ways he was the patron god of the Toltecs, and it was said that the heavens and stars and all the motions of the universe were under his dominion. "He was the master of the winds and of the clouds and the protecting genius of his people."[2]

In Greece the snake was also a symbol of alchemy and healing. The god Hermes carried a staff upon which were entwined two snakes. This caduceus symbol is the primary symbol of modern medicine and doctors. It is a symbol of wisdom expressed through healing.

In India the goddess Vinata was the mother of snakes and a symbol of water and the underworld. Also in India there were demigods, Nagas and their beautiful wives, Naginis, who were usually depicted as half cobra and half deity. The god Vishnu is often depicted sleeping on the serpent of eternity called Ananta. Shiva wears snakes for bracelets and necklaces, representing sexuality.

The serpent and snake has long been a symbol of the sexual/creative life force within humans as is taught in Eastern traditions. The kundalini or serpent fire lies coiled at the base of the spine. As we grow and develop, the primal energy is released, rising up the spine. This in turn activates energy centers in the body and the mind, opening new dimensions and levels of awareness, health, and creativity.

In Chinese astrology one of every twelve years is named for the snake. Those born within that year are believed to have the qualities of compassion, clairvoyance and charm. They usually need to learn lessons associated with forgiveness, superstitiousness and possessiveness as well. A study of Chinese astrology will help you with this.

In Egypt the snake has also had mystical significance. The uraeus is a head band in the shape of the snake. The head of the snake rests and sticks out at the

---

2   Hall, Manly P. *Twelve World Teachers* (Los Angeles: Philosophical Research Society, Inc., 1965), p. 223.

The Snake

The snake has long been a symbol of death and rebirth. Before it sheds its skin, its eyes begin to cloud over, as if to indicate it is entering into a stage between life and death. Snake medicine people were those who learned to imitate the snake and move between the realms of life and death for healing and for enlightenment.

(Photo courtesy of Brukner Nature Center, Troy, Ohio.)

brow area. It was believed to represent a state of inner sight and control of the universe. It was a symbol worn by those who were initiated. Some believe it to be a variations of the eye of Horus, while others see it as the sacred eye of Ra. It represented a certain degree of wisdom and understanding.[3]

Because it sheds its skin, the snake has long been a symbol of death and rebirth. It sheds its skin as it outgrows the old. This death and rebirth cycle is part of what snake represents. It has ties and significance to the ancient alchemists and their symbolic transmutation of lead into gold. This is associated with higher wisdom that comes with the passing of time. This cycle of death and rebirth is often symbolized by the ouroborus, the ancient image of a snake swallowing its own tail. It is the symbol of eternity.

Before the snake begins to shed its skin, its eyes will begin to cloud over. It gives the snake a trancelike appearance. To many mystics and shamans this indicated the ability of the snake to move between the realms of the living and the dead, of crossing over from life to death and then back to life again. As the skin begins to shed, the eyes begin to clear as if they will see the world anew. For this reason, alchemists often believed that wisdom and new knowledge would lead to death and rebirth, enabling the individual to see the world from an entirely new perspective.

The snake has often been depicted, along with its relatives, the serpent and dragon, as a guardian. It is found in myth and lore guarding treasures, the springs

---

3   Hope, Murray. *Practical Egyptian Magic* (New York: St. Martin's Press, 1984), p. 108.

of life or sacred places. The snake/serpent guarded the tree on which the golden fleece hung in the Greek tale of Jason and the argonauts.

The snake is sinuous and fast. Although many people think of them as slimy, their skin is very dry. In fact, humans are slimier than snakes. If a human runs his or her hand on the floor, it will pick up dirt. A snake's skin will not which is why it is able to slide and move in the manner it does.

A snake attacks quickly. It raises itself up and strikes quick, hard, and true to its mark. It is not unusual to find that those with this totem can respond the same way if need be. It is best not to anger snake people. Although slow to lose their tempers, once lost, their bite is quick, sharp, and direct. They almost always hit their mark. They may end up swallowing you whole or just poisoning you in some way.

Anytime a snake shows up as a totem, you can expect death and rebirth to occur in some area of your life. This rarely reflects an actual death but rather a transition. Look for a change in conditions and a movement to new life. examine what is going on around you. Are you needing to make changes but aren't for some reason? Are you trying to force change too quickly? Are you striking out at people and shouldn't? Are you not striking and should? Remember that a snake not only uses its venom and bite to overcome prey, but also for defense. What is needing to be healed? What new opportunities are surfacing that you need to strike out for and take advantage of?

It can also reflect that your own creative forces are awakening. The stimulation of the kundalini usually has physiological as well as spiritual consequences. Physiologically it can activate the sexual drive, bring more energy, etc. Spiritually it can stimulate greater perception of how to apply your insight and intuition. Your own vision and intuition will become more accurate.

To understand the specific role your snake totem will play within your life, first begin by examining the form it takes. This alone will tell you much. Every snake has a head, body, and tail, and there are a wide variety of snakes. Some are poisonous, almost all can bite, and some squeeze and strangle their prey by coiling around it. Examine your snake's markings, and the patterns of its scales. A diamond-back rattler is named for its pattern of scales. Examine the significance of geometric shapes. This will help you to define the role the snake will have in your life.

The rattlesnake, for example, moves around only during the cool hours of the night. Extreme heat is deadly to it. You may find for yourself that becoming more nocturnal would be of benefit. It has a sidewinding motion to its movement. It also has a special sense organ, a small pit in the head that reacts to heat put out by other creatures. This is how it senses its prey. On a symbolic level this indicates for those with this totem an increasing sensitivity to the auras of others. You may start seeing them soon, but you will definitely start sensing them. Trust what you feel around others, no matter how strange it may seem.

Always examine some of the qualities and characteristics of the snake in general. Snakes are carnivorous. They swallow their prey whole. To be able to do this, their jaws will unhinge. The mouth is where we take in nutrition in the form of food. This unhinging ability of the snake reflects the increased ability for those with this totem to swallow and absorb greater amounts of nutrition for the head, i.e., knowledge. Learning opportunities, formal and informal, will surface frequently. Usually with a snake totem, there is little chance of overloading the brain circuits. You will be able to swallow and digest whatever you take in.

Some people have associated hypnotic qualities with the snake because of its stare. The unblinking stare occurs because the snake has no eyelids. Learning to use the eyes to mesmerize and look into the hearts and souls of others directly is part of what traditional snake medicine can teach. It may even indicate a need to look more closely into your own heart and soul.

Snakes have a keen sense of smell. They actually smell with their tongue, which is why it flicks in and out so much. Inside the mouth of the snake in the roof is an organ called the Jacobson's organ. This organ enables the snake to assimilate the air around them. This organ helps them to taste the air and its odors, helping then to locate food sources.

The sense of smell is linked to higher forms of discrimination and spiritual idealism. Individuals with the snake totem will find themselves extremely sensitive to smells and fragrances. Aromatherapy may be a form of healing that is beneficial to explore. They should pay attention to what is going on around them. Do things really smell right around you? Make sure that you are very discriminating about what you say and to whom—and with what you involve yourself?

Snakes are symbols of change and healing. They have speed and agility, so those who have snakes come into their life will usually find the changes and shifts occur quickly and are soon recognized and defined. When snake comes into your life you can look for a rebirth into new powers of creativity and wisdom.

TURTLE

KEYNOTE: *Motherhood, Longevity, Awakening to Opportunities*

As a group, turtles are more ancient than any other vertebrate animal. There are around 250 kinds, 48 of which are found in the United States. Turtles are usually distinguished from tortoises in that tortoises are landbound. Turtles live in and around the water.

A great deal of mythology exists in regard to the turtle. In the Far East, the shell was a symbol of heaven, and the square underside was a symbol of earth. The turtle was an animal whose magic could help you unite heaven and earth within your own life. A symbol of the turtle was an invitation for the blessings of both heaven and earth:

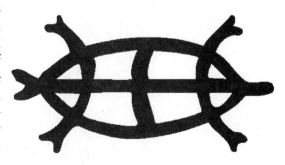

In Japan is a story, "The Tale of Urashima," of a man who stops some boys from picking on a turtle. He chases the boys away and helps the turtle get to the water. Instead of swimming away, the turtle remains close and thanks the man. As a reward for his help, the turtle takes the man on his back deep beneath the ocean to the land of the King of the Ocean. He is honored and rewarded by the king, for the turtle was one of his favorite animals. He gives his daughter, a beautiful water sprite, to him in marriage. He finds true love for the first time.

The turtle is a shore creature, using the land and the water. All shore areas are associated with doorways to the Faerie Realm. The turtle is sometimes known as the keeper to the doors. Turtles thus were often seen as signs of fairy contact and the promise of fairy rewards.

In Nigeria, the turtle was a symbol of the female sex organs and sexuality. To the Native Americans, it was associated with the lunar cycle, menstruation, and the power of the female energies. The markings and sections on some turtles total thirteen. In the lunar calendar, there are either thirteen full moons or thirteen new moons alternating each year. Many believe this is where the association with the female energies originated. Turtle is the symbol of the primal mother.

Because of its great age and its slow metabolism, the turtle is also associated with longevity. Long life and groundedness within life is part of what is associated with the turtle. It does not move fast. It is as if, on some level, turtle knows it has all the time in the world. Turtle medicine can teach new perceptions about time and our relationship with it.

Turtles have amazing survival skills and strategies. They hear well. Actually, they sense vibrations in the water through their skin and shell. Turtles are also able to distinguish some colors, and they do have a sense of smell. Turtle totems hold the mystery of awakening the senses—on both physical and spiritual levels. Turtle stimulates hearing and clairaudience. It can help with vision and clairvoyance. It heightens the sense of smell and higher discrimination.

If turtle has shown up, you may need to ask yourself some questions. Are you not seeing what you should? Are you not hearing what you should? Are you or those around you not using discrimination?

If at all possible, try to identify the individual turtle. Although there are many kinds, with a little effort this can be accomplished, often from the shell. Different turtles do have different kinds of shells. Every turtle has at least one characteristic that makes it stand out, and which usually has great symbolic significance. A snapping turtle may indicate the ability to grab and use the mouth and all associated with it (voice, sound, digestion) in new ways. A box turtle has hinge—like openings in the front and back that it can retreat into, and it can teach how to protect yourself more solidly. A painted turtle may be able to teach you the power and use of color. A sea turtle is fully aquatic, and the symbolism of water should be studied and reflected upon.

Turtles carry their home on their back. Contrary to depiction in cartoons and such, turtles can not leave their shells. The shell is actually the backbone and ribs of the turtle. It serves as home and shelter for it. Although some believe it impossible, if a turtle is flipped onto its back it can right itself. It uses its strong neck and head to flip itself over. For those with this totem, it is a reminder to use your own head and knowledge to right yourself when your world gets topsy turvy. Sometimes turtles show up as a totem to help us during such times.

Turtles are omnivorous. They eat insects, plants, fish, amphibians, and even small mammals on occasion. They are opportunistic. When turtle shows up in your life it is usually a reminder to pay attention or you will miss opportunities. To the Native Americans, the turtle was a symbol of Mother Earth and a reminder that she provides for all of our needs. Sometimes we can't see the forest for the trees, and turtle can slow us down to help us see our opportunities.

Turtles do have a slow metabolism, and this can be a strong reminder. Is our life becoming too hectic? Are we not taking time for ourselves? Are we so busy that we can't really see what is going on? Are we going too slow and need to pick up the pace a little? Turtle can help you to decide.

The Turtle
The turtle is one of the oldest reptiles and thus has one of the most ancient mythologies surrounding. It has been a symbol for Mother Earth, for longevity and for the awakening to heightened sensibilities.
(Photo courtesy of Brukner Nature Center, Troy, Ohio.)

Turtle is the favorite food of raccoons. Those with a turtle totem should also study the significance of the raccoon. It will help you to understand the interplay of energies manifesting within your life. It is believed that turtles use the sun to make vitamin D. Those with a turtle totem may need to check their own vitamin intake and adjust diet and vitamin supplements so that enough vitamin D is taken into the system.

All turtles must come ashore to lay their eggs, and they are usually buried. When the eggs hatch, the young are on their own. They in turn must make their way to the waters. This link between water and land, especially for the purpose of reproduction has great significance. It should be meditated upon by anyone with a turtle totem. The water is the great creative source that we can draw on and live in, but we also have to come out of it and apply that creativity within the physical world—on land. It also hints at needing to think things through carefully before acting upon them.

If turtle has shown up in your life, it is time to get connected to your most primal essence. Go within your shell and come out when your ideas are ready to be expressed. It is time to recognize that there is an abundance out there for you. It doesn't have to be gotten quickly and immediately. Take your time and let the natural flow work for you. Too much, too soon, can upset the balance. Turtle reminds us that all we need for all that we do is available to us, if we approach it in the right manner and time.

Turtles remind us that the way to heaven is through the earth. In Mother Earth is all that we need. She will care for us, protect us, and nurture us, as long as we do the same for her. For that to happen, we must slow down and heighten our sensibilities. We must see the connection to all things. Just as the turtle cannot separate itself from its shell, neither can we separate ourselves from what we do to the Earth.

CONCLUSION

TOTEMS IN A CIVILIZED WORLD

Everything in nature has a purpose. No matter how odd it appears or how strange it behaves, there is some purpose. We may not understand it all, but how often do we understand the behaviors of those around us? People have a tendency to dislike that which they don't understand. Knowledge eliminates prejudices and misconceptions.

No plant or animal is intrinsically bad or negative. Such statements are human value judgments, and usually based upon little contact with or knowledge of a very complex system in which all parts are functional. Humans often know little about an organism's complete role within the ecosystem.

Some believe that there is a danger in exploring the animal world from a mystical perspective. There is often a fear that it will lead to anthropomorphism—endowing the animals with human qualities, or even deifying them in some cases. I believe humans have come too far for us to completely retreat along those lines again.

Yes, there may be a possibility of becoming superstitious, but as I mentioned in part one of this book, superstition usually has no knowledge base. The more we study animals and all of nature, the more our own lives are filled with wonder. Sometimes we endow animals with human, mystical, and even divine characteristics, but this is often due to the fact that our language often becomes quite inappropriate for expressing the awe and wonder of the natural experience.

In our rationalistic society, it becomes difficult not to question the value of some plants, animals, and their interrelationships. We need to ask ourselves whether we need to justify the existence of a plant or animal anymore than the existence of people. Our ability to respect and feel for all of nature should not be based upon its level of "productivity" or intelligence. Who is qualified to determine such?

The natural world is a community of plants, animals, and humans. All are part of an ecosystem. All are necessary for every other aspect. Everything that occurs in nature repercusses upon us. Everything that happens to us, repercusses upon nature. Though we like to remain separate, we are not. We may not recognize the repercussions, but they are real, nonetheless, and she would honor that.

Before we can honor anything, we have to know something about it. We have to see evidence that it is worth honoring. In this book you will have seen that every animal has something about it which can be honored. The following are ways that you can honor all of Nature and help keep all of Nature as your totem:

- Plant trees. (Trees provide shelter and food for animal life, and help filter out pollution.)

- Observe animals and their activities.

- Learn as much about Nature as you can.

- Make bird homes.

- Plant flowers to draw bees and butterflies.

- Pick up litter wherever you go.

- Write letters to public officials to support conservation and environmental protection.

- Help others learn about endangered species.

- Don't buy animals taken from the wild.

- Don't buy products made from wild animals.

- Don't buy products that use animals in testing and research.

- Support organizations that support the environment (zoos, nature centers, non-profit organizations, etc.).

Animal wonders are everywhere. Every animal is a wonder that helps remind us of our own wonderfulness. When we see one aspect of the world with new eyes, we begin to see ourselves with new eyes as well. All of Nature is our totem. Every animal. Every plant. Every time an animal or plant becomes extinct or threatened, the world loses some of its beauty, and we, some of ours. Every time we see the uniqueness of one animal or plant, we also discover something new and unique about ourselves.

Often people question my approach to Nature. Should we approach the animal world or any aspect of Nature from a mystical perspective? I think so. You don't have to believe all of the symbology and mythology of Nature, but by examining it, you touch an ancient primal part of our soul, a part of you that is still capable of responding to Nature with wonder. It can stir a part of the soul that may not have been touched otherwise. This is the power of myth and symbol in Nature.

Sometimes it is more important to feel than to know. By arousing and stirring an ancient ember, the desire for more knowledge will grow; and from that desire will come opportunity to rediscover the joy and the mystery of the natural world.

To speak with the animals and learn from them, we first must be able to see them anew. It is my hope that this book will stir some embers that will build to a fire, for where there is fire there is light; and where there is light, there is joy and wonder!

APPENDIX

(The following are organizations that provide education and support for animals, nature and the environment. It is by no means a complete list, but they are all beneficial.)

Brukner Nature Center
5995 Horseshoe Bend Road
Troy OH 45373

Defenders of Wildlife
1244 19th Street NW
Washington DC 20036

Environmental Defense Fund
257 Park Avenue S.
New York NY 10010

Friends of Earth
218 D Street SE
Washington DC 20003

Hawkquest
c/o Kin Quitugua
15469 E. Oberlin Place
Aurora CO 80013

Beauty Without Cruelty USA
175 W. 12th Street, #15G
New York NY 10011-8275

Raptor Center
University of Minnesota
1920 Fitch Avenue
St. Paul MN 55108

National Audubon Society
950 3rd Avenue
New York NY 10022

National Wildlife Federatioon
1400 16th Street NW
Washington DC 20036

Return To The Sacred
c/o Quenda Healing Woman
Box 6793
Colorado Springs CO 80934

BIBLIOGRAPHY

REALITY OF THE NATURAL WORLD

Angell, Madeline. *America's Best Loved Wild Animals*. New York: Bobbs-Merrill Company, 1975.

Austin, Elizabeth and Oliver. *Random House Book of Birds*. New York: Random House, 1970.

Bantonk, Nick. *Wings*. New York: Random House, 1990.

Blassingame, Wyatt. *The Wonders of Crows*. New York: Dodd, Mead & Company, 1979.

Caras, Roger A. *Panther*. Lincoln, NE: University of Nebraska Press, 1969.

Clement, Roland. *Living World of Audubon*. New York: Grosset & Dunlap, 1974.

Cromer, Richard. *The Miracle of Flight*. New York: Doubleday & Company, 1968.

De La Torre, Julio. *Owls: Their Life and Behavior*. New York: Crown Publishing, 1990.

Di Silvestro, Roger. *Fight for Survival*. New York: John Wiley & Sons, 1990.

Domico, Terry. *Bears of the World*. New York: Facts on File Pub., 1988.

Fourie, Denise. *Hawks, Owls, and Other Birds of Prey*. San Luis Obispo, CA: Blake Publishing, 1989.

Gabb, Michael H. *Creatures Great and Small*. Minneapolis: Lerner Publishing, 1980.

Hines, Bob. *Fifty Birds of Town and City*. U.S. Department of Interior; Washington DC.

Hornblow, Leonora and Arthur. *Birds Do the Strangest Things*. New York: Random House, 1968.

Hoshimo, Michio. *Moose*. San Francisco: Chronicle Books, 1988.

Johnson, Sylvia A. *The Wildlife Atlas*. Minneapolis: Lerner Publishing, 1977.

Kieran, John. *An Introduction to Birds*. New York: Doubleday and Company, 1965.

Limburg, Peter. *What's in the Name of Birds*. New York: Coward, McCann & Geoghegan, Inc., 1975.

_____. *What's in the Name of Wild Animals*. New York: Coward, McCann & Geoghegan, Inc., 1977.

Mackenzie, John. *Birds of Prey*. Minocqua, WI: North Word, Inc., 1986.

Mech, L. David. *The Wolf*. Minneapolis: University of Minnesota Press, 1970.

Merrill, Samuel. *The Moose Book*. New York: E.P. Dutton & Company, 1916.

O'Connor, Karen. *The Feather Book*. Minneapolis: Dillon Press, 1990.

Peterson, Roger. *How to Know Birds*. Boston: Houghton Mifflin, 1957.

Pringle, Laurence. *Listen to the Crows*. New York: Thomas Crowell Comp., 1976.

Scott, Jack Denton and Sweet, Ozzie. *Moose*. New York: G.P. Putnam, 1981.

Seidensticker, John & Lumpkin, Susan. *Great Cats*. Emmaus, PA: Rodale Press, 1991.

Snead, Stella. *Animals in Four Worlds*. Chicago: University of Chicago Press, 1989.

Tanner, Ogden. *Urban Wilds*. Alexandria: Time-Life Books, 1975.

Turbak, Gary. *The Twilight Hunters: The Wolf*. Flagstaff: Northland Pub., 1987.

Weidensaul, Scott. *American Wildlife*. New York: Gallery Books, 1988.

_____. *Birds of Prey*. New York: Gallery Books, 1989.

Wexo, John. *Zoobooks: Birds of Prey*. San Diego: Wildlife Ed. Ltd., 1980.

_____. *Zoobooks: Big Cats*. San Diego: Wildlife Ed. Ltd., 1987.

_____. *Zoobooks: Bears*. San Diego: Wildlife Ed. Ltd., 1987.

_____. *Zoobooks: Endangered Animals*. San Diego: Wildlife Ed. Ltd., 1987.

_____. *Zoobooks: Little Cats*. San Diego: Wildlife Ed. Ltd.,, 1988.

_____. *Zoobooks: Animal Wonders*. San Diego: Wildlife Ed. Ltd., 1988.

Wood, Peter. *Birds of Field and Forest*. New York: Time-Life Books, 1977.

Zim, Herbert. *The Big Cats*. New York: William Morrow & Comp., 1976.

MYTH AND MYSTICISM IN NATURE

Andrews, Ted. *Dream Alchemy.* St. Paul: Llewellyn Publications, 1991.

_____. *How to Meet and Work with Spirit Guides.* St. Paul: Llewellyn Publications, 1992.

_____. *Magical Dance.* St. Paul: Llewellyn Publications, 1992.

Arnott, Kathleen. *African Myths and Legends.* New York: Oxford University Press, 1989.

Baskin, Wade. *The Sorceror's Handbook.* Secaucus: Citadel Press., 1974.

Belting, Natalia. *The Earth is on a Fish's Back.* New York: Holt, Rhinehart and Winston, 1965.

Caduto, Michael and Bruchac, Joseph. *Keepers of the Earth.* Golden, CO: Fulcrum Pub., 1988.

_____. *Keepers of the Animals.* Fulcrum Pub.; Golden, 1991.

Campbell, Joseph. *The Way of the Animal*, Vol. I & II. New York: Harper & Row, 1988.

Christa, Anthony. *Chinese Mythology.* New York: Peter Bedrick Books, 1983.

Cirlot, J. E. *Dictionary of Symbols.* New York: Philosophical Library, 1962.

Coffer, William. *Spirits of the Sacred Mountains.* New York: Van Nostrand Reinhold Comp., 1978.

Cooper, J. C. *Symbolism: The Universal Language.* Northamptonshire: Aquarian Press, 1982.

Doore, Gary. *Shaman's Path.* Boston: Shambhala Press, 1988.

Dulcken, H. W. *Complete Illustrated Stories of Hans Christian Andersen.* London: Chancellor Press, 1989.

Erdoes, Richard and Ortiz, Alfonso. *American Indian Myths and Legends.* New York: Pantheon Books, 1984.

Frazer, James G. *The Golden Bough.* New York: Collier Books, 1922.

Gettings, Fred. *Secret Symbolism in Occult Art.* New York: Harmony Books, 1987.

Godwin, Joscelyn. *Mystery Religions in the Ancient World.* San Francisco: Harper & Row, 1981.

Graves, Robert. *The White Goddess.* New York: Farrar, Straus & Giroux, 1948.

Hall, Manly P. *Secret Teachings of All Ages.* Los Angeles: Philosophical Research Society, 1977.

Hamilton, Edith. *Mythology.* New York: New American Library, 1942.

Hope, Murry. *Practical Egyptian Magic.* New York: St. Martin's Press, 1984.

Ions, Veronica. *Indian Mythology.* New York: Peter Bedrick Books, 1983.

Jung, Carl. *Man and His Symbols.* New York: Anchor press, 1964.

Loewe, Blacker and Carmen. *Oracles and Divination.* Boulder, CO: Shambhala Press, 1981.

McLaughlin, Marie. *Myths and Legends of the Sioux.* Lincoln, NE: University of Nebraska Press, 1990.

Monaghan, Patricia. *Book of Goddesses & Heroines.* St. Paul: Llewellyn Pub., 1990.

Nicholson, Irene. *Mexican & Central American Mythology.* New York: Peter Bedrick Books, 1982.

Nicholson, Shirley. *Shamanism.* Wheaton: Theosophical Pub., 1987.

Opie, Iona & Tatem, Moira. *A Dictionary of Superstititions.* New York: Oxford University Press, 1989.

Osborn, Harold. *South American Mythology.* New York: Peter Bedrick Books, 1983.

Parrinda, Geoffrey. *African Mythology.* New York: Peter Bedrick Books, 1982.

Piggott, Juliet. *Japanese Mythology.* New York: Peter Bedrick Books, 1982.

Poinsias, Mac Cana. *Celtic Mythology.* New York: Peter Bedrick Books, 1983.

Rossbach, Sara. *Feng Shui—The Chinese Art of Placement.* New York: E. P. Dutton, 1983.

Sams, Jamie and Carson, David. *Medicine Cards.* Santa Fe: Bear & Company, 1988.

Spence, Lewis. *Myths of the North American Indians.* New York: Dover Pub. 1989.

Stevens, Jose & Lena. *Secrets of Shamanism.* New York: Avalon Books, 1988.

Sun Bear and Wabun. *The Medicine Wheel.* Englewood Cliffs: Prentice-Hall, Inc., 1980.

Sympson, Jacquelyn. *European Mythology.* New York: Peter Bedrick Books 1987.

Townsend, George. *Aesop's Fables.* New York: Doubleday & Company; 1968.

Tyler, Hamilton. *Pueblo Birds and Myths.* Flagstaff: Northland Pub., 1991.

Walsh, Roger. *The Spirit of Shamanism.* Los Angeles: Jeremy P. Tarcher, 1990.

Waring, Philippa. *Dictionary of Omens and Superstitions.* Secaucus: Chartwell Books, 1989.

Wolfe, Amber. *In the Shadow of the Shaman.* St. Paul: Llewellyn Publications, 1988.

Zipes, Jack. *The Complete Fairy Tales of the Brothers Grimm.* New York: Bantam Books, 1987.

Zolar. *Zolar's Encyclopedia of Omens, Signs and Superstitions.* New York: Prentice-Hall Press, 1989.

INDEX

— E —

eagle dancer, 72
eagles, 136–141
ear canal, 357
Earth (as element), 34, 212, 258
ecology, 43, 58, 310
eggs, 84–85, 338, 341, 350, 352, 366
egg layers, 127, 158, 162, 338, 341
egg stage, 331, 357
electro-magnetic vibrations, 356
elements,
    Air, 37–38, 86, 88, 105, 212
    Earth, 34, 212
    Fire,
    Water,
elephant, 267–269
elephant seal, 311
elk, 270–271
elves, 7, 96, 276
empathy, 239, 243, 245
exercises,
    Beginning the Day, 79–80
    Eggs, Nests, and Divination, 84–85
    Flights of Fancy, 86–89
    Feather Fetish exercises, 100–115
    Power of Imitation, 82

— F —

Faerie Realm, 90, 96, 109, 144, 157, 167, 192, 195,
    198, 200, 303, 311, 330, 339, 364
fairies, 7, 62, 96276,
falcon, 159–161
Farb, Peter, 329, 333
fawns, 263
feather feet, 310
feathers
    as symbols, 69, 107, 143
    exercises for working with, 101–115
    owl and hawk in a dream bundle, 177
    purpose of, 91, 94
feng shui, 58, 59
ferret, 302, 320
Fire (as element), 24, 25, 212, 319
fisher, 300, 320
flicker, 38, 142–143
flight, 91–98
flight feathers, 91
flowers, 47, 49, 57, 62, 307, 327, 339, 351
    see also the List of Symbolic Qualities of
    Different Flowers, 49
forests, 60, 179, 272, 280, 286, 299, 317

fox, 32, 271–277, 317
frogs, 351, 356–357
fur, 3, 240, 253, 272–275, 290, 304, 323, 325

— G —

gardens, 60–61
gecko lizard, 358
geomancy, 58
gifting, 229–231
giraffe, 277–279
goat, 279–280
goatsuckers. 197
golden eagle, 137, 138, 139, 177
goldfinch, 143–144
Gonzalez-Wippler, 25
Goodrich, Norma Lorre, 274
goose, 144–146
goshawk, 153
grackle, 146–147
Grail of Life, 34
grasshopper, 334, 342–343
gray squirrel, 317
gray wolf, 323–324
grosbeak, 148
groundhog, 35, 280–281
grouse, 149–150
grub stage, 338
gulls , 45, 151

— H —

Hall, Manly P. , xiii, 133, 248
hare, 303–304
harems, 242
Harpy eagles, 138
Hawkquest, 32
hawks , 33, 34, 54–55, 76, 151–155, 180, 317
healing, 247
hedgehog, 299
Hermetictists, 2, 73
heron, 156–157, 180
herring, 151
hibernation, 74, 159, 198, 252, 280–281
Hoeller, Stephen, 128
home, 47, 54, 58–59, 61, 62
honey, 337, 338
honeycombs, 338
horns, 240, 242, 243, 257, 258, 278, 307–398,
    309–310, 333
Hope, Murray, 361
horse, 281–282

SACRED SOUNDS
Transformation through Music & Word
Ted Andrews

Sound has always been considered a direct link between humanity and the divine. The ancient mystery schools all taught their students the use of sound as a creative and healing force that bridged the different worlds of life and consciousness.

Now, *Sacred Sounds* reveals to today's seekers how to tap into the magical and healing aspects of voice, resonance and music. On a physical level, these techniques have been used to alleviate aches and pains, lower blood pressure and balance hyperactivity in children. On a metaphysical level, they have been used to induce altered states of consciousness, open new levels of awareness, stimulate intuition and increase creativity.

In this book, Ted Andrews reveals the tones and instruments that affect the chakras, the use of kinesiology and "muscle testing" in relation to sound responses, the healing aspects of vocal tones, the uses of mystical words of power, the art of magical storytelling, how to write magical sonnets, how to form healing groups and utilize group toning for healing and enlightenment, and much, much more.

0-87542-018-4, 240 pp., 5¼ x 8, illus., softcover   **$9.95**

HOW TO SEE AND READ THE AURA
Ted Andrews

Everyone has an aura—the three-dimensional, shape-and-color-changing energy field that surrounds all matter. And anyone can learn to see and experience the aura more effectively. There is nothing magical about the process. It simply involves a little understanding, time, practice and perseverance.

Do some people make you feel drained? Do you find some rooms more comfortable and enjoyable to be in? Have you ever been able to sense the presence of other people before you actually heard or saw them? If so, you have experienced another person's aura. In this practical, easy-to-read manual, you receive a variety of exercises to practice alone and with partners to build your skills in aura reading and interpretation. Also, you will learn to balance your aura each day to keep it vibrant and strong so others cannot drain your vital force.

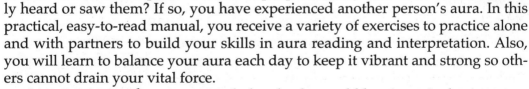

Learning to see the aura not only breaks down old barriers—it also increases sensitivity. As we develop the ability to see and feel the more subtle aspects of life, our intuition unfolds and increases, and the childlike joy and wonder of life returns.

0-87542-013-3, 160 pp., mass market, illus.   **$3.95**

HOW TO MEET & WORK WITH SPIRIT GUIDES
Ted Andrews

We often experience spirit contact in our lives but fail to recognize it for what it is. Now you can learn to access and attune to beings such as guardian angels, nature spirits and elementals, spirit totems, archangels, gods and goddesses—as well as family and friends after their physical death.

Contact with higher soul energies strengthens the will and enlightens the mind. Through a series of simple exercises, you can safely and gradually increase your awareness of spirits and your ability to identify them. You will learn to develop an intentional and directed contact with any number of spirit beings. Discover meditations to open up your subconscious. Learn which acupressure points effectively stimulate your intuitive faculties. Find out how to form a group for spirit work, use crystal balls, perform automatic writing, attune your aura for spirit contact, use sigils to contact the great archangels and much more! Read *How to Meet and Work with Spirit Guides* and take your first steps through the corridors of life beyond the physical.

0–87542–008–7, 192 pp., mass market, illus.   **$4.99**

CRYSTAL BALLS & CRYSTAL BOWLS
Tools for Ancient Scrying & Modern Seership
Ted Andrews

Despite the popular use around the world of the traditional quartz crystal ball and the modern crystal bowl as magical tools, there has been little practical information on their applications and use—until now. *Crystal Balls and Crystal Bowls* takes the ancient processes of divination and scrying out of the realm of the supernatural and places them in the domain of natural knowledge.

This book reveals why crystal balls and crystal bowls are dynamic instruments for transformation, and how they can be used to divine the future, astral project, to connect with spirits, to heal and to balance the human energy system. This book explores their many functions, and reveals the secrets of vibrational energy, as well as its application for increasing intuition and activating creativity. Step-by-step, you will learn techniques for crystal gazing, scrying, attuning to spirit guides, developing clairvoyance, healing and more.

Crystal balls and crystal bowls are two of the most powerful tools for opening to higher states of consciousness. This book provides definitive information on the "hows and whys" of crystal balls and bowls and shows how their magic can enhance your life.

1-56718-026-4, 6 x 9, 256 pp., illus., photos, softcover   **$12.95**